THE MOURNING AFTER

The Mourning After

Loss and Longing among Midcentury American Men

John Ibson

THE UNIVERSITY OF CHICAGO PRESS
CHICAGO & LONDON

The University of Chicago Press, Chicago 60637

The University of Chicago Press, Ltd., London

Published 2018

Printed in the United States of America

27 26 25 24 23 22 21 20 19 18   1 2 3 4 5

ISBN-13: 978-0-226-57654-1 (cloth)

ISBN-13: 978-0-226-57668-8 (paper)

ISBN-13: 978-0-226-57671-8 (e-book)

DOI: https://doi.org/10.7208/chicago/9780226576718.001.0001

Library of Congress Cataloging-in-Publication Data

Names: Ibson, John, author.

Title: The mourning after : loss and longing among midcentury American men / John Ibson.

Description: Chicago ; London : The University of Chicago Press, 2018. | Includes bibliographical references and index.

Identifiers: LCCN 2018000557| ISBN 9780226576541 (cloth : alk. paper) | ISBN 9780226576688 (pbk. : alk. paper) | ISBN 9780226576718 (e-book)

Subjects: LCSH: Men—United States—History—20th century. | Masculinity—United States—History—20th century. | Male friendship—United States—History—20th century. | Homophobia—United States—History—20th century. | Homosexuality and literature—United States—History—20th century. | Burns, John Horne, 1916–1953—Appreciation—United States. | Vidal, Gore, 1925–2012—Appreciation—United States. | American literature—20th century—History and criticism. | United States—Social life and customs—1945–1970.

Classification: LCC HQ1090.3 .I27 2018 | DDC 155.3/320973—dc23

LC record available at https://lccn.loc.gov/2018000557

♾ This paper meets the requirements of ANSI/NISO Z39.48-1992 (Permanence of Paper).

In memory of my sister and brother
NANCY M. COAD (1931–2004)
and
ROBERT C. IBSON JR. (1933–1969)

Contents

Acknowledgments

It's hard to say exactly when work on this book started. I began research and writing with a book like this in mind over a decade ago, and I've received a lot of help that I want to acknowledge.

I refined some of my ideas on men's relationships, the Second World War, and the significance of everyday photographs through presentations at several scholarly gatherings, such as "The Photograph: An International Interdisciplinary Conference" at the University of Manitoba in 2004, at which cordial conversations with Nancy Martha West were especially valuable; "North American Sexualities: Post World War II" at the University of Massachusetts, Amherst, in 2004, at which conversations (and a delightful dinner) with Kathy Peiss were memorably encouraging; "Vernacular Reframed: An Exploration of the Everyday" at Boston University in 2004, where Alan Trachtenberg yet again treated me to his wisdom, generosity, and good company; "Groundwork: Space and Place in American Cultures," the American Studies Association's 2005 national convention, where delivering a paper alongside my friend and colleague in studying masculinity, Jay Mechling, was a highlight; "Symposium on the Art of the American Snapshot," at the National Gallery of Art in 2007; and "Feeling Photography" at the University of Toronto in 2009.

Closer to home, I presented some plans and findings for this book to my department's Graduate Student–Faculty Colloquium in 2012. The American Studies Department at California State University, Fullerton, has been my professional home throughout an academic career that now is well over four decades long, with those years indeed flying by because I was having such a good time. Working alongside talented, dedicated department colleagues has improved this book and enriched my life in countless large and small ways. The university helped the book greatly with a sabbatical leave in 2012 and a lightening of my course load in 2013, supported by Fullerton's Faculty Development Center.

By far the greatest professional satisfaction from my career's earliest days to this moment has come from being with students. This book surely is better immeasurably from the knowledge, perspective, and engagement that teaching has brought my way. To identify students whose company, even lasting friendship, I've especially treasured would be a delightful task, but while I might know where to begin this list, deciding where to stop would be beyond me. I must, though, single out the extremely valuable help I received from two graduate research assistants, David Donley and Judson Barber, and from the outstanding teaching assistants I had while working on this book: Matt Nelson, Tim Schneider, Rich Morales, Heather Andrews, Nathan Kuntz, Emily Starr, Alicia Limon, Manny Sanchez, Adam Vasquez, Patrick Heyer, David Donley, Joseph Meyer, Mike West, Casey Ratto, Danny Juarez, Katya Kuzmina, Paula Beckman, Judson Barber, Jasmin Gomez, and Kai Lisoskie. Manny, Judson, and Kai, I must add, were more like my coteachers than assistants.

The world would be a better place if the rest of us were as generous and committed to knowledge as most librarians and archivists. Helping greatly with my research for this book were Alexander N. Rankin, assistant director of acquisitions, and Laura Russo, manager of public service and donor relations, Howard Gottlieb Archival Research Center at Boston University; AnnaLee Pauls, Rare Books and Special Collections, Princeton University; Heather Cole, assistant curator of modern books and manuscripts, Houghton Library at Harvard University; Paige Roberts, archivist and head of special collections at Phillips Academy; Karen Parsons, archivist at Loomis Chaffee School; Rebekah Kim and Joanna Black, managing archivists at the GLBT Historical Society; Brenda J. Marston, curator, Human Sexuality Collection and head of research services, and Hillary Dorch Wong, reference coordinator, Division of Rare and Manuscript Collections at Cornell University. My research both at Cornell, for which I received a generous Phil Zwicker Memorial Research Grant, and at the GLBT Historical Society was mostly related to what I hope will be a soon-forthcoming book about particular male couples and single men during the "mourning after."

I am grateful to the late Gore Vidal for agreeing to an interview, and to Fabian Bouthillette for arranging that event as well as for later conversations over lunches and a hike. Susan J. Searles, legal administrative assistant at Burns and Levinson LLP, was friendly and efficient in arranging my interviews with Thomas Burns. Getting to know Tom not only became a crucial element of my research but was also one of the more delightful experiences of my entire life. He was a world-class raconteur, a generous host at lunches, a highly distinctive driver on the challenging roadways (and sidewalks) of greater Boston, a wonderful guide to the city of Andover and the campus of Phillips Academy, and a person of rare insight about matters ranging from Massachusetts politics to the joys and burdens of family ties. After his death, it was my great pleasure to share with Tom's daughter Wendy Conquest my high regard for her father and the profoundly moving way he had expressed to me his love for his children.

On another visit to Andover, I got to spend time with Tony Rotundo, a leading historian of American men whose knowledge is as abundant as his good nature, and with his spouse, historian Kathleen Dalton. Enjoyable and instructive as well was my correspondence with journalist David Margolick about his own work on John

Horne Burns, and with my friend Bob Young of Quinnipiac University about his fascinating study of men's attachments in midcentury America. Correspondence with Mike Messner, eminent scholar of American masculinity, was especially pleasant and encouraging. The sudden deaths of Clark Davis in 2003 and Peter Hales in 2014 devastated those of us who had the tremendous good fortune of having those guys as our friends. Clark was a young scholar of men's history, already accomplished and overflowing with promise; Peter, a remarkably young-at-heart expert on seemingly everything, in particular the history of photography and of postwar America. I would have loved to have discussed this book with each of them, and it surely would have been better for that experience.

In countless ways, my Fullerton colleagues and I benefit from the good nature, skill, and dedication of the staff in our department office, Karla Arellano and Aissa Bugarin, both of whom helped me secure the needed authorizations for this book's extensive research travel.

Douglas Mitchell, executive editor at the University of Chicago Press, has been a savvy and supportive friend of this book from when he first heard about it over ten years back. To have mine join the eminent books that Doug has guided into print is a singular honor. A drummer himself, Doug is the Buddy Rich of academic editors, and I have been the grateful beneficiary of his considerable knowledge, patience, charm, and generosity of spirit, to say nothing of his knowledge of the best restaurants across America. His convincing me that I needed fewer words to make a point was no small feat. Kyle Wagner, assistant editor at Chicago, has combined good nature with efficiency, reliability with practicality, and diplomacy with cyber expertise. As my copyeditor, Chicago's Mark Reschke had the curiosity and attention to detail of Sherlock Holmes.

With their judicious criticism, generous praise, and wise suggestions, the two readers that Doug and Kyle recruited to review my manuscript, one of whom was David Doyle, made this a considerably better book in content and structure alike. I am extremely grateful to them both.

I won life's lottery when I met my husband, Steve Harrison, forty years ago. Though I'm the one with the actual hat collection, metaphorically it's he who wears more hats around our house: gardener, interior decorator, haiku maker, baker, dachshund whisperer, and art collector. He is also an astute editor who read and commented elaborately on two entire drafts of the manuscript for this book with meticulous care, candor, and insight, bringing to that task what he long ago brought to my life: a profound commitment to my welfare, a usually unerring and sometimes unnerving perception of how I might do better, and an unmatched ability to encourage, inspire, understand, comfort, and appreciate me. Steve, you are the rose of my life.

Sexual Identity on the Postwar Home Front

Denial's Allure in a Repressive Era

Well over thirty years ago, closer to forty, I discovered the work of John Horne Burns. He had authored *The Gallery*, a 1947 novel about American soldiers in Italy during World War II. With incisive comparisons of conquering Americans and vanquished Italians and a distinctive sensitivity to a war's toll away from the battlefield, *The Gallery* had an entire chapter devoted to a gay bar in Naples. It was a singular work in its day because of Burns's sympathetic treatment of homosexuality, yet this prominent feature of the book encountered little critical scorn. On the contrary, the gracefully written, uniquely constructed novel of penetrating, distinctive insight put Burns in the front ranks of his generation's writers. However, when Burns brought homosexuals home in his two subsequent works, *Lucifer with a Book* and *A Cry of Children*, the critical response was fully as negative as the reception for *The Gallery* had been affirmative. Burns died at only thirty-six in 1953, his once-sparkling reputation greatly diminished. His fame had come quickly; relative obscurity followed just as fast.

A heavy-drinking contrarian who was comparatively open about his homosexuality, John Horne Burns seemed upon my discovery of him to be a paradigmatic Irish American. In my 1976 doctoral dissertation, I had argued that Irish Catholic culture was fundamentally at odds with the dominant culture of the United States, and that the fate of Irishness (and Irish persons) in America was much less happy a tale than most other scholars had seen it to be. Cultural accommodation for Irish Americans, perhaps especially for the males, I thought, had often been painfully, sometimes incompletely, accomplished. A distinctive inclination to self-destruction (often involving alcohol), an ennobling of martyrdom, and a discomfort with material success were to my mind revealingly prominent in the Irish American experience and did not support the widespread view of the Irish as among the more fully and comfortably assimilated ethnic groups in the United States.[1]

Had I known of Burns when writing my dissertation, I would undoubtedly have used him as evidence of the Irish American as cultural misfit. I did mention him, though, in a 1981 *American Quarterly* essay on whiteness in our society, as one of those Irish American novelists from whom "we have much to learn" by approaching fiction as a cultural document. My revised dissertation aroused some initial interest in the early 1980s, but ultimately met universal and unequivocal recommendations of rejection from the scholars to whom a dozen publishers sent my manuscript. I turned away from scholarship for a good while; but I did not forget about Burns.[2]

As the focus of my teaching shifted from ethnicity to gender and sexuality in the early 1990s, I slowly began to rekindle my scholarly aspirations, and to revive my interest in John Horne Burns. No longer, though, was Burns interesting to me simply for what he might reveal about the fate of Irishness in the United States, but rather for how his shifting fortunes as a writer might be linked to the shifting boundaries of male association in the early postwar era. At regional American studies conferences in Reno and Los Angeles, I delivered papers that had Burns as their focal point, maintaining that his descent into obscurity might have involved more than simply a decline in his literary skill.

A pivotal moment in my reawakening as a scholar came at a 1995 conference at the University of Colorado, a gathering that warmly received my proposition that the years of World War II and the period immediately thereafter differed vastly from each other regarding the physical closeness encouraged between American males. That Colorado conference marked the approach of *Life* magazine's sixtieth anniversary; and my paper there, focused on depictions of men in *Life*, marked my growing interest in visual material as cultural evidence. I still found a small place in the paper, though, for the rise and fall of John Horne Burns, noting the significance of a 1965 essay on Burns by Gore Vidal, a rare instance in which Burns had been remembered, fondly so.[3] While my 2002 book *Picturing Men* used everyday photography as its means of exploring cultural shifts regarding men's relationships over an entire century, I did briefly use Burns's experience in that work too, interpreting his fall from critical grace as an instructive example of what I saw as a substantial, and substantially unfortunate, constriction of male affection in the United States following World War II.[4] Wanting to continue my study of men's relationships with each other, I believed that the period right after the war deserved a book all its own, that the era's cultural legacy was long-lasting, powerful, and mostly regrettable. This is that book.

"I'm not no queer." "Me neither." So goes Ennis del Mar and Jack Twist's mutual reassurance following the first of their many sexual experiences together, all of them clandestine, beginning with those during their stay on Brokeback Mountain and then those that took place in either a sleazy motel or on purported fishing trips, in Annie

Proulx's acclaimed 1997 short story and in Ang Lee's celebrated 2005 film adaptation of Proulx's tale.[5] Ennis and Jack's hesitation to identify themselves as sexually different young men is understandable: Ennis had grown up in a rural environment in which a father would take his son to see the corpse of a townsman, his penis severed by the deadly brutality of neighbors who disapproved of the man's living with another male; and Jack had a father who would humiliate a son for a bed-wetting habit by urinating on the boy. Ennis and Jack were nineteen when they first had sex together in 1963; their boyhoods, then, had spanned the 1950s, my focus in this book.[6]

Though fictional, Twist and del Mar were not far-fetched midcentury males. In American real life, however, one did not have to have a harsh rural upbringing in the 1950s, nor did he have to be an impressionable youngster during that decade, to learn denial's allure, even when denials, like Ennis's and Jack's, seemed contradicted by the deniers' own sexual activity. Denials of a homosexual identity were commonplace and intense in the immediate postwar period, even among men who were extensively, sometimes openly, involved sexually with other males and who lived in supposedly cosmopolitan urban environments. To many men, appearing "manly" was what mattered most. Especially disdained in the 1950s was the popular association between homosexuality and mannerisms thought "effeminate": William Burroughs, for instance, once told Allen Ginsberg and Jack Kerouac (with at least one of whom Burroughs had had sex) that "all complete swish fairies should be killed."[7]

Despite all of the heartening advances in gay rights in recent years, this book maintains that the shadow of the 1950s still darkens the American cultural landscape. Some denials born in the postwar years would be long-lasting: Gore Vidal may have gone to his grave in 2012 insisting that "homosexual" is appropriate only as an adjective for activity, not as a noun for personhood, his or anyone else's, even though Vidal's Arlington grave, as he told me during a 2009 interview, would be alongside the grave of Howard Auster, his companion of many years, and not far from the grave of the one alleged great love of Vidal's life, Jimmie Trimble, a boyhood friend (and sexual partner) who died at the Battle of Iwo Jima.[8]

One historian has incautiously accepted such denials of identity at face value, seeing them as refreshing evidence of an incomplete acceptance of binary sexuality in midcentury American culture, said by Barry Reay to have been a largely label-free environment—especially for men like Ennis and Jack, virile-looking guys who didn't swish one bit. According to Reay, that appealingly labelless ambience would, ironically enough, come to an end late in the 1960s and on into the 1970s, when the gay liberation movement and its opponents gave fresh weight to the sexual dichotomy, intensifying the cultural demarcation of difference between gay and straight.[9]

But Ennis del Mar's and Jack Twist's denials that they had a distinct sexual identity of differentness is hardly a symbol of their freewheeling embrace of sexual ambiguity or fluidity. Their refusal to call themselves "queer" was no bold repudiation of the binary, but rather it meant that they were emotional prisoners of a binary firmly in place, men ashamed of which side of an unscalable fence they feared that they might actually be on.

That fence of sexual identity had been under cultural construction at least since the late nineteenth century in the United States.[10] In this book I maintain that the fence was dramatically heightened in the years just following World War II, with the opposite sides of the fence perceived to be radically different during the 1950s as never before. To continue the metaphor, I believe that the fence had been severely damaged during the Second World War, when many men had scaled it, or gone under or through it, with relative ease, enjoying (and sometimes fondly recalling afterward) their time on the other side. When reconstructed in the immediate postwar years, perhaps out of a desire to prevent the reoccurrence of its wartime inefficacy, the fence was made taller than ever—so tall, perhaps, that it was ungainly and destined eventually to begin falling apart of its own weight in the 1960s, a time when other cultural fences also began to topple.

One might argue that Ennis del Mar and Jack Twist were fictional creations, after all, actually born not in 1944 but in 1997, when "Brokeback Mountain" first appeared, and that Proulx wrote from a post-Stonewall perspective that tends to exaggerate the bleakness of all same-sex desire at any time before the allegedly less repressive and increasingly free years of the late twentieth century. Clearly, much recent scholarship has shown, it is a mistake to view all areas of the United States in all eras before the 1970s as uniformly inhospitable to expressions of same-sex lust or of affection of any sort between men.[11]

But the years immediately after the Second World War, my focus here, were a singularly inhospitable time for those expressions, an era not only less hospitable than periods coming *after* the 1950s, but in some ways markedly less hospitable than even those coming *before*, especially immediately before, that time. Men who actually had yearnings for sex with other men might lose their jobs, be subjected to brutal "therapies," or even take their own lives in the postwar climate. And men who had no such yearnings for sex with other men might suffer as well, in an atmosphere of suspicion and inhibition regarding *any* expression of deep affection between men. My central argument in what follows is that male relationships of *many* sorts, not just homosexual unions, were dealt a painful, damaging blow in 1950s America, a blow from which they have not recovered even yet.

In a cruel yet powerful irony, the unprecedented number of same-sex involvements that many American men experienced during the Second World War—involving varying proportions of sex and affection—may have had much to do with creating the fierce proscription of such involvements during the immediate postwar period. And of crucial importance is the fact that so many of the objects of some men's wartime affection or sexual pleasure did not themselves survive the war. Silence is sometimes more revealing than noise, absence more telling than presence: The missing buddy—of whom Vidal's Jimmie Trimble was but one of so many—is a major figure in the pages that follow.

As described in those pages, the immediate postwar period was the *morning after* a highly distinctive night before, a night that had been marked by the pain and peril typical of war yet also by war's customary pleasures of comradeship, all on an unprecedented scale. It is nonetheless on a morning after, of course, that last night's pleasure can become the source of guilt, leading even to pledges of future abstinence. Crucial to recall here is that around one of every thirty men who served in the Second World War did not return home alive; they are prominent characters in this book, their ghosts haunting the postwar years. That so many companions in the pleasure of fellowship did not survive the night also made the immediate postwar period one of widespread grief, of a *mourning after* widespread loss.

Recognizing the power of both loss and longing, sharpened at times by guilt, is essential to understanding postwar American masculinity itself. A marked increase in the space between men—literal and figurative, physical and emotional—occurred during the 1950s, and for some that distancing may have been an effort to assuage wartime losses suffered during the previous decade. When a love affair ends traumatically, future affection is sometimes avoided, with loneliness shortsightedly preferred to the risk of another loss. And when guilt is added to the mixture of loss and longing, the result is far from happy.

My central thesis, then, is that in regard to men's relationships, the immediate postwar period, roughly a decade and a half, may meaningfully be characterized as a prolonged period of *mourning after* the war, with an attendant sense of loss and longing, and may also be viewed meaningfully as a *morning after*, with such a time's own attendant feelings of guilt and penitence. My melancholy characterizations throughout the book regarding the state of American men's various relationships during the late 1940s and through the 1950s range widely, and are usually linked, directly and indirectly, to the huge event that was the Second World War. And yet this is not solely a book about that war's aftermath. Some of the individuals and developments covered in the five chapters to come are not clearly related to the war; although in their melancholy quality they are, I believe, additional manifestations of the sorry midcentury condition of the many sorts of relationships that a disconcerting number of midcentury American males had with each other.

Relying on a vast number of everyday photographs of American males of various ages together in various situations, this work commences with a look at physical manifestations of the altered spaces between American males that emerged in the immediate aftermath of the Second World War. Interpreting those spaces—the visible ones and those less obvious—is a primary purpose of the book, and my reading of the photographs in the first chapter lays the foundation of the entire enterprise. As were the dozens of images in my *Picturing Men*, the photographs in chapter 1 are no mere illustrations for a written narrative; rather, they themselves comprise a narrative, are components or agents of a cultural process. Moving from visual expression to the written word, examining the cultural work that fiction can perform, my second, third, and fourth chapters compare the differing fates of two important American postwar writers, John Horne Burns and Gore Vidal, using the works they produced, together with the reception those works received, as a vantage point for observing the troubled state of postwar masculinity. My two-chapter sojourn with John Horne Burns is necessarily a lengthy one, and I hope its length seems more purposeful than loquacious. My attention to Burns casts a backward glance, deepening my interpretation of the imagery in the first chapter, and the scrutiny of Burns also looks ahead, anticipating what is to come in chapters 4 and 5. In examining at length both Burns and Vidal and each writer's audience, I have sought to place enough signposts along the way to make it clear that my intentions are more than biographical; Burns, Vidal, and those who both appreciated and scorned them interest me primarily for what they reveal about midcentury manhood. The fifth chapter uses a body of diverse evidence to complete my characterization of mainstream American masculinity at midcentury as a sorry mixture of longing and loss. The book's coda examines a novel that appeared at the very end of the 1950s, John Knowles's *A Separate Peace*, a work that in its content and reception suggests some of what occurred culturally during the years that came before its publication.

The sense of loss and longing that permeated midcentury American masculinity is a wounded beast that wanders around to this day. *The Mourning After* is a modest effort to help put the beast out of its misery once and for all.

1

Putting Space between Men
Male Relationships in Everyday Photography at Midcentury

There were once real boys like that, before the great
sullenness spread over the land.
Gore Vidal, writing of a midcentury change in American life

The inability "to just know" who was gay intensified parents'
scrutiny of their children's—especially their sons'—demeanor
for telltale signs of homosexuality. The question of "who was
and who was not" gay extended to grown-ups. (After all, the
Kinsey Report did focus on adults.)
Ralph LaRossa, *Of War and Men*

A snapshot featuring two or more people says something important about their relationship—perhaps not the thousand words that the idiom claims a picture is worth, but nonetheless something substantial, of underappreciated significance. Their body language alone says plenty about the snapshot's subjects. The expressions on their faces (and knowing what those expressions mean to the subjects) is, of course, a good clue. Of particular importance in gauging how close is their relationship is how close to each other a snapshot's subjects choose (or at least agree) to position themselves, and how much comfort they seem to convey in that positioning. Imagine if by some magic we were able to gather and even give a bit of order to every snapshot of two or more American males taken in roughly the decade and a half following World War II; even in those predigital days, we are of course talking about a tremendous, daunting, number of photographs. That enormous archive of images would form a highly revealing group portrait of American males, a portrait from which we could learn much about the nature and meaning of men's relationships, all the more so if for comparison we had another archive of male images from the previous decade and a half, a period that would include the Second World War and the Great Depression.

As anthropologist Edward T. Hall famously maintained, societies differ greatly in culturally defining the amount of preferred space between people in various situations;

it was Hall who coined the term "proxemics" for the study of the culturally distinct ways of defining space in human interaction. By Hall's logic, if the actual amount of space defined and experienced as ideal between persons in a certain situation were to change over time in the same society, a significant cultural change—the change that somehow altered dictates regarding proper space—must surely have occurred.[1] Snapshots and other forms of vernacular photography, then, can be a highly useful tool in what we might call historical proxemics.[2]

In addition to where they are in proximity to each other, also important to observe are what the subjects in vernacular photos wear, how much of their bodies they expose in each other's company, and especially where the subjects are and what they appear to be doing. As Nancy Martha West, a leading historian of the snapshot's significance in American life, has importantly pointed out, snapshots quickly came to be reserved, nearly exclusively, for recording life's happier moments.[3] Snapshots became, almost by definition, not for times of sadness or conflict, with the once-common coffin portraits of dead dear ones, though not disappearing altogether, coming widely to be seen as inappropriate for the family album of snapshots or for more public displays, framed on a wall or a mantle, for instance, or just taped to the door of a refrigerator. However insincere a smile might be, it came to be expected, often explicitly summoned, in snapshots, with the expression of the adolescent unhappy to be along on the family vacation one of the few common snapshot frowns. Where the males in our gigantic collective portrait typically are, as well as where they typically are not, and what they tend to do with each other, as well as what they tend not to do, are crucial considerations. The fact remains, however, with their nearly universal focus on positive or at worst neutral situations, American snapshots have severe limitations as records of the whole of human experience. The best we can do, perhaps, beyond noting all that is present in an image, is also to pay careful attention to what Shawn Michelle Smith has cleverly called the *unseen* in photographs.[4]

Historians and social scientists have yet to widely appreciate the value of everyday photography as cultural evidence. In his 1959 sociological classic *The Presentation of Self in Everyday Life*, Erving Goffman did not even mention everyday photographs as a prime example of self-display.[5] And a later work of Goffman's entirely devoted to visual representation of gender roles was confined to commercial ads, again neglecting vernacular photography.[6] In the half century since the publication of *The Presentation of Self*, Goffman has had plenty of company among social scientists in the continuing failure to recognize the worth of vernacular photographs as social and cultural documentation, as much more than mere illustration for a written narrative. Many have valuably followed Goffman's lead in scrutinizing the performative quality of certain aspects of everyday life, even resulting in the elevation of performance studies to an academic field in its own right; yet the vernacular photograph awaits wide recognition as a performance.[7] While scholars of photography, typically persons trained in art history, have far surpassed other academics in paying attention to snapshots, even their focus on the snapshot has typically been more a matter of aesthetic appreciation than a systematic analysis of social and cultural documentation.[8]

To establish the photograph's value as an object of study and not simply of aesthetic appreciation, scholars first had to address what Marita Sturken and Lisa Cartwright have termed the "myth of photographic truth," realizing that simply because a photograph is created by a machine does not remove it from human intervention and somehow make it an "objective" record of "reality."[9] As photographer, theorist, and historian Allan Sekula put it, "photography constructs an imaginary world, and passes it off as reality."[10]

Seeing a photograph as a representation and not as "reality" itself simply recognizes that the image is hugely dependent on how a photographer frames a subject, and on certain cultural conventions of the moment when a photograph is produced, conventions affecting the choice of what to photograph and—especially for this book's purposes—how the human subjects in a photograph pose. "Culturally standardized systems of visual representations," Nancy Munn has noted, "like other forms of cultural codes, function as mechanisms for ordering experience and segmenting it into manageable categories."[11] In one of the comparatively few considerations of the vernacular or everyday photo as actual cultural evidence, visual anthropologist Richard Chalfen has pointed out that the "redundancy within snapshot imagery, created by the patterned use of participants, topics, and settings, may thus be understood as a reaffirmation of culturally structured values."[12] To the list that includes "participants, topics, and settings," one should add the way that participants in a snapshot typically pose, alone and in relationship to each other.

Of snapshots, photography scholar Marvin Heiferman has succinctly remarked that they "may appear to be naïve, but they are seldom innocent." Snapshots, that is, "reflect the needs and desires of all who make and appear in them, as well as the social, commercial, and visual worlds in which they are produced," so that ultimately "the pictures we take, for the most part, are the pictures we are trained and expected to take."[13] Only rarely and somewhat haltingly have scholars actually applied such insights regarding the nature of vernacular photographs; seldom have they considered the everyday photograph to be something other than an object to be aesthetically appraised, or as something more than a mere illustration of some idea, event, or person, and instead to be a cultural product of independent significance, a form of expression that reflects cultural conventions, to be sure, but that actually may also reinforce or challenge conventions—doing cultural work, just as does the written or spoken word.[14]

Beginning with his remarkable *Wisconsin Death Trip* in 1973, historian Michael Lesy's provocative work has presented photographs as historical artifacts, but typically Lesy has let photographs say what they will to his readers, without much explicit interpretation on his part.[15] Others have taken vintage vernacular photographs wholly out of their historical context and put them in the service of present-day concerns, sometimes quite engagingly, but certainly not as part of historical inquiry.[16] Sometimes with a suggestive written component, a few recent works have used snapshots to create powerful visual ethnographies of past communities—of summer camp goers, mid-twentieth-century New York drag queens, gay leathermen and their motorcycles, mountain climbers, and surfers.[17] Rare, though, has been the book like Deborah Willis and Barbara Krauthamer's *Envisioning Emancipation: Black Americans and the End of Slavery*, which elaborately interprets everyday photos themselves as both indices and agents of cultural meaning, in this case regarding the impact of emancipation.[18]

This chapter addresses vernacular photographs as cultural evidence, documents in the study of American male emotions. More specifically, I am interested in how photos display males relating to each other—that is, how men of differing involvements, ages, races, social classes, and types of sexual yearning literally and figuratively *feel* toward one another, a subject I explored with greater historical sweep in my 2002 book, *Picturing Men: A Century of Male Relationships in Everyday American Photography*. That work examined not only snapshots of men in pairs and groups, and such professional productions as athletic team photos, but also the commonplace studio portraits of men together that preceded George Eastman's 1889 perfection of roll film, the innovation that made snapshots possible and instantly popular. *Picturing Men* paid particular heed to the virtual disappearance in the twentieth century of the studio portrait of men together as a ritual affirming their association, maintaining that such portraits were not so much replaced by snapshots as they were rendered suspect in a culture of increasing anxiety over the meanings of male involvement. While men never stopped posing together for snapshots, changes in the ways that they posed, I maintained, reflected that anxiety, revealed a certain distancing, a moving apart.

Like *Picturing Men*, this chapter's evidence comes from my own collection of vernacular photographs of men together, now approaching ten thousand images, with my interpretations also informed by archival research and systematic attention to the thousands of vintage vernacular photographs of men and boys together offered daily on eBay. As will soon be clear, much to my regret, my evidence slights men of color, a major limitation that in *Picturing Men* I sought to explain. Not only are men of color much less evident in this chapter and throughout *The Mourning After* than I would like, I am also aware, and much regret, that the sources employed throughout this book also slight the experience of working-class males. I can only express the hope that others will be inspired to explore, through other sorts of evidence, whether and how my findings in *The Mourning After* apply to men at various levels of the class structure and with various racial identities.

My photographic evidence has additional shortcomings. The century of images referred to in the full title of my previous book ended around 1950, a time of apparent transition in American male relationships and their visualization in everyday photographs, and therefore an appropriate time, I thought, with which to end that book.[19] As for this book, and specifically this chapter, admittedly even with thorough research, it has been possible—because of formidable limitations of access and energy—to review only an infinitesimal fraction of the two gargantuan archives of male images imagined at the chapter's outset. Yet it has been my goal to view enough of this material to come close to having seen a reasonably representative sample.

This chapter, like those that follow it, extends my analysis of men's feelings in *Picturing Men* further into the midcentury period, documenting through photographs that the 1950s witnessed a drastic change in many men's relationships with each other. An increased distancing between postwar men, along with a certain formality, a regimentation, and frequently a staged quality, was a prominent feature of the period's photographs. As I suggested in the preface, the buddy was a male conspicuously absent at midcentury, making loss and longing, sometimes sharpened by guilt, central elements of midcentury manhood itself. The buddy, and the closeness between men that he represented, was often missing in and out of everyday photos during the 1950s. Though physical intimacy definitely was not wholly lacking in midcentury snapshots of males, when intimacy occurred it was more the exception than the rule, and even then was often cheapened by an exaggeration seemingly intended as a disclaimer.

In its singular way, vernacular photography is one apt means of studying what remains a prominent—if perhaps slowly diminishing—aspect of men's emotionality: the actual and symbolic distance that commonly exists between American males, a lack of intimacy between men that is unfortunate enough in itself and has ramifications for male-female relations as well. This space between men has a revealing history, which is to say that it has experienced changes over time and consequently is by no means inevitable. In *Picturing Men* I wrote that it "is the appearance of empty space between American men that I am out to explain." That goal remains prominent in *The Mourning After*.[20]

Members of the so-called greatest generation, the veterans of World War II who made it home, are today either gone or in advanced old age. But a dramatic incongruity between their wartime and civilian experiences may still, even today, have important cultural consequences. The incongruity was painfully evident in vernacular photos, in a shift from involvement to isolation: wartime closeness in stark contrast to a distancing between men in an America at peace. Though considerably more than half a century has now passed since their return from the war, the cultural time between then and now is brief. Many American men today, especially those millions who had a 1950s boyhood, may continue to be inhibited by a distancing promoted during the years following World War II, perhaps taught and enforced during their formative years by their fathers, often war veterans. One is even moved to wonder whether the quest for community that characterized so much countercultural activity in the 1960s, inside the antiwar movement and elsewhere, may in part have been animated by a search for fellowship born of an unprecedented boyhood isolation from one's fellows in the previous decade, an isolation that is often sadly evident in photos of boys from the immediate postwar period.

Briefly stated, earlier work of mine has shown that American men, old and young alike, once felt no such need for distance. In everyday photographs that likely both reflected and reinforced their feelings, American men indeed were once comfortable holding each other's hands, draping their arms around each other, sitting on each other's laps, and in other ways manifesting physical intimacy—without finding it necessary to pose in such exaggerated ways as to reassure themselves and viewers that they were simply kidding around. *Picturing Men* presented and sought to explain elaborate evidence of an apparently unselfconscious closeness between men present at the very dawn of photography before the Civil War and continuing into the next century. In figure 1.1 are a few representative twentieth-century photos up to the verge of American involvement in World War II, showing comfortable closeness in a pair and some larger groups of younger Americans.

This apparently unselfconscious comfort had begun to diminish—the space between men began slowly to increase, especially in some settings and among males past adolescence—early in the twentieth century. As American culture became more devoted to the fresh concept of sexual orientation, the notion that the more or less fixed direction of one's sexual yearnings actually defined the yearner—the cultural assumption, that is, that *homosexual* and *heterosexual* defined not just actions but persons—took hold. From the binary's beginnings, of course, the heterosexual set of male persons was the preferred of the two, with the homosexual stereotype—weak and womanly—a means of keeping alive American culture's increasingly outmoded gender distinctions.[21]

Among younger males in the twentieth century, however, as in the photos just presented, and also in military culture, and hence in photographs of soldiers and sailors, one continued to see the sort of intimacy between men that had once been much more widespread, no less present among civilians than among servicemen, no less among men of middle age than among the young. If anxiety over homosexuality increasingly inhibited civilian men's expressions of intimacy, a greater acceptance of intimacy in the military may have been promoted, especially during a war, by the reassuring myth that, after all, there were no homosexuals allowed in

FIGURE 1.1

the military (a policy promulgated and sometimes enforced during World War II), by the fact that a widespread concern over who might be homosexual was a luxury that the need for wartime manpower could not afford to consistently permit and promote, and by the intensity of attachments between individuals who so often together faced the distinct possibility of death.[22]

The Second World War was the largest same-sex gathering in American history, involving over sixteen million men, roughly one-tenth of the country's entire population. The war witnessed such intense feelings of male intimacy, elaborately documented in snapshots, photo-booth images, and in the studio portraits revived during the war as a ritual of male belonging, that there may actually have been a resurgence during the 1940s of the nineteenth-century phenomenon that historians refer to as men's "romantic friendships." Scrutiny of World War II servicemen's memoirs and other sources suggests that what appears to be a romantic attachment in countless wartime photos was sometimes, though by no means always, accompanied by an erotic dimension. Wartime memoirs and studies of the war attest that camaraderie among World War II servicemen, whether or not involving sex and romance, was of powerful, pervasive importance.[23] In the summer of 1945, the war nearly over, Sergeant Henry Giles of Company A of the 291st Engineer Combat Battalion made a final entry in the richly detailed journal he had kept throughout his last year of service in Europe. He recorded that a farewell banquet had been "a big flop" because "everybody was too sad over the split-up to have any fun & there wasn't enough liquor to ease the pain." Looking back, then forecasting the future accurately, Sergeant Giles observed that

> what we had together was something awfully damned good, something I don't think we'll ever have again as long as we live. Nobody in his senses wants war, but maybe it takes war to make men feel as close to each other as we have felt. We'll never feel toward anyone else the way we have felt toward each other, for the circumstances will never be the same again. We are all a little homesick for it already.[24]

A certain postwar homesickness, with wartime military service the home for which many men longed, is a theme running throughout *The Mourning After*.

In figure 1.2 are representative examples of the closeness common in World War II images, and of the frequency of coupling in such photos. According to an inscription on the back of both snapshots, the paradigmatic couple who posed reclining on the grass and also with one sitting on the other's lap were together on July 29, 1944, at Indian Point, very likely Indian Point Park, on the banks of the Hudson, a convenient fifty miles north of New York City, a popular getaway spot for picnics, with a swimming pool, halls for beer and dancing, miniature golf, and speedboat and carnival rides, all replaced by a ConEd nuclear power plant in 1962.[25] In another pair of photos (not shown here) of the same young men on the same occasion—which I found, incredibly enough, at a different flea market than the one where I found the other two snapshots—the men sit very close, side by side, at a picnic table. In one shot, the man not in uniform playfully sticks out his tongue at the photographer, while in the other he leans over to kiss his uniformed companion. Across from them at the picnic table sit two middle-aged women, possibly their mothers. These images belong distinctively to the years of World War II: Lighthearted as they clearly are, they surely document a relationship of some affectionate consequence.

FIGURE 1.2

We have no way of knowing, of course, whether the man not in uniform at Indian Point was, like his companion, also in the service. But servicemen's pairing off was reflected and encouraged by the armed forces themselves, in such practices as the distribution of handsome leatherette-bound albums embossed with the word "Buddies," and especially a large pamphlet entitled *My Buddy Book*, with places for names; for lists of "Guys on My 'Good' List," "Guys on My Other List," and "Just a Few Pleasant Memories"; and for "Snaps." There was an individual page devoted to "My Favorite Buddy" and two more for "Another Favorite Buddy." These special pages called for the serviceman to record his buddy's name and home address, of course, but also his physical description, including height, weight, eye and hair color, and complexion, as well as his sports, hobbies, amusements, favorite entertainer, pet expressions, and sixteen possible personal characteristics. The expectation and encouragement of intimate association was striking.[26] Only a decade later, however, such involvement between males had acquired a sinister connotation. Rare indeed would be photos like the ones of the guys at Indian Point. And by the century's midpoint, even younger males, who theretofore had been immune to the increasing inhibitions among civilian men, also began to distance themselves from each other in front of a camera.

To put it mildly, erotic and romantic bonds between men were not widely welcome in civilian settings at the war's end, during those fearful years that witnessed an odd symbiosis between anti-Communism and homophobia; yet while manifestations of such bonds may not have had much of a place in an America at peace, the memory of wartime bonds was perhaps not easily stifled. Regret and resentment over the peacetime loss of male closeness, along with ongoing grief and perhaps even survivor's guilt over the wartime deaths of buddies, was likely pervasive among millions of returning veterans, whether they were married fathers ensconced in the new suburbs that flourished after the war or were instead urban men with new identities as homosexuals living in the same-sex communities that burgeoned in American cities during the same period. Regret, resentment, grief, and guilt, all rooted in wartime service, likely were common, understandably so, among American men of the 1950s.[27]

Among the veterans who were fathers during the 1950s, and during that era of the "baby boom" there of course was an unprecedented number of them, resentment and regret over the loss of wartime's male closeness on the "morning after" the war may often have prompted a distinctly distant quality in relationships between fathers and sons, and may have fueled the era's anxiety over raising a generation of "sissies." In such a cultural setting, not just intimacy between fathers and sons and between adult men but even closeness between boys might be newly stigmatized and feared—and hence proscribed by boys themselves, as well as by parents, teachers, and those "experts" to whom postwar parents often turned for advice. In everyday photos from the 1950s of American males—servicemen, adult civilians, *and* young boys—restraint and lack of intimacy are revealingly common, though assuredly, remarkably, not ubiquitous. The comfortable pleasure of being together that had once distinguished so many photographs of American males of all ages had by midcentury become a rarity, a buried treasure.[28] In *Picturing Men* I displayed the "straightening up" of athletic team portraits that became common even before World War I, an early warning of more widespread anxieties to come.[29] At

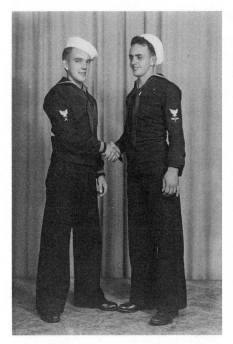

FIGURE 1.3

midcentury a certain straightening up would infect most types of images of American males together—except for photos of self-defined gay men in the privacy of their own homes or other secluded gay spaces.

Even in military culture of the 1950s, distancing occurred. The rapidity with which the intimacy typical of World War II snapshots vanished from images during the following decade is staggering. The military couple's photographic transformation was especially dramatic, beginning with an apparently large reduction in the frequency with which men posed in pairs. If servicemen in couples or larger groups posed close in the fifties, there was commonly an awkwardness or a forced, sometimes staged, quality rarely seen during the previous war and earlier. Service during the Korean War clearly did not arouse, nor did the larger culture encourage, the same unbridled closeness in wartime photographs that had been so pervasive during the previous conflict, such a short time before.

Studio portraits of male military couples, commonplace during the Second World War, apparently once a meaningful way of recording and honoring a relationship, virtually disappeared when the war ended. The contrast between the countless portraits of male military couples taken during World War II and one of the rare such portraits taken during the era of the Korean War, shown in figure 1.3, could hardly be more stark. No heads on a buddy's shoulder now; indeed the only touching was a stiff handshake. In countless earlier studio portraits of pairs of American males, in and out of the military, the couple often sat close together, at times even occupying a single chair. In another studio portrait accompanying the one of the pair of 1950s sailors, however, the buddy is missing, not the chair; the sailor on the left in the photo of the couple sits in a chair all by himself. Incredibly, in yet another shot, shown in figure 1.3, that same sailor sits on one arm of the chair, his arm draped around the chair's back—but the chair is empty! The relatively rare snapshots of midcentury male military couples typically showed either a formality or awkwardness not seen a decade earlier, or else a staged quality, a kidding around that stood in for intimacy (figure 1.4). Once in a great while, however, an intrepid pair had a photo snapped that recalled the romantic involvements seen so often during the Second World War (figure 1.5).

FIGURE 1.4

FIGURE 1.5

Much more often, it appears, midcentury servicemen were photographed in the less personal setting of larger groups, quite often posing in the orderly rows that, as discussed below, became a hallmark of civilian images of males of all ages. According to one man's inscription on the back of a 1953 snapshot from Fort Devens, Massachusetts, three servicemen lined up in civilian clothes, with the virtually interchangeable nicknames of "Daddy," Daddy-O," and "Old Dad," were "all ready for a 'night assault' on the USO women." Sometimes servicemen staged an amusing tableau, or appeared to loosen up a bit with alcohol involved (figure 1.6).

Even 1950s photos of the navy's Neptune Ceremony document a cultural shift. The ceremony was a centuries-old ritual marking a ship's crossing of the equator, with Shellbacks, sailors who had previously crossed the line, initiating Pollywogs, those who had not, the proceedings presided over by King Neptune himself, usually the ship's captain, and Neptune's wife, a comely sailor in female drag; the elaborate ritual featured as well several other specific characters played by members of the ship's crew. The Neptune Ceremony in the past had featured near (or occasionally complete) nakedness or else elaborate costumes, sometimes in female garb, overtones of sadism, and an abundance of homoeroticism. Elaborately and frequently recorded since the very beginning of snapshot photography, Neptune photos were now less numerous and showed little of the well-orchestrated, creative merrymaking of old. Midcentury Neptune photos, in dramatic contrast to their predecessors of the previous half century, seem to suggest a somber, perfunctory, halfhearted effort (figure 1.7).[30]

Photos of adult civilians in the 1950s might occasionally portray men in something approaching relaxation, if not intimacy, but such images often suggest that alcohol

FIGURE 1.6

FIGURE 1.7

was necessary to loosen things up. Even then, these drinking photos frequently featured men in an orderly lineup, in a staged scene, or in some sort of contest, such as arm wrestling. A liquor bottle or a beer mug had been a common prop—along with cigars and firearms—in what I called in *Picturing Men* photographic "pageants of masculinity" of the late nineteenth and early twentieth centuries.[31] While apparent inebriation had been photographed once in a while since then, it was only in the years after World War II that drinking and even drunkenness became truly widespread in vernacular photos of males, perhaps recording a reason for alcohol's loosening of restraint that had not been nearly so necessary before the postwar years (figure 1.8).[32]

A new token of masculinity emerged at midcentury in the automobile—not unlike the liquor bottle, cigar, and firearm in its association with men, despite the fact that of course some women drove, drank, smoked, and shot with as much gusto as some men did. In the unprecedented number of available models of cars, their greatly expanded choice of colors, their extravagant departures in design, and the greatly expanded frequency of middle-class ownership during that prosperous decade, the midcentury automobile assumed a cultural significance previously unknown. Along with liquor, automobiles were frequently found in the era's images of males together, including males clearly too young to drive legally. But happiness, whether induced by alcohol or not, tends to be missing from these photos; males seemed to take cars seriously: The boys of summer, one of them shirtless, who sat on a Pontiac's fender show no elation about either the car or each other's company; and the eleven boys, perhaps members of the Martyrs car club of El Monte, California, who sat close together atop an early 1950s model, are a largely joyless lot, taking no advantage of the closeness to get cozy with their friends (figure 1.9). Indeed the stilted sobriety of many men's snapshots during the 1950s is striking, some of them even challenging the generalization maintaining that snapshots were for happy occasions (figure 1.10). If men occasionally got close, sometimes it was not even with much apparent comfort (figure 1.11). Numerous vernacular photos reveal that American men had for decades enjoyed dressing in women's clothing, with varying degrees of effort to deceive. And dressing in female drag was one midcentury activity when men actually seemed mirthful, as in a 1955 photo of an American Legion drag show, a snapshot of another performance clearly played for laughs, and a team portrait, also from 1955, of the California Cuties, a softball team in drag. (The Cuties had debuted in Guam, to entertain American troops at the end of the war, and came to the United States in 1948.)[33] It is shortsighted to view men in female drag as simply an activity at women's expense, though surely it has sometimes been just that. Some men's drag performances clearly have been more homage than ridicule; and the fun, arousal, or fulfillment that males have derived from dressing as women varies considerably, today and in the past. For midcentury males, bound by their era's singular constraint of men's emotions, dressing as a woman may have provided a welcome escape, as never before (figure 1.12).

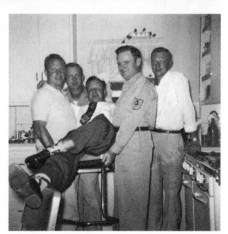

FIGURE 1.8

FIGURE 1.9

Gay males, for some of whom female drag could have a particular meaning—living in a society that derided them as womanly—posed in some distinctive ways in 1950s photographs. In earlier periods, so common was men's expression of physical intimacy in photographs that the sexual disposition of a particular photo's subjects is usually impossible to discern (today's numerous "gay interest" postings for vintage photos on eBay notwithstanding). Indeed trying to impose oriented sexuality on an old photo's subjects based only on their body language and closeness to each other is a fool's errand, often an exercise in anachronism, and always a distraction from my own essential concern as a scholar: the history of intimacy, not sexuality. But such was the cultural state of American masculinity by the 1950s, and such was the developing state of leisure activity and living arrangements among American men attracted sexually to other males, that there is a body of 1950s photos, especially those from an identifiable location—Fire Island in New York, for instance—in which one can be virtually certain to be seeing men who identified themselves as gay or its equivalent. It is primarily in 1950s snapshots of gay men that something of the old comfort of adult males with each other survived, a phenomenon whose significance and very existence I definitely underappreciated in *Picturing Men*.[34]

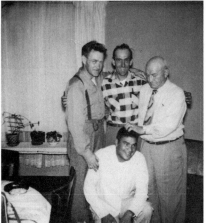

FIGURE 1.10

FIGURE 1.11

In and out of drag, three sets of males, for instance, were photographed on Fire Island, an increasingly popular gathering place in the 1950s for men sexually drawn to other men. In Fire Island's seclusion, theirs are surely some of the more mirthful snapshots of men from this period (figure 1.13).[35] Similarly at ease was a group of four—Gary, Al, John, and Randy—said to have met in each other's homes during the 1950s for games of strip poker, and another anonymous group of five who seem to enjoy the seclusion of private space (figure 1.14). A large number of snapshots reportedly from the collection of a male couple in Chicago show the sort of comfort between men that in an earlier time was confined neither to gay males nor to secluded places (figure 1.15).

Fear of becoming a male like those Chicagoans, shame over actually being like them, or anxiety over simply being thought to be someone like that, was more intense than ever in the United States during the 1950s. It was a period that commonly witnessed the subjection of gay men to severe brutality—at the hands of marauding frat-house gay bashers, government officials, and psychotherapists alike.[36] A best seller worried that what its author saw as the obviously homosexual relationship of Batman and Robin would pervert young readers of comic books.[37] Young boys in some parts of the country insisted on not wearing the colors green and yellow

California Cuties - softball Team 1955

FIGURE 1.12

together, especially on Thursdays, so widely had those colors on that day somehow become associated with being queer.[38] Boyhood was not always a lot of fun in the era; indeed it is in photographs of boys that one sees the most dramatic contrast between images from the 1950s and those of earlier periods. The distancing begun earlier among older American males had now become a part of boy culture as well.

In such typical settings as a campground, beach, dorm room, or simply someone's yard, *Picturing Men* amply documented that snapshots of American boys from before the 1950s, with little variation over the decades, were full of merrymaking and closeness between the subjects.[39] Photos of nineteen camping Boy Scouts in 1953 and of several boys at a church camp in 1957 show that smiles and touching hadn't disappeared, but the more-or-less orderly rows in which the boys posed are noteworthy and quite typical of the time (figure 1.16). Similarly, a charming 1954 image of Louis, Daniel, Raymond, and two boys named Jimmy conveys unselfconscious affection, even though their pose too is an orderly one (figure 1.17). Just as orderly, and much less affectionate, however, were the boys who struck a suggestively common pose as little soldiers during the Cold War (figure 1.18).

Although the would-be soldiers posed shirtless on a bed, the boys in that image conveyed much less intimacy than guys gathered close in a bedroom commonly had shown in earlier shots shown in *Picturing Men*.[40] Likewise, the flexing boys who gathered around another bed seemed to want to say something about themselves other than that they liked each other (figure 1.19). Young males often showed off in other ways during the 1950s, sometimes cleverly, yet rarely conveying the affection of earlier days (figure 1.20). Indeed some common poses of the 1950s seemed designed to keep subjects either apart or else in a stilted closeness (figure 1.21).

FIGURE 1.13

FIGURE 1.14

FIGURE 1.15

Like those young soldiers, boys often had their shirts off in 1950s photos, indeed were shirtless much more often than boys had been in earlier snapshots not taken at a beach or pool; but the distance between subjects, the pervasive lack of touching when shirtless, or the flexing in the midcentury images did not suggest much mutual affection (figure 1.22).

One shirtless midcentury pair, though, Hank and Jerry, with their arms entwined yet still managing to keep most of their bodies apart, remind us that more is sometimes present than immediately meets the eye in a photograph: A message from Hank to Jerry, apparently written on a piece of paper that once covered the photo, has been preserved, as an indentation on the image. "Hank," the hidden inscription says, "I understand just how you feel, Jerry" (figure 1.23).

FIGURE 1.16

As was true of many midcentury photos of older males, if there was to be some disorder and unguarded affection in photos of adolescent boys, alcohol seemed a necessary catalyst as never before, its increased necessity demonstrated by the increased frequency with which adolescents of the 1950s were photographed with a bottle, with a can of beer, or with several beer cans, presumably emptied, arranged like trophies (figure 1.24).

As was also the case with older males of the period, a stilted sobriety characterized many photos of younger males when there was no liquor in sight. Three somber beachgoers from 1954 are a far cry from frolicking boys at the beach in snapshots from every decade since snapshots first were taken. In other images, even Tinker Toys, pajamas, or a high elevation did not inspire smiles; the period's prevalence of regimented posing in a straight line is noteworthy in many snapshots of young males, including those of Oscar, Sparks, Jim, and Porky on a 1949 trip to the Grand Canyon, and of Boy Scouts at 1953's National Jamboree on California's Irvine Ranch (figure 1.25).

Remarkably, however, in spite of the unprecedented barriers the culture placed in the path of midcentury male affection, amid the vast number of photos showing inhibition and somber faces, an occasional snapshot nonetheless captured affection or simply merriment, some—but assuredly not all—of it seemingly halting or subdued (figure 1.26).

Lastly, the numerous group photos taken during the 1950s of young boys away at summer camp, especially when set alongside group photos of earlier campers,

FIGURE 1.17

FIGURE 1.18

FIGURE 1.19 (top) and FIGURE 1.20 (bottom)

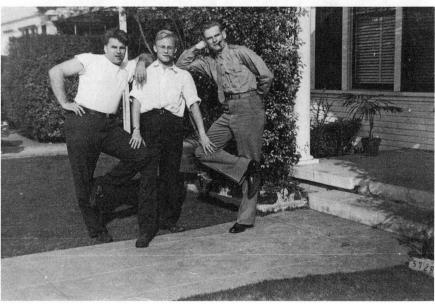

FIGURE 1.21

FIGURE 1.22

captured what had happened to much of midcentury American boyhood, an adjustment of boundaries that had earlier begun to vex manhood in our society, except
for the respite from fearful isolation during World War II. From their inception late
in the nineteenth century, American summer camps were typically a purposeful,
highly structured, gendered experience. The emergence of the American summer
camp may instructively be viewed as an effort to invigorate an American masculinity considered to be endangered by all of the indoor requirements of an urban,
industrial society—along with the contemporaneous creation of the Boy Scouts of
America, the sudden popularity of camping, hiking, and other ways of experiencing
wilderness, the invention of basketball, the birth of a system of national parks, a
fresh interest in "building" a muscular body, the greatly increased appeal and pro-
fusion of college sports, the legalization of prizefighting, and even such linguistic
innovations as "sissy," "pussyfoot," and "cold feet."[41] While there were, of course,

FIGURE 1.23

summer camps for girls, as well as sports for females and organizations like the Girl Scouts, the overall effort to exert oneself physically and to experience more of the "great outdoors" was at its outset primarily designed with males and their supposedly threatened masculinity in mind. Summer camp in the United States had always, then, involved play with a purpose.

If a boy's going away to summer camp had always been expected to involve carefully organized activities and close supervision, photographs from the earliest days of organized camping show that the experience could nonetheless involve affectionate companionship and playful skits. A handsomely mounted cabinet photo of a YMCA camping trip in the late nineteenth century by A. W. Yale, a Northfield, Massachusetts, professional photographer, was a study in relaxation and intimacy, as was a symmetrically posed portrait of six campers during the 1930s. Having more fun, in an eight-by-ten-inch enlargement of a snapshot, was the "seamanship class as pirates," a group of Pasadena Boy Scouts at Camp Cherry Valley on Catalina

FIGURE 1.24

FIGURE 1.25

FIGURE 1.25 (continued)

FIGURE 1.26

FIGURE 1.26 (continued)

Island around the time of the camp's opening in the 1920s, and an expressive pair, also costumed, in another snapshot from the camp on Catalina. Acting something out more cryptically, but seemingly having as much fun, were a group of campers in 1924 at Camp Yukon in Winthrop, Maine, a camp that opened in 1910 (figure 1.27).[42]

Summer camps of the 1950s apparently had become more serious business. A midcentury brochure for Camp Black Point, a summer camp for boys on New York's Lake George, near Ticonderoga, directed by Thomas F. Baker and his wife (called only "Mrs. Baker" in a camp publication), told parents of prospective campers that "under trained guidance and supervision, the boy acquires strength and ability to meet his own personal problems and learn positive adjustments to group living." Camp Black Point was open to boys between six and fourteen, with a tuition of $425 for the usual stay of eight weeks. Clearly there were to be few idle moments or un-structured activities for midcentury boys at Black Point; the brochure's photographs showed boxing, wrestling, hiking, horseback riding, horseshoe tossing, swimming, fishing, campfire talks, shooting, basketball, croquet, canoeing, archery, card games, field hockey, soccer, badminton, volleyball, basket-weaving, and the making of belts and pot holders.[43]

Older photographs in my collection that once belonged to Camp Black Point's Director Baker himself show some affection, spontaneity, and exuberance among the boys. But by the 1950s campers from Black Point and many other camps for boys across the country returned home after as much as eight weeks away with not just the baskets and pot holders they had made but with a group photo, sometimes enclosed in a "Souvenir Photograph" folder. This group photo, in which spontaneity and exuberance, as well as affection, were nowhere to be found, could hardly have differed more from the ones of campers from earlier periods. Maybe this "Souvenir Photograph" was a token of reassurance in that fearful age that nothing untoward had occurred while the boys were away from their parents, nothing like the roman-tic friendships or at least strong attachments to a buddy that so many fathers had ex-perienced during World War II. Photos from such places as Camp Mohican, Camp Equinunk, Kee-Wah Camps, Camp Monomoy, and Brookwood Camps were virtu-ally interchangeable eight-by-ten-inch horizontal portraits, consistently showing boys posed in neat rows, wearing identical T-shirts, doing nothing but sit there and smile blandly, in the same arrangement of "straightening up" that had come to char-acterize the athletic team portrait decades earlier (figure 1.28).

Something of an exception that proved the rule was a vertical eight-by-ten-inch photo, an enlarged 1953 snapshot rather than a professional portrait, from Camp Carlson in the Midwest, in which some campers and their counselors, probably residents of the cabin by which they posed, mostly shirtless, actually looked like they were enjoying themselves (figure 1.29). But such a summer camp photo of re-laxed, unregimented pleasure among young males was unusual at midcentury. It had come to that.

FIGURE 1.27

A popular culture gimmick of the fifties put the high-stakes contestants on TV quiz shows into isolation booths. American males who wanted to cash in culturally during that era were also placed in isolation from each other, increasing the space between them as never before. New material comforts and other distinctive features of white middle-class life during the 1950s, coming so close on the heels of economic depression and war, prompted extensive social research and produced other sociological classics besides the Goffman work with which this chapter commenced. The organization men studied by William Whyte, like the status seekers discussed by Vance Packard, were not notably content in their postwar affluence; their unprecedented material comfort was not always accompanied by psychological satisfaction. As suggested by the title of another classic work of the day, it could be lonely in the crowd.[44]

In his autobiography, Gore Vidal quoted from an effusive letter that his boyhood loved one Jimmie Trimble wrote to his mother—"the swellest Mom in all the world"—during World War II, from Guam, shortly before Jimmie would die in the Battle of Iwo Jima. "This letter could have been written in the Civil War," Vidal observed. "The tone is also that of Andy Hardy in an MGM movie," Vidal went on, "but there were once real boys like that, before the great sullenness spread over the land."[45] There are plenty of "real boys like that"—blissfully unguarded emotion-

FIGURE 1.28

CAMP CARLSON 1953

FIGURE 1.29

ally—in snapshots taken before the 1950s, yet such joyful boys are much harder to find in shots snapped during that decade. As was so often the case in his writing, Gore Vidal's wording was well chosen, his cultural sensitivity acute: It is exactly *sullenness* that pervades 1950s snapshots of American males together, perhaps most starkly so in photos of the nation's boys, with fresh space between them. Something unfortunate was indeed spreading over the land.

2

War as a Cultural Timeout
The Gallery *and Shifting Boundaries*
of Male Belonging

At his best [John Horne Burns] has succeeded in recreating that sense
of utter sadness and loss that everyone in the Army who found himself
overseas, whatever his job, experienced then and everlastingly.
Harry Brown, writer for *Yank* (1947)

Americans were the saddest people in the world in time of war because
they were Magnificent Provincials. That was why every American
soldier who wasn't queer had to have his buddy, with whom he shared
a stream of consciousness in itself meaningless, but which added up
to all the nobility and isolation of a young and idealistic people thrown
into death and destruction.
John Horne Burns, *The Gallery*

As noted already, John Horne Burns has been on my mind for quite a while. I have
long believed that Burns himself and what happened to his reputation—a descent
from acclaim to scorn to obscurity—deserved elaborate attention. Might his be
more than a tale of personal misfortune, and also something of a window onto the
broad landscape of midcentury manhood? Examining him and his fate in detail, this
chapter and the one that follows it give Burns that attention. And the chapter after
that contrasts what happened to Burns with the much longer career of his fellow
veteran and writer, the onetime acquaintance who was among the few who kept
Burns's memory alive, Gore Vidal. My effort here is to place their intertwined tales
into a broad context, one that involves the history of American men and their diverse relations with each other, not simply the history of men, like Burns and Vidal,
who had sexual involvements with other males.

Before journalist David Margolick's *Dreadful: The Short Life and Gay Times of
John Horne Burns* appeared in 2013, Burns had previously been the subject of only
one brief biography and just one unpublished doctoral dissertation.[1] In early stages
of my research, I was excited to discover (as Margolick later did) that John Horne

FIGURE 2.1   Thomas D. Burns and the author, 2010.

Burns had a surviving brother, eminent Boston attorney Thomas D. Burns.[2] Along with our correspondence, three long and informative in-person interviews with him, in 2010, 2011, and 2012, reinforced my conviction of his brother's underappreciated importance (figure 2.1).

Grandsons of Irish immigrants on their father's side and great-grandsons of famine-era immigrants on their mother's, Tom and John Horne (known in the family as Jack) Burns were two of Joseph and Catherine Burns's nine children. Two other offspring, both boys, died as infants, William as a newborn in 1915 and Robert, strangling in his crib in 1923 at only eleven months old.[3] All three of the sisters survived into old age; Cathleen died at ninety-five in 2013; Anne and Constance (known in the family as Connie) are much the youngest of the siblings. With the sole exception of Tom, however, the Burns males, not just the two who died as babies, met harsh fates in contrast to their sisters. Jack died at thirty-six, in disrepute among literary critics, either of suicide or from a stroke hastened by heavy drinking. After his World War II service, another brother, Joseph L. Burns Jr. was diagnosed with schizophrenia and lived a troubled, erratic life, in and out of psychiatric treatment, until he died at fifty-nine. The affable Donald, awarded the Bronze Star for service as a medic in World War II, a heavy drinker who went from being a stockbroker to serving coffee at a market in Kennebunk, Maine, died in 2006 at eighty-two.[4] The postwar period brought distinct difficulty for many American males; Jack, Joe, and Donald Burns are sad cases in point.

The fate of his brothers had haunted Tom Burns. "One of the great mysteries of my family," Tom Burns said to me with some intensity in our first interview, "is the apparent collapse of all the males in the family. None of them were there for the long pull. My father wasn't. Jack wasn't. Joe wasn't. Donald wasn't. And this sounds very vain of me, but I'm the only one that lasted. . . . They couldn't hold it, they couldn't . . . and it has been a mystery, John, to me all my life as to why I could be that way, because they were all talented, they were all bright as hell, all of them."[5] Tom would pose that same question, in some form or another, many times in our three interviews. "What was there about us that nobody [but me] ever stood the test of time" was how he once put it, continuing, "How did that happen?" There was a particular sadness for Tom because something—fate, Irishness, a chemical imbalance—had robbed him of spending an adulthood as equals with his brother Joe, "my closest friend in the family." In contrast to all the soldiers and sailors who didn't return alive from the war, Joseph Burns went missing psychologically, not during the conflict but in its immediate aftermath, a fate he shared with many fellow veterans. For all his material accomplishments and the love he clearly found and gave in his family life, Tom Burns did not escape the weight of loss and longing.

He voiced no longing at all, though, for his mother Catherine Burns, who had died at nearly ninety in 1976.[6] There was a dramatic contrast between Tom's alienation from their mother and the consistently (some would say excessively, even oddly) affectionate tone of Jack's many letters to her during and after his service in World War II. Let it simply be noted for now that in an essay about "the creative writer in the twentieth century," Jack came up with a peculiar analogy: "The good artist, once his work is finished," he wrote, "has no more right to cast his shadow across it than a mother has to blight her son's life by falling in love with him."[7] Their mother's power in the family was as clear in Jack's letters as in Tom's recollections. And in Tom's telling, Jack occupied a position of privilege in the family equivalent to their mother's position of power. Jack also showed early interest and skill in writing, Tom Burns told me. In stories he began writing as a boy, "Jack caught the spirit of the place [Saint Augustine's Parish in Andover]," Tom remembered. "He was, he had, he could be a very biting wit." A favorite target of Jack's was "Father Branton, who was our pastor, who was a drunk. . . . Jack would make fun of him and pick up things he said [in sermons] and he could be devastatingly funny."

This amusing brother also stood out in the family because of his intellect, and for musical talent that was as abundant as his athletic ability was lacking. Jack, Tom said, "was always the brightest one of the class. He was a brilliant pianist. He had a great singing voice. He was soloist for the Harvard Glee Club. He never did anything athletic in his life." Tom continued:

> Joe and I were always very athletic. I mean we played baseball and football and hockey. None of those things did he [Jack] ever do. Joe used to describe him one time when they were both at Andover. Jack was '33, Joe was '36, and I was '38. So we were all there at sort of the same time. And, Joes tells a story, they had something called 'PI' at Andover, which meant physically incompetent. When you couldn't do anything, you became physically incompetent: couldn't do the pole climb, couldn't run the . . . Joe told about Jack with a group of people running around the track, and he is the last one running along, loping along, and talking to someone about some good books that he had read. . . . One summer he was the only one in the family that went to camp because the Depression came along [because] my family thought it would be good for him.

Proudly, though, Tom recalled an occasion "at an officers club in Naples during the war, and I heard him play. . . . There must've been a thousand people there, and he sat down at the piano and he played and played. And I said, 'I have never heard anything like it in my life.' And you know it was like something you would see in a movie."

As veterans both Jack and Tom returned to New England. Back home, they took utterly different postwar paths, each one marked by early accomplishment and considerable promise. Tom quickly began his climb as a Boston lawyer, securing a position with the powerful firm of Friedman Atherton King and Turner in 1946, and Jack was widely heralded as one of his generation's most important novelists when *The Gallery* was published the following year.[8] These brothers, so opposite in their styles, sexual yearnings, and goals, could still greatly enjoy each other's company. Continuing a closeness they had known as boys, "he would come to see me at Friedman Atherton once in a while," Tom remembered, "he would come to talk to me, and we would go drink together, and we would work on an article he was writing for *Holiday* magazine."

Jack's sexuality, however, was a definite barrier for Tom, hardly an unusual situation for two American brothers of opposite sexual interests in the 1940s. The only brother who "never had a girlfriend," Jack had "moved into this coterie, this group, at Phillips Academy, one master and a few men that moved together"; only later on, he said, would Tom realize "that they were all homosexuals." In 1948 Jack shared an apartment with another young man in Boston's West End, in a building that no longer stands on Chambers Street Court. Jack's companion was "some guy that worked in a record store," Tom remembered, "and it was a situation that made me very uncomfortable," though not uncomfortable enough to keep Tom and his wife from having dinner with the two men in their apartment. Surely not atypically for the time, Tom never discussed either Jack's sexuality or his own discomfort with it directly with Jack. To my question about whether Jack was especially fond of his Chambers Street Court companion, Tom simply replied, "I don't know. I didn't allow myself to think about that."

One matter Tom did confront Jack about: the worth of his writing. And in criticizing Jack's second and third novels, Tom may have in fact been indirectly expressing his disapproval of Jack's sexuality.[9] Not unlike the response of many of the era's literary critics, Tom found *Lucifer with a Book* and *A Cry of Children* to be greatly inferior to their predecessor, *The Gallery*. *Lucifer* and *Children*, much more so than *The Gallery*, are both full of homosexual desire and actual activity. And much like professional critics, Tom's assessment of the latter novels may have had less to do with aesthetics than with attitude, setting, and subject matter. Jack, his brother insisted to me, "was a very talented man. But deeply flawed. Deeply flawed. For instance, I told him with *Lucifer*, 'For Christ's sake, don't write this book. It is terrible.' And as far as *Cry of Children*, I said, 'You are not writing about what you know about.'" On the contrary, John Horne Burns knew well the matters with which those two novels dealt, knew them as well as he knew the wartime situations and attitudes taken up in *The Gallery*. Tom Burns and professional critics may simply have found the candor and the domestic settings of *Lucifer* and *Children* too hot to handle at the century's midpoint.

Jack's death at just thirty-six in 1953 was reportedly from a cerebral hemorrhage brought on by excesses of both sun and alcohol, yet there was talk of suicide, even rumors of murder. At the very least, it is accurate to say that self-destruction of a sort marked much of his life, increasingly so as his literary reputation plummeted. He was initially to be buried in Italy, where, as before in Boston, he had lived with another man. In those days, Jack's companion had no way of preventing Catherine Burns from having her son's remains brought back to Boston. After a small Catholic funeral at Saint Anne's Church in Boston's Back Bay, Jack was buried in the elaborate Horne family plot in Brookline's Holyhood Cemetery, a large and sedately lovely place where many of greater Boston's wealthier Irish Catholics (including several Kennedys) are buried. His body retrieved by his forceful mother, John Horne Burns, in death as in life, never got as far from home as perhaps he should have.

In literature and oratory alike, the Irish in Ireland and the United States are not known for parsimony with words, but rather for a "gift of gab" that passes for eloquence in some quarters but for mere wordiness elsewhere. John Horne Burns's writing was rarely lean, and it was also voluminous. Though he had only three novels published before he died, Burns had written many more, along with a substantial body of unpublished poetry; especially useful for my purposes are hundreds of his wartime letters, many of them lengthy, mostly to his parents.

Another American writer, this one not known for corpulent prose, once provided a characteristically pithy assessment of John Horne Burns, a judgment that expressed what for decades has been the central tenet of the dominant narrative of Burns's career: "There was a fellow who wrote a fine book and then a stinking book about a prep school, and then he just blew himself up," Ernest Hemingway told *Atlantic* editor Robert Manning.[10] With more embellishment than Hemingway gave the story, the accepted narrative of Burns's fall has been a simple tale of declension—if, that is, he has been remembered at all.[11] The dominant narrative of Burns since his death has been composed of variations on the themes articulated by Gore Vidal, first in his simultaneously appreciative and patronizing 1965 *New York Times Book Review* essay devoted to Burns and then in a 1975 interview. While Vidal's essay seemed to be an effort to revive interest in Burns, or at least keep his memory from disappearing altogether, the essay, like the interview a decade later, largely blamed Burns himself for the neglect he had suffered. Though Vidal maintained that *The Gallery*, appearing in 1947, had been "certainly the best of the 'war books,'" and that *Lucifer with a Book*, following just two years later, "was perhaps the most savagely attacked book of its day," he assessed 1952's *A Cry of Children* as simply "bad." John Horne Burns, Vidal wrote, "was a gifted man who wrote a book [*The Gallery*] far in excess of his gift, making a kind of masterpiece which will endure in a way that he could not." Burns "seems to have lost some inner sense of self, gained in the war, lost in peace," Vidal suggested, eventually becoming so self-destructive that his death in early middle age "seemed right." In fact, said Vidal, this man who seemed destined to die young, who "chose not to go on," was peculiarly disagreeable, and not even very handsome: "He was a difficult man who drank too much, loved music, detested all other writers, and wanted to be great, . . . [with] a receding hairline above a face striking in its asymmetry, one ear flat against the head, the other stuck out," Vidal wrote in the *Times* essay; later on, to interviewers for the gay press he was even more forthright: "He was an awful man. Monster. Envious, bitchy, drunk. Bitter."[12]

While Vidal might not have allowed himself the introspection to actually recognize a bit of his own temperament in Burns, there may have been identification of a sort. In chapter 4 I will suggest that Burns's harsh fate at the hands of critics, as well as his early death, may have haunted Vidal, to some extent shaping the tone and direction of his own writing, maybe even reinforcing Vidal's fierce public resistance to identifying himself as a gay man. And to characterize Burns, as did Vidal, as the writer of only one good novel, largely blaming Burns's own shortcomings of skill and temperament for his eventual downfall, may shift the burden from where it at least in part belongs: postwar critics, with their failures of imagination and nerve; and postwar American culture itself, with its profound discomfort with men's intimacy.

Fredric Warburg, Burns's English publisher who was best known for working with George Orwell, was, as a Jew, in some ways more familiar with being an outsider than was Gore Vidal. Perhaps consequently, Warburg was much less critical of Burns than Vidal was, finding Burns more attractive both physically and temperamentally. To Warburg, Burns was a "strange, secretive, handsome, vigorous, shy, sensual, puritanical, jesting character, an accomplished pianist with a fine tenor voice." Warburg even refused to see Burns's death as a self-destructive act, maintaining that it surely was just severe sunstroke, not suicide: "A man so full of life as Johnny rarely dies of a broken heart."[13] That cheerful portrait of Burns, however, was the exception, not the rule. Other characterizations of Burns have resembled Vidal's more than Warburg's.

Boston columnist "Uncle Dudley," for instance, thought that Burns was indeed capable of having his heart broken, and that it was the war's aftermath in his beloved Italy, not literary critics, that broke it. Writing in 1955 that *The Gallery* was "still the best" postwar writing, "a permanent work of literature daring in conception and scathing in its outspoken social criticism," "Uncle Dudley" thought that "although he lived seven years after 1945, the war killed John Horne Burns. A young man generous and compassionate, the misery and horror which he saw inflicted on his 'enemies,' the Italian people whom he had come to love, burnt him out and broke his heart."[14] When the Boston Public Library opened an exhibit honoring Burns on the tenth anniversary of his death, "Uncle Dudley" wrote glowingly of the exhibit and of Burns and *The Gallery*, maintaining that the author's death itself "was caused in part by an injury sustained in the war."[15]

In addition to Hemingway and Vidal, two other well-known American writers, James Michener and Joseph Heller, voiced powerful admiration for Burns, lamenting his early death and descent into obscurity. Michener considered Burns no less than "my tragic hero," one of those writers "so overwhelmed by their success that they destroyed themselves." Michener apparently lost track of Burns after the critical denunciation of *Lucifer with a Book*, not even knowing that *Cry of Children* ever appeared. Yet he was so shaken by Burns's death, that "this luminous talent was gone," Michener even fantasized about what Burns's having lived might have meant. In the process Michener expressed a rare understanding of his "alter ego's" cultural significance and potential worth, not seeing Burns's decline as a personal failing, but instead shifting the burden onto the society Burns criticized so severely. If Burns had lived, the popular and utterly conventional Michener was certain

> he and I would have competed, honorably and vigorously, throughout our lives, each checking what the other was doing, meeting now and then as adversaries and in time as friends, each going his unique way, each presenting a mirror image of the other. He would have been one of

the notable aesthetes, I a stolid representative of the stable middle class; he a writer of traceries and shadowy intimations, I of conflicts in blazing sunlight; he the head of a coterie and immensely popular in universities, where his acerbic wit would be appreciated and encouraged, I off by myself plugging away at my own goals. Side by side we would have marched through the decades, and tears fill my eyes when I think of the enormous loss I and the world suffered with his death. My alter ego had vanished in the midst of sunset. I think of John Horne Burns every week of my life.

Although John Horne Burns probably would not have valued praise from a writer so pedestrian, James Michener astutely grasped what Burns might have accomplished with a longer life, seeing the final years of his short life as something more than simply a fall from grace.[16] With none of Michener's sweeping appreciation of Burns, it was perhaps simply Joseph Heller's celebrated sense of irony that inspired his own brief remark in 1999 that *The Gallery*, although "a very excellent novel," had "been forgotten now."[17]

Whether John Horne Burns was soon forgotten in the private memories of the many readers of all three of his novels is a nearly impossible question to answer, though each work was distinctive enough in its time that its being remembered by readers does not seem far-fetched. Apparently eager for more from Burns following *The Gallery*'s publication in 1947 and *Lucifer with a Book*'s appearance in 1949, Yale student Edward Hastings wrote Harper and Brothers in 1951 regarding "the whereabouts and future plans of John Horne Burns."[18] Just twenty when he wrote that letter, Edward Hastings went on to be a founding member of San Francisco's American Conservatory Theater, rescuing it financially after its performance building was destroyed in the Loma Prieta earthquake of 1989. He died at eighty in 2011 in Santa Fe, New Mexico, where he was living with his partner of fifty years, Eugene Barcone.[19] It seems plausible that Burns's work was long present in the private memories of many men of Edward Hastings's generation, maybe especially among those of his orientation.

The possible ongoing devotion of readers notwithstanding, aside from occasional words of praise and remembrance from the likes of Vidal, Hemingway, Michener, Heller, and the *Globe*'s "Uncle Dudley," there were few public expressions of any sort regarding Burns in the first decades after his death in 1953. If not entirely in oblivion, he seemed to be nearly there. Popular Library published a paperback edition of *A Cry of Children* in 1957, with a sensational cover that implied erroneously that the novel was mostly about a woman's sexual escapades. Avon Books revived *Lucifer with a Book* in paperback in 1977, doing the same for *The Gallery* that year. Neither stayed in print for long. In the *New York Times*, only *The Gallery* ever received significant mention from the 1950s through the 1980s, usually in a knowing glance from a reviewer of some lesser work, implying that a reader might well be unfamiliar with this ill-fated masterpiece.[20]

Compelling proof of how quickly Burns's reputation became tarnished and of how little Burns has been remembered is the fact that not only has he had just one significant biographer, David Margolick, but, incredibly, he appears to have been the subject of only one doctoral dissertation, Mark Travis Bassett's at the University of Missouri, completed in 1985. Although Bassett strove to be sympathetic to Burns, he, like so many others, often blamed his subject for the neglect or harsh treatment he received. Had Burns only "been more temperate, more patient, with himself, and with the shortcomings he detected in others," Bassett wrote, his reputation might have not suffered so much.[21] Bassett even largely ignored Burns's work after *The Gallery*; the dissertation in effect ends with it.

Even Frank S. MacGregor, John Horne Burns's close friend and an editor and the president at Harper and Brothers, promoted the notion that *The Gallery* stood far apart from, and probably far above, his two later novels. Shortly after Burns's death, MacGregor wrote an appreciative reader that *Lucifer with a Book* and *A Cry of Children* "were quite different in tone from THE GALLERY and I regret to say that many who admired THE GALLERY so much found a quite different author in his later books." To the reader's question about where he might purchase a copy of *Lucifer with a Book*, already out of print, MacGregor suggested "a second hand store."[22] Even his supportive British publisher Fredric Warburg may have partially blamed the victim when he wrote vaguely that it was "a powerful irritant in Horne Burns' works" that had "turned the critics against him."[23]

Just what might have been such an "irritant" to critics and other contemporaries? At least as much as aesthetic considerations, it was perhaps Burns's dealing so directly with home-front homosexuality in both *Lucifer with a Book* and *The Cry of Children* that did him in with critics and lost Burns many midcentury readers as well. With that proposition of mine on the horizon, it seems appropriate here to consider Burns's own attitudes toward homosexuality. In a manner that surely was common for midcentury American males attracted to other men, he oscillated dramatically between what Kenji Yoshino has aptly called "covering" and unsubtle proclamations of his queerness.[24]

In his *Times* essay on Burns, Vidal recalled a time at a party when Burns declared unequivocally, and Vidal thought seriously, that "to be a good writer it was necessary to be a homosexual." Answering Vidal's dissent, Burns named six well-regarded contemporaries known to be homosexuals: "'A pleiad [an eminent group, of six or seven],' he roared delightedly, 'of pederasts.'"[25] Perhaps "pederast" had merely an alliterative appeal, as a word to be paired with "pleiad"; otherwise, Burns's choice of words may have revealed a guilty sense of himself.

People may of course have many reasons for preferring privacy to disclosure, and Burns by no means sought privacy consistently. Yet in midcentury America, one's homosexuality could be a strong incentive for avoiding disclosure. John Mitzel, a longtime gay bookstore owner and activist in Boston who became Burns's first (and, for many years, only) biographer with a slim volume appropriately titled *John Horne Burns: An Appreciative Biography*, insisted that his subject "was an intensely private person." According to Mitzel, Burns thought it inappropriate to pry into authors' private lives, and of himself reportedly said, "I detest being asked questions."[26] In contrast to the loudmouth recalled by Gore Vidal, others found Burns to be shy. In London for the publication there of *Lucifer with a Book*, Burns reportedly asked Frederic Warburg, his British publisher, if he could leave a party in his honor even before guests had arrived.[27] What appears to be Burns's mercuriality may merely reflect the degree to which queers of his generation often led, in effect, two lives, and had two dispositions: one for queer spaces such as the party recalled by Vidal in his "pleiad of pederasts" story, the other for interactions with the straight world, with each disposition the other's radical opposite, mirroring how radically opposite had become American mainstream culture's estimations of straightness and queerness.

Countless midcentury males who were sexually drawn to other men nonetheless married women, of course; for Burns, who never married or even came close, girlfriends and possible future wives seem to have been wholly imaginary, though often discussed. Just after the war, in a biographical sketch for Harpers when *The Gallery* was published, Burns unbecomingly wrote that he preferred "European women to American ones: they are really more complex and aware of their purpose in life."[28] Around the same time, *Saturday Review* published a portrait of Burns, back home in Andover, that had him writing, listening to and playing music, walking, skiing, skating, and thinking of Italy, where allegedly there was a girl, "daughter of a banker in Milan—'I may go back and marry her yet.'" Both before and after the war, Burns taught at a Connecticut prep school, the Loomis Institute (now the Loomis Chaffee School), an experience that inspired *Lucifer with a Book*. During the second teaching stint at Loomis, Burns displayed in his apartment on campus a photo of an alleged "fiancée," and would even occasionally date women who taught at Chaffee, an adjoining school for young women.[29] Writing Harpers editor John S. Fischer from Loomis in September 1947, Burns recalled a recent party that both Fischer and his wife, Elizabeth, attended. "Your wife is warm, charming, and clever," Burns wrote, observing that such a combination "is a rare trait in women." Referring to the fact that Elizabeth Wilson Fischer was Scottish and had indeed met her future husband in her homeland, Burns closed with a gay man's clumsy effort at "covering": "Perhaps I too should look things over in Scotland."[30] Burns's women were typically only in photos or in countries far away, yet Warburg did report joining Burns for breakfast in Boston in 1951, finding Burns accompanied by "a young man and a flat-chested girl he introduced to me as his fiancée." Warburg found that introduction surprising, "as I had assumed until then that he was exclusively homosexual."[31]

Shortly after leaving Loomis under a cloud late in 1947, John Horne Burns became for the first time one of those comparatively rare American men of the mid-century with the temerity to live with another man with whom he was sexually partnered, this the union that made Tom Burns uncomfortable. Though living with this boyfriend in Boston's West End, in apartment #3 at 4 Chambers Street Court, Burns could still affect a heterosexual pose in some settings. His Loomis job gone, *The Gallery* doing well and *Lucifer with a Book* about to appear, Burns began writing a series of travel pieces for *Holiday* magazine in 1949. Heralding the upcoming series in the "*Holiday* By-Lines" of its February issue, the magazine quoted the "sandy-haired, rugged six-footer" regarding his marital status, a subject about which *Lucifer with a Book* might be expected to arouse some interest: "I am still unmarried and hope to remain exempt until I'm 35—the deadline for men in my family," Burns replied.[32]

For the publicity attending the publication of *Lucifer with a Book*, Burns did not disclose the fact that he lived with someone, but told Ramona Herdman of Harpers that "I live in a five-room apartment done in gay colors; my house, I think, has a feeling of relaxation and well-being about it."[33] In more private settings, Burns might be more candid: Gore Vidal wrote in his journal that Burns usually referred to his living companion as his "roommate," yet once "he told me he was much in love with this boy, that he was tired because they had, that evening sex in the shower."[34] Thanking his close friend and Harpers editor Frank MacGregor for attending a party at the Chambers Street Court apartment, Burns would at least refer to the gathering using a plural adjective, dropping the pose of singleness: "It was kind of you to come to our party."[35]

Neither John Horne Burns nor any other devout American Catholic of the mid-twentieth century needed his religion to inspire guilt over same-sex desires and activity; secular American culture of the day provided more than enough aversion to homosexuality to make miserable the lives of many people who considered themselves gay. But Catholicism could deepen the agony. There seems little doubt that Burns was deeply serious about his religion, especially before he joined the army; and despite occasional efforts to disguise his sexual desires, it seems equally clear that Burns thought of himself as a gay male from an early age. Equally firm commitments to Catholicism and homosexuality were rarely a happy combination at the approach of midcentury. In comparison with "the only perfect thing I know in the world," as Burns described Catholicism in a wartime letter to a former student at Loomis, David Alison Trailsend MacMackin, his sexuality was probably bound to suffer. With teenager MacMackin, still a Loomis student, Burns would use their revealing code word for gay men, "dreadfuls," and in one letter Burns wrote of the dilemma of "so many dreadful people who are ardent Catholics ritually" yet are in "a state of scarlet mortal sin" because of "their peculiar pleasures," putting "their mouths which have received the Body and Blood in unlawful places." Being drawn to those "peculiar pleasures" and "unlawful places" was clearly a source of massive discomfort for the former Saint Augustine's altar boy, who morosely wrote Mac-Mackin about their shared sexuality that "there is nothing spiritual about it—only nakedness and despair."[36]

To Burns, the "20th century homosexual," whether Catholic or not, was just not an appealing person: "Camping is after all," he wrote MacMackin just after V-E Day, "the essence of the tragic spirit contorted into a leer no Greekmask [sic] ever knew. He sets up for himself a tinseled world that has nothing to do with reality, believes himself a golden and divine spirit, gifted beyond other men."[37] "Self-loathing" is perhaps too strong a word with which to describe Burns's estimation of his own sexuality, but to say he was merely ambivalent is to understate. The critical response to his remarkable fiction surely only exacerbated Burns's torturous irresolution over his own sexuality. His talent was rare, but for queer men of his generation the irresolution was not.

Imaginary girlfriends were not Burns's only defense against the scorn heaped on homosexuality; there were also declarations of his own worth and significance so excessive that they must be seen as a sort of desperate overcompensation. The self-absorption and apparently boundless self-regard in Burns's wartime letters to his parents are perhaps in part simply what one might expect from a man who as a boy was made to feel he was the center of his parents' universe. But he hardly confined expressions of his excellence to those letters home. To MacMackin he once wrote that "I have been lonely because I have been excellent"; on another occasion he wrote him that *The Gallery* was "like nothing since King Lear."[38] Authors are prone to various sorts of exaggeration in correspondence with their publishers, and exaggerating his own worth was a common ploy for Burns. He wrote Harpers publicist Ramona Herdman, who was gathering material with which to publicize *Lucifer with a Book*, that he was "brooding over" a new play "which I pray will put me up in Tennessee Williams's league," and that in his future novels he was "aiming at a synthesis of naturalism and anthropomorphic ethics" that be thought achievable.[39] Those excessive estimations of himself, however disingenuous some might have been, were accompanied in Burns by a remarkable wordiness; he seems never to have experienced writer's block. He might have done well to have occasionally substituted reflection, even restraint, for sheer expression. He told Eloise Perry Hazard of the *Saturday Review* that he wrote "on schedule 3,000 words in three hours daily, seven days a week."[40]

While not a memoir, *The Gallery* would nonetheless have been impossible had Burns not served during the war; his service merits attention in its own right, and in any analysis of the novel's cultural work. Burns once called his time in the army "three wild years."[41] But that glib description should not mask the fact that his World War II service was for Burns a multifaceted period of introspection and some heightened self-knowledge, many a dark mood, sexual adventures probably well beyond what he had experienced in New England, a moderated Catholicism, and—from comparisons with North Africa and especially Italy—a recognition of his own country's cultural distinctiveness and shortcomings that would distinguish *The Gallery* as a postwar novel like no other.

For a pampered young man like Burns, wartime must have been simultaneously chastening, challenging, terrifying, disheartening, liberating, and definitely broadening. Beginning his training at Camp Croft, near Spartanburg, South Carolina, Burns was quickly promoted to corporal, and not long thereafter entered officer candidate school, from which he emerged a second lieutenant. He spent some of the summer of 1943 at the Brooklyn Army Base, training in the censoring of correspondence, landing then in Fedallah, North Africa, and by September in Casablanca, where he was a base-bound intelligence officer—while most of those who had traveled with him went into combat. By the fall of 1944 Burns was in Italy, at times with the Censorship Base Detachment in Naples, teaching at GI university in Florence, or translating captured Fascist files in Milan. By June of 1945, the European war over, he began formally writing *The Gallery*, staying in Italy for a bit after his discharge, returning home to New England the following February, and before long teaching again at Loomis.

Leaving the United States for the first time had created for Burns a cultural distancing, not just a geographical one, a separateness that might have particular appeal for an American male with his sexual desires. "In the 19 days, crossing the Atlantic," Burns had *The Gallery*'s narrator recall, "I remember that something happened to me inside. I think I died as an American."[42] While that sort of distancing would serve him so well in *The Gallery* (and, arguably, his two subsequent novels as well), Burns distanced himself as little as possible from his family during the war. He wrote hundreds of wartime letters home, priceless documents of the Second World War.

Like so many soldiers, Burns wrote on the military's "V-Mail," one-sheet stationery designed for easy photographing by censors (of whom Burns himself, of course, was one). Nearly all of the letters that survive were to his parents, though a few were to Cathleen, even a few to his younger sisters Constance and Anne. The overwhelming majority of his letters, not surprisingly, were to his mother, over three hundred of them, beginning with those from Camp Croft in the fall of 1942, through his time in both North Africa, 1943-44, and Italy, 1944-45. Though Burns's letters home frequently contained personal details, even including adventures with sex and liquor, and typically began with effusive expressions of endearment, by 1945 his letters to his parents increasingly sounded like practice for *The Gallery*, in their lengthy descriptions of the Italian populace and landscape.[43]

FIGURE 2.2   John Horne Burns in his World War II army uniform. (By permission of Mark Bassett; portrait now housed at the Gotlieb Archival Research Center, Boston University.)

If his inclination to brag, his frequent resort to hyperbole, was probably at least in part a means for Burns to mask self-doubts and guilt over his sexuality, it also may at times have prevented an emotional intimacy that would have frightened him. Whatever the psychological undercurrents, it is no surprise that he, quite unlike so many other soldiers, once claimed to have few actual buddies in the army. To his mother in 1944, Burns wrote that it was "impossible for me, like most soldiers, to have a 'buddy,' for my arc is too wide and too eccentric to admit of another's presence."[44] Yet despite his own isolation and expressions of superiority, Burns recognized, perhaps with no little envy, the widespread existence and tremendous appeal of wartime camaraderie. He wrote David MacMackin in 1943, still a year before MacMackin's graduation from Loomis, that "I think that those who live through this war—not too sweeping a generality now—will all go off in troops and echelons and live together in a remote fastness. . . . The army ties you in with some strange strong skein of comradeship."[45] And even he claimed he had some meaningful friendships. To "Daddy" in 1945 Burns wrote of "a brilliant Australian captain who now would be my best friend if he didn't have to fly to Austria the other day," and to his mother he had earlier written from North Africa that "one of my more exquisite affinities is for the little Irishman for whom I work. . . . His is the weird wisdom of Roman Catholicism plus bar-room sentiment plus Amherst College plus newspaper work." Burns and the little Irishman, with whom he said he had "altogether one of the most delicious and economical friendships I've known," even gave each other endearing nicknames, Steve and Mike. Some of his affection was apparently reciprocated: Burns wrote his father that "a particularly brusque character" had told him, "You're not the most masculine character I've ever known, Burns. But when you were a platoon leader, you showed what an officer could be. They *loved* you."[46] Even a man of Burns's haughty defenses could not escape the bonds of affection that were often an integral part of World War II service.

Any who would dismiss Burns as a self-absorbed loner would have difficulty reconciling that view of him with how he told his mother of "a quite melancholy pilgrimage" to say good-bye to another officer headed home "as a psych case." Describing his friend's sorry physical state and paranoia with heartbreaking precision, Burns reported that he had urged his friend, also from Massachusetts, to "call on you at 89 Gainsboro when his cure is complete." "He doesn't look like much of anything," Burns told his mother, "sort of a well-mannered baseball player with a boyish face and hair gray in spots." He was, said Jack, "a very lovely sort of guy, gentle and sensitive in the best Irish tradition."[47] At times, the same could be said of Burns himself.

And, in fact, though "buddy" might not be a word that suited him, John Horne Burns did have two intense male friendships formed during the war, two involvements so close that he would dedicate *The Gallery* to these men, along with one of their wives, the dedication made more poignant by the fact that one of the men was killed in battle near the end of the war. While Burns himself would see no time in combat, then, he was not spared battle's emotional toll. The friend who died was Robert MacLennan, killed in Germany in April of 1945; the other close friend was Holger Hagen.

Burns met both men in mid-1943, at Fort Hamilton, Brooklyn, where he was briefly stationed between his training at Camp Croft and his going to North Africa. The friendships were unquestionably intense, fueled by war's own peculiar intensity, its terrifying uncertainties. Hagen, whose wife Beulah was the sister of gay novelist Glenway Wescott (who after the war would introduce Burns and Gore Vidal), said that although his relationship with Burns was not sexual, it was nonetheless "the most intense he'd ever had with another man." Hagen even came up with a reassuring characterization of Burns that is probably not uncommon among the close straight male friends of gay men: "I was never really certain in my own mind: was he gay or was that, too, a mask. His 'swish' way of talking certainly seemed to be deliberate play-acting. It was so very obvious. And God knows he never made a pass at me!"[48] Burns was definitely not beyond posturing, but pretending to be sexually attracted to other men was definitely no mere pose of his.

Nor did his powerful feelings for MacLennan, whatever their parameters, seem to be a pose. The men's wartime correspondence, what Burns called "our furious exchange of letters" has, sadly, apparently been lost. Despite the fact that he and MacLennan "saw so little of each other," Burns wrote Hagen, he had loved MacLennan "with a special flame that will never flare for anyone else." Indeed their involvement had, said Burns, an "essence [that] remains far more perfect than almost any other more protracted rapport I've had with anybody." Learning from Hagen of MacLennan's death on April 7, 1945, Burns said that he thereupon got fiercely drunk.[49] Though he was never in combat himself, its results severely troubled him; the battlefield had just taken Robert MacLennan when Burns wrote his mother, "I think a lot of my depressions overseas have come from looking at leveled towns and brooding on human life snuffed out—the good with the bad."[50]

Like Gore Vidal and countless others, therefore, John Horne Burns left his own dead buddy on the battlefield of World War II, a ghost to haunt the rest of his life, a loved one frozen forever young in time, a standard of affection against which others might unfairly be gauged, and perhaps a self-protective reason for keeping one's distance in future relationships. War allowed, even nurtured, a peculiar closeness between American males that was rare in postwar domestic life. Though, unlike MacLennan, both Burns and Hagen outlived the war—Burns not by much but Hagen by half a century—their close friendship nonetheless ended shortly after the war did.

Dear friends and sexual partners of the same sex were not necessarily mutually exclusive, of course, perhaps especially for some men during the Second World War. But for John Horne Burns, difficulty in making friends did not necessarily preclude sexual relations with other males during the war—or, for that matter, before or after it. Writing MacMackin, who was just seventeen at the time, that Camp Croft was aptly named "Camp Crotch," Burns said that sexual activity between men there was rampant, that "for pure and ecstatic dreadfulness [their code for gay sex], civilian life is a hollow mockery beside it."[51] When in Algiers, Burns thought back to Camp Croft, and wrote a poem about a group of unrestrained gay men he had met there, "The Mad Queens," writing MacMackin that the "Queens" liked to wear their field jackets on their shoulders, so that their jackets would "seem like a mink bolero." When his sexual adventures led to a case of syphilis in 1944, only someone like Burns could write that penicillin's curative powers led to results "more miraculous than anything Bernadette Soubirous saw at Lourdes."[52] If not miracles, more than sexual excitement was clearly part of his relationship with a young Italian, Lino Russo, about whom Burns candidly wrote his father, "I think there's enough sadness in the world that I at least may go all out to make some one happy when I like him as much as I do Lino." By war's end, Burns had another Italian boyfriend, named Mario.[53]

Extraordinary closeness to his family, in particular his mother, was at the center of John Horne Burns's identity. Tom Burns hardly needed to read Jack's letters to realize how close Jack and their mother had been; in fact, he had not yet read those letters when he first told me of what he felt to be their mother's powerful preference for Jack over himself. With occasional comments on Italian politics, Jack devoted most of his letters to his father to just three subjects, which he typically addressed in flowery, sanctimonious language: music, Irishness, and religion. Jack would also talk religion in letters to his sister Cathleen, whom he addressed as "Dee-Dee," her family nickname, but letters to her typically addressed more than the faith: From Camp Croft he reported that "in a bar" he had just finished reading Austrian novelist Franz Werfel's *Song of Bernadette*, about alleged apparitions of the Virgin Mary; then he told Cathleen about a young writer, using a favored nickname for the camp:

> My most recent trophy at Camp Crotch is Peter Paul O'Mara, just a private in the medical detachment. Take a look at his *City of Women*, meretriciously running as a serial in the *Redbook*. But he himself is a good-looking Gael with considerable scholarship, wit, and values. He has fallen away from Rome—perhaps from reading Huxley and Windham-Lewis. He has a very broad wedding ring, but it brooks him no *rede* [does not deter him] at all. He confesses frankly to his whoredom in writing slick serials for money when he has a charming clever mind, but says I can't complain as long as he buys me beer with the proceeds.[54]

To move so swiftly, in the same letter, from discussing the Blessed Virgin to less virginal matters was characteristic of John Horne Burns.

Though he never discussed his "trophies" with his mother, his letters to Catherine Burns were nonetheless by far the most numerous, varied in topic, and peculiarly candid of those to family members. Jack's outsized affection and esteem for her, especially in contrast to Tom Burns's bitter memories of the same woman, was striking. "If your children get a bang out of life and have a simplicity and charm that attracts others, you know whose fault it is," he would write, adding revealingly, "God help the wife who doesn't approach your example! Love and a rain of kisses, Jack." He once reported to "Darling Mother" that he was happily free of the "GI shits" afflicting many others. In an earlier letter on the same topic, he unbecomingly told her that his "greatest enjoyment is to watch those who got diarrhea from neglecting to scald their mess-gear rush past my tent door tearing down their britches." He discussed military politics with her by observing that "the windfall of promotions, the transferring of many plaintiffs and fuckups have engendered an era of good feeling and security in the bosoms of all the girls [Jack's fellow officers]." On another occasion, again regarding some officers, he got philosophical with his mother, saying "to use an Army vulgarism, which is very *a propos*, they think their shit doesn't stink. Shit always has and always will."[55] Jack clearly was aware of both the special place he had in his mother's heart as well as the distinctive nature of his own sexual identity, writing once to "Carissima Dee-Dee" that "I had always thought that she [their mother] knew that my personality is quite a separate entity from the other excellences of my other brothers, and that I do not live in quite the same groove that they do. And that I can't be any other way than what I am."[56]

As noted, Tom Burns was especially struck by Jack's frank discussions of his wartime drinking in letters to their mother, something that must have been troubling to Catherine because of her own mother's alcoholism. (His grandmother's drinking problem had been painfully obvious in some of Matilda Sullivan Horne's visits to the Burns home in Andover, Tom recalled, and was responsible for Catherine's not allowing alcohol to be consumed there.) With an odd candor for a letter to a parent, Jack nonetheless wrote his mother that the watch she had given him at thirteen had "stopped—possibly because I went swimming with it when I was plastered in New York." He would tell his mother of his brief periods of sobriety, during which associates would tell him of "the lucency of my complexion, the sparkle of wit undimmed by hangovers," only to report a week later that he had taken a "Monday off to get drunk." Complete with blackouts, it was by no means light drinking that he wrote her about: "Last night I tied on the worst one in my Bacchic history and woke up this morning at the 6th General Hospital (how did I get there? I don't know) to find my wallet gone, with the $30 I didn't send home." Some months later, interestingly enough, he even told her of having "an almost marijuana sense of eternally unfolding time."[57]

If Jack never showed the frankness with his mother about his sexual encounters with other males that he showed with his sister Cathleen and especially with male correspondents like MacMackin, he occasionally skirted with his mother the issue of his yearnings for men, telling Catherine once that, after a lot of cognac, "my ultimate memory is of a French lieutenant putting his boot in my lap while I tenderly lectured him on the correct way to wear American-made leggings." Only a few days later, he told her that he had just reread *Death in Venice* and "the beauty, terror, and decadence of the work came through even better than they did seven years ago [when he was twenty].” Usually with his mother, though, Burns was awkwardly covering, explaining, for instance, his having extra money to send home from North Africa as the result of the fact that the “wine is death, and so are the Arab gals.” In 1944, he reported that he had heard from Eleanor Brewster, a forty-five-year-old spinster he knew from Loomis:

> I’m in a relatively helpless state now, stripped of my prep school teacher’s armor; so anyone can make kittenish love to me now through the mail. She’s made her claws practically impregnable now by sending me a lot of expensive music, and she won’t hear of payment. Don’t be surprised if I marry an heiress who looks rather like Dante’s bust with a red wig on its skull, and you have a lot of little nutmeg-staters [residents of Connecticut, home of Loomis] calling you grandma. They say a senile love is always the most intense. All kidding aside, she’s always had a soft spot in her boz [bosom, presumably] for me. The feasts she spread at the HMS’s [headmaster’s] picnics were almost comparable to yours.

The following year, from Florence, he claimed to be pursued by one Rose Weiss, by “the elderly Fascist countess,” and even by a “blonde switchboard operator” whose advances had caused Burns to rush “out screaming into the night.”[58] If these covering tales were the boyhood imaginings of a child, they might be amusing, but as the assertions of an adult they are merely sad.

Burns candidly wrote home about his bouts of depression during the war, especially while he was stationed in North Africa; this confrontation with his own psychological struggles surely eventually added weight and texture to *The Gallery*.[59] He thought things started to make sense again in Italy, however, where he “experienced an annihilation of myself and a rebirth in that tragic but four-dimensional country.”[60] He indeed found Florence so soothing, he wrote his mother, that “I can’t imagine that anyone ever had a nervous breakdown” there.[61] In Naples, Burns was stationed near his beloved San Carlo Opera House, which was just across the street from the Galleria Umberto, the huge glass-and-iron-covered shopping area that would give its name, as a metaphor, to the novel-of-a-sort that brought Burns fame. Completed in the late nineteenth century as part of a widespread architectural rejuvenation of the city, the Galleria contained shops of all kinds, along with art galleries, restaurants, and bars, topped by a third story of private apartments.[62] Burns found that appealing sexual opportunities were as varied and abundant in Naples as were shops in the Galleria. Italy, for Burns, was full of possibility, possessing a lack of restraint that he had barely, if ever, experienced in the United States. Using their peculiar religious code for gay sexuality that would later make its way into *Lucifer with a Book*, he told his former student David MacMackin that an area he visited after the Neapolitan bars closed at two thirty "was flea-thick with nuns and prior-esses."[63] And in a poem written then Burns observed that "war mixes up the bestial and divine / and sodomy is just another name."[64]

As the conflict wound down, war's toll, its lessons, and its potential aftermath preoccupied Burns, as *The Gallery* began to emerge in his letters home, as he alter-nated between hope and despair. "The one lesson that war will have taught me," he wrote Catherine Burns, "is that kindness is not confined to any one class of people." The very next day he wrote her that "we can only hope and pray that it doesn't leave the hundreds of thousands of dogfaces so completely demoralized that when they come home they'll be good for nothing nobler than sitting on the front porch and eyeing the girls with a glassy stare."[65] A few months earlier, he had presciently wor-ried to "Daddy" that "if the twenties were a period of post-war insanity, I predict a much higher index this time," observing that "in the men about me, I see seeds of future trouble."[66]

Indeed as the war neared its end, Burns's letters to his father became more sub-stantial, discussing more than his previous trio of topics in letters to Joseph Burns: music, Irishness, and religion. He now told his father of some enlisted men he was working with, "hand-me-downs from the front: too nervous for combat, not nutty enough to go back to the ZI [Zone of Interior, the military area far from the fight-ing]." With the resignation and wisdom that would distinguish *The Gallery*, and that probably echoed the sentiments of soldiers from virtually every one of mankind's wars, he wrote, "I don't regret coming overseas; it's left me without a single illusion except for what I consider abiding things in life." Two months after V-E Day yet before Hiroshima, Burns said he was "terribly tired of the army and of wasting my youth and energy in nonsense," astutely recalling that "in *War and Peace* Tolstoi has a marvelous passage on how a military machine, once in power, desires to keep itself going forever."[67]

As *The Gallery* took shape, its author had high hopes for its success, was not im-modest about its significance, and was coming to see himself as a social critic as well as a novelist. "There's going to be an era of disillusionment, recrimination, and bitterness" after the war, Burns wrote his mother in 1944, "after that wisdom and love must go to work." That *The Gallery* might provide some of the necessary wis-dom was not beyond Burns's goals for the work; he even compared it to John Dos Passos's *U.S.A.* trilogy, "one of America's great novels," saying that Dos Passos "did for the last war what I would like to do for this one." His reformist hopes for the post-war period ranged widely, as his later novels would make clear: "If the American people will direct a little more concern towards cleaning up their own yard instead of criticizing Russia and Great Britain, they will see that after the war their own race and unemployment problems will be quite enough for them to handle, thank you."[68] The depression he experienced in North Africa seemingly gone and Italy having refreshed and enlightened him, Burns was producing in *The Gallery* not only a major expression of the war's deeper meanings but also a penetrating piece of cultural criticism. Upon his return home to the United States in 1946, he returned to teaching at Loomis, finished *The Gallery*, and awaited the response of readers.

The Gallery is no more a traditional novel than the building in Naples that gave the book its name is a typical late nineteenth-century department store. Burns built a gallery of his own in the book, a thoughtfully arranged, subtly linked series of "Portraits," written in the third person, alternating with a set of "Promenades," written in the first. The portraits are vignettes; among them there is no continuous narrative, no sustained plot, no single protagonist. The eight promenades, each one beginning with "I remember," chronicle one man's journey from the United States to Naples, via Casablanca. The nine portraits—some collective, some individual—are a varied lot, mostly depictions of Americans, but a few of Italians: Michael Patrick, a soldier temporarily out of combat; Loella, a Red Cross nurse; Hal, a troubled young lieutenant; Father Donovan and Chaplain Bascom, friends of different faiths; Momma, proprietor of a gay bar in Naples, and her clientele; Captain (eventually Major) Motes, commander of a company of African American soldiers; Giulia, a young Neapolitan woman who takes up with an American captain when her city is liberated by his forces; Queen Penicillin, metaphorical monarch of a VD ward for American soldiers; and Moe (Moses Shulman), an American lieutenant, a Jew, sensitive to the vast cultural differences between Italians and his fellow Americans, dead at the book's end. It was Burns's insight in this melancholy meditation that during wartime it does not take actual combat experience to induce severe disorientation and despair, or at best a grim endurance. *The Gallery* has not one battle scene, but is replete with battle scars.

Burns once told Holger Hagen that he would get *The Gallery* into print "if I have to give a facejob to every publisher and agent in New York City."[69] It apparently took less effort than that: Random House rejected the manuscript, not deeming the work a novel, while Vanguard considered it but wanted many deletions. Hagen's wife, Beulah, by then working at Harpers, urged her dear friend to submit his manuscript there, where it was accepted in October 1946, with Burns receiving a large advance for those days, $2,000. The first printing, in June 1947, was sixty-five hundred copies, and the work eventually reached over twenty thousand more hardcover copies through ten printings, with a paperback edition first appearing in fall 1948. Harpers executives found sales figures encouragingly high, especially since the book sold well even before its initial advertising campaign was complete.[70]

Burns was delighted, and wrote his Harpers editor (and company president) Frank MacGregor that he had been "touched, flattered, and awed by the scrupulous care and tact with which Harpers have handled me and my manuscript." He was eager enough for publication to not even fuss over the fact that timid editors at Harpers had "deleted that most shy-making of all four-letter words."[71] With *The Gallery*, that is, Harpers published an otherwise unflinching work about servicemen, civilians, and the war that was diminished by its not having a single "fuck" to be found. The internal debate at Harpers over inclusion of that word reminds us of what a decidedly innocent age it still was, of how much cultural work there was for *The Gallery* to do, even in its "fuck"-less form. Yet surely its complete absence in *The Gallery* was better than would be the absurd insertion of the nonword "fug" all through Norman Mailer's own war novel, *The Naked and the Dead*, the following year.[72] The sanitizing of both *The Gallery* and *The Naked and the Dead* was a bad omen for the reception that the two subsequent Burns novels would receive in just a few years. Even with its language censored, *The Gallery* was a bold, pathbreaking book, and it definitely did not go unnoticed, being promoted with gusto by a publisher in England as well as the United States.[73]

An early and auspicious indication of the warm reception *The Gallery* would widely receive was the *Saturday Review*'s declaring it the best war novel of its publication year, along with putting a handsome drawing of Burns by Hal McIntosh on the magazine's cover of February 14, 1948. In one of the articles on Burns in that issue, Harrison Smith genteelly declared that *The Gallery* "is not a book for little boys in any school, but for adults who recognize the truth when they see it, and who do not object to blatant four-letter words." Smith thought that compared to *The Gallery*, John Dos Passos's *Three Soldiers*, "the novel that started off the realistic fiction of the First World War, was a fragrant and tender lily." Interestingly, as was the case with most contemporary reviewers, Smith failed to directly mention Burns's bold chapter on Momma and her bar largely frequented by gay servicemen, though he did refer obliquely to the book's encounter with "all the forms of what is lightly known as love."[74]

The potential fame resulting from *The Gallery* at first seemed virtually boundless. The PEN Club, the eminent association of writers, planned "a discussion of books dealing with the war" for its annual dinner in January 1949. Discussants were to be Mailer, Irwin Shaw, Michener, Dos Passos, and Burns.[75] Harpers had sent an advance copy of *The Gallery* to Dos Passos himself, and he had replied enthusiastically that "with the exception of [Australian Godfrey] Blunden's *The Room on the Route* [actually *A Room on the Route*], it's the first book of real magnitude to come out of the last war. It is written with a reality of detail and a human breadth and passion of understanding that is tonic, healthgiving."[76]

Everyday readers were no less enthusiastic. Some appreciated the book's lack of American chauvinism; Lilo Juan Daves, for example, wrote Burns that he hoped *The Gallery* would make readers "a little hesitant of either unconditional praise or rejection of any one group—of damning the strange, or the un-understood." Helen T. Arnold found it "the most honest and decent book I have read about the people in this war," while Marie Whitbeck Clark thought it was "one of the most moving books I have read in years." Taking courage from the book was a common reaction, an interesting response to such a bittersweet work; and its authenticity was praised by fellow veterans Jim Tuck, Hobart Skidmore, and Kenneth Marcom.[77]

There were seventeen major reviews of *The Gallery* by professional critics during the year of the book's publication, ranging from largely negative to effusively positive. Because of the nature of much of the criticism heaped on Burns for his later work—a focus on homosexuality that most reviewers found unseemly—it is important here to note that only five of these seventeen *Gallery* reviews even mentioned the "Momma" chapter at all, and most of those mentions were brief, often vague. Was ignoring the "Momma" chapter a reviewer's effort to deny the very existence of the sort of men, especially among soldiers, who were patrons of Momma's, or else did it simply reflect a reviewer's more pressing concerns in the war's immediate aftermath?

One mention of Momma's, by the *San Francisco Chronicle*'s longtime literary editor William Hogan, was unequivocal in its disdain for such a bar and its patrons, calling Momma's "a bar for the diseased," even though he found that the other parts of *The Gallery* made it "a very satisfying book."[78] A graduate of the University of California, Berkeley, who served with Bill Mauldin in Italy (and later cowrote the 1951 screen version of Mauldin's *Up Front*), Hogan was neither unsophisticated nor unsympathetic to the plight of GIs. Unlike John Horne Burns, however, Hogan perhaps found that his Irish Catholicism got in the way of empathy, or even sympathy.[79] By contrast, an unsigned English review, in the *Times Literary Supplement*, thought "Momma" one of the work's two strongest chapters, "as good as one can hope to find in contemporary literature."[80] Writing in the *Saturday Review*, Lawrence Grant White (son of architect Stanford White), finding *The Gallery* "one of the best" of the many books about the war, also thought that the chapter on Momma's bar was "among the more successful," yet still could only obliquely describe the place as "a Naples bar where the inanities of her customers are accurately recorded." White tried to be affirmative in his review, but a certain reserve got the better of him: "One wonders if the author's school is sufficiently liberal to include 'The Gallery' in its library—it is strong medicine for small boys. But his pupils are fortunate to study English with such a capable writer as Mr. Burns." White found *The Gallery* so shocking that he believed Burns "has no inhibitions; . . . and the reader is spared no details of [the characters'] lecherous conversations or bodily functions. But the ring of authenticity lessens the shock of the brutal four-letter words that appear perhaps too frequently."[81] Whether met by appreciation or disgust, *The Gallery*'s earthiness was universally singled out.[82]

Not surprisingly, Edmund Wilson's review in the *New Yorker* was not faint of heart. Though he found Burns's "gushings over the beauties of Italian love and the Italian acceptance of life" to be at times "maudlin" and perhaps the result of youthful naïveté, Wilson admired Burns's "generous emotion" and not once got censorious over language. To Wilson, *The Gallery*'s best character was Hal, the young lieutenant who ended up in a psychiatric hospital, obsessed with death, a figure who would undoubtedly have been too much for more defensive readers to take. One of *The Gallery*'s more hopeful qualities for Wilson was simply its promise of better books to come from John Horne Burns, "something both solider and more intense than this already remarkable book."[83]

In assessing further the cultural significance of *The Gallery* and its author, and to better understand the fate that awaited him, three matters merit additional consideration: first is Burns's distinctive treatment of male affection and sexual involvement, both in the "Momma" chapter and elsewhere in *The Gallery*; next, the lessons and sensations that Burns took away from the Second World War; and, lastly, the singular breadth of Burns's critique of American culture, a critique begun in *The Gallery*, only to be carried further in his later works.

War changes things—and did so for racial minorities in the Second World War, of course, and even for some of the whitest and straightest young men who served. Participation in World War II changed forever the perspectives and even the self-identification of some of the soldiers and sailors who wanted—and during the war may for the first time have had—sexual experiences with other males.[84] John Horne Burns did not need the army to discover his sexual desires for men or to develop a sense of himself as someone apart, but the war years strengthened Burns's queer identification, and that of many thousands of others. "Momma's boys [patrons of her Naples bar]," Burns wrote, "had an awareness of having been born alone and sequestered by some deep difference from other men."[85] For the first time, the US War Department itself perceived such a "deep difference," seeking, if only halfheartedly and without consistency in a time of war, to keep homosexuals, now considered a distinct type of person, out of the armed forces, rather than simply punishing servicemen for disdained sexual activity.[86] The very idea of oriented sexuality, that there are not simply distinct types of sexual acts but different types of sexual persons, had slowly been working its way into American culture for a few decades, but that idea's acceptance may well have been accelerated greatly during World War II, with its same-sex environments of utterly unprecedented dimensions. Not only might the war have witnessed a widespread revival of romantic friendships among American men, it also surely sent many men home with a new understanding of themselves.

Indeed Burns wrote that Momma's patrons "understood one another, as though from France and New Zealand and America they all had membership cards in some occult freemasonry." His sense of their differentness was profound: these men looked and talked distinctively, at least when within Momma's protective walls. David Margolick has made a convincing argument that an actual place like Momma's, catering exclusively to gay men, was unlikely in wartime Naples.[87] If it bore no resemblance to an actual place, perhaps especially if that were the case, Momma's elaborate development as a fantasy of security and acceptance in *The Gallery* would surely have made that chapter of the book powerfully appealing to certain readers, just as it particularly bothered some others. To reiterate, however, though Momma's came in for some scorn by a few reviewers, it is the absence of any mention of that prominent chapter in some reviews or else complimentary remarks about it in others that is most striking.

Self-pity and chauvinism alike—qualities that became pronounced in American gay male culture for decades after the war—were part of Burns's description of how Momma's patrons looked and talked. Self-loathing surfaced at times, too, perhaps directly from the author's own sense of self. "Their conversation was flashing, bitter, and lucid," Burns wrote. "More than other men they laughed much together, laughing at life itself perhaps. Momma'd never seen anything like her boys. Some were extraordinarily handsome." And yet, beneath "this conversation Momma sensed a vacuum of pain, as though her guests jabbered at one another to get their minds off themselves, to convince themselves of the reality of something or other." At least some of these men, Burns darkly wrote, were doomed, pathetically so, "since the desire to live, in its truest sense of reproducing, isn't in them, they live for the moment more passionately than most." Just as darkly, one of two British sergeants at Momma's, who call each other "Magda" and "Esther," defines camping as "a Greek mask to hide the fact that our souls are being castrated and drawn and quartered with each fresh affair. What started as a seduction at twelve goes on till we're senile old aunties, doing it just as a reflex action." If it was difficult to imagine anybody, other than maybe Burns himself, talking quite like Magda and Esther, other pieces of dialogue by some of Momma's boys were more realistic, comprising some of the most affecting dialogue between men yet to have appeared in print: "I could be faithful all night long." "I looked at you earlier . . . but I didn't dare think . . ." "There's something in ya eyes. I dunno, I just know when I'm happy . . ." "First time for me, ya see. I'm not the lowered-eyelash kind." "Do you remember loathing your father and doting on your teachers? . . . You didn't?"

Away from Momma's, yet in the tender spirit of those comments, was another evocation of men's sensuousness with each other. *The Gallery*'s Sixth Portrait was of Captain Motes, a genteel Southerner who was, as Burns himself had been, stationed in Algiers censoring mail for army intelligence. In an unorthodox living arrangement, Motes shared quarters with one of his lieutenants, Stuki, with whom he also shared fierce devotion and tender comfort. Burns's description of a backrub that Stuki gave Motes, to get him to sleep, was, like some of the dialogue at Momma's, without precedent: "After a while the spasms faded and the horror paled. Captain Motes fell asleep. The last thing he remembered was hands, kind hands that knew him as well as a mold informs a piece of clay to its own image." This humanizing of homosexuality or simply of male affection, Burns's demonstration of such appealing male tenderness and vulnerability, was a huge departure in American writing, perhaps partially responsible for *The Gallery*'s success, but, when placed in domestic settings in his novels to come, may have been much more than many readers were ready to accept.

His gloomy forecasts aside, there was fresh insight in Burns's description of Momma's, a challenge to the binary view of gender and sexuality that was contemporaneous with and similar to Alfred Kinsey's convention-shattering findings. "The masculine and the feminine weren't nicely divided in Momma's mind," Burns wrote. "They overlapped and blurred in life. This trait was what kept life and Momma's bar from being black and white. If everything were so clear cut, there'd be nothing to learn after the age of six and arithmetic." The war had been instructive for Burns, and the teacher in him was at work throughout *The Gallery*. It is an unabashedly didactic novel throughout.[88]

Burns's most significant lesson was that the United States was not nearly as exceptional as many of its citizens flattered themselves into believing it to be, but instead "was a country just like any other, except that she had more material wealth and more advanced plumbing." The notion that, as expressed by Moses Schulman, the disillusioned lieutenant whose portrait is the ninth in *The Gallery*, "we're just like everybody else in the world," is *The Gallery*'s essential proposition—yet its antithesis was the country's bedrock. Out of Americans' naively arrogant sense of exceptionalism, Burns believed, flowed spiritual and emotional bankruptcy, "passion without affection," an empty holier-than-thou sanctimony that made it necessary for Americans to "be taught how to love," so bereft were they of genuinely sensuous feelings. It was, that is, cold and lonely at the top, where Americans believed they resided. Burns's own queer sense of self, perhaps intensified by his wartime experiences, seemed to have made him keenly aware that "in our country there is felt to be something shameful in two human beings taking their pleasure together." In the remarkable Eighth Promenade, the narrator recalls that "I'd known Americans who'd lost their virginity without ever kissing or making love in the old sense of the word. So we came to look upon this Having Sex, this ejaculation without tenderness as the orgasm of a frigidaire." Burns thought that Neapolitans, unburdened by their American conquerors' inflated egos, had a better idea: "They loved love." And Burns's homosexuality surely sharpened his observation, through the narrator, that "the only evil you can do to love is to thwart it by purely intellectual rules or by betraying what your own heart tells you to do."[89]

Not only his queer identity but his Catholicism, a part of his identity with which queerness was of course powerfully at odds, made Burns acutely aware of American mainstream culture and the distance he stood apart from it, intensifying his critique. In his Fourth Portrait, of Catholic Father Donovan and Protestant Chaplain Bascom, he observed that "men who had knocked up a signorina came to Father Donovan for confession. Those desiring advice on their life insurance came to Chaplain Bascom." In *The Gallery* as perhaps in his own life, opera helped Burns further refine his cultural criticism: Michael Patrick, soldier of the First Portrait, seeing a performance of *La Bohème* in Naples, felt "he'd opened a door into a world that had nothing to do with merchandising and selling." It was *as an American*, Burns was arguing, that Michael Patrick was not only starved for what opera might offer, but hungry for "somebody's disinterested hands going all over his body," and he "didn't much care whom the hands belonged to." And in the First Promenade, the narrator maintained that "Americans profess to a neatness of soul because their country is Protestant, spacious, and leery of abstracts." An Irish Catholic raised in greater Boston might well have the sharp sense of marginality that informs *The Gallery* throughout.

It all came back to sex. The radical individualism that Burns came to believe had emotionally crippled so many of his countrymen was something that Italy might help a person overcome. In the Eighth Promenade, Burns developed his cultural critique fully, having his narrator move beyond "the blind preoccupation with my own body and its satisfaction." When a man's "first aim is to please my love," he learns to savor "the sweet slowness of undressing one another," and to appreciate that "sleep's a part of love."[90] A novelist as cultural anthropologist, Burns concluded *The Gallery* with a cultural critique of breathtaking sweep, linking American and Italian notions of the physical and emotional to broader cultural notions of stability, community, and spirituality. A reader who would, as some reviewers did, find such criticisms of American culture to be bothersome was not likely to appreciate a full flowering of Burns's critique—which is one way to read *The Gallery*'s descendants, both *Lucifer with a Book* and *A Cry of Children*. But the fact is that the immediate reception of *The Gallery* was positive, often powerfully so. For Burns and critics alike, *The Gallery* seemed to overflow with promise, to portend a literary career of considerable eminence. Yet within less than a decade of *The Gallery*'s publication, Burns himself was dead, and his literary reputation had begun to suffer the fate worse than disrepute, utter neglect. What became of Burns's career and reputation is more than a tale of personal misfortune, as the next two chapters will seek to demonstrate.

3 Back to Normal
Cultural Work in the Erasure of John Horne Burns

[He] advised me to give up the [two-year] relationship with Larry. Until I did, he warned, any real progress in therapy would prove impossible.
Historian and playwright Martin Duberman on a psychiatrist's advice in 1955

If you loved boys, you could kill little girls.
An Iowa lawyer, justifying in 1955 a special deviants' ward at a state mental institution, even for men convicted of same-sex activity with another adult

The story of a wartime romance that could not survive the peace is common enough in novel and film, and of course typically the tale's loving couple is a man and a woman. Yet if World War II saw a revival of men's romantic association on a scale approaching what I suggested in *Picturing Men* and in this book's first chapter, it seems no exaggeration to say that the end of the war signaled the end of many a love affair between two American males. Juxtaposed alongside the iconic photograph by Alfred Eisenstaedt of the returning male sailor enthusiastically kissing a female nurse on the streets of New York, much to their countrymen's delight, we might imagine two other photos: one of a pair of sailors standing apart, knowing that no such public enthusiasm would greet a similar public embrace between them; the other of a sailor alone, with his wartime lover killed in battle or his wartime romance already dead from the hostile fire of American culture. We are accustomed to thinking of the postwar era as a time of unsettling adjustment for countless American women whose culture expected them to abandon the autonomy many had experienced during wartime, when so many men were in uniform. But the years after the war were also a time of painful adjustment for many of the returned males as well, those who suffered physical and psychological wounds of battle, of course, yet also those who, as had so many women, experienced during the war emotions and a sense of self that had no honored place in an America at peace.[1] The postwar novels of John

Horne Burns became ensnared, fatally so, in the country's transition from the war's warm acceptance of male affection to the fierce fear of men's involvements during the years immediately after the war.

Set in a New England boarding school, *Lucifer with a Book* was as much based on Burns's years as a student at Andover and especially as a teacher at Loomis as *The Gallery* had been informed by his wartime service. Burns's deeper commitment was to writing, not teaching, especially by the time of his return to Loomis after the war; with *The Gallery* completed, hoping for "an immense source of gravy" in "Book of the Month Club, movie rights, serialization and digest rights," Burns wrote his father that "since I hope to be a full-time writer, I suppose that eventually I'll have to pull out of Loomis."[2] As much as he eventually yearned to devote more of his time to writing, and much as he undoubtedly came to aggravate some Loomis colleagues, however, it appears that Burns enjoyed an excellent reputation with his students and many colleagues during his career there. John F. Randolph, in a 1965 letter to the *New York Times* a few weeks after Gore Vidal's appreciative essay on Burns had appeared, declared that Burns had taught him at Loomis before the war, and "was far and away the most outstanding teacher I have ever encountered."[3] Two former students told Mark Bassett of their admiration for Burns when Bassett interviewed them for his 1985 dissertation. "[Burns's] class was brilliant and I could hardly wait to get to it," recalled Taylor Mead. "We aspired to his immense sophistication," said Paul Barstow. "His classes were exciting, and his literary enthusiasms were infectious.... [Burns was] paradoxically caustic and encouraging. He ruthlessly mocked ineptitude and inelegance." Barstow also recalled to Bassett that "at least a few of us 'knew' Mr. Burns was homosexual, like us, if we, indeed, were. And that was immensely significant, at least to me, because he was a fine and greatly gifted man whom I liked and deeply respected—the only 'positive role model' during an appropriately appalling adolescence."[4]

Burns and Loomis figure prominently in *My Well-Spent Youth*, the spirited memoir of David L. Goodrich, an editor at *True* and Doubleday, and one-time member of the army's psychological warfare branch, who was Burns's student at Loomis right after the war. Echoing Randolph, Goodrich maintained that "John Horne Burns was the best teacher I ever had anywhere. He was constantly asking for our opinions and challenging us. He welcomed our questions, and if he couldn't answer them, he'd say so, then answer the next day." On the other hand, according to Goodrich, "if he caught you faking it, he drew a little pile of manure in the margin, with a shovel stuck in it."

Goodrich got to know Burns well at Loomis, and remembered him fondly: "Four other boys and I visited Mr. Burns often, to light up [allowed for seniors, with parental approval], drink coffee, and listen to opera records. He was funny and stimulating, and seemed to welcome our company. We were sure he was homosexual: he was careful not to do or say anything that might confirm that." Away from campus, it became a different story, according to Goodrich. Burns, he wrote, "began going to New York on long weekends, sometimes missing Monday classes. He seemed distracted, and plainly was drinking more. During a New York vacation, I saw him at the opera, liquored up, with an obviously gay man." Goodrich and some of his classmates were also aware of the queerness of Burns's immediate superior at Loomis, English department head Norris Ely Orchard. Of Orchard, Goodrich recalled, "His theatrical side showed when he entered a classroom. He'd start running outside, then—frozen in a pose on his leather heels like a performer on ice skates—he'd glide across the slickly polished wooden floor and come to a grinning halt at his desk." Burns tried to avoid flamboyance of that sort at Loomis, and Goodrich insightfully suggested that "maybe Orchard represented a part of himself that he was ashamed of."[5]

Burns and the flamboyant Norris Orchard had gotten along well enough before the war to join another bachelor member of the English department, Doug McKee, in encouraging students to form an underground group, the Oliver Trisiddien Society, for intellectuals who disdained sports.[6] On at least one occasion after the war, however, Burns seemed more inclined to cultivate a different image of himself. In October 1946, the Loomis *Log* reported that "Mr. Burns came back to school with undoubtedly the most colorful record compiled during the summer. After teaching here at summer school, he flew to Europe to spend a two-week period in Italy in order to see his fiancée and other acquaintances and to testify at the war crimes trial." Shortly before that summer, though, the *Log* had presented a somewhat different picture of Mr. Burns in his room at Loomis, "clad in a night chemise sitting on the mauve ottoman" listening to opera recordings; and in a September 1946 issue of the *Log* it was noted that in addition to teaching summer school a few months earlier, Mr. Burns had "dabbled in interior decorating."[7]

Whereas Burns might sometimes send mixed messages about his sexuality to others, perhaps even to himself, Norris Orchard was not the sort of man ever linked to a fiancée; and, as David Goodrich suggested, that unguarded openness may well have been why Burns grew to dislike Orchard. Orchard was an interesting character, a faculty member since 1933, when he graduated from Yale, and the Loomis theater director from 1939 to 1956. He was an extremely popular teacher over his long career, and the Norris Ely Orchard Theater at Loomis honors him today. Ill with brain cancer and severely compromised from surgery to remove the malignant tumor, Orchard committed suicide near his parents' Cape Cod home when he was just forty-five in 1957.[8] Some blamed not only the cancer but Burns's savage portrait of Philbrick Grimes in *Lucifer with a Book* for Orchard's fatal depression, since Grimes clearly was based on Orchard. Contrasting Burns with Orchard, David Margolick aptly writes of "the somewhat more masculine Burns."[9] Such slight differences had come to mean much in midcentury America.

Like many midcentury men, especially those with sexual yearnings that were widely scorned in their society, John Horn Burns walked a tightrope without a net, usually walking gingerly, yet sometimes with more authority, trying to keep himself and his desires from falling into ridicule, or worse. The delicacy of Burns's situation is captured well in philosopher Alfred Duhrssen's 1967 autobiography in the form of a novel, *Memoir of an Aged Child*. A Loomis student before the war, Duhrssen gave the not-well-disguised name "Mr. Burney" to a teacher at the prep school attended by the book's narrator. "Mr. Burney," we are told,

> is writing a novel about this school which, he claims, will cause him to be fired. Sometimes he invites me into his room and shows me other novels he's written, one every summer, he says, during his vacation. He has given me the key to this apartment and I go there when he is away on weekends, read the books on the shelves, and listen to the phonograph. Hess [a student friend] has insinuated that Mr. Burney has made love to him, but I don't believe it.

"Mr. Burney" later becomes the centerpiece of an intriguing tale:

> After supper a few of us go to Mr. Burney's room, and after drinking black tea, we turn tables in the dark. We have hypnotized Mr. Burney and no one knows what to do with him. . . .
> Suddenly I say, "We have to ask him a question."
> "Ask him if he's a virgin," someone suggests.
> Hess walks up to him and looks into his eyes.
> "Are you a fag?" he asks, and Mr. Burney answers Yes.
> "Stop this! Wake him up!" . . .
> "Where am I," Mr. Burney mutters. "What have I said?"
> "You haven't said anything, Mr. Burney."[10]

It was Burns's fate to be something of a man in the middle. He was not quite as obviously and stereotypically gay as someone like Norris Orchard, for whom convincing covering was not an option, hence not a temptation; although that is hardly to suggest that at that cultural moment being completely and comfortably open about his sexuality was really an option for Orchard either. Yet a man like John Horne Burns could be tempted to wear different masks in different situations: lounging in his night chemise, listening to opera, at one time; still spinning tales of a fiancée at another. It could be confusing, to audience and actor alike.

This was the man who returned to Loomis after the war, someone unlikely to have yet recovered fully from the war's unnerving disillusion, and with memories of its liberating sensuality still fresh as well. At the very center of the place to which

Burns returned was its longtime headmaster, Nathaniel Horton Batchelder, lording over the place since before the First World War. Almost as if he were still in charge, Batchelder continues to loom over Loomis today. The street leading to campus now bears his name. Incredibly, his is even the face of the sensuous, nearly naked, angel who offers sustenance to the sensuous, nearly naked, wounded soldier in the huge, heroic sculpture on campus, *Victory of Mercy*. The sculptor was Batchelder's own wife, Evelyn. According to the *Log* in 1947, the year of Burns's departure, the statue was "a tribute to those Loomis boys who lost their lives in the war."[11] It seems, however, as much a tribute to the artist's husband as to dead soldiers. Interestingly enough, according to Tom Lehrer, the satirist (and brilliant mathematician) who briefly attended Loomis in 1943, before going on to Harvard at the age of fifteen, when someone asked Batchelder, during a dinner attended by both Burns and his gay colleague Douglas McKee, to describe how he dealt with the problem of homosexuality at Loomis, the lordly headmaster decreed, "We don't have any of that here."[12] On the contrary, *Lucifer with a Book* would soon suggest that there was plenty of "that" at the school for which Loomis was largely the model, and maybe plenty of "that" elsewhere as well. Rather than the novel's purely literary transgressions, the remarkable, unprecedented candor of *Lucifer with a Book* may have been what got Burns in so much trouble, not just ending his employment at Loomis but ruining his reputation as one of his country's leading writers.

Was Burns self-destructive? Was an interview he gave the *Boston Globe* in December 1947 not merely impolitic but foolhardy, making it unequivocally clear, before it was necessary to do so, that he was writing an exposé of a school much like Loomis?[13] Did he bring on some of his trouble himself, through overstatement and lack of restraint? Could he be a boor? Of course—a streak of self-destruction is often found in challengers of boundaries: In a savvy description of Lenny Bruce, a contemporary of Burns and a fellow veteran to whom Burns was not unrelated in either temperament or concerns, historian Stephen J. Whitfield once remarked that Bruce "would have self-destructed in Sodom and Gomorrah."[14] The same may be said of Burns, surely.

Clearly Burns had grown increasingly dissatisfied at Loomis, especially with a teacher's inevitable extracurricular tasks. He was probably looking for an exit; indeed before he left Loomis in 1947, he had investigated a faculty position in higher education.[15] Burns appears to have embraced the chance that the *Globe* interview gave him to speak sarcastically and disdainfully of his position at Loomis, telling the *Globe* reporter, "I am now almost immune to the shrieks and guerrilla warfare of nurse-maiding other people's children."[16] It was no wonder that Nathaniel Batchelder, who may have been a tyrant but who nonetheless had hired Burns when so many other prep schools closed their doors to Catholic job applicants, said, in writing his Loomis successor, William Speer, about the Burns affair, that "I don't like to have my hand bitten."[17] Interestingly, Tom Burns told me, "I'm completely in the dark as to why Jack left Loomis in December of 1947, but I suspect the article in the *Globe* had a lot to do with it."[18] Had Burns stuck it out at Loomis, and not given the interview, though, there is no doubt that *Lucifer with a Book*'s publication would still have assured his departure.

As with all recollection, public memory—the way that events and people are remembered collectively, by an entire group—is always to some degree selective. That very selectivity is what makes public memory—what is and isn't recalled—so significant as cultural evidence, so apt an index of a group's concerns, what it honors and what it disdains. The particular way that John Horne Burns and his *Lucifer with a Book* have been kept in mind at Loomis is a story unto itself. The 1947 *Globe* interview, probably what got Burns called into the headmaster's office, terminating his employment right at Christmastime, quickly faded from memory; Burns and his book did not. Public memory at Loomis has not been so selective that it tried to wish Burns and his book away altogether.

Less than two years after Burns's hasty departure from Loomis, and just a month after the publication of *Lucifer with a Book*, the Loomis *Log* published an editorial noting that Burns was a former teacher at the school and had just published a novel on "the ineffectiveness and corruption of the American educational system." The editorial vaguely declared that "Mr. Burns's years of teaching seem only to have embittered him against the profession to which he belonged, and to have convinced him of its utter depravity." Granting that there might be some grounds for Burns's attack, the editorial optimistically called for a remedy in modernizing instruction and learning, and a "greater zest for knowledge" among students. Such was the declared confidence in reform that the editorial forecast that soon Burns would need "to look elsewhere for subjects for satire and vilification."[19]

Fifteen years later, another school publication, L. W. Fowles's "The Harvest of Our Lives: The History of the First Half-Century of the Loomis Institute," without mentioning exactly how Burns had come to leave, declared that

> only one incident disturbed the equanimity of his [Batchelder's] final year at Loomis. Mr. John Horne Burns, a member of the English department who had returned to the Loomis faculty for a short period after the war, completed a satiric novel, *Lucifer with a Book*, which was patently based on life at Loomis and Chaffee, with Mr. Batchelder's personality as the central theme. Reactions to the book were varied: it merely strengthened the opinions of those who disliked the school and headmaster; it irritated others who knew the real worth of Mr. Batchelder; it interested faculty more than it incensed them; and as for Mr. Batchelder—to all outward appearances—he read it and dismissed it from his thoughts.[20]

And perhaps he did. The headmaster, after all, had already demonstrated a certain skill at denial (at least in public), in his declaration that there was no homosexuality at Loomis.

By 2003, the Loomis director of development, John G. Clark, had developed a broader and often-heard interpretation of the *Lucifer* affair, writing that after the richly deserved acclaim for *The Gallery*, "Burns's writing deteriorated. Critics universally dismissed his second novel." Recognizing that *Lucifer* was surely based on Loomis, Clark suggested that "full of acidity and thinly disguised portrayals, 'Lucifer' no doubt had tongues wagging on campus."[21] A director of development, needless to say, has a stake in a portrayal of what had happened with John Horne Burns. When Burns is recalled in any fashion today, the prevailing narrative resembles that of the Loomis director of development, a fact that does not in itself necessarily render the narrative suspect, of course, but does seem to support giving the narrative a fresh look.

Burns had a larger purpose in mind with *Lucifer with a Book* than merely writing a *roman à clef* about Loomis; the novel was animated by a particular philosophy of education, however impolitic Burns might have been in presenting it. Burns's educational philosophy was surely enhanced, perhaps even prompted, by the vantage point of marginality, an ability to see the forest for the trees, that was forced upon Burns as a midcentury queer, his status as a deviant giving him less of a stake in the status quo than a more conventional man would have had. While sex has been more prominent than pedagogy in public memory of the novel, Burns's thorough, well-reasoned pedagogical critique in *Lucifer with a Book* was devastating. That critique may have been what troubled some readers more, even if they did not voice, or maybe even fully recognize, their disagreement with what Burns had to say about schooling, his uncompromising critique of education that prized process over content, that placed practicality and results above less easily measured considerations.[22] And quite importantly, in sharp contrast to *The Gallery*, *Lucifer with a Book* set its cultural critiques and its queer themes in an American context. "It was all very well for me to write about Italy," Burns wrote Rose Orente just after *Lucifer*'s publication, "but when my target was closer to home, I knew I'd be holding the mirror up to many—than which there is, as you say, no more unforgiveable crime."[23] The penalty imposed on Burns would be severe. But the usual narrative, in accord with Gore Vidal's 1965 essay, would have it that Burns's offense was largely his failure of literary skill, not the intensity of his cultural criticism.

In contrast to Gore Vidal's assessment of *Lucifer with a Book* nearly two decades after its appearance—that it was savaged by critics but was nonetheless not very good anyway—two early assessments by American writers who themselves were poles apart in content and audience were revealingly admiring. Poet and novelist Glenway Wescott, brother of Burns's friend Beulah Hagen, having received page proofs of *Lucifer with a Book*, had an interesting reaction to the novel, before any reviews had come out, and well before the notion of its literary inferiority had begun to gain currency. "The new book is very different," Wescott wrote in his journal, "just as shocking, but remarkably different from *The Gallery* in thought and style and construction. Miserable private lives of the faculty and terrible youngsters in a prep school—less like Thomas Wolfe, more like Dreiser—real satire, with moral indignation." Even though *Lucifer* "is not at all my kind of fiction," and while "I have met him twice and not liked" Burns, Wescott said, "I do believe that he is the most talented, the most promising of the youngsters since the war."[24]

Popular writer James Michener had severely strained relations with Burns—first, over Michener's having won the 1948 Pulitzer Prize for Fiction (for *Tales of the South Pacific*), an accolade that Burns and many others had thought would go to *The Gallery*, and also over Burns's bitterly negative review of Michener's *The Fires of Spring* in the *Saturday Review*. In spite of that friction, Michener—whose deep, unselfish admiration of Burns I have already noted—wrote in his memoir that "what Burns did to me [in reviewing *The Fires of Spring*] seemed like a kindness compared with what the older and established critics did to *his* second novel." Michener's own evaluation had been, however, quite different: "His *Lucifer with a Book* was a savage, kinky, vengeful account of a sadistic boys' private school, and the book was so avant-garde and focused on sex, sometimes of an exhibitionistic character, that the critics found the work revolting." Michener even claimed—astutely—that upon reading *Lucifer*, he "found it a logical extension of themes and directions toward which Burns had been moving in his first book."[25] Domesticating those themes, removing them from a wartime setting to an America at peace, made all the difference.

Suggesting the work's breadth of intent, *Lucifer* was not dedicated to specific individuals, as *The Gallery* had been, but instead "to thousands of men and women in America / whose heads are bloody but unbowed," borrowing without attribution a line from "Invictus (Unconquered)," a Victorian poem by Englishman William Ernest Henley. Burns was referring to whom—teachers, nonconformists? Though shrouded in its original Italian, *Lucifer*'s epigraph was more pointed, the passage from the *Inferno* in which Dante meets his own teacher, Brunetto Latini, in hell, among other sodomites. Latini had claimed that all great writers and teachers were sodomites; and Burns himself, of course, had made the same claim to Gore Vidal about novelists.[26] Sexual tension or energy, if not actual activity, between teachers and students, or at least between certain teachers and some students, is one of the primary themes that Burns boldly explored in *Lucifer with a Book*. It was a theme with which Burns was well acquainted, through his intimate association with his own former student at Loomis and frequent wartime correspondent, David MacMackin.[27]

Set in the immediate aftermath of the Second World War, covering one academic year at Miss Sophia's Academy, a New England private school more democratic than elite prep schools, with an eccentric, aging headmaster, Mr. Pilkey, and a protagonist, Guy Hudson, who had just returned from military service, *Lucifer with a Book* bore an obvious resemblance to its author's experience at Loomis. There was one glaring exception, however, one way in which Burns was in utterly unfamiliar territory: He for some reason felt it necessary to give Hudson a girlfriend, fellow teacher Betty Blanchard, whose pregnancy (along with Hudson's refusal to cooperate with the school's new military training program) lost them their jobs—in stark contrast to how Burns left Loomis. Burns's unfamiliarity with heterosexual attraction was obvious; the Hudson-Blanchard relationship was definitely a false note. Much more genuine, distinctive, and instructive was, first, the novel's scathing critique of common notions and practices in American education; second, Burns's singular examination of tensions within postwar masculinity; and last, *Lucifer*'s candid presentation of some varieties of male homosexuality. Rather than any failures of literary craftsmanship, it may actually have been Burns's success—his remarkable prescience, honesty, and insight—in those three aspects of *Lucifer with a Book* that better explain what pushed him off the pedestal on which he had been placed for *The Gallery*. The cultural critique of modern life and the portrayal of same-sex involvement that were definitely present but not always prominent in *The Gallery* were center stage in *Lucifer with a Book*; and while the former novel took place within the confines of a war far away, the latter literally hit close to home.

Burns was keenly aware of the difference that peace had made. A didactic narrator's voice heard only in alternating chapters in *The Gallery* was inescapably pervasive in *Lucifer*, and early in the novel the narration recognized that the postwar period was singular: "It must be the fault of those Veterans! Those returning soldiers from the Second World War have injected something new and anarchic into America! For now the country is jaded and weary and sinister and nervous all at once. And the children are different too." Burns's perception of the war's impact was surely sharpened by the fact that he had been at Loomis both before and after the conflict. Probably projecting some of his own transformations, ideas, and sensations onto his fictional veteran, Guy Hudson, Burns wrote that after a spell of peace and of teaching at Miss Sophia's Academy, "some of his bitterness died like a weed; in its place shot up an agnostic wisdom." Having Hudson, unlike his creator, be a combat veteran, even one who had been wounded, may have been Burns's way of making Guy's "agnostic wisdom," his criticism of postwar American culture, more palatable. As a veteran, did not Guy Hudson, asks the narrator, "know too much of the world to be a bright-eyed scoutmaster for shrieking kids of twelve and thirteen?" Rarely modest about his own powers of perception, Burns made Guy Hudson into a young man of considerable insight.[28]

Interestingly, the most erotic and convincing scenes throughout the novel were between men, not between Guy Hudson and Betty Blanchard, whose involvement seems gratuitous, either Burns's effort to satisfy conventional readers' expectations, or else a reflection of Burns's lingering dissatisfactions with his own sexuality.[29] The most vivid sexual attraction, though not one that ever results in overt sexual activity, is between Guy and his student, a senior, Ralph DuBouchet. Though each is paired with a female at the novel's conclusion, Burns had made the relationship between these males much more subtle, more appealing to the reader and the participants alike, and, though thwarted, more promising as well. Strangely, the relationship with DuBouchet barely appears in the biography of Burns by David Margolick, who seems ill at ease with it, even though Margolick, himself a Loomis alumnus, devotes a substantial portion of his book to the school and to other aspects of *Lucifer with a Book*.[30]

Hudson was oddly smitten, wrote Burns boldly, by "the scholarship boy Ralph DuBouchet, who with his long black lashes and response to Teecher without any attempt at flattery made Guy Hudson almost delude himself into thinking he was a Great Teacher." So smitten that

> sometimes (and he censured himself wrathfully) he caught himself
> teaching only for the response of Ralph. The boy lay open to him like a
> maiden. He had the reflexes of a lover in bed. Sometimes their rapport
> was so sharp that Guy Hudson swore Ralph knew what he would say in
> the next sentence. And when the teacher phrased something extremely
> well the boy would look at his notebook and smile dreamily, as though
> he was Svengali congratulating himself.

When Hudson would wonder about the nature of this attraction, he would reach different conclusions at different times. Though he might vow for a while to avoid Ralph altogether outside of class, "his teaching dropped into a vacuum if Ralph was ever absent." Hudson, quite unlike Burns at Loomis, supposedly did not aspire to have a following of young men, did not want to become a "fading wistful man [who] got a sense of bigness and conquest by surrounding himself with handsome boys, who treated him like their uncle and their pal." Yet immediately following that assurance to the reader, we find Ralph comfortably working on a map in Hudson's room as the teacher grades papers. "It was now much more intimate than those very salons that he didn't approve of," Burns wrote insightfully. Ralph's subsequent admission that he had recently let himself into Hudson's room when Guy was gone, and cleaned it, frightens the older man enough that he calls a halt to that evening's meeting, only to realize afterward that the younger man's activity aroused him, and that "for the past five years he'd never allowed himself or been allowed leisure for the more delicate emotions. He'd known only hate, sex, disgust, boredom." Clearly there was something more, even if Guy was not prepared to quite define it, in this involvement with Ralph.[31]

Whatever its nature, Burns snatches that involvement away by giving Ralph his first sexual experience with a female, over spring break, and ending abruptly, too abruptly to be at all believable, the attraction to Guy Hudson. Echoing countless servicemen at the war's end, with the same air of regretful finality, as they, like Ralph, prepared to embark on the prescribed heterosexual life awaiting them, Ralph tells Guy, as if he were speaking of a time years, and not just weeks, ago, "You know, it was sort of wonderful, those days when you and I were friends." That "friendship" cannot continue, Ralph has decided: "How silly I was about you! I guess I had what my mother would call a crush. But you were silly about me too." That melancholy sense of impossibility, of finality, of a passed "phase," pervades the most appealing male relationship in *Lucifer with a Book*, not unlike the trope in American novel and film, until recently nearly ubiquitous, of the lover who must die at the end of stories with queer characters.[32] Their melancholy endings notwithstanding, surely not unlike many actual male relationships formed during the Second World War, involvements like Guy's and Ralph's did not lose their meaning just by meeting a sad end. Interestingly, Burns made Ralph remind Guy Hudson of another young man he had met during the war:

> The arrowlike beauty of Ralph brought Guy Hudson back to those slim boys of Normandy who in 1944 had mascoted themselves to the American Army for food and security. And he himself had had a young friend, Marcel Bonne, to whom even now he sent CARE packages. But the repetition, the sense of *déjà vu* gave him many a troubled hour. He would examine his conscience as to his motives toward his most remarkable student.[33]

Though Burns, interestingly enough, was able in his actual life to form intimate domestic relationships with other males, relationships more symmetrical than the one between Guy Hudson and Ralph DuBouchet, lasting intimate relationships between males were still far in the future in American literature and film. Rarely saying so, maybe not often even realizing the source of their unease, many reviewers and other readers of *Lucifer with a Book* may have based their dislike of the novel on their discomfort with its candid depictions of male intimacy, a discomfort that may have affected even as astute a writer as David Margolick all these years later.

There were male relationships aplenty in *Lucifer with a Book*, involvements that were tinged with various degrees of eroticism and exhibited various degrees of symmetry, sincerity, and satisfaction. In one typically candid scene, Buddy Brown, who happens to be Ralph DuBouchet's roommate, visits Guy's room, dressed in his pajamas, trying to sit with a knee close to Guy's, hoping for "a little session every evening" to boost his grades—probably not actually with a desire for tutoring but rather with a willingness to do what it might take in exchange for better grades. The narrator comments that "in seductions, mental and physical, you have to play all at once the serpent, the toad, the lion, and the turtle-dove. But what was going on here in the name of scholarship was the most epicene [of uncertain sexual orientation] thing he'd seen yet." A less ambiguous scene, certainly more genuine and less manipulative, involving a more symmetrical duo than Guy and Buddy, or Guy and Ralph, occurs between Ralph and Tad McKinley, the school's only black student, meeting at a barn to smoke together, a strongly forbidden activity at Miss Sophia's Academy:

> They lay side by side, dizzy and exalted by the first cigarette in two days. They hadn't much to say to each other. They never needed to talk. The aloofness of the Negro thawed in the sadness of Ralph DuBouchet. For they gave each other that masculine love, best tasted before twenty, which vests itself in respect, disinterest, and understatement. They never quite knew what they meant to each other—but they knew it was something cool and devoted. So without a word they had another cigarette.[34]

The quiet tenderness, affection, and possible eroticism of that scene, its accurate evocation of many American male relationships, even its recognition that an end to the closeness was not far away, was part of what Guy Hudson most fondly remembered from his wartime experience. Awakening one morning alone and erect in his quarters at the Academy, Guy misses the companionship he had known and needed during the war. We are told that "it didn't much matter with what or with whom" he'd have sex now that he had been to war. "He and other veterans had to touch and be touched the last thing on going to bed and the first thing on waking in the morning. Even when the panic and danger of combat had lifted," Burns wrote, "his indiscriminate desire went on and on like a rocket."[35] An understanding and frank admission of "indiscriminate desire," to say nothing of such a graceful expression of that understanding, was rare enough in American writing, but maybe not so rare in the everyday experience of World War II veterans. Whether Burns's candor in recognizing "indiscriminate desire" would be applauded by his peacetime readers was another matter.

Burns was equally direct and perceptive in describing the pervasive homoeroticism among the boys at Miss Sophia's Academy:

> Roommates under the showers were forever crying out for their *wives* to come and soap their backs. There was a great deal of irreverent bumping and jostling. If anybody went to pick up his soap, the whole shower room roared with laughter. There was something restless and unsatisfied here, and all sorts of odd suggestions, made half in jest, half in earnest. . . .

The maler boys had turned to giggling and passivity; the wiry primping ones were now taking the aggressive in everything. There was also a great deal of courting of little blond boys, and meaningless fights breaking out in the dormitories for no apparent reason.[36]

Burns was careful in *Lucifer with a Book* to confine such appealing presentations of peacetime homoeroticism to adolescent boys, hence to activities "best tasted before twenty," as he had described the bond between Ralph and Tad, seemingly providing the reassurance that, among adults, male homosexuality was either gone or seriously flawed.

Definitely flawed, characterized as a virginal queer, is Guy's colleague Philbrick Grimes, based on Burns's despised colleague Norris Ely Orchard. Grimes is the headmaster's favorite, "his confidante and henchman," someone who "draws his nourishment from panic, gossip, and disorder." As the only male faculty member not expected to coach a sport, Grimes and his real-life counterpart may have made Burns, who was no athlete, feel more manly by contrast. In any case, the portrait of Grimes is so grotesquely overdrawn that it cheapens the entire novel. Need we be told, for example, that Grimes has an underdeveloped penis that is never erect when Grimes, only in his late thirties, awakens in the morning?[37] Nearly as pathetic as Grimes, but not as powerful at the school, was "Doctor Sour, the plump head of the French Department." The school's older students, "who knew more than they guessed, call Doctor Sour Auntie," and Sour is notorious for the "salons" held in his quarters. To these salons

> came boys not yet sure of their sex, athletes desirous of raising their grades, and those young bullies who rejoiced to have a motherly and fussy ear bent to their experimental thuggeries. Wearing a silk mandarin lounging robe over his flabby hips, Doctor Sour served tea, played the piano, and patted them in tempting places. Guy Hudson had heard tales of nude parties in the suite of Doctor Sour, of hard cider and beer, of chasings and titterings in his darkened study.[38]

With Guy Hudson the one faculty member who holds no such salons, in that respect Burns, who did entertain students in his Loomis room with smoking, coffee, and opera, resembled Sour more than Hudson. Unlike the chaste Philbrick Grimes, Doctor Sour has a sex life, but it is apparently confined to schoolboys at Miss Sophia's Academy; when he drunkenly picks up two sailors over spring break, he finds them "not so compliant as his boys at The Academy," and the sailors beat him severely, leaving him without his false teeth.[39] Even with teeth in place, active adult male homosexuality in *Lucifer with a Book* has not one appealing face.

The Academy boys whom Burns characterizes as actively queer have more fun, but are never as appealingly intimate as Ralph and Tad quietly smoking alongside each other. Johnson Tilbury and Edward McWaters are perhaps the most colorful. Nicknamed the Abbott and Abbess, they secretly practice ballet and listen to German music during "Little Evenings at Home," in their dorm room, sex-charged gatherings, full of innuendo and acting out. Also attending these get-togethers is "a handsome blonde upperformer known as The Body, editor of *The Academe*, the school newspaper." The Body's roommate was "a pockmarked muscular Alabaman . . . [who was] a guard on the football team." Present as well is the "tallest and beefiest boy at The Academy," called The Bishop because of an odd bishop's costume he has concocted; he visits the rooms of younger boys wearing this garb, dispensing lollipops and swats on the behind. And there is The Beetle, a "plump little red upperformer . . . [who] was the jest of The Academy in the showers because at sixteen his testicles were as yet undescended." More to the point than their Academy gatherings was another event hosted by Tilbury and McWaters, staying at the New York apartment of Tilbury's aunt during a school vacation: With the aunt out with her friends, "there was a continual little cortege of callers entertained by the two boys: ballet dancers, Y instructors, Marines," and eventually "even bellboys, waiters, and elevator operators" showed up, only to be joined by "famous actors and chorus boys."[40]

Another occurrence away from the Academy, over the same spring break during which Doctor Sour was savagely beaten, and in the same city in which the Abbot and Abbess entertained, finds Guy Hudson and Betty Blanchard, registered under false names, spending ten days together at a hotel, "the gayest and deepest ten days," in fact, "that Guy Hudson and Betty Blanchard had ever known in either of their lives." Not very convincingly, and so briefly that he seems in a hurry to be done with it, Burns described this "gayest and deepest" of times: "Every night till late in the morning these Ameses [the phony name they were using] lay in each other's arms, never using both twin beds," as they "loved, amused, and consoled each other—which is about all that lovers can do."[41] This superficially described and utterly conventional interlude begs the question of whether, in giving his alter ego a girlfriend instead of a male companion, Burns was trying to make *Lucifer* more palatable to some readers or was instead expressing some indecision or discomfort over his own sexuality. Such indecision and discomfort was hardly unusual in 1949; the shame is that Burns was either unwilling or unable to give the novel an interesting complexity by having Hudson wrestle consciously with some sexual uncertainties.

In contrast, there is interesting complexity, even impressive riskiness, and possibly some self-identification by Burns, in another relationship between a male and a female in the novel. This relationship calls to mind Catherine Burns's doting on Jack as well as the comment he once made about mothers who fall in love with their sons. His description of the relationship between Buddy Brown (Ralph DuBouchet's roommate, the athlete who tries to seduce Guy Hudson into bettering his grade) and his mother Cynthia placed Burns alongside Philip Wylie, the contemporary critic of "momism's" destructive impact on American life, this despite Burns's claims to love his own forceful mother unreservedly.[42] It also seems to reveal the same misogyny with which Burns approvingly described Guy Hudson's forcing himself on Betty Blanchard in their first sexual encounter. As Buddy and his mother sit close together in the back seat of the family Cadillac as his father Marlow drives them to the beginning of the new school year at the Academy, the narrator observes that "this tenuous incest had been going on since Buddy's birth eighteen years ago. She called it mother love. . . . Cynthia Brown all last summer had rejoiced in watching her boy's muscles flex when he was on the beach in his swimming trunks." Bothered by what was going on in the back seat, Marlow Brown "called over his shoulder . . . [']Damn it Cynthia . . . Let the kid alone. Or did your analyst tell you to maul your own son?[']"[43]

Though he clung to Freudian notions of a neurotic and juvenile element in queer sex, "momism" critic Wylie had once insightfully declared that the "fact that it [homosexuality] goes on all the time means only that millions of people have dangerously guilty consciences."[44] John Horne Burns seems indeed to have had just such a conscience. Lingering personal concerns over his own sexuality when he wrote *Lucifer with a Book*, concerns that were virtually impossible to avoid in midcentury America, are all too obvious in the novel, in his forcing Guy Hudson to become involved with Betty Blanchard, in the abruptness with which Ralph DuBouchet parts company with Guy Hudson, and in the gratuitously nasty portrayals of Philbrick Grimes and Doctor Sour. *Lucifer with a Book* is nonetheless a work of insight, no little courage, and considerable cultural significance, even value, arguably a worthy enough successor to *The Gallery*, hardly enough to have begun the ruin of Burns's reputation.

It definitely was enough to spark outrage among some everyday readers. Dr. Millicent H. Koenig of Albany, New York, for instance, a minister with the Divine Metaphysical Science Church, wrote Harpers in 1949 "to protest the language that scars the white pages and to express surprise that any publisher would even consider printing such foul language." Revealingly, she feared that "the sadist suggestions are enough to arouse an erotic youngster to stop at nothing to gain his point and satisfy his sex desire . . . [,] arousing the flame of sex into irrationalism." Of Burns, she suspected a lax upbringing, without administration of "the slipper or hairbrush." Frank MacGregor replied for Harpers that "the book was not written or published deliberately to shock, excite, or offend," but instead because Burns "sincerely felt angry about his subject and wrote with genuine emotion." Unconvinced, Koenig replied that Burns's "graphic descriptions of the supposed happenings at the Academy suggest distorted imaginings of a disturbed mind which might result from experiences in the service," accurately recognizing Hudson's assault on Betty Blanchard as a "rape."[45]

Around the time that Koenig was complaining, middle-aged Robert C. Barr of New Canaan, Connecticut, sending a copy to Harpers, conveyed his own displeasure to Orville Prescott, chairman of the New Canaan Library Committee—and principal *New York Times* book reviewer (who, soon to be noted, had already blasted *Lucifer*). Barr called *Lucifer* "the filthiest piece of writing I have ever waded through," and claimed, with the convenient excuse common to censors, that he had only read "beyond page ten" because he had been asked "my opinion of the disgusting thing." Certain that if "such detailed filth were to get into the hands of child, adolescent, or even certain adults it might do irrevocable harm," Barr demanded *Lucifer*'s "immediate removal" from the New Canaan library as well as an explanation of "how such perverted dirt was ever approved for the Library." MacGregor replied to Barr on behalf of Harpers, reminding him of *The Gallery*'s high quality, maintaining that because of Burns's "disillusionment [with teaching, presumably] he became angry and rather bitter. LUCIFER WITH A BOOK is his expression of that emotion," then cautiously adding in longhand, that it "is however not based on any one school." The oddness of the situation prompted MacGregor to add this reassurance:

> We were well aware of the fact that the book would shock some people, but it was not published for that purpose. It was published because it was as a sincere book written by an author of undoubted talent. While some reviews and criticisms have attacked the book there have been an equal number that have commended it highly.[46]

To the limited extent that Burns and his work has been remembered at all, that original balance between denunciation and praise for *Lucifer with a Book* has been forgotten.

The intensity of some of the distaste for *Lucifer with a Book* was remarkable, often documenting inadvertently that Burns was definitely onto something; indeed, the fierce reaction to *Lucifer* was an omen of the queer fear soon to be so widespread. When E. D. Toland of Ashbrook Farm in Concord, New Hampshire, wrote his friend Martha Nicholas of Hairy Hill Farm in Newtown Square, Pennsylvania, about his extreme dislike for the book, he sent a carbon copy to Frank MacGregor. Toland began his critique, interestingly enough, by questioning Burns's military credentials: "I'm sure that anyone so obviously vain, insubordinate, and undisciplined and with an absolutely psychopathic complex about sex (which is brought up upon every possible opportunity, and to the extent of a degenerate or drug addict) was a *rotten soldier*! So much for his character, as revealed by his own pen!"

Toland's own experience teaching history in a private school led to his conclusion, he insisted, that Burns's educational critique was "insignificant and despicable." And he thought that it was surely Burns's experiences "in fourth class brothels" (as opposed, one surmises, to classier ones) that produced a "clinically and psychologically inaccurate" portrayal of "the seduction of an extremely attractive and sophisticated virgin." Several months later, Toland was still exercised, writing MacGregor that he had "had an opportunity to check on the author" yet still had questions such as, "Have *any* favorable reviews of that book appeared?" and "Has the author ever been in a sanitarium, is he a drug addict or a homosexual?" Noting that he himself was both a former student and a teacher at "good" private schools and was hence concerned about the "great disservice" *Lucifer* had done to such places, Toland claimed to have contacted a former Loomis colleague of Burns who had told him that Burns was "a four-flusher . . . never even saw combat . . . about ¾ skunk and ¼ rattlesnake!"[47]

In contrast, another former private school teacher, A. L. Johnsonius of Lockport, New York, wrote Harpers to ask for Burns's address, so that he could "send him my personal congratulations on his picture of life." The novel rang true to Johnsonius, who said he had "spent a number of years teaching in schools of this sort. In fact, he's stolen my thunder, for I had long had it in mind to write such a book."[48] With the formidable full name of Alexander Lodewyke Johnsonius, he was in his fifties when he wrote Harpers about Burns; unmarried at forty-six in 1940, as he had been when he registered for the draft at twenty-three in 1917, he lived as a lodger in Lockport, according to the 1940 census. He died at sixty-four in 1959.[49]

If everyday readers who left evidence behind had mixed responses, what of professional critics who reviewed *Lucifer with a Book*? In the conventional narrative, promoted most vigorously by Burns himself and later by Gore Vidal, restated in David Margolick's recent biography of Burns, the critics were said to be almost unanimously hostile, and, to use Vidal's wording, savagely so.[50] The actual story of the reviews of *Lucifer with a Book*, however, is less clear-cut. *Lucifer* admittedly was not praised nearly as lavishly as *The Gallery*—which itself was by no means unanimously praised, especially in the first year or so after its publication. But Burns's second novel was not uniformly scorned, and it certainly was not ignored.

It was actually more widely reviewed than *The Gallery* had been, surely in part because of the amount of acclaim the first novel had been given, but perhaps also because *Lucifer with a Book* addressed some issues of considerable interest in midcentury America. As with censors and whatever they claim they want to ban, reviewers who were unkind to *Lucifer with a Book* did still get to address its issues, even while covering themselves with a protective shroud of denunciation. No doubt like many other readers, even those of *Lucifer*'s reviewers who could not bring themselves to dispassionately discuss homosexuality at midcentury got license to consider that taboo topic from a stance of displeasure, even disgust. And regarding the literally less sexy topic of standardization in education, a topic on which Burns took a less ambiguous stance than he did on homosexuality, to accept that aspect of *Lucifer with a Book* would require an outright rejection of increasingly common features of contemporary life.

Negative reviews ranged from the snarky and vague to the thoughtful and detailed. It was sometimes all too obvious what was really on a negative reviewer's mind, while some reviewers kept unclear why they were so excited. An unsigned review in the *Atlantic*, for instance, did not mince words in holding that Burns's "Academy is quite the nastiest school in twentieth-century literature, too nasty to be wholly credible." Credibility was lacking, thought this reviewer, because the "imaginative homosexual orgies among the students would, surely, have required more than the available privacy." In contrast to how agitated many American reviewers were, R. D. Charques in the British *Spectator* was perplexed that Americans would bother to care about such matters, but still thought that *Lucifer* was "plainly an ill-considered and immature piece of work."[51]

Hiram Haydn, editor of the *American Scholar*, colleague of W. E. B. DuBois and W. H. Auden in the New School's adult education division, and himself a teacher in a private boys' school for thirteen years, was especially censorious about Burns's creation, "the weirdest collection of freaks to have been brought together since Barnum." "But this book isn't actually satire," maintained Haydn in the *New York Herald Tribune Weekly Book Review*, "it is burlesque," and especially bothersome were "the most unfortunate effeminate students." Sounding like someone from another era, Haydn even declared that Guy Hudson and John Horne Burns were "of the devil's party." Just two days earlier in the *New York Times*, Orville Prescott had used the identical notion of the novel's being burlesque, not satire, in his unrestrained, influential attack on Burns. *Lucifer* was "so drenched in bile and venom that it is hard to take it seriously," Prescott announced, "a wretchedly bad novel, tedious and sometimes ludicrous." Particularly vexing to Prescott was that what he considered "vicious sexual practices were openly indulged in by some of the students, less openly by some of the faculty."[52] Though Burns never went into any detail about such "practices" in *Lucifer with a Book*, his mere suggestion that males were having sex was enough to ignite the imagination of someone like Prescott.

Unlike other negative reviewers who relied mostly on invective and remained vague about what *Lucifer*'s specific faults of content or expression actually might be, Theodore Kalem, a frequent reviewer for the *Christian Science Monitor*, granted at least that "our author is angry about crucial matters," citing standardization, ruthless efficiency, passive conformity, the dominance of sports in schools, the derogation of teaching, undue specialization, anti-intellectualism, and materialism as *Lucifer*'s targets. It was mostly Burns's anger, his avoidance of decorum, that troubled

Kalem so. The novel's potential for significant social criticism was wrecked, Kalem seemed to think, simply because Burns was such an undignified, furious fellow, and his novel was ill-mannered as well: "The result is as tasteless to behold as a racing thoroughbred shackled to an ice wagon."[53]

Less hysterical reviewers managed to get more specific regarding what they liked and disliked about *Lucifer with a Book*. Writing in the *New Statesman and Nation*, Antonia White sensibly cited Burns's sometimes-simplistic view of sex, the misogyny that could present Hudson's rape of Betty Blanchard as a favor he did for her—a point that White was notably alone among reviewers in making. Criticizing Burns much less harshly than did White, indeed maintaining that *Lucifer* bore out the promise of *The Gallery*, Steele Lindsay's review in the *Boston Post* also pointed to the centrality of sex in *Lucifer with a Book*, asserting that "sex is the garlic with which Mr. Burns garnishes everything he writes."[54] Avoiding evasive metaphors like an ice wagon or garlic, Virginia Vaughn in *Commonweal* was direct in citing what had surely been on many other reviewers' minds, though they were too inhibited at that time to say so:

> Mr. Burns tells us what actually goes on in some of the prep schools of today, and he has told the worst and the most incredible of it. He reveals the homosexuality which exists not only among the students as a result of their frustrations (of which the parents are so often unaware), but among the teachers as well, due to *their* frustrations. He reveals too, and this is far more important, the cruelty, the psychotic aggression existing among and between students and teachers as a result of these frustrations.

Vaughn did not cite the precise nature of the "frustrations," nor did she explain exactly how those "frustrations" might prompt the homosexuality, her review was nonetheless more precise than many others. With less genteel wording, Ernest Dewey of the *Hutchinson (Kansas) News Herald* was similarly specific in pointing to what would undoubtedly catch most readers' attention in *Lucifer with a Book*, the goings-on in the dorm rooms of Miss Sophia's Academy. "He visualizes the private school," Dewey wrote of Burns, "as a cross between a prison and a parlor house [a brothel], the teachers as frustrated nincompoops and the young generation, as found therein, are pictured mostly as a bunch of queers!" This "heap of creeps" did not appeal to Dewey in the slightest, but their prominence in the novel did not for Dewey disqualify *Lucifer* as a book to be reckoned with. In fact, Dewey found *Lucifer* to be "clever, ironic, bitter and full of an incensed sincerity," likely to "shock the tender-minded with its outhouse bluntness."[55]

The fact that Ernest Dewey's review from Hutchinson, Kansas, a small town with slightly more than thirty thousand residents, possessed an equanimity missing

among many reviews in media from much larger metropolitan markets is noteworthy. It may be a small piece of evidence to support Colin R. Johnson's provocative
notion that most historians have exaggerated the degree to which large cities were
the first American places to provide a measure of space and acceptance for same-
sex relationships.[56] The number of same-sex neighborhoods and meeting places
may have grown significantly in America's cities in the years after World War II,
along with a nascent homophile movement, but the midcentury American metrop-
olis as a whole was hardly a supportive environment for gay men and lesbians. The
hostility that greeted *Lucifer with a Book* was by no means concentrated outside of
the urban east: instead it originated and flourished there. *Lucifer with a Book*, like
The Gallery before it and *A Cry of Children* to come, appeared at the very beginning
of a transitional cultural moment. The very fact that John Horne Burns, with his
open-yet-conflicted presentation of male homosexuality, found himself a willing
midcentury publisher as important as Harper and Brothers was a sign of the times;
but so too was the hysterical hostility that—sometimes, but not always—greeted
Burns's work, particularly when the setting of the novel in question was the United
States during peacetime, not somewhere abroad during the war.

The conventional narrative about Burns notwithstanding, hysterical opposition
was by no means what *Lucifer with a Book* always encountered. Ben and Estelle Atkins,
writing for another small-town paper, the *Gaston Gazette* (Gastonia, NC), thought that
Lucifer was "written with the same fire, skill, and emotion" as *The Gallery*. Able to
discern "students of varying temperaments" in the novel, they called *Lucifer* "a savage exposé, a biting satire, and above all a completely fascinating story." Writing in
the *Pacific Stars and Stripes*, Marian Orgain agreed with the Gastonia reviewers that
Lucifer was "at least as good a book from the standpoint of craftsmanship, although
its subject matter may not appeal as widely as that of *The Gallery*." The reviewer's
own feelings may have been projected onto Guy Hudson in the suggestion that "he
is shocked at what nasty things the boys do, and well he might be because a weirder
lot of lads one never saw." Shocking behavior aside, this reviewer found *Lucifer* "full
of honest indignation in its attack on hypocrisy in small organizations," and thought
its "implications about the educational system of the country are important" and that
"John Horne Burns is a young author to watch."[57]

One did not have to go to the hinterlands, however, to find positive reviews of
Lucifer with a Book. Writing for the *Saturday Review of Literature*, prominent literary critic Maxwell Geismer favorably compared the Burns of *Lucifer* with Evelyn
Waugh and "the early Aldous Huxley." With none of the hysteria found in the reviews by some others, Geismer found "an inverted Puritanism in Mr. Burns's work,
and a remarkably sophisticated sense of evil and malice." "Meanwhile," Geismer
said, "you can read 'Lucifer with a Book' for entertainment on a high level, or as
an instance of genuine talent among the new writers." In the *Chicago Tribune*, prolific reviewer Victor P. Hass was unequivocal, writing that "John Horne Burns has

taken his second literary hurdle as brilliantly as he took his first," with *Lucifer* "an achievement of the same high order" as *The Gallery*, and "a savagely sardonic commentary on American education." Maintaining that he could not recall "a gamier book," Hass nevertheless was not put off: "Reading it is like being routed from bed with a glass of ice water tossed in your face: it is not pleasant, but it does wake you up." Burns's critique, as Hass read it, was as necessary as it was accurate: "Mr. Burns mocks a stuffy, cliché-ridden, undemocratic system and pleads for a reevaluation of the American way of life." This was not to suggest that Hass liked all the boys in *Lucifer*; he reserved his particular scorn, in fact, for the ones he saw as "lushly effeminate numbers who make your flesh crawl," but neither did he care for the "blond, brainless, moneyed mastiffs popping bubble gum and winning the all-important football games." Just as enthusiastic about *Lucifer* was the *Philadelphia Inquirer*'s longtime columnist, novelist Frank Brookhouser, who considered Burns "a tremendously gifted writer," and who, quite revealingly, thought Burns to be at his best, "one of our great contemporary novelists," when he was angry and bitter—the very attitudes, of course, that dismayed more conventional reviewers. "Never has the private school been castigated so fervently," wrote Brookhouser, who interestingly compared *Lucifer* to *The Gallery*: "What happened in Italy was tragic and inevitable in the process of war. What happens in some ivy-clad preparatory schools, Burns is saying, is totally unnecessary and directly opposed to our educational ideals." Brookhouser's total failure to mention the homoerotic and homosexual themes in *Lucifer* begs the question of whether he saw the same-sex flirtations and activities described in the novel as something offensive that needed remedying in real life or, instead, as too unimportant to warrant a mention in his review.[58]

Two years later, there was not a moment's doubt regarding one influential reviewer's attitude toward homosexuality and his consequent assessment of Burns, in the most significant early evaluation of midcentury American fiction: John W. Aldridge's 1951 book, *After the Lost Generation: A Critical Study of the Writers of Two Wars*. Because of Aldridge's prominence, his harsh judgment of *Lucifer with a Book*, after the praise he had heaped on *The Gallery*, signaled that Burns's reputation was shifting, drastically so, and that the greatly increased, and still growing, fearfulness of the fifties, rather than Burns's deficiencies as a writer, was at the center of what was taking place. Other writers, with Gore Vidal foremost among them, would read the tea leaves and take cover. By contrast, the evolution of Burns's attitudes toward homosexuality continued in his writing and his personal life, marked by an increased openness, maybe occasionally even a fresh measure of self-acceptance. The heavy price he would pay for that evolution was forecast unequivocally in Aldridge's *After the Lost Generation*.

John W. Aldridge was an interesting character in his own right: a combat veteran of World War II, awarded the Bronze Star; an English professor at Sarah Lawrence and, for over two decades, the University of Michigan; a writer for the *Atlantic*,

Esquire, *Harper's*, and the *New York Times*, and the author of several influential books and essays of literary criticism. Additionally, Aldridge's unyielding public disdain for homosexuality was accompanied by a marked lack of success at heterosexual coupling; he was married five times.

An early Burns appraisal of Aldridge was positive: Writing Harpers editor John Fischer, Burns called Aldridge "the keenest critic I have read in a long time."[59] And no wonder, so warmly had Aldridge praised *The Gallery* in a 1947 essay for *Harper's* magazine on "The New Generation of Writers." Fresh from Berkeley, where he had edited the campus literary magazine *Occident*, the twenty-five-year-old Aldridge heaped praise on Burns for seeing "truth with a ferocity of insight any age before ours would have found impossible to bear." Aldridge even saw in *The Gallery* (and in Gore Vidal's *In a Yellow Wood*) a certain optimism, "a new awareness of man's dignity," a realization "that love is the single unshakable truth left to us, the only condition in which beauty and decency have a chance of survival."[60]

Just a few years later, with *Lucifer* in print, Aldridge saw Burns differently and even reevaluated *The Gallery*; it now mattered to Aldridge just what sort of love one might be talking about. He still found *The Gallery*'s "Promenades" full of "faith in the power of human dignity," but was now distressed that the "Portraits" in the work "nearly all end in defeat." Clearly it was the publication of *Lucifer with a Book* that changed Aldridge's mind about Burns, just as the 1948 appearance of Vidal's *The City and the Pillar*, with its queer protagonist and numerous queer characters, made him much less impressive an author to Aldridge as well. Denouncing them both, together with Truman Capote, for a fatal "preoccupation with the theme" of homosexuality, Aldridge was particularly bothered by what he perceived as "the coy posturing and giggliness just behind so much of what John Horne Burns writes." The author whom Aldridge had such a short while ago taken so seriously, whose work he thought offered such hardheaded hope for the future, was now, with *Lucifer with a Book*, just a giggler, the creator of "a world of invented significance."[61]

On the contrary, *Lucifer with a Book* was about several matters of consequence; if anyone was unduly preoccupied with homosexuality, it was John Aldridge. Revealingly enough, reviewing *Lucifer* became for Aldridge an excuse to launch an attack on homosexuality itself, as allegedly a fatal limitation for a writer who would have a wide audience and genuine significance. "At its best," wrote Aldridge, being homosexual

> is probably no more crippling than a strong taste for women or dry martinis. . . . But the homosexual experience is of one special kind. It can develop in only one direction and it can never take the place of the whole range of human experience which the writer is to know intimately if he is to be great. Sooner or later it forces him away from the center to

the outer edges of the common life of his society where he is almost sure to become a mere grotesque, a parasite, or a clown. The homosexual talent is nearly always a precocious talent, but it must necessarily be a narrow one, subject to all the ills of chronic excitation and threatened always with an end too often bitter and tragic.

So troubling had been *Lucifer with a Book*, so intense the postwar period's increasing scorn for queerness, that in retrospect even *The Gallery* now seemed to Aldridge to be "often obsessively concerned with homosexual types and situations."[62]

John Horne Burns was not too long gone before *Lucifer with a Book* would seem tame by comparison with subsequent works by authors such as Philip Roth, Erica Jong, and John Rechy, to name just a few, when an older, if perhaps less wise, Norman Mailer was able to ditch the absurdity of all the fucks-masked-as-fugs in his own World War II novel, 1948's *The Naked and the Dead*. But while Burns lived, the heat surrounding *Lucifer* was intense. In the Burns Collection at Boston University is a sardonic biographical sketch, written by Burns himself in the third person. It has neither a title nor any indication of why it was written, yet it was typeset. (According to David Margolick, "it was written for a reference book called *Twentieth Century Authors*."[63]) In Burns's words in the sketch, "his second novel, *Lucifer with a Book*, met with raucous opposition," not entirely true to what occurred but a foreshadowing of what the conventional Burns narrative would nonetheless maintain.

The same parodic sketch maintained that Burns's "third book, *A Cry of Children* (1952), was admired by practically no one"; and that statement was closer to the truth.[64] Like *Lucifer with a Book*, *A Cry of Children* was much less daring, surely less explicit sexually, than many novels that would appear only a decade or so later. But for a while, in the initial stage of the momentous transition in American life and literature away from an earlier era's restraints, the work of John Horne Burns was simply too bold and sudden a departure to be tolerated. His insightful work, despite its flaws and inconsistencies, deserves to be better remembered, as surely does the instructive way that Burns's own contemporaries reviewed what he wrote.

Though of much less importance than his fiction and the reviews that his novels sparked, the several essays that Burns wrote between 1949 and 1952 for *Holiday*, the handsome monthly travel magazine, merit mention, if only for insight they offer on Burns himself.[65] When Burns's idiosyncrasies and sexual yearnings surfaced in *Holiday*, he was guarded. A 1950 Andover article that probably pleased its author showed ten shirtless seniors, lying in pairs on blankets or directly on the grass, sunning themselves while sleeping or reading, in the "Senior Fence" area of the campus where the older boys could smoke. That essay ended with a long look at two Foxworth Hall roommates, Bill and Hugh, boys who recalled *Lucifer*'s Buddy Brown and Ralph DuBouchet: One, a "handsome, stalwart three-letter man," while the other was "slender and gentle, not too good as an athlete," Bill and Hugh "live in harmony," as Hugh "in almost every respect is the foil for Bill." In his essay on Florence, Burns called the "tiny Italian cars" he saw "*topolini*," or "little mice," the very wording he had used, in a 1948 letter to Gore Vidal, to describe the young men Vidal had said he was picking up in Italy. Burns reported that for "Americans and British, the most glorious bar in Florence is at the Excelsior, a huge and excellent hotel on the Arno."[66] Ironically, the Excelsior bar was where Burns would spend so many of his last days, drinking heavily and furiously.

Heavy drinking had long been a habit of his, but the sorry fate of *A Cry of Children*, published in mid-1952, was enough to make his drinking more intense and frequent. The harsh reception the novel received seems a clear case of killing the messenger, with the intensity of the criticism vastly disproportionate to the novel's shortcomings. Typically reviewed as far-fetched and melodramatic, *A Cry of Children*'s plot may instead have been all too realistic for postwar America: After a wartime romance on Okinawa with Fred Joy, his fellow sailor, David Murray abandons Fred when they come home, trying his best to be a convincing heterosexual with Isobel Joy—no less than the twin sister of the forsaken Fred. Perhaps reflecting Burns's own ongoing ambivalence, it is regrettably never clear whether Burns too wants David to be convincingly straight, or instead intends David's leaving Fred for his female twin to be seen as a sad surrender to convention, a betrayal of self as well as of a lover. *A Cry of Children* also addressed abortion and other forms of birth control, promiscuity, reckless drinking, Catholic repression, guilt, and apostasy, even Boston's political corruption—topics that surely were painfully realistic for certain midcentury readers. It was no far-fetched melodrama.

Even after *Lucifer*'s mixed reviews, Burns was as enthusiastic as ever about his own work, and editors in the United States and England encouraged him with expressions of their keen anticipation for *A Cry of Children*. Frank MacGregor of Harpers had written Burns in 1951 of his eagerness to see Burns's next manuscript, at the same time that English publisher Frederic Warburg wrote him that "I cannot offhand think of any novel coming to us in the next twelve months that I am more anxious to read." Burns wrote Helen Strauss at Harpers that she would "have the book soon, and I think it's a honey. I assure you I haven't gone dry." After the manuscript had arrived at Harpers, MacGregor cabled Burns in Florence of how much he liked *A Cry of Children*, and an elated Burns wrote back that this work was "closer to my heart than anything I've yet done," that in his judgment *Children* was "a much finer work than *Lucifer*." After reading the manuscript, Warburg wrote Burns that he realized "more clearly than ever before how strong a hold the Catholic doctrine has upon you, and how fundamental is your detestation for industrial civilization," thereby thematically linking *A Cry of Children* to both *The Gallery* and *Lucifer with a Book*, adding that he thought *Children* was "a moving and powerful and at times extremely funny novel."[67] Harpers ran a first edition of a respectable fifteen thousand copies in hardcover, and Warburg found the early sales of five thousand copies in England to be "far from negligible."[68] As he had in *Lucifer*, Burns inserted an epigraph in another language, this time in Latin, a stanza from *Dies Irae*, the ancient hymn still sung then at Requiem Masses, a meditation on Judgment Day; the passage expresses hope for the same forgiveness accorded to Mary Magdalene and the penitent thief who had died alongside Christ on Calvary. The ongoing attachment to Catholicism that Warburg noted in *A Cry of Children* thus was evident from the novel's very outset, as was Burns's seemingly unshakable belief that he had a serious sin for which to atone.[69]

Recalling how Burns unconvincingly described the attraction between *Lucifer*'s Guy and Betty, there was a stilted quality to how Burns sought to capture chemistry between David and Isobel. Just as Burns would have done better had he been able to summon the courage to give Guy Hudson a named male lover in *Lucifer with a Book*, he might well have devoted more space in *A Cry of Children* to David's one truly passionate relationship, however riddled it was with guilt and fury, his attachment to his navy buddy, Fred. Summoning such courage, however, was not just beyond Burns; to expect it of Burns or any other American writer at the century's midpoint is simply anachronistic.

Placing the burden more on the men than on their society, Burns was nonetheless right to see that David and Fred were not destined in peacetime America to easily recapture the satisfaction of their wartime association. Isobel voices the country's intolerance for such unions when early in the novel she declares, "What a stinking tiresome crowd you veterans are!" While David tries to convince himself that his "intermezzo in the navy was more frenzied pursuit of sensation . . . [in which] sex loomed huge, blotting out the possibility of love or friendship," Fred is perhaps more honest. He is certainly more affecting than David, in a singular scene for American fiction of the era, in saying, "Remember Okinawa? I was happy withya then. And now I'm lonesome, lonesome, and I hafta pass my time watchin out for others." To David's insistence that "I don't wish it were 1945 again" and that "We were children then, Fred," Fred is unyielding:

> We had something then. And since, we've both worked to destroy it. I guess it was you who wanted to muck it up. I've told ya ya only had to say the word, and we'd be back in '45 again. We shoulda bought a little boat, you an me, and sailed the seven seas. Gawd, am I nuts? Or is everybody else? . . . Sure we were kids in 1945. And from what I've seen after leavin the navy, I'd sooner stay a child than most a grownups I've met. . . . Dopy [Fred's longtime nickname for David], you ain't a child and you ain't a man.[70]

This exchange took place in the apartment David shared with Isobel, but her absence for a night allows David and Fred's candid confrontation with their shared past. "*She's* not here," Fred says of his sister, "We can get drunk for ole time's sake." When Fred had first arrived, David noted to himself that Isobel would have been "irked" to see Fred put his shoes on the couch and even to absentmindedly "pluck at the [stemless] gladioli floating in a brass plate on the coffee table." To David's objection that Fred was "breaking one of the house rules" with his gladioli-plucking, Fred retorts, "Ah, dopey, blow it. She rulesya, doesn't she? Ya used to be so independent."[71]

In a bold scene, after a night of boozy reminiscing about their togetherness on Okinawa, David awakens to find himself bound with rope, about to be beaten by Fred with a piece of rubber hose, with symbolic, carefully considered blows to different parts of his body. Fred explains his actions: "I'm gonna beat ya, dopey. It's the only way. I've thought about it for months. You're off the beam, see, an if anyone can setya right, it's me, for I knowya and I loveya. Forgive me and hate me ifya like." Fred even designates a purpose for each blow: "my sister Isobel, to whom ya done wrong"; "the love ya had and didn't take"; "the love ya have, and have betrayed"; "all the good guys gone wrong"; "all who never try an understand"; "for you and for me."[72]

If this violent encounter between David and Fred symbolizes the difficulty of domesticating wartime male romance, David's relationship with Fred's female twin is no happier: With no appealing future awaiting them, Isobel has an abortion before she and David part at the novel's end. Only Fred and Isobel's mother—seemingly even more than Burns himself—was able to see to the heart of the matter. Visiting David's mother to apologize for Fred's attack on David, with Fred's ceaseless crying ever since the beating making her "think he's gonna have nervous frustration," Mrs. Joy explains what has occurred with a simple insight: "In the navy he was crazy about your son."[73]

If Burns gave David and Fred no way to recapture their Okinawa happiness, he hardly made David content with the sort of coupling that was readily available and encouraged back home. To support his claim that he didn't want to return to 1945, David could express only the shallow rationale that he and Fred "were children then." But in solitary meditation on mornings before Isobel awakened, David did, in fact, relive "something of the personality I had been." And David confirmed Fred's charge that "she rulesya" by recognizing how much he "looked forward to these lonesome reveilles" because "she had so forged my chains by now."[74] That powerful evocation of postwar heterosexual malaise surely accounts for at least a bit of the opposition *A Cry of Children* encountered. And this fundamental deviation from cultural prescriptions was joined in the novel by other departures from mid-century convention, some milder than others: Heterosexual couples lived together without being married; large families were discouraged; blacks and whites socialized; Catholics ate meat on Fridays, and questioned, sometimes rejected, their religion. One harmless departure was notably odd nonetheless: Roy, a handsome young telephone repairman, though never wanting conventional sex, at times liked to have Isobel pose for him to photograph, while at other times he smeared her with olive oil and anchovy paste.[75]

The dominant narrative of Burns's career, reiterated even by David Margolick's recent biography, charts a steep, unrelenting decline from *The Gallery* to *A Cry of Children*, from momentous matters gracefully addressed to small concerns crudely described.[76] The consistency of cultural critique among all three of Burns's novels, however, has been too little noted; additionally, perhaps both *Lucifer* and *Children* received so little praise at midcentury not because they missed the mark but because they addressed—admittedly haphazardly, even at times perhaps inadvertently—so many troubling issues. The Eisenhower years were often an era of denial—of poverty, certainly, and also denial of gross inequities and conceits on matters of race, gender, and sexuality. Not without his own denials, John Horne Burns nonetheless was not inclined to keep still, and for that he paid a heavy price. William Weaver, a fiction editor at *Collier's*, wrote Frank MacGregor at Harpers in 1952 that he was "curious to see the public's reaction to" *A Cry of Children*, and the reason for his curiosity was insightful and worth recalling. Telling MacGregor that "it is a remarkable book and I enjoyed reading it very much," Weaver observed with some understatement that "it's not exactly a pleasant book but I think it is an intense one."[77] Unpleasantness and intensity to the extent possessed by both *A Cry of Children* and its author were not destined to fare well in an age increasingly prizing quiet conformity.

And yet, like *Lucifer with a Book*, *A Cry of Children* was more favorably reviewed than the narrative of precipitous decline would have it. Grasping how Burns wrote on the cusp of cultural change, praising what would bother so many others, William Juengst in the *Brooklyn Eagle*, for instance, thought that "Mr. Burns has mirrored our life and times" with his "pitiless, compassionate reporting," and that "while much of it may be shocking according to the standards of another day . . . all of it is honest, as honest as Mr. Burns' literary style is modern." Similarly, Florence Haxton Bullock, writing in the *New York Herald Tribune Book Review*, thought the novel's lovers to be "as modern—and Isobel as blatant—as a juke box." Properly bothered by Burns's occasionally wooden dialogue in *Children*, Bullock nonetheless found the novel thoroughly engaging, singling out for praise "a very neatly handled, gradual revelation of David's early relationship, while in the service, with Isobel's twin brother Fred." Charles White McGehee, a progressive newspaper editor, NAACP officer, and future Unitarian minister, was also disposed to appreciate *A Cry of Children*, and, affectionately summarizing its story, wrote in the *Birmingham News* that the novel was "both beautiful and cruel, poetic and callous." Literary critic James Kelly reviewed *Children* for the *New York Times Book Review*, and though he considered Burns prone to "excessive malice and nightmarish distortions," he gauged him to be "one of America's gifted young writers" and considered *Children* to possess "great comic blowziness," with its "acid-etched vignettes of the city and its apartment dwellers [and] sin-haunted observations of physical love in all its twists and turns." Kelly was also one of those able to see that *A Cry of Children* was essentially a story of painful cultural change, "the clash between old and new morality." These largely affirmative reviews, three from New York and one by a Southern progressive, together refute the notion that *A Cry of Children* largely went without any acclaim.[78]

It assuredly did not go without severe criticism as well, some of that from people who simply did not care for Burns's attitudes or his story's characters. The unsigned review in *Kirkus Reviews* missed in *Children* the saving graces of *The Gallery*'s "humor, compassion and sensitivity," and therefore thought that *Children*, with its "shockingly intimate close-up of an affair between a sensitive, emotionally immature musician, and a cheap, ruthless, utterly amoral girl," was "not only intensely distasteful but profoundly boring." Isobel, that "amoral girl," along with David's "sensitive" nature, were probably, even if unspoken, at the heart many reviewers' objections.[79]

There was particular ferocity, perhaps understandably so, in the two negative reviews that *A Cry of Children* received from Catholic publications. As John Ford's magnificent 1935 film *The Informer* and Liam O'Flaherty's fine 1925 novel that inspired it demonstrate, there is longstanding hostility in Irish Catholic culture against turncoats, a legacy of centuries of harsh British rule in Ireland, where the temptation to inform on one's neighbors was intense. With *Children*'s powerful critique of official Catholic attitudes toward sex, and in light of the defensive sense of marginality still pervasive at midcentury in American Catholicism, it should not surprise that some American Catholics would issue an angry rejoinder to Burns. Writing in *Books on Trial*, a revealingly titled periodical published by the Thomas More Association that reviewed books deemed to be of particular interest to Catholics, Doris Grumbach might have had particular reason in 1952 to find troubling Burns's own homosexuality and the queerness in *A Cry of Children*: A well-regarded novelist, essayist, literary critic, and World War II naval officer, Grumbach, the mother of four, eventually divorced her husband and became the partner of Sybil Pike, whereupon she began publishing fiction that was notably affirming about its queer characters. The divorce, the female partner, and the affirming novels were twenty years in the future, however, when she wrote unequivocally that *A Cry of Children* was "inept, vulgar, artificial, and totally undistinguished," that it was "a pure synthetic," and was indeed "drivel," with a "crew of humorless, contrived, bohemians and 'upper-class' characters" as well as "degraded and pointless scenes which seem always to hover about the customary private functions of the bedroom and the bath." An Irish American Catholic, John A. Lynch, a frequent *Commonweal* contributor, while not as passionate in his denunciation as Grumbach would be in hers, did little more than indulge himself in unbecoming sarcasm, declaring that *Children* read not like someone's third novel but rather like "a first novel by one of the little boys of the prurient school." Betraying his own bruised parochialism, mired without foresight in his own time, Lynch was distressed to note that, of all horrors, "all of the characters seem to be baptized Catholics."[80]

Burns wrote his friend Beulah Hagen at Harpers that Brendan Gill's review in the *New Yorker* "depressed me with its uncalled-for superciliousness"; more than an author's tender feelings might inspire that characterization of Gill's remarks. As a stylist, Burns would never be confused with Hemingway, and, for anyone who prized lean expression, Gill was surely correct in saying that another 1952 publication, *The Old Man and the Sea*, was better written than *A Cry of Children*. Even to award *The Old Man and the Sea* a designation as "one of the best written books of the year" seems fair enough; but to announce that Burns's novel "should win a place for itself among the worst written" seems gratuitous, suspiciously overstated, mere showing off. It was undeniably clever, but perhaps no more than that, to say that Burns's dialogue in *Children* "is of a sequoian woodenness." And Gill, like many reviewers of many books, probably revealed at least as much of himself as of the author being reviewed by calling David a "prissy young concert pianist," and incongruously bellowing, "No, it is too bad!" right after mentioning a scene in the novel when David passes a gay bar.[81]

If the reviews of *A Cry of Children*, like those of *Lucifer with a Book*, were not by any means unanimous in their criticism, they were surely negative enough to upset an author, especially one who inwardly longed for acceptance as intently as Burns and who felt as much lack of acceptance in his everyday life as did most midcentury American males of queer yearnings. Trained as a Catholic to confess his sins, voice sorrow, and vow not to sin again, Burns was ever one to express exaggerated optimism and a commitment to improve, especially to editors. In character, back in the confessional, Burns wrote Frank MacGregor in early January 1953, that he hoped his next novel "will put me right with the critics, who certainly poured it on me this time. I think, I hope, I've ironed out many of my faults."[82] Not without good reason, though, Harpers rejected the uneven, hastily-submitted *A Stranger's Guise* around six months later; set this time in Europe, it was, yet again, a story of a mismatched man and woman, he seeming like he would be better paired with another man. A month after the rejection, Burns, at just thirty-six, was dead. The widely reported cause was a cerebral hemorrhage, perhaps, some said, brought on by too much exposure to the sun, his overall condition surely weakened by the previous months of drinking that, even for him, had been excessive.[83]

When he died, Burns had been living with another man, Italian veterinarian Alessandro ("Sandro") Nencini, but their relationship was said to have been stormy.[84] Interestingly, Catherine Burns had visited Jack and Sandro in Italy during the last days of Jack's life; whether that visit increased or briefly alleviated her son's malaise is open to question. In a scrapbook that his mother kept of photos and newspaper articles about Jack is a snapshot, with an inscription in Catherine's handwriting alongside it, noting that it is an image of Jack in Andover at age twelve. He is slender and shirtless, wearing shorts. Next to it is a photo described by Catherine as a "view of Florence from 'La Bicocca,' John Horne Burns' villa at Settignano, Italy." In actuality, Burns lived in an apartment that was, according to biographer Margolick, only "a portion of a larger house known as Villa La Bicocca" owned by British composer Reginald Smith Brindle.[85] On the same scrapbook page, directly below the photo of Jack at twelve was a photo of Catherine Burns, Jack, and Sandro, both men in coats and ties, on a patio that overlooked Florence. The inscription by Catherine reads, "Jack (John Horne Burns), Sandro and Mother Burns at Jack's villa 'La Bicocca' Settignano, Aug, 1952."[86] It is an interesting choice and arrangement of photos, complete with a revealingly exaggerated description of Jack's living quarters.

In my last meeting with Tom Burns, over lunch on the Andover campus in 2012, he asked with some feeling whether I believed Jack had killed himself, with it appearing to still matter as much as if his brother's death had been only months or just a few years, not nearly half a century, in the past. Whether Jack's death was literally a suicide seems impossible ever to know, but he clearly had been behaving self-destructively throughout much of his adult life, without a realistic sense of his own strengths and weaknesses, and surely without a joyous appreciation or even a peaceful acceptance of his queer sexuality—an appreciation and acceptance that was sadly elusive for most American men of his generation.

Even after he died, as his work began to be seen in retrospect, Burns's novels continued their cultural work as touchstones. While Burns and his novels had been much too queer for some of his own contemporaries, later on others would unfeelingly find him not nearly queer enough. Only five years after Burns died, an article on "The Ambiguous Heroes of John Horne Burns" appeared in *ONE* magazine, the pathbreaking journal of the just-emerging gay rights movement. The article's author, Daniel H. Edgerton, was utterly unsympathetic to how ambiguous Burns had made protagonists in both *Lucifer with a Book* and *A Cry of Children*, not stopping to consider the origins, possible purposes, and typicality of such ambiguity, in Burns's fiction and in the facts of everyday life at midcentury. Edgerton denounced the "technique of advance and withdrawal in the homosexual treatment of the hero" in *Children*, and merely described, without trying to explain, how "the sexual theme dies of malnutrition, not to say poisoning" in *Lucifer* especially, but really in all three of Burns's novels. Edgerton's was perhaps the understandable approach of a militant activist, urging fellow queers not to imitate Burns's timidity, but if his article was good politics, it made for poor psychology and even poorer history.[87]

Though by no means was his own work always critically acclaimed, Gore Vidal in his much longer life achieved renown alongside which the fame of John Horne

Burns was markedly less luminous. Many, assuredly including Vidal, would claim that this was because Burns had less stamina and definitely less talent. But, the difference in their talents aside, what price, if any, did Vidal pay for his survival and his comparative success? Vidal's 1965 portrait of Burns seemed mostly sympathetic; in his description of the last days of John Horne Burns, drinking nightly to excess in Florence's Excelsior bar, Vidal seemed utterly compassionate in writing, "In those years one tried not to think of Burns. It was too bitter."[88] On the contrary, Vidal may have thought at length about Burns and his fate "in those years" and long thereafter, to some degree making his own decisions about what to write, and even how to describe and comport himself sexually, with John Horne Burns in mind. Suggesting the sweep of his concerns, in his essay "The Creative Writer in the 20th Century," Burns had spoken with some hostility about "our Puritan heritage," and of an attitude "purely American, which feels uneasy in the presence of anything that doesn't contribute directly to the *usefulness* of life."[89] For all his criticism of the United States, especially the country's foreign policy, Gore Vidal, in stark contrast to John Horne Burns, always had an eye out for the main chance; like most survivors, Vidal was a pragmatist. Of the two men, for all the efforts of both for it to appear otherwise, John Horne Burns was much the less conventional of the two. And that was his downfall.

4 What It Took
Gore Vidal and the High Price of Midcentury Manliness

Love is not my bag. I was debagged at twenty-five and turned to sex
and art, perfectly acceptable substitutes.
Gore Vidal (1974)

It takes a romantic to be so angry.
Larry Kramer, of Vidal (1992)

"Our Love Is Here to Stay"
**Favorite song of Vidal's companion of fifty-four years,
Howard Auster**

From its driveway Gore Vidal's Hollywood Hills home was imposing yet shrouded, revealing none of its interior. Inside, though, was a place of spacious complexity, classic decor, and, yes, welcoming comfort. Thus the similarity between the house and its owner went beyond the fact that both were nearly the same age, eighty-four, on the day of my 2009 visit. His exterior self was even more shrouded than the outside of his house, but the inner Vidal I eventually got to see that afternoon was accessible, warm, and sympathetic. Warmth and accessibility were definitely not what I anticipated: Reports and public evidence abounded of his increasing ill temper and of ideas that had gone from brilliantly idiosyncratic to simply odd, especially since the 2003 death of Howard Auster, his companion of more than a half century.[1] I'd come primarily to interview Vidal about John Horne Burns. Though he indeed told me much that was useful about Burns, my afternoon in the Hollywood Hills unexpectedly teased me to think that I might have something fresh to say about Vidal himself. My encounter with Gore Vidal in his old age greatly enriched my understanding of the long-ago years of his young manhood, my focus in this book.

Greeting me at the front door with dynamic warmth was Fabian Bouthillette, Vidal's personal assistant, editor, attendant, handyman, health care adviser, traveling companion, and drinking partner, an Annapolis graduate later active in Veterans against the Iraq War. The living room is sunken, and Bouthillette's difficulty in getting Vidal out of his wheelchair and down into the chair by mine only accentuated the old man's frailty. Gore Vidal looked every one of his eighty-four years that afternoon; he seemed shrunken, dramatically so, in both girth and height, vulnerable instead of formidable.

Vidal had for years insisted adamantly, famously, and frequently that "homosexual" is just an adjective, not a noun, that there are only homosexual acts, not homosexuals. Nonetheless Vidal wanted it understood—he told me several times with emphasis—that his assistant Fabian was "not a degenerate," in contrast, apparent was the implication, to Vidal and to today's interviewer. It was striking enough that Vidal voiced the popular binary view of sexual identity he had for so long rejected, and it was revealing indeed that his reference to Bouthillette's straightness seemed clearly intended as praise. In disparaging William F. Buckley, Vidal called his deceased nemesis a "fag," telling an odd story to exemplify the point, and leaving it unclear whether Buckley was reprehensible for hiding, or simply having, queer inclinations. Nearly as often as Vidal tossed about the word "fag" that afternoon, he frequently exclaimed, "My Lord Jesus!"[2]

I asked Vidal his opinion of John Aldridge, the influential postwar critic who had turned against John Horne Burns once Burns shifted his novels' homoerotic themes from the war to the home front and who had bemoaned the fact, as he saw it, that too many postwar writers, including Vidal, were preoccupied with homosexuality. Recalling that "outing people as fags was sport then," Vidal dismissed Aldridge as "a scandal lover, a bad critic [who] did not deserve to be published anywhere," someone Vidal couldn't imagine "having a serious thought." Not once in any context that afternoon did Vidal use the word "gay," an adjective he had often denounced as a way of referring to homosexuality. But "fag" was not his only use of a word that had preceded "gay" in queer allusion. He referred to contemporary African American novelist Darryl Pinckney as "a black pansy," and the wording, both "black" and "pansy," seemed to be Vidal's unbecoming way of putting Pinckney in his place.

Vidal also relied on a binary sense of identity in discussing his own boyhood, saying that "I started out your normal American boy," implying that there was something abnormal about how he had ended up. Back when this "normal American boy" went off to Exeter, Vidal recalled that—as his protagonist in the largely autobiographical novel *The Season of Comfort* also discovered at prep school—"boys just did it [had sex with each other] and didn't think about it." Eventual thinking about it could rarely be avoided in twentieth-century America, of course, and once the thinking began, Vidal clearly suggested, a particular identity had to be either adopted or denied. There was shrewd insight in his observation that young boys of his era were "paid so much to join the other team," and it was revealing to hear none other than Gore Vidal note that there indeed were wholly separate teams for which one might play.

A bit of the expected Vidal surfaced in his insistence that he himself was no team player, however. When I asked him whether his own sexual desires, practices, and beliefs had ever made him feel guilty, scorned, or queer, his voice got louder when he said, "I made the rules. If you don't like them, go elsewhere." There seemed to be gratitude as well as affection, though, in his warm recollection that whenever people had asked his father, Gene Vidal, about his son, the elder Vidal was always proud, unreservedly so. The explanation for his father's unqualified pride over a son of whom many other fathers of the time would not have been so proud was immediate: "I never saw anybody *less* insecure," said Gore Vidal of his father.

Photographs of his father were prominent in the living room. (Photos of his mother, whom Vidal had often professed to despise, were conspicuous in their unsurprising absence.) A son's pride equaled the father's, as Vidal told me warmly and at length about his father's significance in American aviation history. When I noted the strong resemblance in one photo between Gene Vidal and Gore's dear friend, the late Paul Newman, Vidal agreed, seeming to add another bit of gratitude accompanying affection, alongside another endorsement of binary sexual identity: "I've never known a straight guy like Paul," Vidal said. When it came to the culture's widespread anxiety over homosexuality, his friend insisted, Newman "was absolutely blank on the subject."[3]

A poignant discussion of Newman's death, just a year earlier, preceded talk of Vidal's arrangements for his own interment, a matter I'd read about in his 2006 memoir, *Point to Point Navigation*.[4] I already knew, therefore, that Vidal was to be buried alongside Howard Auster in Rock Creek Cemetery in Washington, DC, and I knew that Vidal's grave also was—quite on purpose—close to the graves of both Henry Adams and the purported great love of Vidal's life, Jimmie Trimble, his boyhood friend killed on Iwo Jima. Our discussion prompted Vidal to tell me several times, as he had so often thought it necessary to aver in print, that he and Howard may have lived together for five decades but had never had sex during that time. Hearing this odd insistence in person, yet seeing the sadness in his eyes when he spoke of Auster, and then having Gore Vidal himself describe for me his so famous, allegedly lifelong, devotion to the memory of Jimmie Trimble, made Vidal's sentimentality and romanticism almost tangible, in spite of all of his talk over so many years about *not* being a romantic ever, at all: ice water at the core, love's not my bag, and so on. If ever a lady—a word he fancied using for Truman Capote, by the way—protested too strongly, it was Gore Vidal about his lack of a sentimental side.

While much else got discussed that afternoon, some of it unrelated to the concerns of this book, Vidal did contribute to my understanding of John Horne Burns, to whom Vidal had been introduced after the war, he told me, by the older gay novelist Glenway Wescott.[5] As had happened when I interviewed Tom Burns, I was quickly reminded of the importance of the fact that Burns was Irish: "Burns was a sensation with that first book," Vidal recalled. "I might've thought 'competition.' I thought

'Irish Catholic' and I had no desire to meet him." When I asked Vidal about some of the differences between himself and Burns, he quickly said, "I'm ruling class and he was bog Irish. Nervous about everything. He was servant class. I didn't *need* to know anyone. I thought he'd misplaced himself," Vidal insisted, refusing to let go of the ethnic theme, and the slurs: "Should have been cutting peat." For a moment we were transported back to the 1940s, indeed to a bit of the 1840s. The descendant of peat-cutters of course, had graduated from Harvard, while Vidal had not attended any college; much to the consternation of his relatives, Vidal would, for reasons yet unclear, leave his entire estate, including his papers, to Burns's alma mater.[6]

More compassionately, still to his own advantage but without insulting the Irish, Vidal continued to discuss the differences between himself and Burns, replying to my inquiry about whether Burns had succumbed to the era's hostility to homosexuality while Vidal himself had not. "I was a little too strong," said Vidal, with a different, if inadvertent, implication than his simply saying that he "was strong" would have had, while "[Burns] was a little too weak." Vidal knew Burns well enough to have met his younger sister Cathleen, and Vidal recalled her spreading the rumor that Jack was "in love with a countess," as well as her insistence that her brother "was a completely normal man." These remarks of Cathleen's, Vidal offered, were "the usual nonsense that the Irish are good at."

When I inquired about Vidal's motivation in writing his largely affirmative 1965 piece about Burns for the *New York Times Book Review*, an essay that had been singular in remembering Burns at all, he said simply that "I was furious that he was ignored." I listened for some identification with Burns by Vidal, not simply a remembered desire to set the record aright, but I detected no such thing. It was only much later, after I had carefully examined the way that Vidal himself was actually treated by critics in the 1950s, that I suspected more nuance in his ongoing, usually lonely, support for Burns over the years.

For now, I simply heard Vidal supporting my desire to take a fresh and long look at John Horne Burns—and perhaps to even, I suggested tentatively, attempt a fresh look at Gore Vidal himself, in tandem with my analysis of Burns. "I lived a different life," Vidal stated, suggesting, I thought, that exploring the contrasts between Burns's experiences and his own could indeed prove instructive. Only later on would I decide that discerning the differences and similarities between Vidal and Burns would be both more challenging and more interesting than first appeared to be the case. Regarding my planned examination of postwar hostility to Burns and to men's same-sex involvements in general, Vidal said of Burns: "He's your Dante, getting you into the Inferno." That clever analogy's meaning was simple enough to grasp. Not so clear was Vidal's next analogy: "I'm the snake." Regrettably, I did not ask Vidal what he meant. Could it have been that he, as the snake, was actually an agent of the Inferno, as Dante's own snakes clearly are? Burns, my Dante, could show me the hellishness of the postwar era; was Vidal, with his "different life," admitting to having been a more sinister creature?

Sadly, I was unable to interview Gore Vidal again. Talking to Fabian Bouthillette on August 1, 2012, the day after Vidal died, I heard more about Vidal's rapid decline in the months just after our November 2009, conversation, a deterioration of body and mind that precluded another fruitful meeting by early in 2010. I had seen Vidal in one of his last good moments.[7]

It is not simply the sheer volume of his writing that makes Gore Vidal such a daunting subject to write about. Often claiming to resist the confines of sexual categories, he wore enough hats to make difficult any sort of categorization. Foremost, Vidal was a writer, but a writer as adept at the essay as at the novel, at historical fiction as at cultural criticism, at screenplays and television scripts as at plays for the stage. But he was also at times a politician, as well as one of those distinctly twentieth-century creations: the person famous for fame itself. Quite appropriately, he was also an actor, with roles in at least nine films and four television programs.[8] Trite as it sounds, his best role was simply as Gore Vidal, a role of many facets. He could be slippery, so accomplished was he at the pose.[9]

An American male of the twentieth century's second half who wanted sex with other males could get plenty of practice at posing, at pretense, much as Gore Vidal might claim that he was above all of that. The same guilt and insecurity, the frequent need to cover, that bedeviled John Horne Burns was difficult to elude for nearly all members of Burns's—and Vidal's—generation, though the covering might manifest itself in various ways. That Gore Vidal outlasted John Horne Burns for so long may indeed have been in part because Vidal was the more gifted writer, but perhaps it was also because Vidal was the better poseur. I am mindful of Vidal's admonition to journalist Tim Teeman: "Don't make the error that schoolteacher idiots make by thinking that gay men's relationships are like heterosexual ones. They're not."[10] This schoolteacher, however, will nonetheless challenge that position of Vidal's, maintaining that Gore Vidal was in many ways, in relationships and otherwise, actually a conventional American male, not nearly as eccentric as he might claim and often appear to be. Not unlike John Horne Burns, Gore Vidal—for all that has been written by and about him—is not yet well known.

Norman Mailer was often an unreliable guide to the sexual terrain of postwar America. One of his moments of insight, though, came when he observed of Gore Vidal that

> as a homosexual, he's very much a man. He insists on that and he acts that way. In sex, he does it. . . . No one does anything to him. So he's just as much a male as any "convict," so to speak, any strong male.[11]

The convict analogy was apt, because Vidal, quite like Mailer, was a prisoner of certain postwar sexual conventions.[12] Sounding like one of those "schoolteacher idiots" who see the sexual notions of American males as largely unrelated to sexual orientation, Vidal himself tried to demonstrate his conventionally male sexuality by maintaining in a memoir that

> in a recent biography of Jack [Kennedy], *Reckless Youth*, I was struck by the similarities between my youthful self and his, particularly in sexual matters. Neither was much interested in giving pleasure to his partner. Each wanted nothing more than orgasm with as many attractive partners as possible.[13]

And yet Vidal then revealingly recalled a small bedroom at Merrywood, the Virginia estate where his mother lived with her second husband, Hugh D. Auchincloss, once also the stepfather of Jacqueline Bouvier: Vidal noted that Jack and Jackie had shared that bedroom when attending her mother's marriage to the man once married to Vidal's mother. Vidal had himself had that room when living in the house; and Vidal's prep school friend—allegedly the sole love of his life—Jimmie Trimble had slept there too when Gore had brought him home from Saint Alban's for the weekend. That "small bedroom," Vidal wrote, "reminds me that, unlike Jack, I had once been (in this very room—and ever since?) in love."[14] Whether Vidal, in invoking the memory of Jimmie Trimble, dead on Iwo Jima, was simply being melodramatic or instead was being genuinely wistful is one of my central concerns in this chapter.

Determining the truthfulness of a poseur as accomplished as Vidal is tricky. One would do well to keep in mind Glenway Wescott's 1957 comment in his journal about Vidal:

> Gore Vidal, ever the same odd character: intelligent but inaccurate; virtuous in a way but cheap; with the great pusillanimity of wanting to have, even succeeding in having his cake, while at the same time eating it; and with the bothering question of whether he does not simply lie.[15]

Gore Vidal took his actual feelings toward Jimmie Trimble with him to his grave—a grave not far, one must recall, from Trimble's own in Arlington. Much closer still, though, is the grave of Howard Auster, with whom Vidal lived for a half century, the person who would have inherited Vidal's entire estate had Auster not died first.[16] Trimble and Auster both of necessity figure prominently in my forthcoming examination of Vidal's masculinity. As for the elusive veracity of what Vidal had to say about each man, I am more interested that Vidal elected to say what he said than in whether he was speaking something called the truth.

The Second World War, from which he returned at only twenty-one, is the central event in both of Vidal's first novels, *Williwaw*, in 1946, and *In a Yellow Wood*, just a year later.[17] Both are short and crisply written: neither attempts the range or the depth of several other more ambitious World War II novels. *Williwaw* is set aboard an army ship in Alaskan waters, where Vidal had served, the novel's title the name of the fierce offshore winds common in the area. Though on countless occasions Vidal would express loathing for his mother that in its intensity matched the fervor with which John Horne Burns expressed love for his, Vidal made *Williwaw* "For Nina," the allegedly despised (and truly despicable) mother, Nina Gore Vidal Auchincloss Olds.[18] With this literary debut, interestingly enough, Vidal affirmed his manliness in the eyes of some reviewers, presenting a self-contained and humorless tale, virtually without affect among its characters, men who rarely swear or even express themselves strongly. Utterly without heroes and deeply pessimistic, the brief novel is entirely about self-protection. There is no romance or even discernible affection between men, only a vague, ill-founded love between a man and a woman. It was precisely because the emotions in *Williwaw* were as cold as the water around the Aleutians that the unnamed reviewer for *Kirkus* declared that the novel was "peculiarly masculine in its appeal."[19] John Aldridge, who would later disparage Burns and Vidal for what he discerned as their perverse and parochial sexuality, was fond of *Williwaw*, believing that the author of this "slight and unpretentious" novel "seemed to have learned early the trick of the narrow scope, the tight portrait."[20]

The title of Vidal's second novel, *In a Yellow Wood*, referred to the place in Frost's poem where two roads diverge; as short as *Williwaw* but seemingly with grander aims, it is, in fact, a novel about dichotomy, a stark choice between convention and fulfillment in postwar America. The novel was dedicated to yet another maternal figure, coincidentally with a surname remarkably close to the first name of Vidal's mother: Anaïs Nin, the writer twenty-two years Vidal's senior with whom he had been living for a time, perhaps in one of his few halfhearted efforts, early in life, to establish a sexual relationship with a woman.[21] A little too neatly, *In a Yellow Wood* covers just one symbol-packed day in the life of Robert Holton, a recently discharged veteran trying to balance his wartime desires with the dictates of his postwar employment as a stock broker. Reunited during that single day with both Jim Trebling, an army buddy visiting from Los Angeles, and Carla Bankton, a wartime lover, Holton must decide whether to stick with his boring but financially secure job or instead join either Jim or Carla for a life promising more genuine satisfaction. Robert, and Vidal himself, seem confused about exactly what either Jim or Carla has to offer, though the alternative to them, Robert's job, seems clearly to represent tedious routine yet a good salary. Robert had had sex with Carla during the war, and has it again on this day of their reunion, but Vidal describes it awkwardly, with no more appeal than work at the brokerage: "They kissed and began the act of completion."

With Jim Trebling—whose name is too close to Jimmie Trimble's to have been given inadvertently—Robert seems to have warmer wartime memories: of plans to open a pottery business together in California, to work "just a little to get enough ahead," being "careful though not to get bogged down, not to get too interested in working." A previous romantic attachment between Robert and Jim seems plausible, more so, on Robert's part, than between him and Carla. In a paradigmatic postwar reunion between former military buddies, Robert and Jim keep up straight men's appearances, shaking hands upon meeting "with Anglo-Saxon restraint, muttering monosyllables of greeting, each asking of the other's health." "You've certainly changed," Jim tells Robert, "I don't know if I'd have recognized you." Robert's changes sadden Jim as he leaves the office, "because they had once been very close," but Jim drives away the sadness—and perhaps other feelings for Robert—by reminding himself, after all, that he has just made a date with Caroline, one of Robert's female coworkers. He reassures himself that "the Carolines are the important things."

Robert too refreshes his heterosexuality when that evening Vidal sends him with Carla to a "fairy night club" along with George Robert Lewis, a highly stereotypical gay man whom they had met at a party. An unappealing person of extravagant physical and verbal gestures, Lewis publishes an avant-garde magazine and is the novel's only unequivocal representative of homosexuality and of the flight from convention. Thus, with the misleading dichotomy Vidal has established, it is easy for Robert to decide that he "would not have said that being a broker was a productive life but if, to be an artist, it was necessary to be like Lewis, he had no desire to be an artist." If only by default, then, Robert opts for convention, deciding to stay in place at the brokerage, ending his day as he began it, alone.[22]

Like *Williwaw*, *In a Yellow Wood* is a book of little wisdom and less resolution, mirroring its youthful author's extreme restraint and uncertainties—as, differently, did all three of John Horne Burns's novels. So restrained was the emotionality that Vidal brought to *In a Yellow Wood* that it made *Williwaw* seem colorful by comparison; *In a Yellow Wood* was not simply lean, it was emaciated. It gave reviewers little to review, and it received scant notice; the few reviews it received were typically brief. In the *Saturday Review*, Nathan Rothman did take time to denounce one aspect of *In a Yellow Wood* that particularly offended him, and in this he was joined by most of the book's other reviewers. What troubled Rothman was that "fairy night club"; he resented having to experience "a visit to one of the more dubious night clubs and a view of its perverse habitués." John Aldridge, his distaste for homosexuality not yet fully developed, went beyond the mere handwringing of some others. Aldridge found George Robert Lewis, "an extremely sensitive homosexual," to be something of an antidote to the "numb purposelessness" of postwar life, yet thought that "such a theme cannot be adequately objectified in the cold and mechanical style in which Vidal wrote the first half of the novel, just as the idea it signifies cannot be made meaningful to the cold and mechanical person Vidal has shown [Robert] Holton to be." Perhaps without fully grasping his own point, Aldridge did seem to see that Vidal was in over his head in this novel, not yet sure enough of himself and his own disposition and desires to be able to look freshly at the bourgeois-bohemian divide.[23]

No reviewer was angrier at Vidal for *In a Yellow Wood* than Father Victor Yanitelli, writing in *Best Sellers*, a journal published at the University of Scranton, a small Catholic institution. Only thirty-three himself when he wrote the review, Father Yanitelli, a Jesuit with a PhD from Fordham, was no mere parish priest: He went on to be named Jersey City's Man of the Year in 1966, only a year after he had been named president of that city's Saint Peter's College, a post he held until 1978. For a time a New York Port Authority commissioner and a lifetime member of the NAACP, Yanitelli showed how ensnared he was in the burgeoning bigotry of his era and in his church's own peculiar deceit about homosexuality. Hysterically, he declared that "twenty-two pages of homosexualism have nothing to do with the case [of finding purpose in contemporary life], and could well have been left in the gutter where they were found." He seemingly could not let go:

> The publishers refer to the book as "the tragedy of a generation striving for freedom and self-expression" whereas the only tragedy is that the book was written. They inform us too, that "Gore Vidal has no fixed home; he travels and writes." Would that he only travelled![24]

The country's homophobia epidemic was just beginning; the fearful fury of Father Yanitelli was no anomaly. The "homosexualism" that so upset Yanitelli was, as his careful count showed, confined to just twenty-two pages of *In a Yellow Wood*, and it was not, after all, an especially becoming portrait of men who felt and acted on same-sex desire. If someone like Yanitelli could become so exercised over a minor work in which queerness played a minor role, what might happen with a more substantial novel that examined American queerness more sympathetically and in more detail, one in which a protagonist's sexuality was explicitly a primary issue?

The nature of Vidal's very next novel, *The City and the Pillar*, published less than a year after *In a Yellow Wood*, and the common critical response to it, made for a livelier and hugely more significant story. At over three hundred pages, *The City and the Pillar* was much more substantial in narrative and ambition than either of its predecessors, with the breadth and bravado that came to be associated with its author. Rather than being dedicated to a literal or figurative mother, *The City and the Pillar* was "For the memory of J.T.," Jimmie Trimble, dead but a year when Vidal began writing, a potent rejoinder to those who decades later might think that Vidal's devotion to Trimble was only a contrivance of old age. Largely written when Vidal was just twenty-one, while he was living in a dilapidated Guatemalan convent, it was a novel without precedent in Vidal's own writing or even in American literature as a whole. Despite an unfortunate, artless ending and an occasional departure from its engaging story that made the work sound like a didactic academic monograph, *The City and the Pillar*'s appearance in 1948 marked a major cultural moment.[25]

The novel begins and ends with Jim Willard and Bob Ford, friends since boyhood who become lovers late in their teens, just as Bob, a year older, is about to graduate from high school. When Bob leaves for the merchant marine, the novel becomes only Jim's story. After failed attempts to become involved sexually with women, Jim recognizes with clarity that his only genuine attraction is to males; during the course of the novel, as he travels the country, spends time at sea and in the army, and teaches tennis successfully enough to eventually buy into some tennis courts, Jim has three intense relationships with other males and simply has sex with several more, all the while becoming well acquainted with communities of queer men around the United States. Bob, meanwhile, after five years in the merchant marine, returns to his and Jim's hometown, and marries a girlfriend from high school days. He and Jim meet in New York City, and eventually share a hotel room where they drunkenly reminisce about their intimacy as teenagers. When Bob not only rejects Jim's physical advance but denounces him as "nothing but a damned queer," a furious Jim accidentally yet purposefully kills Bob by choking him. Thus does Vidal starkly end a long story that otherwise is marked by subtlety, with moments of sublime tenderness, as well as brutal candor and pain, moments that all make sense—unlike the novel's utterly senseless conclusion. The absurd ending seems to be Vidal's awkward attempt in one incongruous scene to placate readers bothered by all that has gone on before. Lest we miss the point, right after Bob's death, *The City and the Pillar* concludes in a bar, where a pathetic, older, "little man" from Detroit—who lives with his mother, no less—tries to pick up Jim. If not as an effort to placate readers by punishing both Bob and Jim, Bob's death might also be viewed—more reasonably so, sadly—as a reflection of Vidal's unyielding pessimism about the possibility of a lasting romantic involvement between midcentury American males. The novel's ending was surely, however, more than simply an abstract matter of Vidal's exercising "artistic integrity," as his biographer suggests that Vidal himself felt it to be.[26]

Central to understanding the novel is the fact that Vidal began writing it within just a year of the death of the young man to whom it would be dedicated, Jimmie Trimble, whom Vidal was surely still in the depths of mourning. If *Williwaw* and *In a Yellow Wood*, in their own dedications, were restrained tributes to Vidal's cruel, unstable mother and to another woman with whom he had an ambiguous rapport, *The City and the Pillar* may instructively be seen as an expression of love, bereavement, and, with that ending, perhaps even of survivor guilt and irrational anger at the deceased Jimmie for having had the inconsideration to die, leaving Vidal alone at barely twenty-one, utterly without hope of a postwar resumption of their involvement, whatever its dimensions and future prospects had actually been. Though Jim Willard carries Trimble's first name—and despite Vidal's frequent insistence that actual people in his life, including himself, did not show up in his novels—it seems likely that Jim was meant to represent Vidal in some ways, in his evolving queer identity and certainly in his steadfast attachment to a lover from his youth; as did Vidal, Jim even contracts arthritis during his time in the army.[27] With his less certain sexual identity, his centrality in the protagonist's dream life—and, of course, in the fact that he must die—Bob Ford might in some ways be seen as a stand-in for Jimmie Trimble.

Vidal described Jim and Bob's teenage love affair with a tenderness he had never shown, or even hinted at, in his writing before, and would rarely allow himself to display again. Though male couples have conspicuously abounded in American writing at least since the appearance of Hawkeye and Chingachgook, there had never been a pairing like Jim and Bob in American literature before *The City and the Pillar*. His previous two novels had certainly not prepared Vidal's readers for the weekend that Jim and Bob spend together following Bob's high school graduation, at a cabin by a river, with a pond nearby. It was a place where "they could swim without clothes" because "almost no one ever came to this pond." In a scene outside the cabin, by firelight, "their faces met, their cheeks touched and with a shuddering Bob gripped Jim tightly in his arms and the magic was made: both were aware." At least for Jim, the weekend was no anomaly, no impulsive adventure soon to be forgotten, no "situational homosexuality"; instead, for Jim it was the culmination of long-simmering desire. When Jim "looked at Bob's strong white body, [he] did not envy; rather he felt a twinship, a similarity, a warm emotion which he could not name. He had always felt this way about Bob." Vidal describes their first sex together, at seventeen and eighteen:

> Then, as in a dream, they took their trousers off, not looking at each other, not thinking of the outer world, and finally, shuddering, their bodies came together and for Jim it was his first completion, his first discovery of a twin: the half he had been searching for. He did not think if it was the same for Bob. He did not think. He felt.[28]

For someone like Vidal, this graceful description of male intimacy was only slightly more of a departure than the elevation of feeling over thinking. Bob is present only in the single early chapter that describes that weekend with Jim, briefly in a much later chapter that notes his marriage, and then when he returns to die near the novel's end. But Bob is never far from Jim's mind throughout the five years of their separation—the bulk of the novel. He is Jim's recurring point of reference, the gold standard against whom Jim measures all other lovers, a foreshadowing of Vidal's own life to come, if we are to believe his insistence that he had a lifelong obsession with the memory of Jimmie Trimble.

A bit heavy-handedly, clearly conscious that his was the first book of its kind, Vidal at times sets the plot aside in *The City and the Pillar*, and becomes an ethnographer and social historian. As part of his effort to make the novel something of a guide to gayness in the United States, and perhaps an affirmation of self for the novel's young author as well, Vidal has one of Jim's lovers, journalist Paul Sullivan, expound on the "certain similar beginnings" that queer men in America tend to share:

> Well, often you start out in school. You're just a little different from the other boys. Sometimes you're shy and a bit frail; sometimes you're too precocious to get along with them; or in a few cases, you're handsome and a popular athlete: a regular little narcissist. Then you have erotic dreams of a certain boy and you get to know him and you often become friends and if he's sufficiently ambivalent and you're sufficiently aggressive you'll have a wonderful time experimenting with each other: there it begins. Then you have another and another and as you grow older, if you're talented or handsome or dominant, you become a hunter. If you're none of these things but rather pretty you might become a kept boy. If you're hopelessly effeminate you join a group of others like yourself and accept being marked and known. No, there are many types and many different patterns but there are certain similar beginnings.

Indeed, in an extraordinary scene at Chenenceaux's, "their special bar" in New York, on Jim's twentieth birthday, Vidal through Paul Sullivan delivers a long, intense, and poignant call and justification for what later would be commonly called "coming out":

> We live a short life and it's hard enough to find love in the world without there having to be the added hazard of continual pretense.... [Homosexuality is] censured because the others are afraid, afraid for themselves. They're afraid of their own dreams, their unlived past.... As it is here in America we're sick with fear: sexual, professional, on the surface and beneath. We are very sick and frightened and we condemn what we don't understand or what we feel endangers us. We cannot even love. The men cannot love women, cannot love one another, cannot love themselves. All they have left is hate; hate of the ones who try to love; hate of the few who succeed. No, we must declare ourselves, become known; allow the world to discover this subterranean life of ours which connects kings and farm boys, artists and clerks. Let them see the im-

portant thing is *not* the object of love but the emotion itself and let them respect anyone, no matter how different he is, if he attempts to share himself with another.[29]

Through a person Jim meets at a New York "fairy party" that he attends with another of his serious boyfriends, actor Ronald Shaw, Vidal even delivers an early, remarkably insightful interpretation of World War II's impact on American sexual boundaries. The war actually produced more homosexuals, the man declares, men "who might have remained hidden all their lives, who never practiced but remained latent . . . normal-looking young soldiers in bars who, back in their home towns, are married and engaged to girls, have respectable reputations and would never be, in any way, connected with anything as repellant as homosexuality, but whose inhibitions have now been broken down." Vidal even has one of his favorite targets, an "effeminate man" at the party, "squeal" that he was "thankful for the war" since he had "had some perfectly wonderful experiences which I know I wouldn't have had if all these boys had gone on being frustrated back home."[30] It is hardly surprising that some would claim to be either horrified or disgusted, but to read these passages in *The City and the Pillar* could mean the world to other readers, those who actually had been "young soldiers in bars" or the men they met, or had simply been men guiltily hiding their sexual desires for most of their lives. With *The City and the Pillar*, then, Gore Vidal not only told a story the likes of which Americans had not seen in print before, but unequivocally staked his own claim to a queer identity. His bold, unprecedented novel—sometimes graceful, sometimes merely preachy—would be applauded by some as intensely as it would be denounced by others.

I have Vidal himself to thank for the suggestion that I consult the letters he received from readers of *The City and the Pillar*. Rarely are those who examine literature as a cultural document presented with evidence as copious and instructive as that correspondence. The abundant correspondence prompted by *The City and the Pillar* attests to the considerable cultural work performed by this novel. Considering the dearth of publications of any sort that dealt at all sympathetically with homosexuality before the 1948 publication of *The City and the Pillar*, the letters Vidal received form a singular body of evidence, anticipating the letters to *ONE* magazine a few years later that historian Craig Loftin has interpreted.[31]

Vidal began receiving letters from readers of *The City and the Pillar* as soon as it was published in 1948, and letters continued well into 1952. Some were from physicians and clerics, some from other writers, but most were simply from other queer men, some of whom sought advice or wanted a meeting with Vidal, or at least a photograph. Though overwhelmingly from the United States, these several dozen letters in Harvard's Vidal Collection include mail from England, South Africa, Denmark,

Canada, Ceylon, Germany, and Switzerland. Together they are not simply a measure of the novel's early impact, but are also something of a window onto a gay community that was still largely unorganized, often overflowing with misinformation and fear. To a revealing degree, one finds in these letters expressions of relief, gratitude, guilt, self-pity, loneliness, and naïveté. Despite *The City and the Pillar*'s emphasis on diversity among American men who shared with each other only their common desire for sex with males, many of Vidal's correspondents, having internalized their culture's undiscerning stereotypes of queer men, assumed a considerable, automatic degree of emotional, intellectual, and sometimes even physical compatibility between Vidal and themselves.[32] Many seemed to lead lonely lives, especially understandable in 1948 and several years thereafter, with their feelings of isolation reflected by the very fact that they wrote Vidal, a stranger, sometimes at such length and with such self-revelation. While queer enclaves had been developing in parts of the United States for over half a century, it is clear from the letters Vidal received that many American men with queer yearnings lived far outside the gates of those communities.

Thus did twenty-four-year-old navy veteran George Gaillard of Greenwich, Connecticut, write "Dear Gore" that "I have your picture and to say I would fall for you is putting it mildly. If only we two could meet as did Jim and Bob but with a happy ending." In accord with what Vidal had written about the war's impact, Gaillard reported that "when I did my bit in the Navy as an Ensign away from this Country I found ever so many young [men] eager to do it themselves and to submit. I sure have some lovely memories even tho I am just turned 24." "Having been taught to do it by an older boy and still pursuing it," he said, now "I have a lovely High School boy of 17 whom I have broken in. . . . He is a little more obvious than I would like but he loves me so that is what counts." Like this correspondent, most of the men who wrote Vidal were not seeking advice or even a meeting as much as they simply wanted to tell their queer story, some as if for the first time, apparently believing that anyone who would write *The City and the Pillar* would appreciate hearing it.[33] Joseph A. Bochert of Lancaster, Ohio, for instance, an aspiring writer himself, observed that the novel's story "could well be my own" yet could never be shared with "one's everyday acquaintances, especially in a small town." Having already read *The City and the Pillar* "again and again," Bochert, who signed himself "sincerely yours in confidence," touchingly asked Vidal to send him an autographed photo, so he would be able "to glance at your photo as I reread 'The Pillar' again."[34]

It is crucial to recognize the staggering paucity of sound information and consequent lack of perspective among the men who wrote Vidal, and among the millions more whose lives resembled theirs. With appalling rarity did they ever encounter empathy or compassion. Decades later, Vidal himself was still touched enough by the letter from one man, Charles S. Marlor of Oxford, Ohio, that he displayed it in his 2009 volume of memorabilia, *Snapshots in History's Glare*. Grateful to Vidal "for presenting to the general public a picture of the homosexual as a human being," Marlor wrote simply that his thanks came "from the bottom of my heart" and that from *The City and the Pillar* he had found "a bit of new hope in my life that someone else feels the same."[35] Such was the power of this one book.

A young physician who also taught biology at Clark University, Fred H. Howard, told Vidal that he had "been acutely aware of the so-called underground of homosexuals and of the stupidity in the methods with which they are handled in our courts of law." Some years before the pathbreaking research of Evelyn Hooker would find no significant difference in psychological adjustment between homosexual and heterosexual men, it is noteworthy that Dr. Howard wrote that "I would further number among my close friends quite a number of so-called queers, all very intelligent and interesting people."[36] Another correspondent whose professional experience made him grateful for Vidal's novel was Edmund Randolph Laine, rector of Saint Paul's Episcopal Church in Stockbridge, Massachusetts. "In the years of my ministry," he wrote, "I have come in contact with people who were homosexual and turned to religion and the Church for help. I fear they received little because of the often unmerciful and unscientific on the part of the so-called good people to this complex and mysterious problem." Laine told Vidal of a man who was previously "one of the leading athletes of the High School" in Stockbridge who later sought Laine out when he was a "young Naval officer" for advice about being "hopelessly homosexual." When psychiatric treatment "got nowhere," Laine had advised the young man to accept "that you evidently were made that way" and should "order your peculiar love life in the best way possible, and keep in touch with goodness, beauty, and truth": Laine thought that *The City and the Pillar* expressed the same "humane understanding" he had tried to summon.[37]

Among accomplished or aspiring writers who contacted Vidal was Sheldon F. Eckfeld, forty-six, from Columbus, Ohio; in the 1940 census, Eckfeld was living with his mother Olegene, and when he died in 1967 his death certificate noted that he was never married. Homosexuality, he declared to Vidal, "is something that cannot be eliminated by psychiatry, surgery, or imprisonment and while it is perhaps unfortunate that most of us cannot be so-called normal in our sexual relations, it should not necessarily mean that anyone with homosexual tendencies should be banished to a sexual Siberia." Eckfeld told Vidal that *The City and the Pillar* "is not a brilliantly written book but it lets the uninitiated know there is such a thing as homosexuality, that it is more widespread than most people think and that it is here to stay." Most interesting were Eckfeld's comments on the war, which, he thought

> did more to give thousands of young men homosexual experiences than anything else. I have loads of friends who before the war would have

turned away in horror at the very idea of going to bed with a homosexual. Now that they are back in civilian life, they continue to seek such experiences as diversion from their normal sexual activities and this is especially true of young married men who seem to grow tired of being completely dominated and owned by a woman. They seem to enjoy the freedom and relaxation that comes to them with a casual homosexual experience with no permanent strings attached.

Complimenting Vidal again for doing "a damned good job," Eckfeld concluded by saying he would "like to talk with you sometime when I'm in New York as I have two unfinished novels on tap, one has a distinct homosexual theme."[38]

More modest was Harry Miele of Bethel, Maine, who wrote Vidal a few years after *The City and the Pillar*'s publication. Miele said he had "stopped counting the number of copies I have bought for friends" and that he "was particularly attracted to your novel because of its clear exposition of life and people without condemnation nor condonement." His own novel was "along the same lines" as Vidal's, and Vidal's success had emboldened him, Miele said, whereas before he had feared its depiction of "promiscuity" would doom it. "Much of the background of my 'would be' novel," he reported, "is material gathered from my three and one half years in the service and my travels around the world." Like Eckfeld, he hoped for a meeting. A licensed pharmacist who in 1951 taught English, Spanish, French, and Italian "in a private school," Miele was teaching at Westbrook High in Westbrook, Maine, by 1953, and was an assistant professor when he lived in Sanford, Maine, in 1961. In no surviving record of Miele is a spouse ever listed.[39]

One of those who sought Vidal's advice seemed to have more on his mind than just writing a novel. Corporal Irvin S. Sterling, who eventually served in Korea as a sergeant, wrote from Elgin Air Force Base in Florida that *The City and the Pillar* was, of Vidal's first three works, the one from which "I derived my greatest pleasure." "So far I have found that many men in this Air Force," he maintained, "as well as in the other branches of the service, are far from what most people would call 'normal.'" "One of my closest buddies is a homosexual," he went on, "and he tells me that he is not only in love with a man but he is married to him. Both are in the service and the 'husband' is overseas. At the present time he is just waiting to get out of the service so he can have a home ready for the both of them when the other gets out. . . . Perhaps I, myself, have come to act like one from being around them as much as I am." Sterling asked Vidal whether *The City and the Pillar* were "an autobiography," since he also wanted "to write a book on the same theme," but believed he still had more to learn. Planning a trip to New Orleans, he wondered whether the "particular cafe there" described in *The City and the Pillar* "actually does exist," believing that if "I could get acquainted with them in civilian life where they can be much more themselves I could get much more material." In closing, he told Vidal that "your suggestions would be appreciated more than you know."[40]

Another advice-seeker was more direct. Paul Edwards of New Haven was grateful for *The City and the Pillar* because "for the first time I have found a character, although he is fictional, to whom I feel myself very similar." Having kept his desires a secret, Edwards told Vidal that "although I go out on dates with girls (because of social pressures) and am considered very personable, I have thus far *not at all* been sexually attracted to them." It was just the opposite with "many of the fellows I come in contact with both at college and other places." Without yet having had sex with either a woman or another man, Edwards asked Vidal for the names of some "higher class" New York City gay bars, so that he might "find out once and for all whether I am basically a homosexual or not." If he did not discover his actual nature soon, he feared, "under present conditions my nerves will crack."[41]

A dislike of men considered effeminate permeates *The City and the Pillar*, and was expressed in writing and in more private activity throughout Vidal's life. The previously quoted remark of Norman Mailer's that Vidal was "very much a man" would have pleased Vidal greatly, since by that Mailer meant that Vidal did not act like the stereotypical queer; Vidal in his way sought to avoid any appearance of vulnerability and weakness, even tender sentiments, almost as much as Mailer did. Opposite sides of the same coin, each man clearly had something to prove: Mailer was forever trying to prove what he *was*, a virile male through and through, while Vidal often seemed desperate to prove what he *was not*, a sissy. In a 1960 interview, Vidal even aligned himself with Mailer as the "other writer who had the same problem," critics who "really turned on him . . . for radical statements about life, and sex, and so on." In the same interview, Vidal sought to explain why another writer, Truman Capote, nemesis of both Vidal and Mailer, had not encountered the same hostility Vidal experienced. Critics "don't mind hairdressers," Vidal explained. "They are not threatened by someone who is effeminate and freakish and amusing. . . . I was a six-foot soldier with a much-admired war novel who had suddenly written a book of the sort that nobody else had ever done, showing the normality of a certain sort of relationship."[42] There was some accuracy, of course, in Vidal's point about the particular threat of the straight-appearing queer, but his need to make his point at the expense of hairdressers and Truman Capote attests to Vidal's own insecurities.

The stereotype of gay men as effeminate, an equation of male queerness with weakness, seeing all gay men as womanly inverts, is, of course, both misogynistic as well as homophobic, a two-for-the-price-of-one bigotry that at its birth relied on existing negative attitudes toward women as means of stigmatizing homosexual men and affirming the strength of their straight brothers. The fairy, descendant of the nancy boy—an unmanly, hence womanly creature—was the first American queer, a creature of the late nineteenth century's division of gendered labor, someone with whom a manly male could even have sex and keep intact his own conventional masculinity, as long as the manly male always took (or said he took) the dominant, penetrating position in sex. Only well into the twentieth century did America's queer maleness come to include any male who had sex with another male, regardless of position or demeanor.[43]

The City and the Pillar, then, like all three of John Horne Burns's novels, appeared at a momentous time: just as American men who had sex with other males were freshly contending with the broadened indictment of their sexual activity, wrestling with what had come to be seen as their very nature, not just their engaging in an activity they enjoyed and some scorned. This nature of theirs, lest we forget, had during the recent war been officially declared to be so offensively unmanly that it was incongruent with military service. In letters to Vidal, it seemed especially to be American males of his immediate generation, those in their late teens and their twenties, for whom this new meaning of being queer—any male who had sex with another male—was particularly vexing, worth writing Vidal about.

Anxiety over effeminacy—in voice, language, and gestures—was revealingly frequent in the letters Vidal received.[44] The fundamental concern was not as much queerness per se, but rather how one's maleness was performed. Clearly one of the reasons many readers appreciated Jim Willard, and Gore Vidal so appreciated the character's probable inspiration, Jimmie Trimble, was that both were athletes whose conventional masculinity seemed unassailable. Neither was a stereotypical queer, Trimble perhaps not an actual one either. C. S. Maxon, a philosophy professor at Michigan Tech, sent Vidal some "academic mutterings" on the topic of effeminacy, suggesting that the novel had drawn a valuable distinction between "normal homosexual love" and "under-ground" homosexuality, where effeminacy was more prevalent. A womanly queer man, to Maxon, was the genuine deviant.[45] Poet Carl Selph, then a Columbia undergraduate, thanked Vidal for *The City and the Pillar*, for treating "the homosexual male as a decent human being and not as some kind of freakish pseudo-woman."[46] The misogyny, of course, was obvious, but deeper was the concern over what sort of male one was to be, over whether rigid gender boundaries would be maintained, apart from the source of one's sexual arousal.

Others were stronger in their disdain for effeminacy, and hence their approval of how Vidal had characterized Jim Willard. Don Macintosh, a twenty-seven-year-old air force and merchant marine veteran who was studying piano at the American Conservatory when it was in Chicago in 1949, told Vidal that he wished "I could shake your hand and say thanks for the wonderful non-fiction" in the way Jim had been portrayed. Hating effeminacy in men, Macintosh identified strongly with Jim: "These characteristics I have always hated, and destroyed them whenever they were found in myself."[47] Donald Michie Mackintosh went on to receive his BA and MA from the American Conservatory and had a lifetime career as a public school band director in Florence, Waterboro, Macedonia, and McCormick, South Carolina. A member of the New Wappataw Presbyterian Church, Charleston's French Huguenot Society, and the Society of Antiquaries of Scotland, Mackintosh, who never married, eventually died at seventy-eight in a Greenwood, South Carolina, nursing home.

Less successful at emulating Jim Willard was Victor Andrzejewski, twenty-five, of Detroit. He wrote "Dear Gore" that he was "EFFEMINATE—BUT *NOT* THE GIDDY TYPE," and indeed felt that he "had a woman's soul trapped in my male body." Deeply troubled by how the novel ended, he asked Vidal, "Do you abhor men such as I? I sincerely hope not, for I want to be your friend. Words can never adequately express how greatly I admire you." Sadly self-effacing, he went on: "Unabashedly, I beg for your friendship . . . you delineated homosexuals so understandingly that I am hoping my loneliness will strike a responsive chord in you. . . . Please, won't you write to me—even if it's only to tell me to go to hell?" Andrzejewski poignantly revealed that at twenty-five his "one and only affair ended with him maturing into the heterosexual stage. Similar to Jim's experience with Bob. . . . Since then I have lived on the boundary—desiring men desperately but never having the confidence to approach them." *The City and the Pillar*, however, had given him "hope and courage."[48] When he wrote Vidal, Andrzejewski was still living with his widowed, Polish-born father and four older siblings. Apparently living his entire life in Michigan, Andrzejewski died there at eighty in 2003.

More poignant still, and probably representing the situation of many midcentury males, was the letter Vidal received in 1952 from Frank Peterson, thirty-four, of Santa Monica. Having learned of *The City and the Pillar* from reading, at his doctor's suggestion, Donald Webster Cory's *The Homosexual in America*, Peterson told Vidal that he had

> been to seven psychoanalysts . . . , and they have all told me I am a congenital sexual invert, incurable, and the only hope I have for happiness is to locate some one of my type, love him and spend the remainder of our lives together, sharing and helping one another. . . .
>
> I do not drink nor smoke, and have no interest in the perverts who abound by the hundreds of thousands, I am friendly and try to help them, but I cannot agree with them in their flippant attitude, feminine qualities, and their sexual promiscuity. I feel sex is, like the kiss, an expression of love. I see nothing in the idea of sex, unless it expresses love. Hence, I live without sex until I have mutual love to express. . . .
>
> I am alone, and do not know how I can stand it much longer, as nothing is as fun when I am alone, yet I have nothing in common with the heterosexual world, or the world of perverts, hence I stand alone,

between both worlds, fitting in neither one, and alone and unhappy. I hope you can help me, and you may perhaps know of someone similar to myself in feelings, who is searching for someone to share his life, not merely for sex, but for love and companionship and mutual helpfulness.

If you do, kindly show him my letter. . . . In closing, I might add that I am attracted to huge and massive men, or overpowering masculinity. The less masculine, the less I feel attraction.[49]

The lack of information and open discussion about homosexuality in the United States in the late 1940s was evident throughout the letter Vidal received from Laurence Poinsette, a New York City college student who confided that "I am confused, wholly confused. My whole concept of life has been altered." Though fascinated by sex since middle school, Poinsette nonetheless claimed that he had "only recently heard about" the existence of "homosexuality in men," and even insisted as well that he did not "believe I could have sexual relations" with a woman, even though "I like girls and hope to be married someday." The continuing attention of "a handsome blonde boy of the college I attend," someone he had first noticed in gym class, was what troubled Poinsette enough to write, certain that Vidal would surely be able to tell him whether "effeminateness" was "inborn or caused by a domineering mother," as well as whether homosexuality was "an immature love which the possessor hasn't outgrown for fear of sex relations with the opposite sex." Since Poinsette had "learned far more from your book than I ever knew before on homosexuality," he was sure Vidal could explain the blonde boy's attentiveness as well as his own inability to "look directly at him."[50]

A revealing number of letter-writers, after reading *The City and the Pillar*, sought the author's friendship, or at least a friendly meeting. Charles Beckwith Jaqua of Paterson, New Jersey, for instance, still in his twenties, asked Vidal how he thought "a homosexual person (male or female) should handle their problems?" Jaqua elaborated, asking "should they live their affliction or sickness" and find "one of their own . . . or should they isolate themselves . . . and suffer the torture of loneliness." Desiring a vote against isolation, Jaqua hoped that he and Vidal might meet.[51]

An intrepid seventeen-year-old high school student, Richard Donald LaConte of Worcester, Massachusetts, wrote that "I have read your book 'The City and the Pillar' which I enjoyed tremendously. It was beautifully written. In fact of all the books I have read on that particular subject, I must say that yours was by far the better. I have passed the book down to friends and they have enjoyed it as much as I." Claiming to "read about 4–5 books a week mostly Historical Biblicals and Shackespears [sic] works," LaConte said his hobbies were "Tennis, golf, Sailing, swimming, skiing, horse back riding," along with "Music (classical), Opera, Ballet, Art and reading." After that list, he asked Vidal, "Do we have anything in common?" adding that "I hope someday to become a Prof. of Fine Arts." If LaConte were to be believed, *The City and the Pillar* had something of a young fan base in Worcester. "I have told all the kids that read the book after [me] that I would write to you, but they do not believe that you will bother to answer me. So lets [*sic*] show them." He signed himself "Fondly, Dick."[52] LaConte, whose parents were both born in Italy, was the youngest of eleven children, a situation that perhaps fostered his outgoing nature.

Interestingly enough, another seventeen-year-old, Bill Harclerode, also had a group of friends who appreciated the book; he told Vidal "myself and my friends have enjoyed your book ememncely [*sic*] and that 'gay' escapaid [*sic*] in reading." Harclerode found Jim Willard "a fascinating and very desirble [*sic*] young man" and said that *The City and the Pillar* was the "type of reading [that] is best for my age and it has also taught me a great deal that I didn't know about the life of a homosexual." Were he ever to be in New York, Bill Harclerode told Vidal, "I would very much like to meet you."[53] Still another teenager, nineteen-year-old Jack Brenner of Saint Petersburg, Florida, wrote that he had found *The City and the Pillar* "very interesting and very frank," and found Vidal's "writting [*sic*] very serious and understanding." Wondering if "you have written any other novels on the same subject," Brenner asked Vidal for an "autographed photo of your self or a personal note and a snapshot," even enclosing postage. He also enclosed a small studio photograph of his handsome self, probably a high school graduation portrait, inscribed, "Me! Jack Brenner."[54]

Leonard Selzer of Hancock, New York, was no reader, but was eager for a meeting with Gore Vidal nonetheless. Teasingly saying at first that he was an "old man," he later revealed that he was just six years older than the author. He admitted that he had read none of Vidal's works, but had become acquainted with his writing and good looks in a *New York Herald Tribune* "write-up." As for himself, Selzer said,

> I tower 6′3″ into the atmosphere, have a slim hard build. My beautiful orbs (gad!) are blue. I have slightly wavy thick medium brown hair sprinkled with gray, a mustache and long sideburns. . . . I have at least one advantage over you; I know how good-looking you are, but you have no idea of my looks. Now quit blushing. I can see it way up here.

Noting that the *Herald Tribune* article had not indicated whether Vidal was married, Selzer had "an idea you enjoy the blessings of single life the same as I do." The letter was typed, but he closed with a note in longhand, giving Vidal his phone number "for your little black book."[55]

Much less lighthearted, and also hoping for a meeting, was musician Philip R. Macy, twenty-five, of Scarsdale, in his 1949 letter. "Being an introvert," wrote Macy,

> much of my sex life is realized vicariously through music and through my main outside interest: reading. This, plus the fact that I have come to consider myself a latent homosexual (latent, that is, except for an

occasional like-minded or just plain frustrated pal) impelled me to start collecting books dealing with the homosexual. . . . Up to the time I read PILLAR (and now the SEASON [*of Comfort*] has contributed even more), aside from recognizing my irresistible attraction to male beauty and the phallus, I had never been able to clarify in my own mind just what it was that I was looking and longing for with regard to a companion. The PILLAR performed this service for me brilliantly, and Jim's twin conception is mine now, too.

Macy hoped to meet Vidal "for a real bull session," he said, and suggested that "if you ever want your ego pumped by an unashamed admirer, or if you ever need a secretary who doesn't write shorthand, or a typist who types with two fingers, or even a companion to travel around the world with (trouble is, no money), just write, wire, or phone (Scars 3-3755) and I'll be in NYC in forty minutes." Like Leonard Selzer, Macy had typed his letter, and then ended with a longhand note, his saying, "P.S. That *personal* on the envelope is the understatement of the week!"[56] After a year at Cornell, Macy had left to spend a year on the road with a dance band; in 1943, he enlisted in the army where he spent three years. He lived to be eighty-seven, only dying in 2010.

C. W. Randolph Benson, another man about Vidal's age, a student at the University of Virginia, wrote to complain about the ending of *The City and the Pillar*, and what he reasonably saw as its pessimistic implications. "I was really very upset when Jim killed Bob," he wrote,

> probably because I saw so much of my own experiences in Jim's. But I did not kill my "Bob," nor do I think Jim had to. Why could Jim have not had the experience that thousands before him have had—losing that which he had wanted so bad for so long, and with it his dream and hope, but accepting it all eventually and going his way alone, disillusioned but still seeking. . . . I am a young "hopeful," and any words of advice you can give me will be more than appreciated. I would like very much to meet you and talk with you. . . . I think that we would get along well, since our interests are so similar—except that your efforts have been so very successful. I am twenty-four [he was actually 26], a college student, 5′11″, athletic, not handsome, not homely, . . . I first became interested in your work when I saw your picture in LIFE some time ago, and I do not believe that the admirable things I saw in your face could be absent in your personality.[57]

Later a biographer of fellow Virginian Thomas Jefferson, Benson became a professor at Trinity University in San Antonio and at Roanoke College. He died at eighty-five in 2007, leaving only nieces and nephews.[58]

Another "young 'hopeful'" writing Vidal was Charles K. Winter of Bridgeport, Connecticut. Returning to the United States on the *Queen Elizabeth* after his army service in World War II, Winter had just graduated from Duke, and believed he had a guaranteed future in his brother Alpheus's machinery manufacturing business. Simply reading *The City and the Pillar*, however, had "forced" Winter to decide whether to leave his hometown of nearby Fairfield, or stay put, and "pretend to be content, and ever wonder what might have been." As with so many correspondents, Charles Winters's identification with Jim Willard was powerful: "Physically and mentally I am the closest thing to jim [*sic*] that could be imagined—closer, I suspect, than the real model. It is amazing that I even read the book, for my reading is restricted generally to certain sporting magazines." After "three weeks of sitting on the idea," Winters boldly asked Vidal to meet him shortly in New York City: "I can come into the city any evening or weekend. My Saturdays and Sundays are still free. I marvel at my frankness on bare paper. I hope such frankness draws an answer."[59] It is not clear whether Charles Kofold "Koke" Winter ultimately decided to stay close to Bridgeport for most of his long adult life or not. Although he is known to have lived in Denver when in his late fifties, and his ashes were scattered in the "troutfishing headwaters of the Colorado River," he died, in 2007 at eighty-five, of prostate cancer and Alzheimer's, back home in Bridgeport.[60]

Less famous correspondents than Thomas Mann seem often to have found, as Mann confided to his diary, that *The City and the Pillar* had "stirred the banked fires" of their pasts.[61] Two correspondents somewhat older than many of the others, old enough to have already established themselves in careers and a family, wrote especially significant letters to Vidal that were stimulated by *The City and the Pillar*. For Kennard Lewis, a thirty-six-year-old Pennsylvania lawyer, the novel's impact had been considerable, moving him to wonder whether "all sex is a snare and a delusion [that] never satisfies" and telling Vidal that

> I shall not exceed the boundaries of simple good manners, by saying anything much about myself, except that I have been troubled for some years searching for something I have not found in spite of much hunting and searching, marrying and reproducing, and living a useful (I hope) life in a profession requiring good judgment and hard work. It has much reward but I never expect to find the brother you refer to in your book although I have tried for years.

The City and the Pillar may well be among a handful of fictional works in the United States—*Uncle Tom's Cabin* and *The Catcher in the Rye*, for instance, among them—that have had truly extraordinary impact on their readers, indeed on the culture at large. The novel's effect on Kennard Lewis was clearly remarkable. "I shall remember the book forever," he wrote Vidal, "and probably read it many times. . . . You have put more of my own thoughts in writing than I ever thought anyone else on earth ever could or would." He began to get more specific, revealing to Vidal that

> I have a great love for my wife and enjoy full completion of sex; but I am still a rover at heart, and yet I know I wouldn't be happy roving either. There is no answer, I swear. I really believe I expect too much out of life, and a book like yours is the only possible answer, viz: a discussion of the topic, a sharing of experience with someone else who knows what I am talking (thinking) about.

Thereupon he proposed a meeting, if Vidal should ever "come to the Pocono Mountains for a vacation." He offered "a good meal" and "some slight conversation," promising not to reveal Vidal's identity to townspeople. "Think it over," he wrote, "I am not making any kind of proposition. . . . I am looking for a friend in the best sense. . . . Maybe we could bat an idea back and forth, like a tennis ball."[62] Whatever thoughts the novel stimulated in Lewis, it apparently did not prompt a move away from East Stroudsburg in Pennsylvania's Monroe County, the place from which he wrote Vidal. From 1974 to 1978, in his sixties, he was president of the Monroe County Bar Association, remaining married to his wife, Eloise; he died ten years later.

Vidal received a similar letter from another middle-aged, seemingly well-established correspondent, Hathaway Turner, forty, an executive with a New York machinery manufacturer who was a married father of two. *The City and the Pillar* had so affected Turner that, in awkward prose, he told Vidal that

> I know that in the future I shall re read many parts of it. So frankly, simply, and beautifully, yet often with dreadful and deadly thrusts, you express conflicting thoughts and emotions which have tortured me, that I deeply respect your understanding and the manner in which you as so gifted a writer can present it.

Somewhat evasively, he wrote that "being somewhat older than you," he already had "led a full and widely varied life with many friends of all types in [Union] College, Europe, New York City, and the Army" before settling in "this little village in rural New York," Montour Falls. Despite the experience he claimed and his being older than Vidal, he said "I marvel at your grasp and comprehension." Coincidentally, he revealed that "only once before have I written to the writer of a book and that was after being revolted by the exaggerations of John H. Burns's 'Lucifer with a Book,' when only a short time before I admired his 'The Gallery.'" He had questions, not complaints, about *The City and the Pillar*, including uncertainty about Vidal's "complete intent in writing" it. To address that uncertainty, he thought that "meeting you and talking with you is what I would most appreciate." There was more on Turner's mind: Asking what "I hope is not too presumptuous a question," he touchingly wondered whether "you believe there is only unhappiness or disaster for those whose lives have fallen or been led into the direction of those dealt with in your book?"[63] Strikingly handsome in his 1929 yearbook photo from Union College, nattily attired as an older man "on a trip to Italy," Turner stayed with Shepard Niles, the hoist manufacturing company he had joined as a young man, becoming a vice president just a few years after writing Vidal. He died at only sixty-four in 1972.

For many of Vidal's correspondents, *The City and the Pillar* had clearly brought a welcome, even life-altering, sense of alternatives that were previously unknown, along undoubtedly with countless questions—about themselves and American society. For others, like Hathaway Turner, perhaps the book mostly brought just troubling questions, an encounter with sensations that had been repressed more or less successfully, and an ultimate decision that it was too late for them to explore possibilities the book presented. Whatever the book's various effects on its readers, it definitely was no ordinary work of fiction.

In the novel's original hardcover, publisher Dutton apparently sought to make the book appear as unthreatening as possible. There were no images, no clue of what the novel was about, just geometric designs, the author's name, and the book's title, all in four different colors. Inexplicably, a Signet paperback in 1950 even featured a woman in a low-cut dress in its cover's foreground, with a young man, presumably Jim, seated behind her. Another Signet/New American Library paperback in 1955 had Jim sitting alone on the cover, while a new version in 1961 had on its cover Jim alone, holding a tennis racket. Uninformative covers notwithstanding, there was the matter of the novel's title, unambiguously a reference to Genesis and the fate of Lot's wife (turning into a pillar of salt) when, defying an angel's instruction, she turned back to look at Sodom, the burning city associated with its inhabitants' wicked ways; she and her family were fleeing Sodom, to escape God's punishing destruction of their former home. Of huge significance was the particular form of wickedness that had over centuries come to be associated with Sodom, the sexual act to which the city gave its name. Vidal's novel was divided into two parts, literally "The City" and "The Pillar," that latter section commencing with Jim's and Bob's returns, for different reasons, to the Virginia town of their boyhoods, setting in motion the circumstances of their ultimately violent reunion.

Not unlike Vidal's frequent use, whatever the reason, of "My Lord Jesus" when he and I met all those years later, his giving *The City and the Pillar* its particular title shows, if nothing else, religion's continuing hold on his consciousness. What the novel's title meant more specifically, indeed what Vidal intended the novel as a whole to be about, and to say, is more elusive. Much later on, with hindsight's benefits—or its delusions—and with either the insights or the conceits of older age, Vidal would come up with explanations, at times contradictory ones, about his original intentions in *The City and the Pillar*. If the author himself was not always of one mind about his creation, is it any wonder that reviewers in 1948 had varying reactions? Just as he had a specific interpretation of the negative nature and destructive effect of the reviews of John Horne Burns's *Lucifer with a Book*, Vidal would often say that *The City and the Pillar*, when it was not denied attention altogether due to its unpopular topic, encountered such widespread hostility to homosexuality that his future work suffered guilt by association, and that he was even blackballed to such an extent that he was driven away from writing novels for his entre livelihood, having to resort to writing stage plays, teleplays, or screenplays, or else to publishing mystery novels under a pseudonym. He once wrote, for example, regarding *The City and the Pillar*, that "*The New York Times* would not advertise it and no major American newspaper or magazine would review it or any other book of mine for the next six years."[64] There was, however, a revealing similarity, even synergy, between his separate accounts of how reviewers mistreated Burns and himself. As with Burns and *Lucifer with a Book*, there was more nuance than Vidal claimed in the story of *The City and the Pillar* and its reviewers.

How well and how often during "the next six years" were *The City and the Pillar* and its immediate successors reviewed? Was there derision or outright neglect sufficient to drive Vidal into the exile of a pseudonym or the job of writing scripts for the movies, the stage, or television? Quantitatively, this is easily determined. In 1948 and 1949, *The City and the Pillar* received twelve reviews in important forums: not an abundance of attention, especially in light of the novel's importance in retrospect, but surely not neglect either, especially in light of how much discomfort and denial the topic of homosexuality generated at the time that *The City and the Pillar* came out. After the anxiety aroused in some reviewers by even the relatively brief and largely unbecoming attention to homosexuality in *In a Yellow Wood*, much greater ill ease in reviews of *The City and the Pillar* was surely no surprise. Admittedly some of those reviews of *The City and the Pillar* were strikingly brief and did not, as Vidal often pointed out, include magazines with large circulations such as *Time* and *Newsweek*. But the dozen reviews were nevertheless more than double the number that either *Williwaw* or *In a Yellow Wood* had attracted, and, like *The City and the Pillar*, neither of those earlier works had been reviewed in the major newsmagazines. Additionally, reviews notwithstanding, *The City and the Pillar* reportedly sold a hefty thirty thousand hardcover copies, while the much less sensational four novels by Vidal that followed it each sold around ten thousand copies, "not bad," as Christopher Bram has observed, "for the hardcover book slump of the early Fifties."[65]

Neither Vidal nor his publisher (again, E. P. Dutton) were enough intimidated by the reception *The City and the Pillar* had received to keep another novel of his, *The Season of Comfort*, from appearing the very next year, 1949. Generally viewed as the story of a young man's effort to break away from a cruel mother, not unlike Vidal's own, it also had a homoerotic dimension, though that little noticed theme admittedly was not central in *The Season of Comfort*. It received eleven reviews in its year of publication—once again, not a record of outright neglect. The year after that, in 1950, came a departure, *A Search for the King*, Vidal's first published foray into historical fiction, a simple quest tale of the lyricist Blondel's legendary twelfth-century search for the imprisoned Richard the Lionheart. Garnering more attention, it was reviewed fourteen times, mostly in important places. That very same year came *Dark Green, Bright Red*, a departure of another sort, a novel about a revolution in Central America, an area where Vidal had lived while writing *The City and the Pillar*. Appraised less often than *A Search for the King*, it nonetheless received eleven reviews. Then in 1952 Vidal published a coming-of-age novel set in postwar France and Italy, *The Judgment of Paris*. Taking its title from Greek mythology's contest among the three most beautiful goddesses, the novel involves its protagonist, a young male lawyer, with three women, from each of whom he learns important lessons. It was reviewed twelve times, yet again hardly an indication of Vidal's being shunned altogether. Finally, roughly at the end of the six years that Vidal mentioned in his claim of being ignored or disparaged as punishment for *The City and the Pillar*, came *Messiah*, still another Dutton publication. Impressively, with *Messiah* Vidal gave his work yet another fresh direction; this was an unrelenting satire of organized religion and mass media, a dystopian tale of a death cult that rapidly replaces the world's dominant faiths. No neglect of it either; although it had fewer reviews than its predecessors, it still received eight.

The quality of the sixty-eight reviews given to *The City and the Pillar* and the five Vidal novels that followed over the next six years was by no means as uniformly disparaging as Vidal's blackball narrative would have it. Vidal did decide to begin writing additional novels—mysteries—under a pseudonym during this period, and he also took to writing scripts for the stage, television, and film, even moving eventually to Hollywood, a place he had first visited when in the army. Something other than unfair criticism or critical neglect—the allure of high salaries—may also account for his choosing to do something besides just writing novels under his own name. Even novelists as luminous as Fitzgerald and Faulkner had, after all, turned to Hollywood for work. To view Vidal's life in the aftermath of *The City and the Pillar* as simply a noble and sadly inevitable retreat in response to his being either unjustly shunned or unfairly criticized for a courageous novel is unfounded. In his declining years, Vidal went so far as to write—wholly inaccurately—that, under duress after *The City and the Pillar*, "I vanished from the scene and wrote a number of novels under pseudonyms."[66] When he revived the story of John Horne Burns in his 1965 *New York Times Book Review* essay, and characterized Burns as yet another the victim of postwar prejudice against homosexuality, Vidal may have also been thinking about his own postwar choices, maybe trying to build a reputation for himself as a man of principle, as much as (or even more than) he was trying to keep alive and enhance the memory of John Horne Burns. Or, more charitably, one might just suggest that the essay on Burns was Vidal's effort to ally himself with Burns, as two victims of what clearly was rampant hostility to homosexuality in the years right after the war.

As Christopher Bram has astutely observed, Vidal often wrote of his own past "as if he were born wise," and also, one might add, as if he had consistently risen above petty concerns of making money and achieving notoriety.[67] As he did in my interview with him in 2009, Vidal also was inclined to insist that throughout his life he had been fearless enough to dodge the hurt of antigay bigotry and not succumb to the sad self-loathing, self-doubt, or covering that could result from being bigotry's target. Scrutiny of how his early novels were actually reviewed, something that occurred more often than he usually implied, reveals that he encountered something other than uniform, unreasonable criticism—except for *The City and the Pillar*, on which the critical verdict was, in fact, almost entirely negative and laced with bigotry. Scrutiny of his life during the 1950s and beyond, furthermore, suggests that indeed Gore Vidal was, after all, human enough to have internalized much of the culture's intense midcentury disdain for sexual desire and activity between men—and disdain even for any form of male intimacy. Like so many of his male contemporaries, including men like Mailer and JFK, Gore Vidal paid a price to affirm his manliness in that climate of fear, sacrificing intimacy for notches on the bedpost.

Some of the reviews of *The City and the Pillar* were brief enough almost to count as neglect. *Kirkus* issued a "storm warning for P.L.'s," presumably public libraries, terming the novel a "serious treatment of the problem of homosexuality," and giving Vidal a compliment of sorts because "instead of highlighting the more ordinary types of perversion, [he] concentrates on the lesser recognized love of men for men." The New York Public Library's Robert Kingery, who had been disturbed by the "perversion" readers encountered in the visit to the queer club in *In a Yellow Wood*, did not surprise when in *Library Journal* he advised that "each library must consider whether this subject," which he had defined as "the road to homosexuality," would be "locally admissible." Despite the warning, Kingery still found the novel to be "serious, discerning, and obviously courageous," a work "having no counterpoint in the recent rash of similarly concerned novels." L. A. G. Strong, in *The Spectator*, wrote an even briefer review, saying little more than that the novel was "a serious work of literature, with a theme which some readers may dislike."

Another British reviewer, P. H. Newby in *Listener*, said cryptically that a British equivalent was unlikely for this "wise and sober book about homosexuality."[68]

Whereas one Irish Catholic reviewer for the *San Francisco Chronicle* who had served in World War II, William Hogan, had been repulsed by Burns's chapter on "Momma's" bar in *The Gallery*, another *Chronicle* reviewer with a similar background, Edward Dermot Doyle, found *The City and the Pillar* to be "a straightforward, unimpassioned appeal for understanding," a story of a male homosexual "as it has not been told before." Believing that "solutions to problems of any variety are more frequently discovered in the light than in the dark," Doyle hoped that Kinsey's figures and works like Vidal's might end the taboo on discussion of the phenomenon he chose to label a "problem." While Doyle's review, and certainly the others already mentioned, hardly gave Vidal either the attention or the approval that an author might like, the Doyle review was at least entitled "An Honest Approach."[69]

The *New Yorker*'s unsigned review, buried in its "Briefly Noted" section, today seems far from a demonstration of the sophistication for which that magazine has always liked to congratulate itself, but of course few midcentury definitions of "sophistication" included acceptance of homosexuality. Indeed it is a revealing sign of the times that even a *New Yorker* review solidly supports Vidal's claim that *The City and the Pillar* was a bold breakthrough that commonly received short shrift. This "disappointing third novel," said the review, charts "a young man's gradual development into an unflinching homosexual"—apparently preferring queers of the flinching sort. Jim and Bob's affecting love scene at the cabin was just the "first, puzzled experience of inversion," with the novel's sole merit said to be "sociologically," as "an amazingly thorough compendium of the kind of dreary information that accumulates on a metropolitan police blotter." Artistically, the *New Yorker* complained, Vidal's work documented a "stage in the decline in the literature of homosexuality to the level of unadorned tabloid writing," a deterioration that the magazine declared began with *Death in Venice*.[70] It is no wonder that it would be another thirty-four years before the *New Yorker* would see fit to publish its first short story highlighting gay characters, David Leavitt's "Territory."[71]

"Abnormal Doom," the title of Richard Gehman's review of *The City and the Pillar* in the *New York Herald Tribune Weekly Book Review*, suggested what was to come. A prolific journalist, World War II veteran, writing teacher, and much-married friend of both Humphrey Bogart and Hugh Hefner, Gehman granted that "few readers will put down this book unmoved or untaught." With sensibilities more delicate than his experience might suggest, he found Vidal's story, covering this "vast half world of furtive, unnatural love," to be "tragic and terrifying," indeed "one of the most astonishing collections of strange men ever to people a novel." Not only "frank, shocking, and sensational," Gehman even thought it was "often embarrassing," and also "extremely sympathetic, penetrating, and exhortive [presumably exhortative]." The love affair of Jim and Bob was, to Gehman, a matter of Jim's discovering "his damnation at seventeen," interestingly enough something that an alarmed Gehman thought "could happen to more young men than the disinterested observer might imagine." Shrouded by his hysteria was Gehman's not unreasonable observation that *The City and the Pillar* had some "careless" writing, "stylized and unreal" dialogue, and "a narrative effect," which Vidal always claimed was quite intentional, "that is almost a monotone."[72] But the review made clear that literary criticism was not what was most on Gehman's mind.

Similarly severe anxiety over homosexuality marked another review, one that reportedly especially annoyed Vidal. In an odd coincidence, in the very same year, 1948, that he published an essay in the *Kenyon Review* that included *The City and the Pillar*, controversial critic Leslie Fiedler also published his well-known essay, "Come Back to the Raft Ag'in, Huck Honey!" A snickering look at the alleged prevalence of male couples in American writing, with implications of barely veiled homoeroticism, the essay probably revealed more about Fiedler's and the culture's discomfort with male intimacy at midcentury than it expressed anything profound about the history of American literature back when male intimacy was not frightening. With closeness between males not veiled at all in *The City and the Pillar*, it was rough going for Fiedler, who tried to make it rough on Vidal. Fiedler's was one of those reviews that say very little but say it with flair, if not with much grace or insight. In Vidal's novel, according to Fiedler's cumbersome, pompous prose, homosexuality "is not an aspect of a fancied Greek world, but the seedy torment of an underground City; the very cartoonishness of the characters, the formal settings, labeled neatly: Hollywood or New Orleans or New York, give a pathos to the real terror they falsify." To Fiedler, Jim Willard's open embrace of his sexuality was nothing more than "animal awareness"; what seemed to alarm Fiedler most, in anticipation of latter-day opponents of gay rights, was that homosexuality might someday be given "free play."[73] According to Vidal biographer Fred Kaplan, "Fiedler's harsh review" was evidence to Vidal of "a homophobic cabal to wound him by attacks or eliminate him by silence."[74] Midcentury discomfort with male intimacy was severe and widespread enough, however, to make an actual "homophobic cabal" superfluous.

But there may still have been scheming against Vidal. According to Kaplan, "an admirer [of Vidal] with close contacts at [the *New York Times*] executive level reported that the decision had been made by the owner himself, Julius Ochs Adler, who had decided that the *Times* would accept ads for *The City and the Pillar* but not review it." It was a year of tough decisions for the *Times*; Kinsey's *Sexual Behavior in the Human Male* also first appeared in 1948, and the *Times* decided to review that, but not advertise it.[75] Though the daily *Times* indeed never reviewed *The City and the Pillar*, C. V. Terry, a pseudonym for celebrated medical novelist Frank Slaughter, gave the book a perfunctory glance, an essay of less than two hundred words, in the

New York Times Book Review. This novel "as sterile as its protagonist," he wrote, features "a doomed young ox who seems suspiciously in love with his doom, and worries the reader beyond endurance with his endless self-questioning." Apparently in an effort to infantilize (or simply insult) Jim, the review repeatedly calls him, with inadvertent cruelty, "Jimmie"; and so inattentive a reader was Terry/Slaughter that he erroneously described journalist Paul Sullivan as "a fashionable novelist."[76]

Lonely dissents from the widespread criticism or neglect given *The City and the Pillar* came from Julia Strachey, a novelist and the niece of Bloomsbury's Lytton Strachey (John Maynard Keynes's lover) in the *New Statesman and Nation*; Charles Rolo in the *Atlantic Monthly*; and, most notably, Richard McLaughlin in the *Saturday Review of Literature*. Strachey was anything but expansive, maintaining calmly that "Mr. Vidal's writing is not at all up my street, but from this story one learns interesting things, and I think we ought to give both author and publisher our respectful gratitude for breaching literary territory against which there is still such mistaken prejudice." Rolo was similarly unexcited, finding Vidal's work "an entertaining story," believing that "essentially it's an attempt to clarify the inner stresses of our times, of which the increase in homosexuality and divorce are symptoms." Only McLaughlin was largely affirmative, commending Vidal "for his realism and honesty," yet still seeing the novel solely as a "social tract," hardly excellent literature. Though perhaps sensing there to be more current novels about homosexuality than there actually were, McLaughlin thought that thanks to the "astounding revelations" of the Kinsey Report, Americans needed soon to realize "the variety of changes in the American sex patterns" and the consequent need for "greater public and private tolerance" of sexual difference.[77] With Vidal's bold (and admittedly cold) novel complementing Kinsey in 1948, conventional morality could understandably feel itself under siege.

Finally, when John Aldridge, as if under protest, let himself evaluate *The City and the Pillar* in his *After the Lost Generation* in 1951, he essentially dismissed the novel as "purely a social document that was read because it had all the qualities of lurid journalism and not because it showed the craft and insight of an artist." As he did with Burns, Aldridge characterized Vidal as a writer of narrow interests and skill, producing a novel with "no master design, no unifying philosophical principle." According to Aldridge, no work that had a queer protagonist could possibly be of general interest or importance, for the "young homosexual is always and only the homosexual." In Aldridge's mind, and surely in the minds of most of his countrymen, the wall between the conventional and the queer was high and solid.

"Always and only the homosexual" was the common thread, a damning stereotype, that ran through nearly all of the critical responses to *The City and the Pillar*. Reviewers were not, however, about to dismiss Vidal himself—as long as he no longer made an "unflinching homosexual" his protagonist. And though he did begin writing for the screen, television, and the stage, by no means did Vidal stop writing novels under his own name. However, behaving as either an artist, a pragmatist, or a coward, Vidal did not feature another queer protagonist, unflinching or otherwise, for well over a decade following the critical scolding or shunning he received for telling Jim Willard's story. Some writers might ignore reviews, but skillful performers are always attentive to their audiences. Not only did Gore Vidal read his own reviews carefully, whatever the lessons he took from them, but it seems certain that he also paid careful attention to how reviewers dealt with John Horne Burns. Though Burns had no protagonists as openly queer in their desires as Jim Willard, queer characters and themes were variously prominent in all three Burns novels, works that were increasingly unpopular with critics. Vidal later characterized how Burns fared with critics as a steep decline, an exaggeration that in its overstatement was perhaps more of a projection of what might have happened to Vidal had he kept queerness prominent than it was simply an accurate description of Burns's fate.

Following *The City and the Pillar* by only a year, *The Season of Comfort* was Vidal's fourth novel in three years, declared on its otherwise dull dust jacket to be "the best novel Gore Vidal has yet written." Though it definitely examined a queer dimension to one of its protagonist's relationships, even John Aldridge could not say that this novel was entirely about homosexuality. More importantly, it would be the last novel to have a queer dimension of any discernible sort during the six-year span following *The City and the Pillar*. Among its other concerns, *The Season of Comfort* is the decidedly *un*comfortable story of a son's efforts to free himself from an overbearing, spiteful mother, surely Vidal's effort, as was *The City and the Pillar*, to put art in his life's service. With "no real home to be sick for," the novel's protagonist, Bill Hawkins, is sent to a Washington, DC, prep school that resembles Saint Alban's, where he eventually befriends none other than another Jimmy, one Jimmy Wesson. This Jimmy is, much like Jimmie Trimble had been, "an important baseball player . . . considered the best athlete in the school," a boy who "moved easily through this world, his short, sand-colored hair curling and uncombed . . . [and] accepted admiration naturally, pleasantly." Bill and this Jimmy's sexual discovery of each other, at the home of Bill's grandparents, differs greatly from Jim and Bob's erotic weekend in the woods in *The City and the Pillar*. No love affair, certainly no lifelong obsession, would follow, nor does Vidal describe their sexual doings in any detail, though their activities do continue when they return to school. Although Bill and Jimmy differentiate their involvement from the "dirty" doings of their schoolmates in the dormitory, they simply agree that "you ought to try everything once." Recognizing that "it was important for both of them to begin to learn the need and the boundaries of love," and even though Bill "vaguely" recognizes "that he and Jimmy were in love," Vidal reassures his readers—and a crucial reassurance it is—that their coupling is but a way station on the road to heterosexuality.

Young women soon enter the lives of both Bill and Jimmy, as Vidal notes with resignation that this new attraction must "destroy the relationship" of the boys. While at another school, surely modeled on Exeter (which Vidal attended, but Trimble did not), while the boys remain roommates, they develop friendships with other young males, Jimmy with the athletes, Bill with his fellow painters, guys that Jimmy derides a "the queers." Thanks to Jimmy's athlete buddies, Bill "had his first woman," and later meets another girl, Kay, with whom he shares a compatibility that goes beyond sex; she is a Boston college student who, like Bill, paints. His attraction to Kay, however, is inhibited by Bill's haunting, recurring recollection of his abusive mother's grasping insistence that "no one else will ever love you as much as I do." Only when Bill goes to war, indeed is wounded in the Battle of the Bulge, does he feel strong enough to finally break away from this horrid parent, and stop altogether his letters to her. In a direct parallel to Vidal's experience, Bill then learns of Jimmy's death, as a marine in the Pacific, oddly pairing the mother's symbolic death with Jimmy's actual one. Yet despite Bill's earlier feeling that he and Jimmy had split up, each developing quite separate friendships, learning that Jimmy is dead renders Bill unable even to finish reading the letter informing him of his friend's death. Then, in an ending in its way as depressing as the conclusion of *The City and the Pillar*, Bill, with utter passivity, decides to go on a date he had previously declined, with a woman whom a buddy describes as "a real nice girl and you can do anything to her you want." Though Bill's date occurs in the springtime, the novel tells us that "the sky was almost black and a cold wind blew," whereas "only yesterday the weather had been warm. . . . Spring, like the other seasons, was bitter."[78] Heterosexuality by default.

Better, certainly less hysterical, even more benignly titled reviews rewarded Vidal's change of tune. In the wake of eclectic writer Philip Wylie's controversial attack on American "momism" in 1942's *Generation of Vipers*, reviewers uniformly accepted the publisher's dust-jacket description of *The Season of Comfort* as being about "the emotional conflict centered around a son's urge to sever the psychological umbilical cord which ties him to a selfish and possessive mother." Most slighted or even altogether ignored the relationship between the protagonist and his friend Jimmy. Without mentioning Jimmy at all, and urging that this was "not a book to be inadvertently left about the house for the kiddies," Richard Cheatham in the *Carolina Quarterly* maintained that *The Season of Comfort* reinforced the notion that "Gore Vidal is one of the most skillful story-tellers in the league of young writers today."[79]

There was no apparent shunning of Vidal after *The City and the Pillar*, and most reviews that did respond negatively to *The Season of Comfort* did so with comparative restraint.[80] The *New Yorker* approached *The Season of Comfort* with an attitude recalling the magazine's censorious review of *The City and the Pillar*; this one, at least, was signed and somewhat lengthier, but was strikingly conventional nonetheless. Focusing on a theme other than the mother-son conflict, John Broderick found Bill to be unappealing because of his dislike of sports and because of "his uncertainty, from age twelve to age seventeen, about which sexual direction he intends to take," an uncertainty that made Bill "perhaps too special to arouse widespread sympathy." The threatening sexuality of *The City and the Pillar* that had so bothered the *New Yorker*'s unsigned reviewer was now absent, thought Broderick, since this annoying coitus was just a boys' game; he saw no need for Vidal to have made Bill so struck by the death of Jimmy, since they had only been "friendly after the private school fashion." Broderick was so unyieldingly narrow-minded that he did not even want someone with Bill's tastes to have had the distinction of being wounded at as grand and consequential a battle as the Battle of the Bulge![81] As was shown in the larger number of reviews of John Horne Burns's work, there was no guarantee at midcentury that publications from large urban areas would be any more receptive to same-sex involvements than hinterland publications would be.

In his own first public appraisal of *The Season of Comfort*, in the *Saturday Review of Literature*, John Aldridge thought that Vidal retained his great promise, having "made more than a fledgling attempt to discover the sensibility of the Forties," even if this novel really was too dull to be of much interest. Just two years later, however, in *After the Lost Generation*, Aldridge's hostility toward anything he sensed to be at all queer had grown apace, and he declared *The Season of Comfort* to be "an even emptier and [more] chaotic novel than *The City and the Pillar*." What bothered Aldridge now was that Vidal seemed "uncertain"—as indeed he did—about what Bill's relationship with Jimmy actually meant. That Bill "acquires a homosexual tenderness for his best friend, Jimmy Wesson" was just too much for Aldridge. Noting that it was "neither the war nor his break with his mother" that "releases [Bill] from the past and prepares [him] for a new life of freedom," Aldridge suggested that the actual problem for Bill, and maybe for Gore Vidal as well, is not an excess of mother love or a mother's domination, but simply "William's homosexual feelings for Wesson."[82] Broderick and, especially, Aldridge, then, were virtually alone in grasping the importance of Jimmy Wesson's character to the novel and its author; but their singular insight was drowned by the era's typical bigotry. While not escaping criticism altogether for having hinted at a queer attraction, Vidal managed to dodge the bullets sent his way for *The City and the Pillar* by literally killing Bill's chances with Jimmy and, however implausibly, concluding the novel by sending Bill off with a female on his arm.

For the themes in *The Mourning After*—postwar longing, loneliness, and intensified antipathy to any sort of closeness between males—*The Season of Comfort* is a text of crucial importance. Its significance in Vidal's oeuvre and in his emotional development has been underappreciated, by biographers and by Vidal himself, who, as already noted, gave *The Season of Comfort* no attention in *Palimpsest*, his memoir, beyond observing that *Season* was one of his rare autobiographical novels. A key to *The Season of Comfort*'s importance appears on its penultimate page, when we are told that on learning of Jimmy's death, Bill "would have cried but he'd forgotten how."[83] Vidal too seems to have experienced an emotional shutdown, in his work and beyond, after the excessively harsh critical response to his openness in *The City and the Pillar*, followed by his melancholy surrender in *The Season of Comfort*.

In his next novel, 1950's *A Search for the King: A Twelfth Century Legend*, Vidal retreated seven and a half centuries to craft a quest tale, his distinctive rendering of the legendary adventurous search by the lyricist Blondel for imprisoned Richard the Lionheart. The story apparently seemed harmless enough to the several reviewers who evaluated the novel, generally quite positively; there surely was nothing to equal the outrage that greeted *The City and the Pillar*, or even *The Season of Comfort*. Vidal himself barely mentioned *A Search for the King* in *Palimpsest*, noting simply that he finished writing it at Shepheard's Hotel in Cairo.[84] Many thought *A Search for the King* well written, such as Winnifred Rugg in the *Christian Science Monitor*, who praised Vidal's "exquisite prose." The New York Public Library's Robert Kingery, by then an experienced Vidal reviewer, thought it was "an historical novel of substantial grace and penetrating imagination." And for that genre, Edward Wegenknecht in the *Chicago Tribune* declared Vidal "just the man to redeem the historical novel from the lushness and bad taste into which it is always in danger of falling." Probably the silliest reviewer's comment was George Miles's remark in the *Commonweal* that the "book is a trivial and pretentious thing which gives little evidence that the author has the ability with words or images or rhythms." Inexplicably beginning the review with an epigraph of Christopher Isherwood's praise of *The City and the Pillar*, Miles and the Catholic *Commonweal* seemed to betray a lingering resentment over that novel, not this one. And Robert Langbaum in the *Nation* also appeared to still be looking back at Sodom, oddly maintaining that the fantastic monsters described in *A Search for the King* "symbolize by their grotesqueness the abnormal types of the earlier novels." Unsurprisingly, John Aldridge also could not shake the memory of *The City and the Pillar* as he addressed *A Search for the King*: The latter work was "a simple exercise in light historical fantasy," said Aldridge, that "does not solve the problem which all the other [Vidal] novels were unsuccessful attempts to solve; it is simply a momentary avoidance of the problem."[85]

Aldridge's typically pompous pronouncement notwithstanding, *A Search for the King* did indeed address, surreptitiously, a recurring concern, if not actually a "problem," prominent in every one of Vidal's earlier novels: the boundaries and meanings of male attachment. Vidal managed to traverse terrain that had become hazardous in the immediate postwar period, and to do so with some fresh subtlety, without overtly addressing the great distraction of homosexuality, the form of male intimacy that was making so many midcentury Americans so uneasy. Vidal appeared to know exactly what he was doing: In a preface to *A Search for the King*, he said that one reason the new novel pleased him was because "stories about friendships are not common: dark loving has always been the more popular theme." By seeming to avoid "dark loving," Vidal was thus able to avoid the fuss that his last three novels had caused. In another mood, in another year, Vidal might have less cautiously written of King Richard, perhaps examining the sexual relationship some scholars think actually existed between Richard and Philip II of France. Speculation regarding Richard's sex life was perhaps not irrelevant in Vidal's choice of someone to write about, though he claimed simply to have been fond of the Blondel legend since reading of it as a child in the attic of his grandfather's Washington, DC, home.[86]

The bond between the king and "Richard's Blondel" clearly was one of profound affection; Blondel would stop at nothing, would be intimidated by no man or beast as he looked for the imprisoned monarch. And along the way he found a dear companion for himself, Karl, another troubadour. Samuel Putnam, who had himself translated *Don Quixote*, praised Vidal in the *Saturday Review of Literature* for crafting this "little epic of friendship," no less than an allegory about how friendship could be the remedy for modern loneliness. John J. Maloney in the *New York Herald Tribune* wanted even more, thought Vidal too restrained, needing to have better "kindled" the "warmth of this friendship." As long as there was apparently no addition of sex into the association, most reviewers eagerly embraced the male involvements Vidal had presented.[87]

And yet *A Search for the King* may be read as a male romance, with even some elements of a war novel. When Blondel finds Richard and they are reunited at the Austrian castle where the king had been kept, "Blondel heard a pulse beating in his ears. The blue eyes were the same and the world was the same again." In celebration, Blondel "sang a song of an imprisoned heart, and he looked directly at Richard as he sang." Vidal may have had someone else on his mind as he wrote of returning the world to an earlier state of bliss: Like King Richard, Jimmie Trimble had had blue eyes.[88] But Richard would not become a lost friend.

There would be a buddy lost in this tale, though. In the guise of fantasy, Vidal had established an intense and clearly erotic attachment between Blondel and Karl, an attachment in one appealing scene that even recalled Jim and Bob's weekend in the woods in *The City and the Pillar*, and the actual Vidal-Trimble tryst on which that scene was said to be based. In the scene in *A Search for the King*, Karl has gone swimming while Blondel sleeps, then returns to lay beside Blondel "on the rock drying off in the sun." Blondel awakens to see a unicorn, which Karl, still naked from his swim, is riding. Karl stays astride that unicorn, Blondel recalls, "all over the woods and it was all different . . . I . . . well, I don't know how to explain but everything was different." After this shared experience, and then with the freed King Richard back in England, Blondel's beloved Karl is killed in a battle between Richard's army and the forces of John, his brother and rival for the throne. Finding Karl's dead body after the battle, perhaps a surrogate for Iwo Jima, where Jimmie Trimble had died,

Blondel put his head in his lap. A cold rain fell, an early spring rain, but he was not aware of it. He remained a long time. It had ended; his own youth lay dead in the rain and he'd be old now, unprotected, centered in himself and never young again.

Richard arrives on the scene, first telling Blondel that "I'll see he's buried here," then that "We have to go now" to "Nottingham and the victory feast." The war has ended.[89] Interestingly, in Vidal's actual novel of World War II, *Williwaw*, there had been no such intense, loving attachments as that between Blondel and Karl, and between Blondel and Richard; and had there been, reviewers might not have been nearly as bothered as they were by the domestic, peacetime love between men in the novels that came between *Williwaw* and *A Search for the King*. Critical responses to John Horne Burns's work, after all, showed that the fictional setting of male attachment could make a large difference. Shifting both locale and century, writing metaphorically about riding naked on a unicorn, Vidal may in *A Search for the King* have pulled off a bit of literary legerdemain akin to the thinly veiled homoeroticism that, a few years later, he famously slipped into the scene between Charleston Heston's and Stephen Boyd's characters in the screenplay for *Ben Hur*.[90] Such evasions, such covering, had become necessary.

Direct allusions to male intimacy of a sexual sort did not disappear altogether from two of the three of Vidal's next novels, the remaining ones of the six for which he claimed, with considerable exaggeration, to have experienced uniform neglect or derision. But sexually charged love between males, indeed male intimacy of any sort, was no more than a small topic in these remaining works, and the uneven critical response these novels received did not hinge on anyone's being repulsed (or pleased) by queerness.[91] The culture's postwar constrictions had silenced Vidal.

After publishing his first collection of short stories, *A Thirsty Evil*, in 1956, Vidal finally spent a considerable length of time writing a novel, *Julian*; published in 1964, it was a great critical and popular success, the first of his majestic historical novels.[92] The next year, perhaps emboldened by the success of *Julian*, a more mature Vidal decided, curiously enough, to publish a line-by-line revision of *The City and the Pillar*, a rare move by a novelist. Gone was the cumbersome sociology, with that important information now readily available elsewhere; and no longer did Vidal kill Bob at Jim's hands at the novel's end. The new ending, Jim's rape of Bob, was nearly as problematic as Bob's death had been; utterly conventional, it was no less of an attempt by Vidal than the original ending had been to discredit "the romantic fallacy," especially for males, the primary purpose he often claimed to have had in mind for both versions of the novel.[93] But his alleged disbelief in the romantic ideal may have been at heart a matter of sour grapes, ultimately a gay man's surrender to the disdain his country's dominant culture had for male intimacy.

If the ponderous polemics of the original version of *The City and the Pillar* were excised, so too was much of the original anger: In the original, Jim Willard had returned home "to come out and tell them [his mother, sister, and his mother's boarders] what he was and defy them; to fight them if they dare be horrified." In the revision, this passage simply became, "How he longed to tell them exactly what he was." Paul Sullivan's eloquent declaration in the original that "we must declare ourselves, become known" was watered down into "why should any of us hide?"[94] Admittedly better written, with dialogue that usually sounded more natural, the revision was yet considerably less powerful than the original, an odd attempt at cosmetic surgery that, like many a face lift, would have been better left undone, letting the age show rather than be unconvincingly covered up.[95]

This begs the question of why Vidal ever attempted to revivify *The City and the Pillar*, a work that belonged peculiarly to the immediate postwar period. Perhaps it was Vidal's attempt, not a successful one, to resolve a tension in the novel, and a lifelong tension in the novel's author (and in his country's culture), between romantic idealism, Whitman's cohesiveness, and a pursuit of selfish satisfaction, Emerson's self-reliance taken to its frequent American extreme. An unprecedented number of American men, Burns and Vidal among them, had experienced war's unique cohesiveness or camaraderie, only to return to a domestic life in which such a sense of belonging was hard to find, with their missing the camaraderie compounded by missing and mourning actual comrades, buddies who died in the war. A common psychological response to such a sense of loss and longing, Gore Vidal's apparent response, was a self-protective rejection of deep caring itself, as a hedge against more painful losses in one's future. Adding to Vidal's emotional dilemma was a professional one: his witnessing the spectacle of critics' turning on John Horne Burns. In the margin of the typescript of his 1965 essay on Burns, alongside descriptions of Burns's increasingly heavy drinking at the Excelsior bar as he approached his death, reads a longhand passage in Vidal's own hand: "He literally disintegrated, night after night."[96] It would understandably be a fate he wanted to avoid for himself. When Vidal wrote his essay remembering Burns, he was just publishing the revised version of *The City and the Pillar*, with its reminder of the penalty for too much caring.

Vidal's frequent—perhaps suspiciously frequent—denials of caring, such as his insistence in this chapter's epigraph that "love is not my bag," could be convincing, to others and sometimes maybe even to himself. Complementing his claim of rejecting romance were the frequent assertions that he was invulnerable to the guilt that his country's prejudice could instill in its male lovers of other men. No less a sexual expert than Alfred Kinsey "was intrigued by my lack of sexual guilt," Vidal claimed, insisting, as he did to me in our 2009 conversation, that his being so guiltless "was probably a matter of class." He was above all that. He was oddly pleased, actually glamorizing his own isolation, because supposedly "Dr. Kinsey told me I was not 'homosexual'—doubtless because I never sucked cock or got fucked. Even so I was setting world records for encounters with anonymous youths, nicely matching Jack Kennedy's girl-a-day routine. I would not have had it otherwise, since, even then, I did not believe in fixed sexual categories."[97] Vidal's frequent argument against sexual categories—an argument challenged by remarks he made in my meeting with him—may have been no more than a reflection of Vidal's having internalized the nation's midcentury bigotry against homosexuality.

And he did not convince everybody. In a 1992 conversation with AIDS activist, playwright, novelist, and something of a scold himself, Larry Kramer, the transcript of which is aptly titled, "The Sadness of Gore Vidal," Kramer astutely observes, "But I bet there is a big romantic streak in you. Perhaps that's why you're so angry. It takes a romantic to be so angry." Revealingly, in that conversation with Kramer, Vidal had gone out of his way to ridicule, as "one of the funniest books I've ever read," historian Martin Duberman's *Cures*, a memoir in which Duberman recounts his fervent but ultimately unsuccessful efforts to be "cured" of his homosexuality as a young man in the 1950s.[98] "I've never understood psychotherapy," claimed Vidal, "I mean there's no one's advice I want on anything to do with my life. And he [Duberman] took it so seriously—that white picket-fence dream he has." Just moments before that—and maybe by no coincidence—Vidal had referred to the rampant antihomosexual prejudice that had "practically destroyed" him in the 1950s, the time when that same bigotry had sent Duberman to psychiatrists. "My friend John Horne Burns," Gore Vidal then recalled "*was* destroyed."[99] He who seemed so to relish proclaiming the downfall of the American empire was yet the elaborate chronicler of much of his nation's history. Those historical novels are not an iconoclast's work.[100]

Any characterization of Vidal as a disbeliever in romance must, of course, contend with his allegedly lifelong devotion to the memory of his Platonic twin, Jimmie Trimble, his prep school friend and sex partner whom Vidal last saw when both were just seventeen. Admittedly Vidal only began to write extensively about this devotion to Trimble rather late in his life, in his two memoirs. And many, some who knew Vidal well—not surprisingly, Vidal's companion Howard Auster among them—have dismissed Jimmie Trimble as a harmless fantasy, an annoying affectation of a man prone to affectation, merely a safely dead abstraction, a symbol of the unattainable, of lost youth. Yet fantasies are rarely meaningless, and it must be recalled that Vidal's dedication of *The City and the Pillar* to Trimble, unrevised in 1964, originated in 1948. There are few combat deaths from the entire war that have haunted American writing more than Trimble's; yet remembering all the deaths of all the buddies, for how many men of Vidal's generation, one wonders, was there a Jimmie Trimble, a symbol of Whitmanesque cohesiveness lost and longed for, the memory serving as a self-protective barrier to future association and potential loss? Vidal would claim that "by the time I was twenty-five, I had given up all pursuit [of

FIGURE 4.1   The author's desk: John Horne Burns and Jimmie Trimble loom over this work. (Photograph by the author.)

a perfect 'other half'], settling for a thousand brief anonymous adhesions, as Walt Whitman would put it, where wholeness *seems*, for an instant, to be achieved." Vidal maintained that he and Jimmie were reunited just once, in a thoroughly romantic hallucination brought on by some potent Kathmandu marijuana: "Jimmie materialized beside me on the bed. He wore blue pajamas. He was asleep. . . . The simulacrum opened its blue eyes and smiled and yawned and put his hand alongside my neck." Perhaps in hopes that it might prompt another visit, at the top of the stairs in Vidal's Hollywood Hills home, as the last thing he would see before retiring to his bedroom, Vidal kept a large picture of Jimmie.[101]

In his Italian villa, "on the wall beside my bed," had earlier hung this same image, a life-size reproduction of the prize-winning portrait of Jimmie by Clayton Alexander, the sittings for which, Vidal recalled, would get Jimmie excused from their classes at Saint Alban's, when their friendship was blooming.[102] I purchased that huge print of the Trimble portrait at a 2016 auction of Vidal's estate, and it hangs nearby in my study as I write these words (figure 4.1). I purchased as well the desk chair from Vidal's study: The desk itself, interestingly, was a partners' desk, its double-wide top practical, of course, in giving an author ample room for papers, books, and other objects, but the use by a single man of a piece of furniture meant for use by two did also symbolize the empty space in Vidal's life that Jimmie Trimble's death had brought about.[103]

Another bedroom in the Hollywood Hills house had belonged to Howard Auster, Gore Vidal's longtime companion, the man with whom Vidal realized something of the "white picket-fence dream" he so derided in the interview with Larry Kramer. In his magnificent presentation of photographs from their long life together, Vidal indeed referred poignantly to "the fifty-four years that Howard Russell Auster and I shared a life."[104] Much more affecting still is how Vidal remembered Auster, who had just recently died of cancer, in a long chapter of his final memoir, *Point by Point Navigation*. The chapter begins with the guarded tone of pompous self-importance that was all too characteristic of Vidal. The upcoming account of Howard's passing will be, Vidal wrote, his "surrender to Montaigne's request" for the details of someone's dying. He quickly adopted a more endearing tone, though, noting that Auster "remains permanently present in my memory." In an Italian hospital, awaiting surgery for his brain cancer, Auster had asked Vidal to kiss him. Vidal, who had always found it necessary to insist, almost to anyone who would listen, that he and Auster had a relationship devoid of sex since nearly the very beginning of its half-century duration, recalled this of the request for a kiss: "I did. On the lips, something we'd not done for fifty years." Some of the cancer removed, back in their Hollywood Hills home, Howard

> still sang; he had a repertoire of several hundred songs and despite all the recent surgeries and hallucinations he never forgot a lyric. Cole Porter, Sondheim, and his favorite, "Our Love is Here to Stay," echoed through the house at the end.

"Near the end," Vidal remembered, Auster had remarked about how fast their time together seemed to have gone by. "Of course it had," Vidal wrote. "We had been too happy and the gods cannot bear the happiness of mortals." That part of Vidal's personality that fancied himself something of a god had had a problem with human happiness as well; yet the other part of Vidal's personality—the gentle, genuinely endearing part—emerged when he wrote of speaking to Howard after his heart had ceased but, Vidal believed, Howard's "optic nerves were still sending" signals to his brain. After Vidal said to Howard, "Can you hear me? I know you can see me," Auster "had the sort of wry wiseguy from the Bronx expression on his face which said clearly to me who knew all his expressions, 'So this is the big fucking deal everyone goes on about.'"[105] Auster and he "who knew all his expressions" now are buried side by side, but not far from Trimble's grave.

Vidal always presented himself as sui generis. Though he claimed to recall being born, traveling down his despised mother's birth canal, he often spoke and wrote as if instead he had come down from Olympus. He was undoubtedly in many ways one of the more singular Americans of his era or any other. But it has been my guiding assumption in this chapter that for all his idiosyncrasy, Gore Vidal was instructively representative of American males of his generation. As with many of them, the price he paid for midcentury manliness was exorbitant. Despite Vidal's efforts to distinguish himself from John Horne Burns, ironically enough the ends of both men's lives, though nearly sixty years apart, were hauntingly similar: hastened by excessive drinking and unhappiness. Obsessing over missed opportunities is perhaps the saddest burden of old age, a burden to which Vidal surely doomed himself by deciding never to risk love again after Jimmie Trimble's death. Though he claimed that an unemotional pragmatism inspired his decision, its actual inspiration may simply have been his surrender to midcentury America's disdain for male affection.

5 Mourning the Loss
The "Great Sullenness" and the Contours of American Manhood

His walk through fire and blood is what bound Dad to his
comrades for life, and forever isolated him from the rest of us.
Julia Collins, daughter of a World War II veteran

World War II is an example of the way American war
spills beyond tidy time boundaries.
Mary Dudziak, *War Time*

Men's isolation from each other was not brand new, just worse than ever, in the aftermath of World War II. American males had been encouraged to go it alone ever since the modernization process in the eighteenth century began to shrink the appeal and extent of what Anthony Rotundo has aptly termed the "communal manhood" of the colonial era, a time when dependence on others was imperative, a fact of life and not something of which to be ashamed.[1] The notion of "self-reliance" that gave Emerson a title for his famous 1841 essay is a modern cultural contrivance, and a peculiarly American one at that. Beginning around a half century later, as the nineteenth century turned into the twentieth, another cultural contrivance—the notion of fixed, oriented sexuality—and its attendant anxiety over the possible implications of male closeness, only gave a fresh rationale to American men's isolation from each other. By this logic, coziness between males was only for losers and queers. To make matters even worse, following war's usual reprieve from individualism's constraints, the loss of so many buddies during World War II likely made some returning veterans even more isolated, hesitant to risk yet additional loss, hence avoiding intimate attachments to other males with a renewed resolve. For American males, the middle years of the twentieth century, then, must surely rank as a period of particular loneliness, intensified by postwar feelings of loss and longing.

Perhaps as old as war itself, the camaraderie of soldiers was nothing new in the Second World War; but the sheer number of American comrades, their high proportion of the male population of their society, and perhaps their need for fellowship, as modern American males, was distinctive. No significant examination of World War II should ignore the importance of buddies, and few have. Even social scientists, sometimes adept at robbing human experience of its nuance and poetry, were quick to recognize, even when their language was stilted, how important buddies were in the Second World War. Right after the war ended, Howard Bortz and Everett Wilson, for instance, wrote in the *American Journal of Sociology*'s special 1946 issue on the war, that the "complete severance of accustomed social relations finds compensation in part in the acquiring of 'buddies.'" "It is rare to see," they continued, "a soldier or sailor alone, whereas most psychoneurotic servicemen have few or no friends."[2] In a 1944 collection of his World War II essays, *Still Time to Die*, war correspondent Jack Belden wrote succinctly what countless war participants and analysts have maintained: "War binds men more tightly together than almost any other branch of human activity."[3] There was something about the experience of servicemen in World War II that made remarks like Belden's seemingly more common than ever.

And when the war ended and the men began coming home, an army of social scientists, more numerous than ever and organized and influential as never before, in the wake of both the war and the Great Depression, took up the issue of how best to help the returnees adjust. One important diagnosis, if not also a prescription, regarding what might most ail a veteran was 1944's *The Veteran Comes Back* by renowned Columbia sociologist Willard Waller. Recognizing that American culture's powerful emphasis on individualism could make servicemen particularly appreciative of the sense of community and common purpose the military had provided, Waller saw as well that their return to a civilian life with such different priorities could make veterans feel like "immigrants in their native land," making the returnee "estranged from his loved ones." So important was wartime's sense of belonging, thought Waller, that "the comradeship in war remains the high point of their lives," to the extraordinary extent that "the soldier-returned-to-civilian life will never be quite the same." Waller entitled one section of his book "Chances of Success of Post-War Marriages"; and he believed that the chances were definitely not encouraging, with a veteran's marriage "immediately after his return" best described as "hazardous."[4] Echoing Waller's points about the particular appeal that wartime camaraderie could have in a capitalistic society was yet another postwar critique of American culture's virtually unqualified stress on individualism during peacetime, political theorist Sebastian de Grazia's 1948 work, *The Political Community: A Study of Anomie*. In de Grazia's apt wording, war was "the Great Association."[5]

Had there ever been such attention to the importance of friendship in American writing of various sorts? And it was attention typically voiced in the past tense, with a sense of profound loss, loss not only because of wartime deaths but loss due to an inhospitable peacetime culture.[6] Leon Uris's *Battle Cry*, a novel about World War II that was published in 1953, only a few years after the first batch of war fiction had appeared, was nonetheless already far enough removed from its war that it could seem like a visit to an alien planet, a place where there were

> guys that loved each other in a way that no woman could understand. Guys who had been through hell together, and could give a tenderness to each other that even a woman couldn't duplicate. Many a night I lay half shivering on my cot with my head on the lap of L.Q. or Danny or Seabags while they tried to force some fruit juice into me.[7]

With passages like that in mind, Allan Bérubé, the foremost authority on those whom he defined (and most of whom probably would have considered themselves) as "gay men and women in World War Two," observed that "veterans of all kinds describe the love they felt for each other with a passion, romance, and sentimentality that often rivaled gay men's expressions of their love for other men and made gay affections seem less out of place."[8] Whatever ambiguities, complications, uncertainties, fluidity, and hazy definitions the war had introduced into people's sense of their own and others' sexuality, however, homosexuals were back to seeming "out of place," often literally with a vengeance, during the 1950s. As John Horne Burns discovered, something happened, and happened quickly, between the end of the war and the early years of the following decade, something that this chapter will explore from various angles.

If one of the stages of grief is denial, it is understandable that many Americans at times grew weary of dwelling on all of the losses attributable to the Second World War. Nonetheless, there were plenty of these losses, and, as I have already suggested, the missing buddy, and missing a buddy, is a primary motif in the story of midcentury American masculinity. The enormously popular wartime cartoonist and essayist Bill Mauldin wrote that "when you go through the line companies in those outfits [such as the Forty-Fifth Division, in which he served] you find, as I did in my old company, only four or five men who have been through the whole war. The rest have died or been crippled."[9] If, as so many suggested, love of each other was prominent in servicemen's lives during the war, mourning for loved ones who died must therefore have been prominent in the war's aftermath—whether or not the mourning was recognized as such at the time or later on. The marine corps, which took such pride in its toughness, "generally warned their troops against forging too many friendships," not to demonstrate that a marine could go it alone, but rather because the marine corps recognized that "combat would rip huge, heartbreaking holes in these networks." The US Marine Corps did recommend that "each man identify one other" marine, to give him a "close ally, eyes and ears, his alter ego in combat"—and someone to comfort his parents if, as the odds suggested might well occur, the worst were to happen.[10]

In absolute numbers of the dead from battle or disease—and hence as a substantially greater proportion of the male population of military age—the Civil War was the costliest conflict in American history, with deaths variously estimated from a half million to well over six hundred thousand. The number of dead in World War II was similarly huge, over four hundred thousand.[11] Although over sixteen million men served during the entire war, only about 10 percent of that number saw "extended combat," making the number of dead, in proportion to those serving in combat, especially dramatic.[12] These figures underscore the point made by philosopher Jesse Glenn Gray, in his classic 1959 work *The Warriors: Reflections on Men in Battle*, informed by his own experience in army intelligence in World War II, that in

> every slain man on the battlefield, one can recognize a possible friend of someone. . . . Therefore in love as friendship we have the most dependable enemy of war. The possible peaks of intensity and earlier maturity which war may bring to friendship are as nothing compared with the threats of loss it holds. . . . Friendship cut off in its flower by war's arbitrariness is likely to seem the height of unreason and madness. . . . Hence no ultimate consolation is possible for the loss of a friend.[13]

Closer to our own time, philosopher Jacques Derrida went so far as to maintain that death is inherent in all friendship, since, barring a simultaneous demise, one friend will outlive the other. "To have a friend," wrote Derrida in his funeral oration for his own friend Jean-Marie Benoist, who had died of cancer at only forty-eight, "to look at him, to follow him with your eyes, to admire him in friendship, is to know in a more intense way, already injured, always insistent, and more and more unforgettable, that one of the two of you will inevitably see the other die."[14] Less grandly, legendary featherweight boxer Willie Pep, who had served in both the army and the navy in World War II, once observed, "There are three things that go on a fighter: first your reflexes go, then your chin goes, and then your friends go."[15]

Drew Gilpin Faust has compellingly maintained that the staggering magnitude of dying during the Civil War was so extraordinary that it altered the meaning of death itself in American culture.[16] If the amount of death in World War II was not sufficient to do that, it may nevertheless have been traumatic enough to have affected what it meant to be a man for millions of veterans. Further, from the Civil War era to the years of the Second World War, American society had experienced nearly a century more of modernization—with its longer life spans, diminished belief in an afterlife, greater material stake in the trappings of earthy existence, and greatly increased discomfort with even recognizing the existence of death. The deaths of hundreds of thousands of young men in World War II, consequently, were probably more shocking, more incongruous, and therefore more difficult to accept, than had been the deaths of soldiers in the Civil War.

At the end of World War II, Private First Class Edward Thomas (Tom) Moore wrote Mrs. Esther Redmann about the death of her son Morris, his dear friend, at nineteen, in combat in "Monkey Wrench Woods" in Luxembourg, during the Battle of the Bulge. A college graduate at just eighteen, Morris had left law school to join the army the year before he died. Tom Moore wrote, he said, "to tell you about my friendship with Morris." In France, "we occasionally had time off, and it was almost like living. Morris and I spent all of our off time together." Morris was killed, said Tom, by German shrapnel, close to Moore, who was the first to reach his buddy's body: "We called a medic, but I knew it was useless. Smith, Gallagher, Hambly, De-Mase and I were like lost babies after that. These boys were other friends of Morris's." Almost a year later, Vincent A. DeMase, one of those "other friends of Morris's" wrote Esther Redmann and her husband, Morris Sr., about the loss of their son. "Morris's passing was a great blow to me," said DeMase, "a shock from which I don't think I'll ever recover. I've tried to forget it, but never knew that forgetting could be so difficult—but—that's my problem. Anyway, it'll take time."[17] For many of the war's deaths, there must have been letters like these, with reverberations that might be felt in ways subtle and obvious for a survivor's lifetime.

In a time less given than ours to the expression of feelings, especially male feelings, the impact of a buddy's death might often be subtle, or hidden, or actually unfelt. Even the emotionally articulate might have difficulty permitting the feelings of grief to surface. Bringing buried feelings home sent some veterans to various sorts of therapy, for variously named disorders, but many sufferers tried to tough it out—and therefore took it out on spouses and children. Those wise enough to seek help often had great difficulty in dealing with the deaths of comrades. And even some professionals, who should have known better, were not always adequately attuned to the significance of losing a buddy. Although the eminent psychoanalyst Therese Benedek, of Chicago's Institute for Psychoanalysis, in her book about life during and after wartime service, devoted an entire chapter to "mourning for the soldier," she dealt only with mourning by wives and parents, so apparently reticent was she to recognize, let alone examine, the depth and extent of comradeship and the trauma of its loss.[18] Benedek's omission was glaring, but understandable in light of her stern belief that a soldier's "spending his psychosexual energy among men stimulates his homosexual tendencies. These may be expressed only in dreams, or they may cause severe anxieties and neurotic reactions." Out of her disdain for homosexuality came Benedek's regret that "living only with men in such close quarters is a threat to the not yet well entrenched heterosexuality of the late-adolescent."[19]

By contrast, in their own important *Men under Stress*, published at the war's end and dedicated to the "Combat Crews of the Army Air Forces," Chicago psychiatrist Roy R. Grinker and psychiatrist John P. Spiegel of the Harvard Medical School told of one returning veteran who "dismisses his personal exploits from the conversation [with friends] and is reticent about talking of himself, not because of any inherent modesty, but because 'Joe,' who died on the very same mission, haunts his memory with reminders that he has not done as much." Another "patient kept thinking of his dead friend; his face constantly appeared before him." Of the sixty-five case studies in *Men under Stress*, all army pilots, several involved reactions, typically depression, to a comrade's death. "The stress of war," the authors wrote, "tries men as no other test they have encountered in civilized life." Identification with deceased buddies was "the source of their greatest strength, supporting them in their resolution to face the stress of combat, and of their greatest suffering, if that resolution should fail." Frequent therapy then was the administration of sodium thiopental, so-called truth serum, which on occasion could valuably unleash memories and feelings. Grinker and Spiegel told of one patient whose "severe depression resulting from repeated loss of comrades in combat" was deep and persistent, with the "only clue" being "that the two boys [the patient and each of the deceased buddies] were so closely identi-fied."[20] Other early professional efforts to wipe away the psychological stains of the war were hugely more severe than sodium thiopental, and just as inclined to strive for a quick "remedy." Along with widespread use of ECT, electroconvulsive therapy or "shock treatments," psychiatric "use of lobotomy on the veteran population was at its highest point in the ten years following World War II, and only began to diminish with the advent of pharmaceuticals for the treatment of mental illness."[21] Thus were some of the mourners of the war dead permanently silenced.

Whether as a response to the death of a buddy or to one of the other strains of warfare, around 1.3 million, roughly the same number as all of those who served in combat, "suffered debilitating psychological disorders" during the war, with the war in the Pacific taking the higher toll by far.[22] Interestingly, in the special 1946 issue of the *American Journal of Sociology* devoted to the recently ended war, the longest article was S. Kirson Weinberg's "The Combat Neurosis."[23] With the large number of American men suffering psychologically, then, and because strength, toughness, and resistance to any form of adversity, especially since the late nineteenth century, had come to be seen as central attributes of the ideal American male, the very defi-nition of American masculinity was often at stake whenever the various psychologi-cal traumas endured by the men of World War II were discussed and dealt with.

Three films made during or soon after the war, either commissioned or created by the armed forces themselves, one of them occasionally noted by historians but the other two rarely mentioned, are highly revealing demonstrations of the way in which masculinity was negotiated when the psychological distress of soldiers was addressed. In 1945, after the army had had extensive experience with emotionally wounded personnel in the war, the US Army Air Services released *Combat Exhaustion*, an hour-long training film that was simultaneously compassionate and unrealistic in how it dealt with identifying and treating a multitude of symptoms, ranging from mild neuroses to severe psychoses. The film did not flinch in recognizing the remarkable extent of emotional trouble in the ranks, especially as the war had worn on, yet it delivered an upbeat message: that 70–80 percent of the "emotionally exhausted" soldiers could be back to duty within a matter of days or weeks, as long as their trouble was recognized and treated early enough. The film's faith was steadfast in the "cures" imposed—primarily narcosis, days of twilight sleep induced by drugs such as sodium amobarbital. The primary message to the troubled soldiers, played mostly by actors in the film, was simply that "you're just worn out." *Combat Exhaustion* barely alluded to the possibility that there might be men more seriously, even permanently, disturbed.[24]

John Huston's more elaborately produced *Let There Be Light*, the single film in this genre to which historians have already paid some attention, was a 1946 documentary recording the allegedly efficient and effective ten-week stay in a psychiatric hospital of several dozen psychologically disturbed soldiers. Whereas *Combat Exhaustion* addressed the return of troubled soldiers to combat, *Let There Be Light* was about returning such men to productive postwar lives. Though the film opened with somber music and the equally somber narration of the director's father, actor Walter Huston, *Let There Be Light* was actually a superficial narrative of reassurance. Total cures of serious-appearing disorders were made to seem quick in coming and without resistance, through hypnosis and, as in *Combat Exhaustion*, the miraculous effects of sodium amobarbital. At first embarrassed about their "weakness" and pessimistic about their chances to be cured, seeming haunted and frightfully alone, the men soon came to share their doctors' faith in postwar therapy and technology; not a single failed cure was shown. Though a racially mixed group, the film showed not a hint of racial tension; therapy sessions were more integrated than the wartime army itself had been. The film showed several thoroughly optimistic "before and after" shots of patients, playing baseball with gusto whereas just a few weeks earlier they had exhibited ticks, tremors, paralysis, dark moods, uncontrolled crying, and muteness. With the soundtrack playing happy music, soon a busload of released patients departed from the hospital, waving to encouraging and encouraged nurses, all of them women. The men—and their masculinity, for which strength was integral—were made to appear completely restored, virtually without scars, sound as ever.

Urging prospective employers to hire men such as these, *Let There Be Light* had been made with civilian audiences primarily in mind, to promote smooth postwar readjustment and to reassure the nation about masculine strength and resilience, for which any setbacks had been only temporary. In spite of its vagueness about the exact cause of the men's disorders, and its unrestrained, unfounded optimism about their being quickly cured, *Let There Be Light* was nonetheless determined to be too much for postwar civilians to bear, and it was not released—apparently out of the army's fear that even such a sanitized version of the topic would severely hurt future military recruitment. Interestingly, novelist and film critic James Agee was outraged at the suppression of "this fine, terrible, valuable non-fiction film about psychoneurotic soldiers."[25] Unrealistic as it actually was, however less "terrible" than was the reality of veterans' psychological turmoil, the film was not made available for viewing by the general public until 1980.[26]

A year after *Let There Be Light* was made, another army documentary was released, *Shades of Gray*, this one a "professional medical film," with reenactments, not actual cases, apparently designed mostly for those who cared for emotionally disturbed veterans. It too is a revealing cultural document, espousing a particular definition of masculinity while it addressed the issue of mental illness in the military. As its title implies, the film took the progressive stance that no one is entirely "well" or "sick" psychologically, but instead that there are countless, subtly differentiated "shades of gray" in humans' mental well-being. Emotional difficulties could befall anyone, the film maintained, "no man is without some fear or tension," and "nobody is 100 per cent perfect." As with boils, sinus trouble, and dental problems, every person has particular psychological weaknesses or conditions. Military induction, said the film, aims to discover those with obvious emotional as well as physical disqualifications, those who are already casualties; the goal was that before combat, "the weak have been eliminated." While "even the toughest man" may break in combat sufficiently severe, the film maintained, certain kinds of child rearing make a break more likely, and the film took out harshly after mothers who would make their sons overly dependent, too "sensitive," unreasonably tied to their families, and not inclined to "go out with girls." If not suitable for combat, the film maintained, men such as that were still salvageable, for "women's work" as clerks, stenographers, or secretaries. As had both *Combat Exhaustion* and *Let There Be Light*, *Shades of Gray* approached its topic with rock-solid optimism: A soldier named Bill Brown, suffering severely at the beginning of the film, seemed fine again at the end, supposedly after just three weeks of care. "It took a lot to knock me down the first time," said Bill, speaking not for himself, but for his fellow American men—perhaps especially the white ones, since not a single man of color appeared in the film. "Now how are you?" a psychiatrist asked. "Pretty good," Bill replied, described by the film's narrator as "an end product" of the military's psychological reconstruction.[27]

In spite of the fact that one of them was suppressed, these three military films had a virtually identical message: The American man and his emotions were indomitable, though a bit of care and compassion might be necessary in extreme circumstances. With such officially expressed wishful thinking, even among those in a position to know better, it was no wonder that countless veterans who returned home in pain stayed that way, their pain undiagnosed, even unnoted, for years to come, even for the rest of their lives.

Those with the gumption and the means to seek psychiatric care after the war were, of course, often treated by other men who had served in the armed forces. Indeed the connection between wartime and postwar psychiatric care is highly significant. Making wartime psychiatric service unique in its intensity and scope were the sheer scale of military mobilization, the stress of combat and of other aspects of military service, the army's inaugural attempts to discover and weed out homosexuals, ideally before induction, and the armed forces' need to salvage, even return to duty, as many men with psychic scars as possible. William C. Menninger, MD, general secretary of the Menninger Foundation, son of its founder, had been a brigadier general, the chief consultant in neuropsychiatry to the army's surgeon general during the war. Just as soon as the war had ended, General Menninger was not about to let his unprecedented experience—the rare "residency" that so many had also had—go to waste in peacetime. Already important nationally in psychiatric care before the war, the family's psychiatric services expanded hugely afterward, beginning with the establishment of the Menninger School of Psychiatry in 1946.[28] So famed became the Menninger facilities in Kansas that simply the name Menninger became synonymous with psychiatry in postwar America. William C. Menninger's 1948 book, *Psychiatry in a Troubled World: Yesterday's War and Today's Challenge*, is, even more than the three army films, an instructive document of its times—powerful, often disturbing, evidence of the impact of cultural values on psychiatric care. Like the films, Menninger preached certain notions of American manhood, espousing particular beliefs regarding men's gender and sexuality as he dealt with what he believed the war's manifold lessons had been.

Acutely aware of his profession's freshly increased significance, Menninger wrote that "my conscious purpose in writing this book was to record the evolution of psychiatric practice in the Army. Psychiatry struggled from the rear seat in the third balcony to finally arrive in the front row at the show." The primary reason for the profession's move to that better seat, of course, was simply the volume of psychological injury that a worldwide war caused; but another reason for psychiatry's enhanced significance brought about by the war was the decision to try to identify a group of potential inductees, a certain type of men newly deemed unfit to serve: homosexuals. Following his chapters titled "The Psychoses," "Other Maladjustments," "Behavior Disorders," "The Lowest Eight Per Cent [Intellectually]," and "Malingering," Menninger took up what he clearly thought was yet another "problem": "Homosexuality." After detailing the army's wartime effort to balance its manpower needs against growing prejudice against these men, to determine the proper workings of the dishonorable (blue) discharge, using a noun to describe a type of person, not an adjective to describe a type of action, and mincing no words, Menninger wrote:

> Homosexuals, in the opinion of the psychiatrist, have immature personalities which make them and their lives and some of their personal relations grossly pathological. Like any sick person, they deserve understanding instead of condemnation. At the same time it is necessary to realize that as citizens they vary in their usefulness. Some have unusual talent and may make important contributions to society. At the other end of the scale is the homosexual who is a menace, and society has a right to be protected from him. Persons afflicted with a homosexual make-up should not be condemned wholesale but instead should be considered individually.

Striving to sound therapeutic rather than punitive, yet still betraying a massive bias, Menninger conflated emotional attachment and sexual attraction, patronizingly characterizing the "predominance of homosexual interests" as a normal part of early adolescence; it was, after all, "the age of 'crushes' and of hero worship," and of membership in groups like the Boy Scouts. He even proposed a novel, to say nothing of cold and mechanical, theory of adult friendships, maintaining that when, as adults, "we enjoy emotional attachments to members of our own sex," we exhibit "residuals" of the "earlier stage," the one he called "the homosexual stage of object interest." This "homosexual stage"—just a phase, really—was definitely not, in Menninger's scheme, to be confused with full maturity.[29] The nature and goal of therapy based on these prevalent, privileged assumptions is not difficult to imagine.

Menninger trivialized certain forms of same-sex activity as merely situational, little more than accidents of the moment, the participants assumed to be innocent until proven guilty of a more lasting disposition. Whether "autoerotic, homosexual, or heterosexual," Menninger wrote, soldiers during the war had found "outlets or sublimations for their normal sexual energies, drives, and interests." There was a line, he insisted, between perfectly normal "homosexual buffoonery" and the sort of "homosexuality which represents an arrest in psychosexual development." Though Menninger assumed its existence, that line was difficult to locate, even to define, for Menninger. In an important footnote, he cited Kinsey's recently released "amazing findings" about widespread homosexual activity among American men. Kinsey's "remarkable and revolutionary document," Menninger thought, instead of suggesting that shopworn prejudices against same-sex activity ought to be revised, showed instead that there was massive arrested development abroad in the land. Heterosexual sex was at the heart of Menninger's world; anything else was but a poor substitute, including the war's much celebrated camaraderie, whose disappearance, he seemed to assume confidently, would quickly occur in peacetime.[30] At best, then, for a leading American psychiatrist, wartime attachments between men were of no lasting consequence. Clearly many American men who had had such attachments felt otherwise. Few wartime experiences of any sort could be shaken off with ease.

Perhaps the war's most gifted memoirist, marine veteran E. B. "Sledgehammer" Sledge, wrote that for "the first twenty-odd years of my return, nightmares occurred frequently, waking me either crying or yelling, always sweating, and with a pounding heart. . . . Old comrades wrote me that similar troubles drove many of them to drink and to the ensuing misery of alcoholism, which they beat with sheer self-discipline." For Sledge, the "embedded trauma" he brought home from the war was "the emotional equivalent of a sliver of steel shrapnel lodged near my heart."[31] Countless articles appeared, in postwar scholarly journals and the popular press alike, on similar adjustments returning servicemen had to make to civilian life. John F. Cuber, an Ohio State University sociologist, observed that "the 'road back' is seldom questioned by the analyst of human behavior, but also seldom appreciated by the person who travels it." Interestingly, Cuber's research revealed that returned veterans "report that they lack both the motivation and the habit necessary to accomplish the day-to-day duties of the husband and father."[32] Despite Menninger's privileging heterosexual relationships and marriage, J. H. S. Bossard, past president of the Pennsylvania Federation for Planned Parenthood, thought that the "war marriage"—a form of situational heterosexuality, after all, a reminder that all sexual experience is really situational—was both common and inherently problematic.[33] Similarly, Edward C. McDonough wrote in the *American Journal of Sociology* that it "is probable that many of the marriages contracted under the exigencies of wartime are dominated more by sexual desires than by enduring affection."[34] As the war neared an end, *Parents* magazine had announced in its January 1945 issue that it was publishing "A Supplement for Fathers in Uniform," smaller in size and printed on lighter-weight paper than its regular issue, to be "easily inserted in a letter," with articles such as "You Will Be Different" and "Strategic Problems on the Home Front."[35] Obviously the end of wartime sexual involvements, romances, and simple friendships with fellow servicemen—some now dead, some trying elsewhere to stage their own return to conventional life—was but one of many reasons that returnees had problems with postwar adjusting; what is striking is that it was a reason whose very existence went virtually unrecognized by those seeking to ease the return of veterans to civilian life.

One guide to postwar adjustment did address wartime closeness, even intimacy that had involved sex, but managed to both scorn and trivialize such closeness by treating it as simply an unfortunate expedient. In their guide to postwar reconstruction of the veteran, Irvin Child and Marjorie Van De Water's 1945 anthology, *Psychology for the Returning Veteran*, there was a chapter just for former prisoners of war, taking up the "unnatural sex experience"—that is, sex among themselves—that POWs had experienced. Offering little more counsel than a confident "that was then, this is now," Child and Van De Water merely declared that such previous practices would not be appealing "when normal sexual outlets are once more possible." That some veterans might still prefer their wartime ways was simply not contemplated. Masturbation or "attachments with other men," said Child and Van Der Water, were merely "a temporary makeshift satisfaction."[36] Most published advice, then, assumed either the resumption or fairly quick adoption of married life. Such was midcentury culture that, to most experts, all adult life outside of marriage was considered abnormal. In addition to the advice literature already mentioned, a book with as generic a title as 1946's *Sex Problems of the Returned Veteran* by Howard Kitching was entirely devoted to heterosexual sex between married persons.[37]

An instructive example of how powerfully repressive midcentury culture could be, how overwhelming was the force of heteronormativity, is the experience of Allard Lowenstein, the liberal activist instrumental in President Lyndon Johnson's decision not to seek reelection in 1968. Born in 1929, Lowenstein was just barely too young to have served in World War II, missing wartime's singular opportunity to act upon sexual yearnings for other males. When American males only slightly older than him were in the war, Lowenstein wrote wistfully in his diary, at fourteen in 1943, that "the urge I get when I see certain boys is getting out of control. Good God, what will I do? . . . This can't go on. I can see only one solution, very good friendships."[38] Lowenstein tried to keep up appearances, dated women, even married early in middle age and became a father, yet he always recognized the nature of his most fervent desires.

Stifling those desires while not denying them as he entered young adulthood in the 1950s, Lowenstein would have intense, apparently sexless relationships with other males, continuing to have what his biographer has called "the problem with intimacy." Blocking any erotic fulfillment, not an unusual act for persons of various inclinations in the 1950s, Lowenstein made his professional political associations into intensely personal attachments. Becoming more pathetic as time went on, as he traveled extensively in his organizational efforts in the civil rights and antiwar movements, Lowenstein reportedly would try to maneuver younger, handsome Waspy males into cuddling in bed or at least into a wrestling match. The culture that so severely scorned his desires had reduced this gifted man to that.[39]

It was a challenging era when it came to what seemed to matter. Lowenstein's sympathetic biographer, William Chafe, has maintained that for some of Lowenstein's former male protégés—including David Harris, Stanford student leader, imprisoned antiwar activist, and spouse of Joan Baez—it "took years to work through their sense of guilt and ambivalence over what Armin Rosencranz [once Stanford student body president] correctly described as 'just hugging Al in bed,' but which the individuals themselves clearly felt was illicit activity."[40] It was one of those former protégés, Dennis Sweeney, determined at his trial to be mentally ill, who fatally shot Allard Lowenstein, at fifty-one, in 1980.[41]

Considerable ambivalence, outright repression, evasion, and denial regarding sex between men was not confined to conservatives, moderates, or even liberals like Lowenstein. That it was also prevalent even within a group of self-styled cultural radicals like the Beats suggests the sorry state of men's intimacy at midcentury. The relationship of Jack Kerouac and Neal Cassady—basis for the pivotal association between narrator Sal Paradise and Dean Moriarty in Kerouac's *On the Road*—was one of the more renowned love stories of the postwar years. Neither man was as blissful in any woman's company as in each other's presence, and both often seemed as if nothing would make them more content than to spend the rest of their lives together. But the sexual dimension of their involvement, and of Kerouac's erotic connection to several other male contemporaries, among them Gore Vidal, was not openly acknowledged, then or sometimes even later on. Allen Ginsberg was the only well-known Beat to openly acknowledge his queerness; Ginsberg and Peter Orlovsky were the only male couple among the Beats who were openly acknowledged to be lovers, compelling evidence of what a cultural transgression sex between men had become at midcentury.[42]

An omen of homophobia on the horizon and of ambivalence even among the Beats on the issue of homosexuality was evident in the bizarre circumstances surrounding the 1944 murder of Dave Kammerer by Lucien Carr, an early member of the Beat circle, a student at Columbia and friend of Ginsberg, Kerouac, and William Burroughs. With delicate, androgynous features in stark contrast with the rougher faces of Ginsberg and Kerouac, Carr, born in 1925, was a young man of wide-ranging physical appeal. Though he did have a girlfriend, Celine Young, when he was in his late teens as a Columbia undergraduate, he had also for some time been pursued, allegedly sexually, by Dave Kammerer, whom he had met in Saint Louis when Kammerer was Carr's scoutmaster, twenty-five to Carr's mere eleven. Reportedly attempting suicide in Chicago when Kammerer had followed him there, Carr seemed troubled and victimized by Kammerer's attention; whether he was also oddly empowered by it is something else again. Kerouac, for one, said he thought that Kammerer's pursuit of his friend was "just a lot of fun."[43] Kerouac himself was drawn powerfully to Carr, as was Ginsberg, whose sexual desires and poetic gifts were burgeoning just as he met Carr; Carr apparently nurtured both the desires as well as the gifts. A recent biographer of Kerouac has maintained that Ginsberg's early journals suggest that he had had "a few tentative sexual encounters with both Lucien and Kammerer."[44] Carr's own yearnings seem virtually unknowable, perhaps were not wholly recognized even by Carr himself in those cloudy days.

What is knowable is that Lucien Carr eventually murdered Dave Kammerer in 1944, stabbing him to death before he weighted his body with rocks and threw it into the Hudson River. Carr's lawyers presented the popular defense that their client, himself wholly without perverse inclinations, had killed Kammerer in self-defense against the older man's perverse advances. The murder weapon was no less than Carr's own Boy Scout knife. Not only were detectives greatly interested in whether Carr had any perverted inclinations himself that might weaken his defense, they were also interested in Kerouac's leanings, since he had given Carr sanctuary after the murder and had even helped Carr dispose of his victim's eyeglasses. "Hetero-sexuality all the way," Lucien reportedly mouthed to Kerouac as they both "waited to be arraigned in a courtroom on Chambers Street on August 26[, 1944]."[45] None too subtle was Kerouac's decision to hurriedly marry his girlfriend Edie Parker when he was released from jail on bail as a material witness to the murder.[46] The maid of honor was Lucien Carr's girlfriend, Celine Young. The marriage lasted two months.

According to the first press reports, in the *New York Times*, Carr confessed even before Kammerer's body was found, "peacefully reading poetry most of the night" as he "stayed in the district attorney's office." Carr was described in the press as a "slender, studious youth . . . a quiet, well-behaved, intellectual type who had been classified 4F by Selective Service on medical grounds." Kammerer, on the other hand, was said in the press to be "a homosexual who had recently earned his living by helping the janitor at 48 Morton Street." Carr reportedly told the assistant district attorney's office that he had known Kammerer "for several years in St. Louis," seeing him on his trips home from Phillips Academy, Bowdoin, and the University of Chicago. Carr claimed that "several times" Kammerer "had made improper advances to him but that he had always rebuffed the older man." Kammerer was said to have followed Carr to New York, and thereafter "steadily deteriorated," becoming "little more than a derelict." When they sat on the bank of the Hudson, shortly before Carr killed Kammerer, as they were "enjoying a breath of the cool, morning air," Kammerer allegedly yet again "made an offensive proposal." With the "slender blonde youth" at 140 pounds no match for Kammerer at six feet and 185 pounds in the fight that followed Kammerer's lewd overture, Carr's stabbing Kammerer with the Scout knife, "a relic of his boyhood," seemed utterly reasonable. The *Times* piece even made it seem reasonable that Carr had disposed of the body, with the help of "John Kerouac, a 23-year old seaman."[47]

Carr's "gay panic" defense worked—if not as well as his friends had hoped, since in their thinking he would be acquitted or given a suspended sentence. The press had even referred to the murder as an "honor slaying," the wording that the *New York Daily News* screamed in a headline. Carr was found guilty, not of murder but of manslaughter, and was sentenced to the state reformatory in Elmira, serving there for just two years.[48] After his release, Lucien Carr changed course, beginning an association with United Press International that would span nearly a half century, until he died of bone cancer in 2005. Though maintaining his friendships with Ginsberg and Kerouac, Carr did ask that his name be removed from the dedication page of *Howl*. He married and fathered three children. Though surely few had such a sensational prelude, there must have been many such midcentury marriages of the mismatched.

Even before Carr died, literary historian James Campbell departed from the standard narrative of Carr as predator's victim, observing astutely that

> Lucien himself did not act as if he was being hounded. He spent a lot of time with Kammerer. His vanity was flattered by the attention. When he did something outrageous, Kammerer beamed and asked all around, "Isn't he wonderful?" Visitors to [William] Burroughs's Bedford Street apartment often came away having watched the two men, one [Kammerer] overweight, the other [Carr] slender but muscular, wrestling on the floor like Birkin and Crich in *Women in Love*. Kammerer would get up from these contests sweating with lust, Lucien fired with adrenalin and ready for further mischief. When they went out into the street and headed uptown to the West End bar, opposite the [Columbia] campus, Carr might burst into song, and Kammerer would join in [in a weird folksong of anonymous authorship, popular at midcentury]:

> *Violate me*
> *In violent times*
> *The vilest way that you know.*
> *Ruin me, ravage me,*
> *utterly savage me,*
> *on me no mercy bestow.*[49]

It seems no wonder that Carr was extremely fond of Rimbaud. As for Kammerer, this game had much higher stakes than he realized.

In his obituary for Carr, literary and cultural historian Eric Homburger suggested that the standard "version of the relationship" between Carr and Kammerer— "the story of a predatory homosexual"—is largely "doubtful," made up of tangled "strands of insinuation, legal spin, and lies." Homburger even suggested that Kammerer "was not gay," that "Carr enjoyed his ability to manipulate the older man," and was himself "a troubled and unstable young man" whose alleged suicide attempt in Chicago, with his head "in an unlit gas oven" was just a bit of drama. Whatever the truth of those assertions, Lucien Carr's postprison turnaround was an abrupt shift from an appreciation of transgression to a preference for conformity, a morning-after conversion, suffused with the same melancholy air of repentance found in other aspects of postwar masculinity, mirroring the shift that animated the altered critical fortunes of John Horne Burns discussed in chapter 3. In his obituary, perhaps with tongue in cheek, Homburger called the Carr who left the Elmira correctional facility "a changed man," who "alone among the Beats . . . became the sober one who held down a job, and cautioned against excess," even advising Ginsberg, "don't let yourself go mad, and keep hustlers and parasites at arm's length."[50] Carr's walk on the wild side was over, the "New Vision" he had once urged Ginsberg to cultivate was a thing of the past. Conventional masculinity's triumph was apparently complete for Lucien Carr, if oddly so, and it had cost Kammerer his life.

Testimony to irresolution (or at the very least cynicism) among the Beats on the issue of homosexuality is the possibility that, according to historian Campbell, it was William Burroughs who first advised Carr to "make a self-defense based on unwanted homosexual advance." "Where the judge was concerned," Campbell has written, "two homosexuals fighting on a riverbank in the early hours was an entirely different proposition to the one being presented by the press, of a morally upright young student fighting off the advances of a thirty-five-year-old pederast."[51] "Heterosexuality all the way!"

Even Allen Ginsberg, who later seemed at such utter peace with his sexuality, had thought in 1944 that "I should have to commit suicide" should anyone discover the direction of his desire. He later recalled that before he had had sex with anyone, Lucien Carr "took me to his room and took off all his clothes and said, 'Get in *bed*,' and I sat there like a frightened creep. I guess Jack [Kerouac] was the first person I really opened my mouth to and said, 'I'm a homosexual.'"[52] Regardless of how bold Ginsberg would become in his poetry later on, the sexual attraction between Ginsberg and Carr in the mid-1940s, interestingly examined in the 2013 film, *Kill Your Darlings*, should be seen as a boys' game, full of the uncertainties and obtuseness that might so easily accompany being nineteen, especially in 1944. The very day before he would kill Kammerer, for an attraction that may well have been mutual, Lucien Carr may have impotently tried to have sex for the first time with his purported girlfriend Celine Young—who then reportedly "climbed into bed with [Lucien's apartment mate] John Kingsland," who later told Ginsberg, himself infatuated with Carr, of what had (and had not) transpired. With the insight of retrospect, decades later Kerouac's former lover Joyce Johnson speculated that when the murder occurred the next day, "perhaps Lucien had never hated Kammerer more; perhaps he had never felt closer to yielding to him." Long before that, focusing on a symbol that in its triteness ill-suited a poet of his gifts, Ginsberg would speculate in his diary whether Kammerer had actually handed the Scout knife to Carr, with the injunction, "Choose to love me or to kill me." Later on Ginsberg reimagined the murder with more subtlety in notes for a novel he planned about the Carr-Kammerer affair, describing Carr's having "conflicting ecstasies of fear and desire, revulsion and attraction, hatred and love, wish and well, emotion and counter-emotion, open and close, straining their sight, blinking the confused turbulence of the body they mirrored."[53]

Jack Kerouac, of course, was no innocent bystander in the Carr-Kammerer tragedy himself, much as he tried to side with the angels. As did Ginsberg and Burroughs, each in his own way, for his own reasons, Kerouac identified wholly with Carr, the beautiful supposedly straight man, with Kammerer representing the dreaded perversity of queerness. Shortly after the murder, when police, trying to figure out who was what, asked Kerouac's girlfriend Edie Parker whether "your boyfriend" might "like boys," she reportedly said, "Are you nuts? Do I look like a boy to you?" She stuck up for Lucien as well: When police had said that Carr "knocked off his lover," Edie hotly replied that, "Lucien is not queer, he likes girls, and especially Celine."[54] Though Ginsberg never wrote the novel he planned about Carr and Kammerer, Kerouac late in life did write such a novel, his *Vanity of Duluoz*, a largely autobiographical story based on Kerouac's life between the mid-1930s to the mid-1940s. Kammerer's surrogate in the novel was a disgusting villain, Franz Mueller, "that no-good pederast." Carr was represented by the character Claude de Maubris, "blonde, eighteen, of fantastic male beauty like a blonde Tyrone Power with slanted green eyes and the same look, words, and build . . . actually like Oscar Wilde's model male heroes I s'pose." Beautiful as he was, Claude was "no fairy and he was strong and wiry," the novel's protagonist and representative of Kerouac, Jack Louis Duluoz, continuously insisted, sometime in descriptions that sounded like arousal:

> What's amazing about him is his absolute physical male and spiritual, too, beauty. Slant-eyed, green eyes, complete intelligence, language pouring out of him, Shakespeare reborn almost, golden hair with a halo around it, old queens when they saw him in Greenwich Village bars wrote odes to him starting, "O fair-haired Grecian lad." Naturally all the girls went for him too, and even this old dreamy hard-headed seaman and footballer, Jack, got to like him and drop tears over him.

When the district attorney investigating Mueller's murder asked Duluoz if Claude, Carr's stand-in, is "a homo," Duluoz replied, as if it would be conclusive, "No, no, not in the least, if he was he'd have tried to make me." Art imitated life from two decades past, when at their arraignment, "Claude takes advantage to say to me out of the corner of his mouth: 'Heterosexuality all the way down the line.'" In a genuinely bizarre scene, Kerouac put Duluoz at the morgue to identify Mueller's corpse: After "some fifty hours" in the river, the body was "all bloated and blue," yet "his dong's still preserved." Having Duluoz turn away from the corpse, Kerouac then has the morgue attendant inquire, "Wassamatter boy, ain't you never seen a weenie before?"[55] It was a question whose implications Kerouac never seemed to recover from dreading. Drinking himself to an early grave at only forty-seven, Kerouac died just a year after *Vanity of Dulouz*, the last work to appear in his lifetime, was published; he had begun it more than twenty years earlier. Joyce Johnson has claimed that the novel was "ahead of its time," in that its protagonists, based on Kerouac himself and his close associates, "struggle to work out what it means to be a man outside the conventional definitions of masculinity."[56] An early, and interesting, indication of Kerouac's unconventional streak was his wartime discharge from the navy, after only eight days of active duty in 1943, on the grounds that he possessed "an indifferent character," that is, that he was judged psychologically incapable of submitting to the discipline that military service required.[57] And Kerouac and his buddies were indeed distinctive in their pondering of escapes from American manhood's prescriptions for material success, and their search for sensation over security. Yet with the exception of Ginsberg later in life, the others, Kerouac in pathetic particular, were the most conventional of American men when it came to acknowledging, to say nothing of savoring, the full range of their erotic desires. On that, Jack Kerouac was not ahead of his time at all.[58]

The claimed disdain for queers in the 1940s by men like Jack Kerouac, and by public policies like the wartime declaration of homosexuality's incompatibility with American military service, became ubiquitous in the United States once the war ended, during what I have characterized as the literal "mourning after" as well as the metaphorical "morning after" the war, with the air of repentance, guilt, renewed zeal to "behave," and also the longing and loss that appropriately accompany a period with such a double meaning of regret and sorrow. The "mourning after" notion, I believe, can add to our understanding of why the postwar period saw such a dramatic increase in hostility against affection between men. "Homosexuality" was not even a subject heading in the *Reader's Guide to Periodical Literature* until 1947, and then it only instructed a reader to "see Sex Perversion." By the 1950s, "homosexuality" had its own entries—almost always references to negative, alarmist reports, appraisals, or recommendations—and the *Reader's Guide* entries grew apace through the decade.[59] In actuality, the issue at stake at midcentury was gender, not sexuality, the experience of queer men simply an especially graphic example of a shift in cultural boundaries that affected nearly all American males.

Fear was the fundamental emotion of the era. Yet again, as had happened so often in the past, Americans who needed to think of themselves as conventional believed themselves, self-servingly so, to be surrounded by "savage neighbors," Peter Silver's apt term for Middle Colonists' attitudes toward indigenous people.[60] Similarly, in examining how three different generations of Massachusetts Puritans turned on themselves in the seventeenth century, Kai Erikson smartly observed that "men who fear witches soon find themselves surrounded by them."[61] American society, with its continuously shifting demographics and consequently ever-shaky sense of national identity, has found a remarkable number of "savages" or "witches" to be alarmed over throughout its history, useful deviants whose hugely inflated threat attested to—and temporarily helped to ameliorate—the uncertain sense of identity among those doing the worrying.

In midcentury America, the savages or witches of the moment—set against those who needed to feel either virtuous, less mournful, or both—were Communists and homosexuals, a monstrous conjoined twin created wholly by the twisted logic of bigotry, all the more horrifying because of its dual nature. To expect the duality to make sense, to try to understand *why* Communists and homosexuals actually would be allies, is to expect rationality of bigotry, an inherently irrational phenomenon. Despicable as the junior senator from Wisconsin was, and as much damage as Joe McCarthy and his supporters caused all by themselves, the term "McCarthyism" is nonetheless highly misleading. The fear he exploited was broad and deep, preceding and outlasting him. Paralleling how the Truman administration's "loyalty security" policies for ferreting out Communists in the federal government anticipate Joseph McCarthy's agitations, Truman showed personal concern, barely a year into his presidency, about a link between political disloyalty and alleged sexual perversion—stereotyped by Truman as a certain kind of man. In his own hand, as an entry in a daily diary on White House stationery, Truman expressed concern on September 19, 1946, that "all the 'Artists' with a capital A, the 'parlor pinks' and the soprano voiced men are banded together under the Art Club and call themselves 'leftists.' I am afraid they are a sabotage front for Uncle Joe Stalin."[62] Accompanying the Red Scare—as opposed to simply a realistic concern about Communism—that was part of the Cold War, there also was indeed a Lavender Scare, historian David K. Johnson's term for a furious fear of homosexuals and rampant discrimination against them; the term was inspired by Illinois senator Everett Dirksen's supposedly amusing wording—"lavender lads"—for homosexuals working in the federal government, especially in sensitive positions in the State Department.[63] Fear of homosexuals didn't always accompany fear of Communism, and vice versa, in midcentury America, but in tandem they were potent and complementary.

The Communist and the queer were creatures of such frightening fantasy, such was the national ignorance about their actual existence, that it was assumed that they couldn't be like ordinary people, despite the fact that they were feared to be lurking around virtually everywhere. What a homosexual or a Communist might really look like was the stuff of stereotypes, jokes, speculation—and sometimes, with homosexuals, agonizing self-doubts. Unlike racial "others," at least those not devilish enough to "pass" for white, Communists and queers were creatures of mystery, much like the abundant space aliens of the era's popular films. It was a time of such extraordinary denial and repression regarding sexuality of all sorts—the era, after all, when even Lucy and Ricky had to be filmed in separate beds—that not only was the queerness of Rock Hudson and Tab Hunter hidden, but Liberace, of all people, was popularly characterized as a ladies' man.[64]

As has still been the case much closer to our own times, in discussions of marriage equality and gays in the military, any consideration of homosexuality in the 1950s was much more often about males than females, and seems in essence to have really been more about masculinity than sexuality. In 1955 journalist and screenwriter Ted Berkman—best known for writing 1951's *Bedtime for Bonzo*, starring Ronald Reagan—took to the pages of *Coronet*, a popular midcentury monthly magazine owned by *Esquire* that published brief, accessible articles on a variety of topics, to address the unsettling fact that, as he put it, "homosexuality is probably increasing in the United States," or was at least "being practiced more and more openly." Berkman echoed the era's dominant disparaging views of homosexuals, sounding at times like an everyman's William Menninger. They were, he said, likely the victim of some glandular disorder as well as "stunted emotional growth." The gendered nature of Berkman's concern was clear when he declared that the homosexual "has a childlike emotional equipment in the body of a grown man." Overly strong attachment to female family members, notably mothers, was pronounced to be a likely contributor to male homosexuality. Another environmental contributor, he observed, sometimes was involvement in places "where large groups of men are confined together," as in "prisons, army camps, boy's schools and on shipboard." "Experts agree," Berkman counseled, "that proper upbringing of children is the best safeguard against homosexuality." In his eight recommendations to parents, a specific sex was mentioned in four—and it was always boys. "Provide growing boys with the consistent interest and company of a man," urged Berkman, "so that they will naturally absorb masculine attitudes—especially regarding parenthood and the responsibility of forming a home." While "warmth and love" from mothers was encouraged, lest a boy not turn to women for affection later on, "fostering overdependence" was scorned, while self-reliance was encouraged.

An aura of danger surrounded Berkman's article, more than most pieces in *Coronet*. The stakes were high, the diligence demanded was constant. Parents must watch their sons, Berkman urged, for "overt signs of psychological difficulties, such as a violent aversion to little girls, . . . or an insistence on playing exclusively with them." Middle ground was best, then, but it obviously was difficult to be a boy and to be the parents of one. Berkman wrote vaguely but gravely that a parent should "give your son particularly sympathetic attention during adolescence, when his glandular system is going through enormous readjustment." This was a risky time to be a boy, he said, for "the latent female component has the most opportunity to come to the surface because the dominant male element has not yet developed full power to repress it."[65] What was not so latent here, obviously, was misogyny, the image of women and womanliness as utterly corrupting, while society's boys were nevertheless to be trained to one day desire one of these scary creatures.

This national concern over sissy sons was intense and widespread in the fifties, and punishments for unmanly sons, disguised as remedies, could be severe. Young Lou Reed's parents, conservative New Yorkers Sidney and Toby, worried that he was beginning a walk on the wild side, and sent their unconventional Lou "to a psychiatrist, requesting that he cure Lou of homosexual feelings and alarming mood swings." The doctor prescribed the era's customary treatment for such a "disorder," twenty-four electroshock treatments at two-day intervals spread over the eight weeks of Lou's confinement in Creedmoor State Psychiatric Hospital in Queens. Creedmoor was "equipped to handle some six thousand patients," with the treatments administered in "a majestically spooky edifice that stood eighteen stories high."

In a "treatment" whose precise workings and efficacy are still not fully understood, but whose cost and efficiency have had appeal, young Lou's dose of twenty-four treatments was typical of the period. The teenager's immediate sensation was the common loss of memory, and he would recall thinking "he had 'become a vegetable'" as he left Creedmoor. One Reed biographer reported that "Lou suffered through eight weeks of shock treatments haunted by the fear that in an attempt to obliterate the abnormal from his personality, his parents had destroyed him."[66] He became a lifelong insomniac. In a 1996 interview, Reed observed that

> they put the thing down your throat so you don't swallow your tongue, and they put electrodes on your head. That's what was recommended in Rockland County [New York] then to discourage homosexual feelings. The effect is that you lose your memory and become a vegetable. You can't read a book because you get to page seventeen and you have to go right back to page one again.[67]

His sexuality, along with depression over the parental concern that led to the shock treatments, would for Reed remain a mixture of confusion and self-disgust until he died in 2013 at seventy-one. When Reed developed a following with the Velvet Underground in the late 1960s, there was quickly speculation about his sexuality. His roadies were reportedly asked frequently by fans whether Reed was bisexual. "Bi?" one of them is said to have replied, "The fucker's quad!"[68]

Fifteen years after the shock treatments, Reed recalled the experience in a song recorded for his 1974 album, *Sally Can't Dance*. In his aptly titled "Kill Your Sons," his haunting anthem of unconventional masculinity's fate in the immediate postwar years, Reed would warn

Don't you know they're gonna kill your sons
don't you know gonna kill, kill your sons
They're gonna kill, kill your sons
until they run, run, run, run, run, run, run, run away[69]

So demonized had female and male homosexuality both become at midcentury that the white, middle-class feminism of Betty Friedan in the 1960s was embarrassed by queerness in women and repulsed by it in men. Gay men and even lesbians were definitely excluded from the list of those who stood to gain from feminism as people like Friedan understood it. There was little difference between the unselfconscious bigotry of Senator Dirksen's fretting about "lavender lads" in the midst of the anti-Communism frenzy of the early 1950s and Friedan's bemoaning the fact, in *The Feminine Mystique* a decade later, that male homosexuality was "spreading like a murky smog over the American scene."[70]

The midcentury mood of alarm that unsettled Betty Friedan, subjected Lou Reed to such brutal "treatment," and prompted Ted Berkman to urge such close scrutiny of the nation's boys was pervasive. Bois Burk, a gay man who lived his entire life close to San Francisco, kept a file of clippings of mainstream newspaper and magazine articles from the late 1950s, mostly pertaining just to the Bay Area, articles whose very titles and sheer number suggest the tenor of the times. They suggest as well the fearfulness that might be felt by any reader, especially a man like Burk, who might reasonably feel he was a target of such writing: "UC Official in Morals Case Resigns Post"; "UC Professor Arrested—'Lewd Vagrancy'"; "Teacher's Ouster Upheld in Sex Case"; "The Third Sex—Guilt or Sickness?" (Berkman's *Coronet* piece); "Homosexuality Reported Widespread in Britain"; "Homosexuals Can Be Cured"; "S.F. Bars Accused in Vice Drive"; "Fifth Tavern Called Hangout of Perverts"; "S.F. Teacher Fired on Old Sex Offense"; "17 Swoop Down, Find One Suspect"; "Muir Beach Raid Nets 30 Men Dancers"; "Police to Continue Roundups"; "Bar Loses Plea for License on Morals Charge"; "State Accuses Eddy Street Bar"; "Bay Teacher Arrested in Lewd Case"; "Schoolteacher Arrested on Morals Charge"; "Marin Tavern Operator Gets Jail Sentence"; "Turk Street Club Loses License"; "Bar Appeals License Loss in 'Perversion'"; "Hormone Pills May Be Used to Curb Homosexual Urges in Men"; "Berkeley Police Brand Aquatic Park Moral Cesspool"; "New Drive against 'Shady' Bars"; "S.F. 'Pervert' Charge Denied."[71]

This official orgy of repression at midcentury entailed even more than just police raids on bars and public toilets, with attendant issues of entrapment and the actual involvement of vice squad officers in same-sex activity, ironically all in the name of safeguarding morality. There were full-fledged sex panics around the country, two in 1955 alone, one in Boise, Idaho, the other throughout Iowa.[72]

"In this social climate," overstating only slightly the situation's severity, Neil Miller has written in his study of the Iowa panic, it was no wonder that a gay man or a lesbian in Sioux City and a thousand towns like it lived lives of fear and desperation. There was virtually no avenue for articulating the view that being homosexual was anything other than a mental illness or pathology. If you were a gay man in Sioux City, you married your high school sweetheart and tried to put away sexual desire for men out of your mind, or you never married and lived quietly with your mother, cultivating an interest in antiques or community theater, or you simply left town.[73]

As those Bay Area newspaper clippings collected by Bois Burk—and no less celebrated an event than the Stonewall Rebellion itself—demonstrated, however, midcentury harassment of gay men and their meeting places was in significant ways an urban phenomenon, by no means just a feature of small towns. In the papers of Donald Stewart Lucas, a midcentury member of both the Mattachine Society and the American Civil Liberties Union and a resident of San Francisco, is further evidence of urban hostility to queerness. The Mattachine Society distributed cards, about the size of a business card, with instructions about "what to do in case of arrest": Do not resist, give only your name until you have secured an attorney. Along with his membership cards for both the ACLU and the Mattachine Society, Lucas also carried cards, presumably to distribute, from San Francisco Suicide Prevention, Inc., with a phone number, and the name "Bruce," following the query, "Thinking of ending it all?"[74]

As noted in chapter 3, regarding the relatively warm reception John Horne Burns received for his *Lucifer with a Book* from a small-town Kansas paper, some recent scholarship has convincingly challenged the long-held assumption—articulated without equivocation, for instance, by Neil Miller in his study of the Iowa sex panic—that rural America was peculiarly inhospitable to expressions of same-sex desire, that the city has always offered queerness greater freedom of expression. On the contrary, in his *Men Like That: A Southern Queer History*, John Howard has convincingly shown that throughout Mississippi, one of the nation's most rural states, during the twentieth century's second half, men "interested in intimate and sexual relations with other men found numerous opportunities to act on their desires, and did so within the primary institutions of the local community—home, church, school, and workplace."[75] To challenge the notion that urban America was always a safer place for transgressive sexuality is not to suggest that queerness, and queer identities, have thrived in rural spaces; it is simply to suggest that queerness may have found a tolerable rural home to a greater extent than has been realized. Whether or exactly how regional differences might have shown themselves at midcentury, during the mourning after the war, is perforce beyond this project's scope, but the nationwide existence of a panicky postwar sense of sexual propriety under siege, a sweeping view of any departure from sexual convention as "perversion" seems clearly established.[76]

That postwar siege mentality, an integral component of the mourning after, was the mentality on which the era's epidemics of moral panic were based and which those epidemics in turn fostered. Employing a separation between "us" and "them" on which all forms of bigotry depend, the siege mentality of course characterized "perverts" as "the other," as much aliens as if they had arrived on a spaceship from Mars. "Othering" of all kinds requires some degree of denial, at a minimum a denial of our common humanity, but treating homosexuals as wholly distinct, perverted others also required a process of denial more elaborate than that, a process that required some individuals to deny their own histories and, in some cases, even their current doings. It is unclear just how many Americans were actually familiar with the findings of the Kinsey Reports, and hence might have been disposed to indulge in a fervent denial of its remarkable assertion that "perhaps the major portion of the male population has at least some homosexual experience between adolescence and old age."[77] Even American men who had never heard of Alfred Kinsey, however, especially if they had served in the wartime armed forces, might well have had some research experience of their own on this score, some experiences that had to be named or recalled or misremembered in a particular way if the person himself were to escape designation as a queer "other," that is, escape inclusion in cartoonist Walt Kelly's insight, in his 1953's *Pogo Papers*, that "we shall meet the enemy, and not only may he be ours, he may be us."[78] Did some of a man's own experiences during the recently concluded war include him in that freshly stigmatized group, making him a part of "them," or exclude or excuse him somehow, retaining the much preferred designation "us"? What exactly—anything?—might distinguish a genuinely homosexual man from a man who simply had had sex with one or more other men? Frequency? Fantasy? Self-identification?

Let us pull back now from the more expansive meanings of the mourning after and consider an especially significant way in which veterans returning in a state of mourning might have an impact on American domestic life: veterans as fathers, a sizeable group, in light of the period's well-known increase in the birthrate. Adjusting to parenthood is challenging in the best of circumstances, but fatherhood could pose a particular challenge for many returning veterans, especially those who had seen combat and, as would often have been the case, those who were mourning the loss of a beloved buddy—a loss either to death in battle or because of a decision by one or both parties to end a wartime relationship thought to be too intimate for continuation by civilians.

Forums from popular culture to professional advice literature addressed the adjustment of veterans to being married and a father, sometimes to a child they had just met. The strain of adjustment by children and fathers alike could understandably be severe: "Children described their fathers as 'solemn,' 'intolerant,' 'frustrated,' 'abusive,' 'very nervous,'" historian William M. Tuttle Jr. has written. "Especially devastated were those who had been prisoners of war." Not surprisingly, "alcoholism was rampant among returning fathers; indeed, alcohol abuse throughout the postwar population was a significant—though largely unacknowledged—feature of American family life."[79] Alcohol abuse may have been just one manifestation of the psychological burdens carried by many returned veterans who were fathers. Psychologist Francine Shapiro has recently written of the "distant dads" of the 1950s, a common description of midcentury fathers, "disciplinarians, who maintained a firm sense of control in the household, but were either silent or emotionally withdrawn or angry." Shapiro suggested that in many cases fathers' "distance" was probably not merely the result of being absorbed by peacetime occupations but also of their suffering from undiagnosed post-traumatic stress.[80]

Some professional advice urged that postwar fathers make sure they were manly enough for the job—with a highly traditional, rigid sense of manliness prominent in this advice. *Hygeia*, the official "health magazine" of the American Medical Association, had expressed concern even during the war that there were too many "maternal fathers" who had their roles confused and were too attentive to their children. A "distant father," according to the unnamed *Hygeia* author, was altogether appropriate, and the "maternal father" was the result of "a loss of balance between the sexes" that "naturally followed the emancipation of women." If "few fathers seem to be outwardly interested in the tiny baby," thought this author, that was "rightfully so."[81] Such a traditional notion of masculine emotionality and of a father's proper role would obviously contribute to an interpretation of a veteran's emotional reserve as normal behavior, not a war wound.

Indeed one historian has maintained that "many returning fathers believed that their two most important functions, in addition to being the breadwinner, were to discipline the children and to enforce what they considered to be appropriate sex-role behavior."[82] For such a father, then, his job was to reinforce emotional reserve in his son, and to be especially watchful for any signs of the son's being a sissy. A father's own emotional turmoil from the war, especially if exacerbated by a desire to make up for lost time as a disciplinarian because of wartime absence, might make his sissy-watch all the more intense, and make the consequences of his discovering alarming signs of weakness in a son all the more serious. As William M. Tuttle Jr. has observed,

> One would think that these hazards alone [being seen as a stranger to his own kids] would challenge any father-child relationship. But there was still one more obstacle—one exemplified by the homecoming father who railed that his son had become a "sissy," surrounded as he had been by women and in the absence of a strong male role model.[83]

And if a father were feeling psychologically weak himself—from mourning, loss, and longing associated with the war—and further was reticent to admit that feeling, his treatment of a son considered a "sissy" might be especially harsh, in an act of overcompensation. Born in 1946, novelist and Vietnam veteran Tim O'Brien has even suggested that a World War II veteran's son could have a peculiar significance, bear a particular burden: O'Brien considers himself "one of millions come to replace those who had just died."[84] Boys of the late 1940s and the 1950s, then, might sometimes be casualties of their fathers' survivor sorrow and guilt, with distancing imposed between themselves and their combat-veteran fathers to protect the fathers against another painful loss, on the one hand, as well as to assure that no weakling, no sissy, was being raised.[85]

Not surprisingly, Benjamin Spock weighed in on the issue of gender roles and child rearing; comparing his advice in the 1946 edition of *Baby and Child Care* to that given a decade later is revealing. Interestingly enough, "Timidity and Sissiness" had a section of its own in 1957, although there had been no such section at all a decade earlier. Indeed the overall tone of the 1957 edition implied that child rearing had become a more serious business, with higher stakes, than it was in 1946.[86] While Spock's opposition to the Vietnam War in the 1960s was early and vigorous, his notions of gender roles were thoroughly conventional in 1957. Though he recognized that "a father may be upset if his son at two likes to play occasionally with dolls and doll carriages," wrote Spock, he counseled that age two was "too early to start worrying"—begging the questions of whether such activity would be worrisome later on, and whether more dramatic departures from masculinity than playing with dolls would be worrisome even at two. Spock, whose training was in psychiatry, maintained that although gender differentiation should typically show itself increasingly by age three, "it is perfectly natural for a boy of 3 or 4 to play with girls part of the time . . . but if they are playing house he should be wanting to play father or son." Spock's potential concern, though, increased with a boy's age:

> If a boy of 3 or 4 or 5 is avoiding boys or is regularly preferring to take
> the part of a mother or girl in house play, he is probably afraid of being a
> boy and needs child-guidance help. He also needs a friendlier relation-
> ship with his father. Sometimes the mother is being too protective or
> enveloping.

To correct his son's inappropriate behavior, however, Spock advised fathers not to resort to the kidding that he said men "in civilized life" often used to control their greater "fierceness" in comparison to women. Tempting as it might be with a sissy for a son, it was better for a father to "go light on kidding." A father's alternative approach was left vague.

But Spock was hardly suggesting that either parent lighten up too much on a son. A mother should not "show too much concern or sympathy" for a timid son, should not "fight his battles for him," should not even "tell him he must share" but instead "suggest casually that he go and get the toy back." Odd advice for the soon-to-be peace activist, perhaps, but neither Spock nor anyone else was inclined to perceive a link between conventional masculinity and belligerence in 1957, especially not if the pressing mission was to guard against having queer sons. Preventing such an outcome was the unstated yet clear purpose of the section on "timidity and sissiness," which mentioned only sons, not daughters.[87]

Anxiety over the possibility of that outcome—having a queer son or being a queer son—had grown tremendously since the war. The disappearance of one simple piece of advice from Dr. Spock, from the 1946 edition of *Baby and Child Care* to its 1957 version, captures the dourness of midcentury masculinity with chilling succinctness. In 1946 Spock urged parents, not just mothers, referring to the baby as "him": "Don't be afraid to kiss your baby when you feel like it."[88] In 1957, there was no more mention of kissing.

As historians have recognized increasingly, literature of advice—even advice as popular as Dr. Spock's—has distinct limitations as historical evidence of the actual lived experience of the people to whom the advice was directed. A new, specialized genre of American writing has recently emerged that—like autobiographies, diaries, letters, and everyday photographs—is a more direct avenue to how certain people actually lived, as opposed to simply how they were advised to live. This new genre is a quest literature of sorts: chronicling a search by the children of World War II veterans for better understanding of their fathers, of men whose silence, moodiness, or outright absence in the lives of their children suggested that there were wartime stories untold, secrets undisclosed. The number of fathers about whom such a quest might meaningfully be undertaken is unknown, and is perhaps only a small sample of the 16.5 million men who served during the war; the number about whom books have already been written is admittedly much smaller still. Significant as those limitations are, this fresh body of American writing does provide a new way of looking at the experiences of the men who served in the Second World War—during and long after the war itself. This literature is eloquent confirmation of a point made by Mary L. Dudziak in her singular *War Time: An Idea, Its History, Its Consequences*: "World War II is an example of the way American war spills beyond tidy time boundaries."[89] In cultural time, the distance from us today back to World War II has been brief, and it is an important assumption of mine that American masculinity of the twenty-first century is still affected by that war in ways both obvious and shrouded.

Of the books that have so far appeared by World War II veterans' children trying to make some sense of a father's troubled family life, linking the trouble to the trauma of the war, more have been written by veterans' daughters than sons. The overall number of books in this genre has not yet been large enough, nor is the gender difference in authorship substantial enough, to be significant, nonetheless it may well be that the fathers' continuing denial or at least silence about wartime trauma has been more thoroughly absorbed by their sons, inclining them to be less curious about their fathers, or at least less willing to investigate the roots of their fathers' malaise, in some cases themselves adopting their fathers' emotional style rather than recognizing its problematic nature.[90]

A veteran's son without such reticence is professional historian Thomas Childers, whose own father is one of the three veterans whose postwar adjustment is the focus of Childers's exceptional study *Soldier from the War Returning: The Greatest Generation's Troubled Homecoming from World War II*, a book of remarkable empathy and insight that convincingly refutes today's superficial, and ultimately patronizing, pieties about the so-called greatest generation, generalizations that rob veterans of the Second World War of the dignity of their own considerable travail. Purely from a historiographical standpoint alone, Childers's work is notable in how gracefully and meaningfully, never with self-indulgence, he places the historian squarely in the middle of his own inquiry, as one of the historical actors himself.[91]

One of the more bravely candid of the recent "quest for the father" books is Carol Schultz Vento's well-titled *The Hidden Legacy of World War II: A Daughter's Journey of Discovery*. Addressing the war's lingering impact, Vento, a political science professor, remarks that ironically "during the 1950s, my father wanted to forget. The same war which preserved his historic legacy also cut a swath of suffering and silence through my life." With his burial at Arlington awaiting, Carol Schultz Vento kept her father's ashes in an urn on her mantle in 2005, "the longest period of time my father and I lived in a house together since my parents' divorce when I was eleven." A paratrooper who landed at Normandy on D-day and then fought in the Battle of the Bulge, prominently and cheerfully portrayed in the 1962 film *The Longest Day*, Arthur Bernard "Dutch" Schultz had only told his young daughter "tedious and predictable" stories of the war, leaving her unaware that those stories were just "an abbreviation," merely "the version that fit comfortably into his middle-class life—the version where everyone lives happily ever after." Only when he was eighty-one did she begin to learn what had for years been left out, as he urged his daughter to write her book, explaining "what it was like to grow up with a combat veteran of World War II."

What it was, was hell—for Schultz, his wife, "whose letters had sustained him through the long years of the war," and for their children:

> But the soldier coming home was no longer a carefree, happy boy with big dreams of a major league career. He was a man who had been profoundly affected by war. My father's battle to integrate his warm nature with the horrors he had seen at war would last all his life.

Haunted incessantly by the combat he had seen, Schultz self-medicated, with alcohol and the company of comrades from the war: "Dutch drank and drank," his daughter would write, "only happy when he spent evenings with other paratroopers. These men, all veterans of sustained combat, imbibed all night, talking incessantly about the war, while the young wives waited impatiently to take their inebriated husbands home in the wee hours of the morning." When Schultz and his first wife divorced, he married another alcoholic, so that his drinking could continue unimpeded. After a serious breakdown, he joined Alcoholics Anonymous and then another rehabilitation program called Today; his second marriage ended, and that was perhaps what led his second wife to commit suicide on his birthday. At fifty in 1973, he vowed to "start over," but the horrific memories of the war, Dutch Schultz's own mourning after, did not end. Carol Schultz Vento's book about her father was an effort to bring the mourning to a close. As Thomas Childers wrote in his foreword to Vento's book, with characteristic eloquent restraint, "In the end, children bore many of their father's scars."[92]

Like Bernard Schultz, Murray Fisher had to wait until his eighties to bear to recall the war's full horror, in his case the specific instance of watching his navy buddy Mal die from a shrapnel wound suffered when a kamikaze plane went down near their ship. Only with the events of September 11, 2001, the war over for nearly fifty-six years, would Murray Fisher begin to seem agitated, plagued by nightmares. When he turned eighty, he gave his daughter Karen a large number of the letters he had written home during his time in the navy, spent mostly in the Pacific. Carefully reading those letters, his daughter began to uncover the horror of a buddy's death in 1945, a trauma that her father, all those decades later, at last allowed himself to consciously mourn. As his daughter, Karen Fisher-Alaniz, wrote in her *Breaking the Code: A Father's Secret, A Daughter's Journey, and the Quest That Changed Everything*,

> He held his dying friend in his arms. He cradled him like a baby. "Oh, Murray" were Mal's last words. In the mind-numbing scene that followed, he couldn't let go of his friend. He couldn't leave him. His hands clenched tight to him until a comrade pried them open. The next thing he knew he was waking up in a military hospital some time later. This was the secret he kept.

Having at last uncovered her father's repressed memory of losing his buddy Mal, "the greatest tragedy of my father's young life," Karen Fisher-Alaniz accompanied her parents to Hawaii, where they held a memorial service for Mal, sixty years after he had died at twenty—twenty—in Murray Fisher's arms. They placed some flowers into the Pacific, and the flowers flowed out to sea. "'They're going to Okinawa,' my father said softly," wrote Karen Fisher-Alaniz. "'He never forgot you,' I whispered. 'Rest in peace, Mal.'"

FIGURE 5.1   World War II pencil sketch by "Dickson," in Ralph S. Green's scrapbook of the army air corps. (Courtesy of Gay, Lesbian, Bisexual, Transgender Historical Society, San Francisco.)

"Something profound happened as he felt life leave his friend," according to Murray's daughter. "He carried it with him for more than fifty years, never letting light penetrate that dark, dark place. But as he remembered his friend, with flowers that pushed against the tide toward Okinawa, light slowly penetrated the darkness." Back home, his daughter asked Murray Fisher if in Hawaii he had said good-bye to his buddy: "'Never good-bye,' he said, 'Just . . . see you later.'" Fisher-Alaniz dedicated her exceptional book to her father, her mother, and "my father's comrade, Mal."[93] Many a Murray fought in that war, and left behind many a Mal, only to return home to a society whose culture made it difficult to grieve the loss openly, to acknowledge fully—perhaps even to recognize—the affection the buddies had shared (figure 5.1).

It was an exceptionally bloody land battle in the Pacific, the nearly three-month-long Battle of Okinawa in 1945, with its horrendous carnage and in particular the death of a close buddy, that altered the rest of the life of Jeremiah (Jerry) Collins, prompting yet another gorgeously terrifying biography by a questing daughter, freelance writer Julia Collins's *My Father's War: A Memoir.*

"Many a family," she wrote,

> like mine, can trace to World War II the root causes for the remoteness,
> anger, depression, despair, alcoholism, violence, even the suicide of
> their husband or father. Like my dad, the unlikeliest of warriors, many

men did not belong in combat and were altered forever by its brutal exigencies.

The unlikely warrior had studied chemistry at Yale before becoming a marine, "but something irrevocable had happened to the boy famous for his energy and ambition, and for whom high school classmates predicted a career as a world-renowned chemist." Julia Collins wrote:

> His life came to a standstill, the clock stopping in 1946. He had brought the war home, where it grew inside him, usurping part of his soul. With the self-abnegation typical of World War II vets, Dad didn't let on to his wife, parents or three sons about the nightmares or survivor's guilt that haunted him. He began to lose himself in booze and other diversions. Eventually, however, as he hit middle age and saw that all his plans were coming to naught, Jeremiah Collins was driven to share his war, in full bloody splendor, with his two youngest children, both daughters.

The combat was especially ghastly for Sugar Loaf, a strategic spot on Okinawa, with torn-off "limbs and heads, gouged eyes, seared flesh," men "sliced in half," "intestines spilled from exploded chest cavities," and the "stench of putrefying flesh quivering with maggots." The horrible combat death of John Terence, a buddy he had known since they trained together at Maryland's Camp Ritchie, "especially haunted him." As a civilian, for years he took no more chances with male affection: "For as long as I could remember," his daughter recalled, "my father had no friends. I'd always thought he was the loneliest man in the world." He found some solace in an extramarital affair, years of heavy drinking, and telling grisly war stories to his young daughters, with whom he forged an odd bond.

Only in old age did Jerry Collins "suddenly burst out of his isolation, to socialize with a small group of Branford [New Jersey] men, some of them fellow vets." And among her father's fellow veterans, Julia Collins came to realize,

> My father was not alone in his defeat. There were many other vets like him, emotionally and invisibly scarred by the "Good War," who failed to live up to the impossible standards set for men of their era. . . . Most loved ones were kept in the dark. World War II vets are notoriously close-mouthed, the stoic product of the Great Depression and wartime when ideals of honor, courage, patriotism, sacrifice, and self-reliance fostered impregnable reticence.

Her voyage of discovery complete, Julia Collins returns each year "to our mutual hometown, looking for Jerry Collins. . . . All along my route I imagine the tenderhearted boy who went off to become a Marine, and the soul-weary man who came back."[94] Their fellow citizens, including their own spouses and children, often had little understanding of the weary souls of men like Jerry Collins; there surely were many such men, whose moodiness was misunderstood, and who left a lingering mark on what it means to be an American male.

Conversations about the war, especially about its trauma, however slow they were in coming, may well have been more common between fathers and their daughters than were similar talks between fathers and their sons. According to journalist Thomas Matthews Jr., "My father hated war stories. He was a soldier with a code, a brave man who wouldn't talk about World War II." This brave, silent man bullied his son, and the years of conflict between them led Tom Jr. to use their tense experience, and that of nine other father-son pairings, for *Our Fathers' War: Growing Up in the Shadow of the Greatest Generation*. The senior Matthews was part of the legendary Tenth Mountain Division; though the division's losses in Italy were unusually high, the younger Matthews reported that "none of this my father ever mentioned." Not all of the fathers in *Our Fathers' War* were cruel and distant, but they were all either reticent to talk about the war or else they would deliver only fabrications.

Weyman Watson, whose father Spann was one of the Tuskegee Airmen, thought that on "the Kelvin scale, the chill between fathers and sons ran close to absolute zero." He remembered that "all of my friends were going through the same thing," and that "we thought all of our fathers were sore at us all of the time." As a black man who had triumphed over powerful racist resistance to become a pilot, Spann Watson "expected his own sons to always be above reproach, to prove the racists wrong in their demeanor, even their clothing." Ed Person, a former infantryman who served in France, was so closemouthed about the war that until he was an old man near death he showed no one his war snapshots, though he kept several in a "secret album"; many of those photos were pictures of his buddies, "arms draped around each other, shoulder to shoulder in the hot, white light of the overexposed frames. . . . Young men with open, innocent faces, draftees and volunteers, GIs, not officers." When his son Bob asked about a photo of the French countryside, his father broke down: "We lost sixteen men in that field," he said through tears, the first time his son had ever seen the old man cry.

Another veteran whose story Tom Matthews recounted, Murray Greenberg, came home to Brooklyn after having been in a German prison camp for over a year. He continued to have an especially strained relationship with the son born while he was away. It was another son, born after Murray's return, who brought his father's war memorabilia to Matthews for his book; it had been hidden from the family. Murray's wife Shirley had a simple explanation of her husband's silence: "The war killed him," she would say. "He was never the same man."

Of his own father, the silent bully, Matthews wrote, "when a son is as afraid of his father as I was, love can curdle, producing obedience and something close to awe." As a tribute of sorts, the younger Matthews became as much of a heavy drinker as his father, and, at least until his inquiries for his book broke his father's spell over him, he probably was no less emotionally constrained than his father had been. And yet his father had gone "into the war an innocent, an idealist full of hope and energy," even though "he came home an elusive shape-shifter." Perpetually looking sad, sitting in his chair at night, "reading Proust, belting gin, brooding," his father could not "show the simplest expression of fatherly affection," seeing "poker and life as the same game," keeping his sons guessing, expecting of them "a commander's due: obedience and admiration." His son Tom was in therapy, no wonder, for twenty years; he had the same therapist for all that time, "a strong woman from Texas" who finally was moved to ask, "Tom, when are you going to get your daddy's dick out of your ass?" Though they might not have been in therapy for two decades, other sons of World War II veterans that Tom Matthews met while writing his book were also deeply troubled, moving Matthews to conclude that "there was something darker going on below the heroic surface of the Greatest Generation":

> And if the war was still seething somewhere inside [the fathers], how much collateral damage could be detected among their sons? Did a kinetic force from the war run through the GI Generation to the Boomers, and X-ers, maybe even to the Nexters, one generation after another of fathers and sons tuned by the war to the same pitch?

Research for his book introduced Tom Matthews to many fathers and sons, and, he said, "the more I talked to, the more I felt a small shock of recognition," leading him to "wonder whether the Last Good War might be the Last Best Kept Secret."[95]

The Battle of Iwo Jima in 1945, where Gore Vidal's Jimmie Trimble died, setting for one of the most iconic images of World War II or of any war, was the focal point of still another book by a veteran's child seeking to better understand his parent, and hence himself, James Bradley's *Flags of Our Fathers*. Interestingly, though John Bradley, a marine medic, had been in the battle for the island, no copy of the famous flag raising hung in the Bradley home.[96] James Bradley's interest in his father's role in the battle was generated by boxes of photographs and letters that were discovered only after his father had died in 1994—yet more secrets that had been kept hidden away for decades. James Bradley recalled the response when he asked his father's medical supervisor, the battalion surgeon on Iwo Jima, James Wittmeier, why his late father might have been so secretive about the war: "Finally, after many long minutes, he turned to me and softly said, 'You ever hold a broken raw egg in your hands? Well, that's how your father and I held young men's heads.' The heads of real heroes, dying in my father's arms."

Having told his son that "the heroes of Iwo Jima are the guys who didn't come back," but not ever wanting to say more, John Bradley at last and for once in 1970 opened up to sixteen-year-old James with the sort of specific memory his son had so often asked for:

> I have tried so hard to black this out. To forget it. We could choose a buddy to go in with. My buddy was a guy from Milwaukee. We were pinned down in one area. Someone elsewhere fell injured and I ran to help out, and when I came back my buddy was gone. I couldn't figure out where he was. I could see all around, but he wasn't there. . . . A few days later someone yelled that they'd found him. They called me over because I was a corpsman. The Japanese had pulled him underground and tortured him. His fingernails . . . his tongue. . . . It was terrible. I tried so hard to forget all this.

The younger Bradley, researching his father's life a quarter of a century later for his book, was told by Cliff Langley, his father's co-corpsman, that the buddy's injuries were even more severe: "'Both his arms were fractured,' Langley said, 'They just hung there like arms on a broken doll. He had been bayoneted repeatedly. The back of his head had been smashed in.'" Once when James Bradley was visiting Japan, having learned to savor its complex culture, he had invited his father to join him there. John Bradley declined, telling another son, Steve, why he could not accept: "Jim wants us to come visit him. They tortured my buddy. The Japanese stuffed his penis in his mouth. I'm not too interested in going to Japan."

The buddy's name was Ralph "Iggy" Igatowski. As James Bradley would learn,

> It was at Camp Pendleton that Doc Bradley met the doomed youth who would become his best buddy in the service and perhaps a key to his lifelong silence on the subject of his World War II experiences. It was here that my father met Iggy. . . . They bunked together, ate ice cream together, went on liberty together, and generally came to know each other's deepest hopes, fears, and joys.

"Some veterans cope with pain via alcohol or drugs," James Bradley has written. "Others seek psychiatric counseling—or don't seek it. Here is where my dad may have been a little different. He coped by making himself not think about the war." But there was a price for such nearly total silence. Incredibly, he spoke of Iwo Jima only once to his wife, Elizabeth, and that was for just a few minutes on their first date. "But," James Bradley wrote, "after they were married, my mother told me, he wept at night, in his sleep. He wept in his sleep for four years."[97]

Sixteen and one-half million men served in World War II, and of course many, especially those millions who saw no combat, slept more peacefully than John Bradley. Those who literally mourned a buddy who had died in the war or mourned a relationship with a buddy that had ended when peace came were surely numerous enough to merit more mention than they have received. But this book merits its title only if an attitude, an emotional pitch, that resembled mourning was more widespread among members of the World War II generation, widespread enough to have cast its pall over midcentury masculinity, and widespread enough to still be influencing how we American males perform our masculinities. To show that such was the case has been my central purpose in these pages.

A suggestion of the broader significance of the "mourning after" notion is contained in the autobiography of Tom Hayden, *Reunion: A Memoir*. Some of the spirit animating the 1960s counterculture, for which Hayden was a leading voice, may have been a particular yearning among young males like Hayden who had come of age amid the constraining melancholy of 1950s masculinity. The preface of Hayden's countercultural manifesto, the Port Huron Statement, had noted the discontent felt by midcentury children of the American middle class who, though "bred in at least modest comfort," nonetheless found material comfort unsatisfying. In *Reunion* Hayden recalled the symbolic significance of C. Wright Mills's early death in 1962, just as Hayden was composing the Port Huron Statement:

> It struck me that Mills was describing the world of my father, especially in *White Collar*, a book about the new middle class typified by accountants and clerks. . . . As I pored through Mills, I saw an image of my father, proud in his starched white collar, occupying an accountants' niche above the union work force and below the real decision makers, penciling numbers by day, drinking in front of the television at night, muttering about the world to no one in particular.

Crucially important for *The Mourning After* is that Hayden did not simply attribute his father's discontent to the nature of his postwar work, but rather to the contrast between the (dis)satisfactions of that work and what he had experienced in the war:

> But something about the military changed my father. . . . While he had not been overseas, the excitement and camaraderie of the war years was enough to break and replace the moorings of family which bound us together before. When he finally returned home [after hitchhiking from San Diego to Michigan], he became president of the American Legion

Post in Royal Oak, a flat and spreading suburb twelve miles north of Detroit, where we settled in a tree-shaded, two story, white wood-frame house. Spending time at the Legion Hall socializing with the other veterans seemed to allow my father to relive the war he missed. For many of them, life seemed to have peaked somewhere in the Pacific. Like many of them, my father began drinking heavily.

In light of the comparative shortcomings of the white-collar existence that awaited so many veterans like John Francis Hayden after the war, even those who saw no combat, those who mourned no lost buddy, a disengaged posture of mourning might be adopted nonetheless. His father came home drunk one night, Tom Hayden remembered, "came into my room, whispered to me that he and Mom were getting divorced, kissed me for the first time I could remember, and quietly was gone."[98]

Unkissed boys like young Tom Hayden in the 1950s typically had fathers whose parenting faced a sense of surveillance largely unknown before midcentury. As Ralph LaRossa has written,

> The question of "who was and who was not" gay also extended to grown-ups. (After all, the Kinsey Report did focus on adults.) Thus, in the fifties, fathers tended to be scrutinized differently than they might have been before: people wanted to see men adopt a demeanor that supposedly established that they were heterosexual.

The surest way to convey that insisted-upon demeanor was through the severity of a drill sergeant. In LaRossa's words, "With the burgeoning of the Little Leagues [in the 1950s], however, playing catch became an instructional activity. Learning how to throw and catch 'correctly'—which generally meant 'not like a girl'—ascended in importance."[99] Midcentury sons like Tom Hayden, then, may have had singular yearnings of their own. Add to that the fact that these sons were the first generation of American males to be raised with homophobic barriers between themselves and their male friends, sometimes even between themselves and their brothers and fathers, barriers that fostered their own feelings of loss and longing. Sensations of loss and longing—a yearning literally for *fellowship*—were definitely not a prerequisite for responding warmly to Martin Luther King Jr.'s 1957 call for the Beloved Community, King's rendering of a concept named decades earlier by philosopher Josiah Royce. Devotion to equity, a hunger for social justice, would have been enough to answer King's call, but a void in the emotional lives of certain American men may have provided an additional incentive.

In vivid contrast to Hayden's autobiography, a compelling reminder that being a veteran and a veteran's son in the 1950s did not inevitably entail a dreary sense of mourning, loss, and longing—and hence that many of my generalizations in this book demand significant qualification—is a different sort of questing memoir: sociologist Michael Messner's smart, sensitive, and utterly charming *King of the Wild Suburb: A Memoir of Fathers, Sons, and Guns*. Guided by his keen awareness of the degree to which a child may be shaped by a parent, yet, with rigorous self-awareness, not be fated to be that parent's clone, Messner recounts hunting trips with his father and his grandfather that were important parts of his childhood. A teacher ever willing to learn himself, Messner observes that in writing his memoir, "I learned how those hunting trips with Dad and Gramps were actually about fathers and sons finding a way to love each other. Those outings were not so much about hunting for deer: they were about hunting for each other." Wise enough not to read history backward and expect more of persons in the past than they could possibly have exhibited, Messner savors how well his father played the hand he was dealt; the son does not bemoan any limitations of the fathering.[100]

The magnitude of the antiwar movement during the Vietnam War may have contributed to the notion that the Second World War was not only the nobler venture, a war so just that Saint Augustine himself would have approved, but also was a war without troubles and controversies of its own. It has seemed somehow sadly fitting that a war about which Americans were as conflicted as they were over the Vietnam misadventure would have a large number of psychologically damaged veterans, victims whose emotional turmoil would even receive its own acronymic title, PTSD (post-traumatic stress disorder), a full-fledged diagnosis, rather than the euphemisms employed in previous wars, "shell shock" and "battle fatigue." Popular histories still romanticize the World War II generation as "the greatest," the same grandly vague salute that Ralph Kramden would give his wife, Alice, on *The Honeymooners*. But professional historians and persons who lived through World War II tend to see the conflict with more subtlety. Studs Terkel's designation of World War II as the "Good War" was filled with irony, whether he intended it to be or not; and probably only people who never wore a military uniform, men like Tom Brokaw and Ken Burns, could so unreservedly and patronizingly characterize those who did suit up as "the greatest generation," treating their cause as something as majestic but as lacking in emotion as Yosemite's Half Dome. The title of historian C. C. Adams's *The Best War Ever* is meant to be highly ironic, not a celebration of the "greatest" generation's grand adventures. But a society's public memory is a matter of serviceable collective perception; accuracy is not simply secondary, it is irrelevant. The war served up by Terkel, Brokaw, and Burns is an exercise in wish fulfillment, the war we wish we had fought. In Terkel's collection of veterans' recollections, as well as those of others alive during the war, the phenomenon of psychological distress barely appears in a book of nearly six hundred pages. "Battle fatigue" or its equivalent is not even in Brokaw's index, let alone not receiving a section of its own. Stephen Ambrose might be excused for naming a World War II book for children *The Good Fight*, but that is the implied title of most popular histories that are intended for adults as well, by Ambrose and most others.[101]

Warm recollections of camaraderie's vital importance are prominent in veterans' memoirs and in some popular histories, such as Ambrose's several volumes; he even devoted an entire book to the subject, *Comrades: Brothers, Fathers, Heroes, Sons, Pals*, and of course he famously and movingly borrowed from Shakespeare for titling his *Band of Brothers: E Company, 506th Regiment, 101st Airborne from Normandy to Hitler's Eagle's Nest*.[102] Any suggestion that sexual activity or romantic love might have accompanied some of the comradely affection was consistently beyond Ambrose, however; he apparently was too squeamish to bring that up, yet of course a historian as well versed as he in military culture was well aware of it. That narrative gap limited the completeness of his many tales.

Similarly, there is no attention whatsoever to same-sex affection in the monumental evocation of World War II by the nation's popular documentarian, Ken Burns. A filmmaker who has taken on no less of a task than capturing the essentially American quality of the nation's wars, games, parks, monuments, music, and heroes, Burns's histories recall the celebrations of consensus and conformity that were popular among professional historians before the cultural turmoil of the 1960s. The 452-page book *The War*, companion to Burns's fourteen-hour PBS documentary about World War II, is thin despite its girth, oddly bland and self-congratulatory. Thirty-five photos of persons featured in the book and film adorn the book's frontispiece. Not one is of a pair of buddies, to say nothing of a pair that might seem to have shared something other than friendship. Glaringly missing from the book's bibliography is Allan Bérubé's definitive history of gay men and lesbians who served in the war. Missing from the index are such benign yet crucial words as "buddies" and "camaraderie." "Homosexuals" shows up, but only in reference to Nazi persecution; missing as well are "sex," "venereal disease," and "battle fatigue" or any of its synonyms. Missing too in this nationalistic extravaganza is the simple yet essential word "allies." Although *An Intimate History* is the book's subtitle, only one form of intimacy is countenanced, and even that in a highly chaste fashion: Women are seen, from the rear, waving to servicemen on an arriving or departing ship on the dust jacket, and on the full page opposite the book's table of contents is a photograph of a soldier holding an infant, presumably his child, while a young woman, presumably the child's mother, looks on.

Candid and thoughtful veterans of many wars have rejected efforts to see melodrama, romance, or greatness in what they experienced. Karl Marlantes, formerly an American marine in Vietnam, and also a Yale graduate and Rhodes Scholar, has written with unusual grace and insight about the meaning of being in combat—

whatever the war. "Warriors will always have to deal with guilt and mourning," Marlantes wrote in *What It Is Like to Go to War*. "It is unfortunate that the guilt and mourning reside almost entirely with those asked to do the dirty work," he said, making someone like former defense secretary Robert McNamara highly unusual in his expressions of responsibility, sorrow, and regret for the abundance of mistakes the country made in the war Marlantes was asked to fight.[103] Writing further about the aftermaths of any war, not just an unpopular one, Marlantes observed that

> We cannot expect normal eighteen-year-olds to kill someone and contain it in a healthy way. They must be helped to start out what will be healthy grief about taking a life because it is part of the sorrow of war.[104]

In yet another generic approach to warfare's impact on the warrior, *The Warriors: Reflections on Men in Battle*, Jesse Glenn Gray, a World War II veteran who received confirmation of his doctorate in philosophy the very day that his draft notice arrived in 1941, worked some fourteen years after the war ended to "comprehend my experience as a soldier," recalling that in his journal of 1945 he had grown "bitter and sarcastic in the war," and would "often despair of myself." He noted as well that in the 1940s an American could still go to war and be struck profoundly by the diversity present in his own country: "I had not known their like before, nor have I met them since." Echoing John Horne Burns in *The Gallery* and E. B. Sledge in *With the Old Breed*, J. Glenn Gray was also unprepared for discovering his countrymen's capacity for cruelty in the Second World War, a discovery whose disorienting impact he brought home with him: "The enemy was cruel, it was clear, yet this did not trouble me as deeply as our own cruelty. . . . I felt responsibility for ours much more than for theirs."

And undoubtedly like many of his fellow warriors, but unlike his countrymen who had not served, Gray held onto his feelings of remorse from the war. "I am afraid to forget," he wrote, "I fear that we human creatures do not forget cleanly, as the animals presumably do." And for Gray, odd though it might seem to outsiders, peace at midcentury had provided no substitute for "the old days of conflict." For him, the war had had three essential appeals: aesthetically, as a grand spectacle; a highly disconcerting delight in destruction; and the pleasures of camaraderie. The spectacle and the destruction might be timeless in their appeal to all soldiers, but the warm memories of fellowship might be bound to the twentieth century, especially in the United States, with its inordinate emotional constrictions in civilian life for males.

"With the boundaries of the self expanded," Gray believed, World War II veterans could "sense a kinship never known before" in modern America. "Many veterans who are honest with themselves will admit, I believe," said Gray, "that the experience of communal effort in battle, even under the altered conditions of modern war, has been the high point in their lives." The war had even provided Gray a promise of immortality that modern civilian life simply could not, a chance to go "forward and [live] on in the comrades for whom I gave up my physical life," satisfying a "yearning for communion," an opportunity to "discover some of the mysteries of communal joy in its forbidden depths [because] comradeship reaches its peak in battle." Noting that the war had lifted "civilized controls over sex impulses," Gray treated the experience of love in war as steadfastly, unyieldingly heterosexual, ignoring same-sex erotics altogether, even though he did recognize that the war could nurture a genuine, lasting friendship between men much deeper than a comradeship of the moment. Interestingly, though he failed to recognize the sexual component of some male attachments in the war, he saw in camaraderie a bond greater than sex, one that exposed comrades "to an anxiety even greater than that of other lovers": "In every slain man on the battlefield, one can recognize a possible friend of someone. . . . The possible peaks of intensity and earlier maturity which war may bring to friendship are as nothing compared with the threats of loss it holds."

Whereas the death of friends in old age is comprehensible, in a wartime death,

> friendship cut off in its flower by war's arbitrariness is likely to seem the height of unreason and madness. What earlier had been luminous, ordered, and purposeful in experience becomes suddenly emptied of meaning. Unlike other loves the preciousness of friendship has no connection with its precariousness. Hence no ultimate consolation is possible for the loss of a friend.

So it seemed to be the most treasured form of love, in its irreplaceability. Though Gray claimed that the "true domain" of love in friendship is "peace, only peace," it actually was the experience of war that prompted Gray's powerful celebration of its singular appeal. "It may be the death of an acquaintance in his arms," wrote Gray with considerable historical perspective, "where the transition between life and death is made imaginatively viable for the first time."[105] Thus, out of the coming together of memories of the intense fellowship that inheres in virtually all war and the unprecedented, desperate intensity of midcentury America's resistance to fellowship in the domestic world to which veterans returned could arise the distinctive mournfulness that has been my subject in *The Mourning After*.

America before World War II and the society after it were vastly different places. In one of his memoirs, Gore Vidal quoted a passage from a letter Jimmie Trimble wrote to his mother during the war, signing it, "All my love to the swellest Mom in all the world. Your devoted son, Jimmie." Vidal observed that "this letter could have been written in the Civil War. The tone is also that of Andy Hardy in an MGM movie, but there were once real boys like that, before the great sullenness spread over the land."[106] To Vidal's everlasting sadness, this particular "real boy like that" did not make it home, but for the millions who did, the "great sullenness" in the country to which they returned was in various ways an aftermath of the war to which they had been sent.

We now have moved beyond midcentury America, but how far? Developmental psychologist Niobe Way found a "crisis of connection" to be a common feature of becoming an adult male nowadays, a crisis generated by the loss of and longing for the intimacy of younger male friendships. Writing of late twentieth- and early twenty-first-century boys' friendship, Niobe Way maintains that "late adolescence for the boys in my studies is a time of disconnection and loneliness. Rather than being simply a period of 'progress' as scholars of human development emphasize, adolescence for these boys is also a period of profound loss."[107] The sense of loss that Way found to be so common today became integral to American manhood in the aftermath of the Second World War.

Because they are inherently studies of change, histories of whole societies are an essentially subversive study—because they demonstrate that things can always be different than they are, or were. Distinctively among the many descriptions of the troubled state of boyhood in contemporary America, Niobe Way's *Deep Secrets: Boys' Friendships and the Crisis of Connection* rises above its sad descriptions of boys breaking away from each other, and is a profoundly subversive—and hopeful—work, because Way demonstrates so compellingly that there is no inevitability to men's isolation, that males are fully capable of circumventing cultural obstacles and of loving each other. The obstacles themselves are not inevitable, either, one of my primary points in this book.

The common portrait of the mainstream American male in the 1950s is essentially benign, if somewhat sad and one-dimensional. If troubled by the anonymity of the corporate work world and the scary exclusivity of his role as family breadwinner, the 1950s male of the middle class is typically seen as freshly exposed to the culture of consumption and, especially if he has remained unmarried, to the enticements of life as a playboy. These portraits, drawn largely by female historians and cultural critics, may claim to look into the "hearts of men" of postwar America, but the look has remained an incomplete and sometimes patronizing one, an assessment perhaps unduly shaped by comparisons between the admittedly more privileged economic positions of mainstream men and the material status of midcentury women and men of color.[108] Too often we make a contest of disadvantage, arguing over who has, or has had, it the worst, distracting ourselves from complex causes and remedies. To maintain that the lives of many midcentury males could be filled with buried sadness and thwarted desire is no plea for pity, simply a hope for better understanding.

Bookend for an Era

As the fifties, an era of various postwar cultural adjustments, drew to a close, the nation verging on a new decade that would be celebrated by some, denounced by others, for its cultural clamor and apparent change, a novel was published that described in lovely language the hiding place where affection between males had been put—better said, the place to which men's affection had been relegated in the war's lengthening aftermath. *A Separate Peace* by John Knowles, which so quickly came to be loved and taught with highly revealing frequency in the United States, aptly concludes this book's consideration of the cultural work performed by some important pieces of midcentury American literature, work on the cultural meanings and boundaries of male association.

In part because it came to be so frequently assigned in American English classes, commonly to high school sophomores, *A Separate Peace* has had a large readership, far in excess of that for any work by Burns or for any of Vidal's early novels. Already made into a film twice, in 1972 and in 2004, and even performed on the stage, the story has been told frequently in the United States over the past half century and more, becoming a minor cultural phenomenon. Yet, as with Burns and Vidal, much remains to be said of John Knowles, and especially of the most celebrated, by far, of his several novels. As with other works of literature that some English teachers and critics consider timeless, *A Separate Peace* has been seen as a work of everlasting significance, for its examination of themes as broad as loyalty, adolescence, friendship, rivalry, and responsibility. Be that as it may, it is also a work rooted firmly in the cultural particulars of World War II and its aftermath. It is a novel that might best be seen as an elegy—to a time, a companion, and an emotion.

Set in Devon, an elite prep school modeled on Exeter, the author's (and Gore Vidal's) alma mater, the novel deals neither with soldiers in combat nor with soldiers anywhere else, but rather with boys in late adolescence who yearn to become soldiers, who are preparing for their graduation and eventual service in the Second World War. Although the novel is set in the early 1940s, *A Separate Peace* reflects, as does all historical fiction, the time when it was written—in this case, the 1950s—at least as much as it captures the time written about. Gore Vidal, two years ahead of

Knowles at Exeter, claimed not to recall the younger man from those days, though as adults they became friends. According to Vidal, "*A Separate Peace* remains an eerily precise reconstruction of how things were in that long ago world before the Second World War."[1] Perhaps so, but it also captures much of how certain things turned out in the decade after the war had ended.

Knowles graduated from Exeter in 1945, just as the war was ending. He served less than a year in the army air corps before going on to Yale, never having, then, anything approaching the sorts of military experiences of Burns or Vidal. After Yale, he wrote for the *Hartford Courant* and then for *Holiday*, until the great success of 1959's *A Separate Peace*, Knowles's first published novel, allowed him to become a writer of fiction full-time. Though he published seven more novels, one of them a sequel to *A Separate Peace*, a collection of short stories, and a book about his foreign travels, nothing came remotely close to his first book, in either critical acclaim or sales. Though he at times sounded bitter about the comparative failure of his subsequent work, blaming a mistaken notion by critics that he was an upper-class writer, he was usually upbeat about his early success. "It's paid the bills for 30 years," he said in 1987. "It has made my career possible." Never out of print, *A Separate Peace* had sold ten million copies when Knowles died at seventy-five in 2001.[2]

A Separate Peace is narrated as a reminiscence by Gene Forrester, a Devon student during the early 1940s, who returns to his alma mater fifteen years after he graduated and went off to war. At its heart the novel recounts the intense, loving friendship between Gene and his Devon best friend and roommate, Phineas, or Finny, a boy who differs from his classmates not only because of his exceptional good looks and athletic ability, but in his confident disdain for competition and other cultural requirements of twentieth-century masculinity.

Gene's and Finny's love for each other, and each other's company, is never in doubt. They unashamedly admire each other's considerable good looks, and Finny especially is unguarded in expressing his affection. Once, having surreptitiously ridden their bikes to an off-limits beach hours away from the school, finding "a good spot among some sand dunes at the lonely end of the beach" and having "settled down to sleep for the night," Finny with his typical directness tells Gene that he is Finny's "best pal." "It was a courageous thing to say," Gene recollects. "Exposing a sincere emotion nakedly like that at the Devon School was the next thing to suicide. I should have told him then that he was my best friend also and rounded off what he had said. I started to. I nearly did. But something held me back. Perhaps I was stopped by that level of feeling, deeper than thought, which contains the truth." There are many such moments "deeper than thought" for the boys throughout the novel. Though we are told of no overtly sexual involvement between them, Knowles describes their pleasurable physical intimacy without restraint. Walking once to dinner at Devon, they stop occasionally for some playful wrestling: "I threw my hip against his, catching him by surprise, and he was instantly down, definitely pleased. This was why he liked me so much. When I jumped on top of him, my knees on his chest, he couldn't ask for anything better."[3] There is virtually as much, maybe more, loving intimacy in that scene between Gene and Finny as in Vidal's portrayal of Jim and Bob having sex by the river in *The City and the Pillar.*

Knowles has each boy pay careful attention to what the other wears. When Gene pulls off a sweatshirt, then removes an "Army fatigue shirt" that Finny sarcastically describes as "very topical," he wears "just my undershirt, stained with sweat." Finny "smiled at it for a while and then said . . . , 'There. You should have worn that all day. Just that. That has real taste. The rest of your outfit was just gilding the lily of that sweatshirt." No article of clothing seems more symbolic in the novel, however, than Finny's pink shirt, something nobody else at Devon would have had the gumption to wear. Not only is Finny undeterred by Gene's insistence that the shirt "makes you look like a *fairy*," he even wonders "what would happen if I looked like a fairy to everyone." In one remarkable scene, with Finny out of their room, Gene "decided to put on his clothes," dons the pink shirt, feels that he thus becomes "Phineas, Phineas to the life," so transformed, so emboldened, that "I would never stumble through the confusions of my own character again."[4]

And yet, in spite—*or because*—of the fierce bond between them, Knowles makes Gene at least indirectly the agent of Finny's death. When they—together, holding hands—are about to jump off a high tree limb into river water below, a popular ritual for Devon boys, Gene shakes the limb enough to send Finny falling alone, onto the ground, not into the river, breaking his leg. Surviving that fall, Finny nonetheless breaks the weakened leg a second time, sending a bone fragment into his bloodstream, killing him. As I have previously written of Finny's death, "many an object of homoerotic desire was similarly dispatched in American fiction until the 1970s, when the stigmatizing of homosexuality in the society at large began slowly to diminish."[5] But is it instructive to view Gene's and Finny's attraction to each other as "homoerotic"? Nearly three decades after the novel's publication, Knowles denied that the boys were gay, insisting that if they were, "it would have changed everything, it wouldn't have been the same story."[6] As for why or whether Gene meant for Finny to fall, surely a matter of discussion in countless English classes over the past half century, John Knowles consistently refused to provide an answer. When he died, his brother-in-law Bob Maxwell observed that "John used to say he would never answer that question. He took that one with him."[7]

This begs the question of whether Knowles himself actually realized in full why he had Gene jump on that branch. Interestingly, Knowles did acknowledge that Gene's character was based on himself, and that his friend David Hackett, a Milton Academy student (and longtime friend of Robert F. Kennedy) who spent the summer of 1943 at Exeter, was the model for Phineas. There was even a tree at Exeter from whose branches boys would jump into water, but neither Hackett nor anybody else suffered an injury like Finny's. Knowles, in fact, would insist that "the summer of 1943 at Exeter," when he was almost seventeen, "was as happy a time as I ever had in my life." Additionally, he maintained that "the only elements in *A Separate Peace* which were not in that summer were anger, envy, violence, and hatred. There was only friendship, athleticism, and loyalty."[8] Having Phineas die, becoming another missing buddy of the World War II era, especially to have him dead from friendly fire, admittedly gave the novel a moral complexity it otherwise would not have had. But whether Knowles destroyed his idyll in the way he did solely to give his novel more depth is unclear.

An explanation of Gene's action was by no means all that John Knowles took with him to the grave. Though so silent about the orientation of his own sexuality that he made his friend Gore Vidal seem like Harvey Milk, Knowles never married, and apparently was never publicly known to have had any romantic or sexual interests, male or female. As far as we yet know, he left fewer explicit public clues about his own sexuality than about Gene's and Finny's. What John Knowles did acknowledge was that it was his friend Thornton Wilder, the author most famous for *Our Town* and *The Bridge of San Luis Rey*, who had urged him in the 1950s to write *A Separate Peace* in the first place. A generation older than Knowles, Wilder was also extremely private about his sexuality, though he is widely assumed to have been mostly attracted sexually to other males.[9]

Apparently in the home of John Knowles's boyhood, privacy was a virtue, so much so that his later silence about his sexuality is no surprise. His younger sister Dorothy recalls that while "there was lots of conversation, mostly history, politics, and current events and lots of laughing" at the family dinner table, "there was never personal conversation by anyone of us. I believe we were a very private kind of family with parents and with siblings." To my questions about why she thought he never married, and whether he might, in fact, have been "a very private gay man," Dorothy Knowles Maxwell replied simply that while her brother "was part of a very active social group who lived in our town [Fairmont, West Virginia], mostly made up of boys and girls who went away to prep school and partied when they got home," she nevertheless had "no idea why John never married, he dated a lot." As reticent as was her brother to discuss his "private" life, she added that, "if I were to guess, I would say he was determined to be an author and put his energy toward that goal. He always seemed to have an active social life and met interesting people along the way, but writing was what he wanted and he was fortunate to be allowed to live the life he wanted." And that was that. Dorothy Maxwell considered her brother's succinctness admirable. Of the fact that "he always used one word rather than five," she observed that "I really liked that trait in him, he was never 'wordy' in his books and everyday life." Whether she, and he, were covering something they thought shameful, or were simply choosing not to discuss a matter that they considered no-body's business, is unclear. What seemed utterly unambiguous was Dorothy Max-well's concluding declaration to me that "[A Separate] Peace is special and I think he had a happy life because of it. Needless to say, I loved John, I am very proud of the kind of brother, author and man he was."[10]

Whatever ambiguity might still surround Knowles, however, some recent schol-arship has been unreserved in seeing Gene and Finny as queer lovers and Finny's death as the penalty typically meted out in a society riddled with homophobia. While occasionally insightful, recent readings of A Separate Peace have sometimes had about them an air of presumptuous omniscience that can blithely ignore what an author himself claimed for his work, ignoring as well the historical context within which a cultural product emerged, paying more attention to the cultural workings of the present moment than to those of the past one.[11] And while A Separate Peace has tended to remain a favorite of the generations of students for whom it has been as-signed reading, at least one group of latter-day parents, in a New York school district in 1980, had the book banned as "a filthy, trashy, sex novel" that has "homosexuality as an underlying theme."[12] Additionally, advertisements and theater lobby cards for both of the film versions of A Separate Peace typically showed the actors playing Gene and Finny without their shirts.

For my purposes here, however, what is important—and remarkable—is that crit-ics reviewing A Separate Peace at the time of its publication were as silent about the possibilities of a sexual attraction between Gene and Phineas as John Knowles ap-pears to have remained about his own sexuality throughout his life. Reviews were vague—studiously vague, it seems. So toxic had male affection of any sort appar-ently come to seem by the end of the 1950s that reviewers commonly ignored the pivotal, incontrovertible fact of the story, the profound affection between the novel's main male characters. Like Knowles did about himself, most reviewers kept still.

Just as he had ignored sexuality in reviewing John Horne Burns's A Cry of Children, the New Yorker's Whitney Balliett not only managed to skirt any possible sexual implications of A Separate Peace, he ignored the boys' friendship as well, merely praising Knowles for how accurately he captured the look and feel of Ex-eter, Balliett's own alma mater too. It "is Exeter," he insisted, "down to the last ivy leaf and lights-out time." Donald Yates of the Chicago Tribune was similarly super-ficial and largely descriptive, noting the novel's "delicate, heightened, poetic style," at least recognizing Gene's fondness for Finny yet inexplicably calling Gene Fin-ny's "reluctant worshipper." For Yates, this was essentially a story of competition gone wrong, in "an intense, eventually self-destructive friendship." Granville Hicks skimmed the surface as well in the Saturday Review, simply pointing to the fact that Finny is "the boy who hasn't been corrupted by life" as all the while the cruel war is raging. The unsigned review in Booklist also merely described how "a personal relationship" managed to exist on "a campus increasingly touched by the restiveness of war." More unsigned reviews, in *Bookmark* and *Kirkus*, could address only the "blind impulse" in Gene's moving the branch and the fact that the boys' "close friendship . . . is not unmixed with resentment."[13]

A few reviews actually mentioned the intensity of the friendship. Anne Duchene, for instance, of the *Manchester Guardian*, praised how Knowles had drawn "with tenderness and restraint the pure joy of affection between the boys," yet sounded a cautionary note by pointing to "the hostility latent" in the affection. In the *New York Times Book Review*, Edmund Fuller, a private school English teacher and author of *Man in Modern Fiction*, declared without explanation that Knowles had been "sensitive without being delicate, subtle without being obscure," even adding the distracting point of a supposed "parallel between the impulse that moved Gene and the impulses that move men to war." Simon Raven of the *Spectator* did manage to note that "the quietly told story of the boys' relationship" had "its crises," but said nothing regarding what the crises might have been about. The *San Francisco Chronicle*'s Douglas Aitken was perhaps the vaguest reviewer of all, noting that the boys were "close friends," then adding without explanation that the "interpretation of the messages [of the novel] must be highly subjective, which holds true of all major works of art." The *Christian Century*'s unnamed reviewer praised Knowles for recognizing that "suspicion, jealousy, malice, cruelty can indeed be compatible with heightened sensitivity and self-consciousness," but explained too little of how the novel demonstrated that fact. The unnamed reviewer in *Horn Book Magazine*, which evaluated books for young adults, simply wrote teasingly that "not all readers will catch the allegorical aspect beneath the surface of the story, but it will spark discussion among those who do." For this reviewer, Gene had a "hidden resentment against Finny," simply for being a better man. Jean Holzhauer, a prolific reviewer for *Commonweal*, found Knowles's work just "one more foray into the territory of guilt earned in adolescence," and declared it to not be on a par with *The Catcher in the Rye*, yet provided no evidence for this harsh judgment. And the *New Statesman*'s unnamed reviewer was one of the very few who viewed the novel negatively, finding its story of this "fatal relationship" unconvincing, and yet declaring unconvincingly and with aggravating vagueness that Gene and Finny "interpenetrate and exchange roles with conscientious significance."[14]

The evasiveness that characterized so many reviews was especially apparent in screenwriter and playwright Harding Lemay's piece in the *New York Herald Tribune*. Lemay wrote that *A Separate Peace* possessed "a theme" that he would not explicitly name but "which echoes in every sensitive man's experience." He then proceeded to criticize Knowles for what he himself had just exemplified: "a somewhat cautious approach which insists on gazing from a distance upon the seizing cauldron of adolescent nature." However, Thomas Houlihan, a librarian for the Council on Foreign

Relations writing for the *Library Journal*, did not just gaze from a distance. Calling *A Separate Peace* "an extraordinarily perceptive and sensitive story about the relationship between two 16-year old boys," Houlihan was the singular reviewer from that era who actually noted that Gene and Phineas were in love: "Mr. Knowles has captured the feeling of friendship and love that sometimes develops between adolescent boys, a kinship that is peculiar to the young." This single recognition of what lay at the novel's heart, while not possessing the reassuring evasiveness in other reviews, had a reassurance all its own by defining as inherently temporary the love between the boys, even if both, and not just Gene, had lived.[15] The greater reassurance, of course, was provided by Knowles himself, by removing Phineas from the scene.

The contrast between *A Separate Peace* and another book published the very same year, on the cusp of all the cultural ferment of the 1960s, is suggestive. That other book, Philip Roth's novella *Goodbye, Columbus*, was also a love story, but one that made it unequivocally clear that its youthful main characters, Neil Klugman and Brenda Patimkin, had a sexual relationship even though they were not married, a relationship that was tremendously satisfying to them and surely to most readers.[16] Neil and Brenda encountered serious obstacles in their relationship: their considerable differences in social class and the eroding but still strong cultural opposition to sexual intercourse outside marriage. Their particular relationship indeed could not surmount those barriers, but nobody had to die in the attempt, and readers were intended to sense the tragedy of convention's triumph. Further, it would be only another decade before Roth would publish a novel, *Portnoy's Complaint*, that would be enormously popular, well known for an explicit depiction of heterosexual sex (and male masturbation) that was without precedent in American writing. While of course it was not without its opponents, *Portnoy's Complaint*—in its popularity, even its very appearance—signaled the considerable loosening of cultural constraints regarding sex between males and females. By contrast, that same year of *Portnoy's Complaint*'s publication, the event that best symbolized the plight of same-sex involvements in the nation was no book, but rather the Stonewall Rebellion. Queerness was decades away from affirmation in American popular culture.

The furious opposition that had so often, though not universally, greeted Burns's *Lucifer with a Book* and Vidal's *The City and the Pillar* was not an element of any critical response to *A Separate Peace*. In small part, this was surely related to the simple fact that Knowles's novel was by far the best written of the three. But Knowles also escaped criticism because, a decade later than they, hostility against same-sex love having increased greatly over that period, he was so much less clear than Burns and Vidal in what he was writing about. He placed his characters in the closet, joined them in there, and shut the door.

Notes

Preface

1. John Duffy Ibson, "Will the World Break Your Heart? Dimensions and Consequences of Irish-American Assimilation" (PhD diss., History of American Civilization, Brandeis University, 1976).

2. John Ibson, "Virgin Land or Virgin Mary? Studying the Ethnicity of White Americans," *American Quarterly* 33, no. 3 (Bibliography Issue 1981): 284-308, 306. My dissertation was finally published in 1990, largely unrevised but with a lengthy new preface in which I sought to soften the work's claims and yet demonstrate that some of my interpretations of 1976 had been corroborated by subsequent events and scholarship. See John Duffy Ibson, *Will the World Break Your Heart? Dimensions and Consequences of Irish-American Assimilation* (New York: Garland Publishing, 1990). My approach to the Irish American experience has lately been endorsed by some scholars younger than those whose fierce criticism delayed the work's publication by a decade. See esp. Marian R. Casey, ed., "The Genealogy of Scholarship: An Oral History with Kerby A. Miller, David N. Doyle, and Bruce Boling, March 27, 2003," *Radharc: A Journal of Irish and Irish-American Studies* 5, no. 7 (2004-6), 309-65, esp. 350-51.

3. Ibson, "Masculinity under Fire: *Life*'s Presentation of Camaraderie and Homoeroticism before, during, and after the Second World War," in *Looking at "Life" Magazine*, ed. Erika Doss, 178-99 (Washington, DC: Smithsonian Institution Press, 2001), esp. 192-93.

4. Ibson, *Picturing Men: A Century of Male Relationships in Everyday American Photography* (Washington, DC: Smithsonian Institution Press, 2002; Chicago: University of Chicago Press, 2006), 175, 185-86, 191.

5. Annie Proulx, "Brokeback Mountain," *New Yorker* 73, no. 31 (October 13, 1997): 74-80, 82-85, 76. The screenplay altered Ennis's disclaimer to, "You know I ain't queer." Larry McMurtry and Diana Ossana, "*Brokeback Mountain*, the Screenplay," in Proulx, Larry McMurtry, and Diana Ossana, *Brokeback Mountain: Story to Screenplay* (New York: Scribner, 2005), 29-128, 50.

6. I examined the significance of their 1950s boyhood in "Lessons Learned on Brokeback Mountain: Expanding the Possibilities of American Manhood," in *Reading "Brokeback Mountain": Essays on the Story and the Film*, ed. Jim Stacy, 188-204 (Jefferson, NC: McFarland, 2007), 190-91.

7. William S. Burroughs, *The Letters of William S. Burroughs, 1945-1959* (New York: Viking Penguin, 1993), 298, quoted in Barry Reay, *New York Hustlers: Masculinity and Sex in Modern America* (Manchester and New York: Manchester University Press, 2010), 171. Burroughs was not denying being sexually different, but rather was denouncing those who

seemed to fit the stereotype of effeminacy. On the denial of a homosexual identity by men who nonetheless had sex with men, see Reay, esp. "Conclusion," 234–61.

8. Interview with Gore Vidal, Los Angeles, November 9, 2009. On Vidal's insistence that "homosexual" is only an adjective, and on his utter disdain for the adjective "gay," see, e.g., John Mitzel and Steven Abbott, "The *Fag Rag* Interview," in Gore Vidal, *Sexually Speaking: Collected Sex Writings*, 194–218 (San Francisco: Cleis Press, 1999), 195, 196.

9. Reay, *New York Hustlers*, esp. 234, 253. Other significant studies of postwar American masculinity include, K. A. Cuordileone, *Manhood and American Political Culture in the Cold War* (New York: Routledge, 2004); James Gilbert, *Men in the Middle: Searching for Masculinity in the 1950s* (Chicago: University of Chicago Press, 2005); Michael Messner, *King of the Wild Suburb: A Memoir of Fathers, Sons, and Guns* (Austin, TX: Plain View Press, 2011). For fresh considerations of the postwar period in general, see, e.g., Peter J. Kuznick and James Gilbert, eds., *Rethinking Cold War Culture* (Washington, DC: Smithsonian Books, 2010).

10. George Chauncey, *Gay New York: Gender, Urban Culture, and the Making of the Gay Male World, 1890–1940* (New York: Basic Books, 1994). Also see Jonathan Ned Katz, *The Invention of Heterosexuality* (Boston: Dutton, 1995), and Katz, *Love Stories: Sex between Men before Homosexuality* (Chicago: University of Chicago Press, 2003). For the proposition that distinct identities dependent upon the sex of the person with whom one has sex may actually precede the late nineteenth century, see Thomas A. Foster, *Sex and the Eighteenth-Century Man: Massachusetts and the History of Sexuality in America* (Boston: Beacon Press, 2007), and esp. Richard Godbeer, "The Cry of Sodom: Discourse, Intercourse, and Desire in Colonial New England," *William and Mary Quarterly* 52, no. 2 (1995): 259–86.

11. The most complex and detailed discussion of shifting perceptions of same-sex involvements is still Chauncey's. Also see, e.g., Katz, *Love Stories*; D. Michael Quinn, *Same-Sex Dynamics among Nineteenth-Century Americans: A Mormon Example* (Champaign: University of Illinois Press, 2001); John Donald Gustav Wrathall, *Take the Young Stranger by the Hand: Same-Sex Relations and the YMCA* (Chicago: University of Chicago Press, 2000); Colin R. Johnson, *Just Queer Folks: Gender and Sexuality in Rural America* (Philadelphia: Temple University Press, 2013); and Ibson, *Picturing Men*.

Chapter One

1. Hall defined "proxemics" as "the word I have coined for the interrelated observations and theories of men's use of space as a specialized elaboration of culture." Edward T. Hall, *The Hidden Dimension* (New York: Random House/Anchor Books, 1969; originally published, 1966), 1.

2. As I am using the words here, "vernacular" or "everyday" photography may include images produced by amateurs as well as by professionals who have no critical recognition. Thus there were vernacular or everyday photographs even before there were snapshots at all, with snapshots only emerging with the tremendous democratization of photography brought about by George Eastman's invention and marketing of roll film in 1889.

3. Nancy Martha West, *Kodak and the Lens of Nostalgia* (Charlottesville: University Press of Virginia, 2000).

4. With impressive imagination, as difficult as it is to argue for a negative proposition, Shawn Michelle Smith has recently explored the significance of the unseen in photography. Shawn Michelle Smith, *At the Edge of Sight: Photography and the Unseen* (Durham, NC: Duke University Press, 2013).

5. Erving Goffman, *The Presentation of Self in Everyday Life* (Garden City, NY: Doubleday, 1959).

6. Goffman, *Gender Advertisements* (New York: Harper and Row, 1979).

7. Specifically regarding the performance of gender, a leading figure has been Judith Butler. See, e.g., Butler, *Gender Trouble: Feminism and the Subversion of Identity* (New York: Routledge, 2006); and see also, e.g., Victor Turner, *The Anthropology of Performance* (New York: PAJ Publications, 1988); Richard Schechner, *Between Theater and Anthropology* (Philadelphia: University of Pennsylvania Press, 1985); and esp. Diana Taylor, *The Archive and the Repertoire: Performing Cultural Memory in the Americas* (Durham, NC: Duke University Press, 2003).

8. A catalog of a seminal exhibition is Douglas R. Nickel, *Snapshots: The Photography of Everyday Life, 1888 to the Present* (San Francisco: San Francisco Museum of Modern Art, 1998). See also Thomas Walther, *Other Pictures: Anonymous Photographs from the Thomas Walther Collection* (Santa Fe, NM: Twin Palms Publishers, 2000); Robert Flynn Johnson, *Anonymous: Enigmatic Images from Unknown Photographers* (New York: Thomas and Hudson, 2004). California public libraries have led the way in recognizing the significance of snapshots, preserving either original prints or copies of snapshots gathered from local residents. See Carolyn Kozo Cole and Kathy Kobayashi, *Shades of LA: Pictures from Ethnic Family Albums* (New York: New Press, 1996), and Kimi Kodani Hill, ed., *Shades of California: California's Family Album* (Berkeley, CA: Heyday Books, 2001). The catalog of another important exhibition is D. J. Waldie, *Close to Home: An American Album* (Los Angeles: J. Paul Getty Museum, 2004). Yet another exhibition catalog represents the most substantial recognition to date of the snapshot's importance: Sarah Greenough et al., *The Art of the American Snapshot, 1888-1978: From the Collection of Robert E. Jackson* (Washington, DC, and Princeton, NJ: National Gallery of Art and Princeton University Press, 2007). For a thorough evaluation of the snapshot from the perspective of an imaginative art historian, see Catherine Zuromskis, *Snapshot Photography: The Lives of Images* (Cambridge, MA: MIT Press, 2013). A conventional yet interesting collection of over 350 snapshots, along with a brief but useful text, is Michael Williams, Richard Cahan, and Nicholas Osborn, *Who We Were: A Snapshot History of America* (Chicago: CityFiles Press, 2008).

9. On the "myth of photographic truth," see Marita Sturken and Lisa Cartwright, *Practices of Looking: An Introduction to Visual Culture* (New York: Oxford University Press, 2009), 16-22. As promising as the field of "visual anthropology" sounds, that field typically considers the use of the camera simply as a tool in conducting ethnographic research, not the study of images already produced. See, e.g., John Collier et al., *Visual Anthropology: Photography as a Research Method* (Albuquerque: University of New Mexico Press, 1986).

10. Allan Sekula, "Reading an Archive: Photography between Labour and Capital," in *Visual Culture: The Reader*, ed. Jessica Evans and Stuart Hall, 181-92 (London: Sage Publications, 1999), 181.

11. Nancy Munn, "Visual Categories: An Approach to the Study of Representational Systems," *American Anthropologist* 68, no. 936 (1966), quoted in Richard Chalfen, *Snapshot*

Visions of Life (Bowling Green, OH: Bowling Green State University Popular Press, 1987), 141.

12. Chalfen, *Snapshot Visions*, 98.

13. Marvin Heiferman, *Now Is Then: Snapshots from the Maresca Collection* (New York: Princeton Architectural Press, 2008), 41, 48. The photo-booth photograph should also be considered a type of snapshot. A collection of wonderful photo-booth imagery, along with a valuable interpretive text is Nakki Goranin, *American Photobooth* (New York: W. W. Norton, 2008).

14. Stacey McCarroll Cutshaw and Ross Barrett's *In the Vernacular: Photography of the Everyday* (Boston: Boston University Art Gallery, 2008) is an excellent review of the growing scholarly interest in the genre.

15. Michael Lesy, *Wisconsin Death Trip* (New York: Pantheon Books, 1973). Also see, e.g., Lesy, *Dreamland: America at the Dawn of the Twentieth Century* (New York: New Press, 1997).

16. See, e.g., Sebastien Lifshitz, *The Invisibles: Vintage Portraits of Love and Pride* (New York: Rizzoli, 2013), and David Dreitcher, *Dear Friends: American Photographs of Men Together, 1840–1918* (New York: Harry Abrams, 2001). A wonderfully imaginative use of found photographs as part of a fictional narrative is Ramsom Riggs, *Miss Peregrine's Home for Peculiar Children* (Philadelphia: Quirk Books, 2013).

17. Roger Bennett and Jules Shell, *Camp: Where Fantasy Island Meets Lord of the Flies* (New York: Crown Publishers, 2008); Michael Hurst and Robert Swope, eds., *Casa Susanna* (New York: Powerhouse Books, 2005); Scott Zieher, *Band of Bikers* (New York: Powerhouse Books, 2010); Yvon Chouinard and Steve Pezman, *California Surfing and Climbing in the Fifties* (Santa Barbara, CA: T. Adler Books, 2013); C. R. Stecyk and Don James, *Surfing San Onofre to Point Dume: Photographs by Don James, 1936–1942* (Santa Barbara, CA: T. Adler Books, 2008).

18. Deborah Willis and Barbara Krauthamer, *Envisioning Emancipation: Black Americans and the End of Slavery* (Philadelphia: Temple University Press, 2013). Though short on interpretive text, much more than an arresting string of images is also Catherine Smith and Cynthia Greig, *Women in Pants: Manly Maidens, Cowgirls, and Other Renegades* (New York: Harry Ambrams, 2003).

19. John Ibson, *Picturing Men: A Century of Male Relationships in Everyday American Photography* (Washington, DC: Smithsonian Institution Press, 2002; Chicago: University of Chicago Press, 2006). In that work, I noted that "every photograph that a subject knows is being taken is something of a performance," and I used a theatrical metaphor for titling the chapter in which that remark appeared: "Pageants of Masculinity: Photography as Cultural Performance," 50–75, 51. See also Ibson, "Picturing Boys: Found Photographs and the Transformation of Boyhood in 1950s America," *Thymos: Journal of Boyhood Studies* 1 (Spring 2007): 68–83. On the race of photos' subjects, see Ibson, *Picturing Men*, x, 43–45. In essence, my explanation of the predominant whiteness of subjects in my work's evidence has to do with possible differences among ethnic groups in the extent to which photos were taken in the first place; the race of most photographers in the days when many studio portraits were taken; cultural differences that might prompt persons of color to hold onto the photos of deceased relatives more often than have whites, thus

making photos differentially available to private collectors and archives; and, lastly, the greater collectability nowadays of images of persons of color, reducing the availability and raising the price of such images on internet sales, at in-person vintage photography sales, and at flea markets.

20. Ibson, *Picturing Men*, 2. The literature on contemporary males of all ages and how they deal with intimacy (with each other and with females) is extensive. See, e.g., Sam Keen, *Fire in the Belly: On Being a Man* (New York: Bantam, 1992); Robert Jensen, *Getting Off: Pornography and the End of Masculinity* (Boston: South End Press, 2007); Geoffrey Greif, *Buddy System: Understanding Male Friendships* (New York: Oxford University Press, 2008); Peter F. Murphy, *Studs, Tools, and the Family Jewels: Metaphors Men Live By* (Madison: University of Wisconsin Press, 2001); William Pollack, *Real Boys: Rescuing Our Sons from the Myths of Boyhood* (New York: Henry Holt, 1999); Malina Saval, *The Secret Lives of Boys: Inside the Raw Emotional World of Male Teens* (New York: Basic Books, 2009). Singular in its insights and findings is Niobe Way, *Deep Secrets: Boys' Friendships and the Crisis of Connection* (Cambridge, MA: Harvard University Press, 2013). Studies of the matter's history are much less numerous, but see William Benemann, *Male-Male Intimacy in Early America: Beyond Romantic Friendships* (New York: Harrington Park Press, 2006); Richard Goodbeer, *The Overflowing of Friendship: Love between Men and the Creation of the American Republic* (Baltimore: Johns Hopkins University Press, 2009); Caleb Crain, *American Sympathy: Men, Friendship, and Literature in the New Nation* (New Haven, CT: Yale University Press, 2001); Jonathan Ned Katz, *Love Stories: Sex between Men before Homosexuality* (Chicago: University of Chicago Press, 2001); George Chauncey, *Gay New York: Gender, Urban Culture, and the Making of the Gay Male World* (New York: Basic Books, 1994); and E. Anthony Rotundo, *American Manhood: Transformations in Masculinity from the Revolution to the Modern Era* (New York: Basic Books, 1993).

21. The history of whether—and, if so, why—women were permitted, even encouraged, to have more fluidity in defining themselves sexually and in displaying same-sex affection is beyond my purview here, but the considerable significance of that matter must be noted.

22. On the emergence of the notion that sexuality is oriented, see, e.g., Chauncey, *Gay New York*, and Katz, *The Invention of Heterosexuality* (New York: Penguin Books, 1995). For a compelling contemporary assessment of the notion, see Edward Stein, *The Mismeasure of Desire: The Science, Theory, and Ethics of Sexual Orientation* (New York: Oxford University Press, 1999). On the widespread presence of gay men and lesbians in the armed forces during the Second World War, see Allan Bérubé, *Coming Out under Fire: The History of Gay Men and Women in World War Two* (New York: Free Press, 1990).

23. E. Anthony Rotundo, first to use the term "romantic friendships" in discussing American men, was also the first historian to demonstrate the nineteenth-century pervasiveness of the phenomenon. See his *American Manhood*, esp. chapter 4, "Youth and Male Intimacy," 75–91. My notion that the phenomenon reappeared on a large scale during World War II is at the heart of my interpretation of World War II and its aftermath. See Ibson, *Picturing Men*, chapter 7. In that chapter I also discussed the evidence of sexual activity as one aspect of wartime attachments. For a sample of the emphasis on camaraderie's wartime importance, see, e.g., Stephen E. Ambrose, *Band of Brothers: E Company, 506th*

Regiment, 101ˢᵗ Airborne: From Normandy to Hitler's Eagle's Nest (New York: Touchstone, 2001); Paul Fussell, *Wartime: Understanding and Behavior in the Second World War* (New York: Oxford University Press, 1989); Gerald F. Linderman, *The World within War: America's Combat Experience in World War II* (New York: Free Press, 1997); John C. McManus, *The Deadly Brotherhood: The American Combat Soldier in World War II*. Three of the best memoirs are Douglas Allanbrook, *See Naples: A Memoir of Love, Peace, and War in Italy* (Boston: Houghton Mifflin, 1995); Robert Kotlowitz, *Before Their Time: A Memoir* (New York: Alfred Knopf, 1997); and E. B. Sledge, *With the Old Breed: At Peleliu and Okinawa* (New York: Oxford University Press, 1990).

24. Janice Holt Giles, ed., *The G.I. Journal of Sergeant Giles* (Boston: Houghton Mifflin, 1965), 376–77.

25. Randal C. Archibold, "Before Power Plants, Glory Days at Indian Point; Where Neutrons Now Dance, a Grand Amusement Park Stood on the Hudson," *New York Times* (April 9, 2003), online.

26. *Buddies* album and *My Buddy Book*, personal collection of the author. For additional discussion of the singularity of the buddy phenomenon in World War II, see Ibson, *Picturing Men*, 164–69.

27. On the cohabitation of anti-Communism and homophobia, see David K. Johnson, *The Lavender Scare: The Cold War Persecution of Gay and Lesbians in the Federal Government* (Chicago: University of Chicago Press, 2004); Robert J. Corber, *Homosexuality in Cold War America: Resistance and the Crisis of Masculinity* (Durham, NC: Duke University Press, 1997); and Neil Miller, *Sex-Crime Panic: A Journey into the Paranoid Heart of the 1950s* (Los Angeles: Alyson Books, 2002). For one cotemporary expression of the concern, see Jess Stearn, *The Sixth Man* (New York: Macfadden Books, 1962). On the Second World War's loosening of sexual restraint, see Bérubé, *Coming Out under Fire*; Ibson, *Picturing Men*, chapter 7, "Men Set Free: World War Two and the Shifting Boundaries of Male Association," 158–95. On the difficulties veterans had in adjusting to life in peacetime, see esp. Thomas Childers, *Soldier Home from the War Returning: The Greatest Generation's Troubled Homecoming from World War II* (Boston: Houghton Mifflin Harcourt, 2009). Certain memoirs of 1950s boyhoods challenge the notion that the era was entirely dreary. See esp. Bruce Clayton, *Praying for Base Hits: An American Boyhood* (Columbia: University of Missouri Press, 1998); Bill Bryson, *The Life and Times of the Thunderbolt Kid: A Memoir* (New York: Broadway, 2007).

28. On the era's excessive concern about raising a generation of "sissies," as well as postwar parents' reliance on child-rearing "experts," see, e.g., Elaine Tyler May, *Homeward Bound: American Families in the Cold War Era* (New York: Basic Books, 1999), 129–31, 140–42 .

29. Ibson, *Picturing Men*, chapter 5, "The Evolution of the Team Portrait," 98–117.

30. On the history of the Neptune Ceremony and for photographs of the ritual in earlier times, see Ibson, *Picturing Men*, 87–92, 176–77. Also see Simon Bronner, *Crossing the Line: Violence, Play, and Drama in Naval Equator Traditions* (Amsterdam: Amsterdam University Press, 2006); and William P. Mack and Royal W. Connell, *Naval Ceremonies, Customs, and Traditions* (Annapolis, MD: Naval Institute Press, 1980), 186, 188, 189.

31. On these "pageants" and the props, see Ibson, *Picturing Men*, chapter 3, "Pageants of Masculinity: Photography as Cultural Performance," 50–75, esp. 68–71.

32. In an American Male class of mine, a student who had tended bar for several years once told of how common it was to see male patrons, stopping in for drinks after work, leave an empty barstool between them when they began drinking, only to kick the stool out of the way and move closer to each other after a few drinks.

33. On earlier images of men in drag, see Ibson, *Picturing Men*, 73-75, 134. On the Cuties, see https://www.hakes.com/Auction/ItemDetail/52235/CALIFORNIA-CUTIES-SOFT BALL-TEAM-PHOTO-AND-PENNANT.

34. On my thin appreciation of photography's role in postwar gay male culture, see Ibson, *Picturing Men*, 194.

35. On the nationwide increase in gay spaces during the postwar period, and the increasing popularity of older gathering places like Fire Island, see esp. John Loughery, *The Other Side of Silence: Men's Lives and Gay Identities; A Twentieth-Century History* (New York: Henry Holt, 1998), 175-82. On the postwar increase in political awareness and organization among gay men, see John D'Emilio, *Sexual Politics, Sexual Communities: The Making of a Homosexual Minority in the United States, 1940-1970* (Chicago: University of Chicago Press, 1983).

36. On the severe hostility toward homosexuality during the 1950s, see, e.g., D'Emilio, "The Homosexual Menace: The Politics of Sexuality in Cold War America," in D'Emilio, *Making Trouble: Essays on Gay History, Politics, and the University* (New York: Routledge 1992), 57-73, and Loughery, *The Other Side of Silence*, chapter 9, "The Postwar Scene," 158-82. For an individual story with a tragic end, see Calvin Trillin, *Remembering Denny* (New York: Farrar Straus Giroux, 1993), and for a story of victory, of one man's triumph over the era's psychiatry, see Martin Duberman, *Cures: A Gay Man's Odyssey* (New York: Dutton, 1991).

37. Fredric Wertham, *Seduction of the Innocent* (Port Washington, NY: Kennikat Press, 1954).

38. Author's recollection from his own 1950s boyhood in Des Moines, Iowa.

39. See, e.g., Ibson, *Picturing Men*, 126-27, 129, 132-35, 141-42, 148-49, 152, 154-55.

40. See, e.g., Ibson, *Picturing Men*, 154-55.

41. The first historian to identify and examine a "masculinity crisis" in the late nineteenth century was John Higham, in his influential essay "The Reorientation of American Culture in the 1890s," in *The Origins on Modern Consciousness*, ed. John Weiss, 25-48 (Detroit: Wayne State University Press, 1965). Of the many works that have applied Higham's ideas well, especially valuable are Gail Bederman, *Manliness and Civilization: A Cultural History of Gender and Race in the United States, 1880-1917* (Chicago: University of Chicago Press, 1996), and John Kasson, *Houdini, Tarzan, and the Perfect Man: The White Male Body and the Challenge of Modernity in America* (New York: Hill and Wang, 2002). On the history of summer camps in the United States, see Abigail A. Van Slyck, *A Manufactured Wilderness: Summer Camps and the Shaping of American Youth, 1890-1960* (Minneapolis: University of Minnesota Press, 2010), and Leslie Paris, *Children's Nature: The Rise of the American Summer Camp* (New York: NYU Press, 2010).

42. On Camp Cherry Valley, see https://www.facebook.com/campcherryvalley/info/?tab=overview. On Camp Yukon, see http://www.manta.com/c/mm57grv/camp-yukon-cottages.

43. "Camp Black Point," a large, twelve-page booklet.

44. William H. Whyte, *The Organization Man* (New York: Simon and Schuster, 1956); Vance Packard, *The Status Seekers: An Exploration of Class Behavior in America and the Hidden*

Barriers That Affect You, Your Community, Your Future (New York: D. McKay, 1959); David Reisman, *The Lonely Crowd: A Study of the Changing American Character* (Garden City, NY: Doubleday, 1954).

45. Gore Vidal, *Palimpsest: A Memoir* (New York: Penguin Books, 1995), 37.

Chapter Two

1. David Margolick, *Dreadful: The Short Life and Gay Times of John Horne Burns* (New York: Other Press, 2013). The previous published biography is John Mitzel, *John Horne Burns: An Appreciative Biography* (Dorchester, MA: Manifest Destiny Books, 1974). The dissertation is Mark Travis Bassett, "John Horne Burns: Toward a Critical Biography" (PhD diss., University of Missouri, Columbia, 1985).

2. Tom Burns died of cancer, close to his ninety-fifth birthday, on February 27, 2016.

3. Catherine had eleven pregnancies; her first ended in a miscarriage, and one child was stillborn.

4. My characterizations of Donald Burns are largely based on my interviews with his brother Tom. Donald died at the Veterans' Home in Scarborough, Maine. "Obituaries for August 10, 2006," www.seacoastonline.com/article/20060810/Obituaries.

5. Interview with Thomas D. Burns, Boston, May 27, 2010. All subsequent quotations from Tom Burns are largely from this interview, our first, or from an interview in Boston, January 11, 2011, or from our final interview in Boston and Andover, Massachusetts, April 23, 2012. Quotations from our written correspondence are noted as such.

6. In family photos, snapshots and formal portraits alike, Catherine Burns is a formidable woman. Not heavyset but by no means slight, she was at least as tall as her husband. Family photos, John Horne Burns Collection, Howard Gottlieb Archival Research Center, Boston University. Abbreviated hereafter as JHB Collection, BU.

7. John Horne Burns, "The Creative Writer in the Twentieth Century," typescript, n.d., JHB Collection, BU, 5.

8. Tom Burns reached a summit when, with his close friend Lawrence Levinson, he was a cofounder in 1960 of Burns and Levinson, a law firm that had become so large and potent by the time of my interviews that its five-floor dominance in the large building it occupies on Summer Street was marked by a sizeable plaque set in stone at the building's entrance. Along the way, Tom had exchanged Catholicism for the Episcopal Church and even managed, so he would insist to me, to stop considering himself Irish.

9. John Horne Burns's three published novels are *The Gallery* (New York: Harper and Brothers, 1947); *Lucifer with a Book* (New York: Harper and Brothers, 1949); and *A Cry of Children* (New York: Harper and Brothers, 1952).

10. Robert Manning, "Hemingway in Cuba," *Atlantic*, August 1965, online, pt. 1, 1–8; pt. 2, 1–11. pt. 2, 5.

11. Burns receives but a single sentence in Christopher Bram's survey of gay writing, *Eminent Outlaws: The Gay Writers Who Changed America* (New York: Twelve, 2012), 4. The very designation "gay writer" is a misleadingly narrow description for Burns (and many others), a mistake promoted by the patronizing and tone-deaf subtitle of Margolick's book: *The Short Life and Gay Times of John Horne Burns.*

12. Gore Vidal, "Speaking of Books: John Horne Burns," *New York Times Book Review*, May 30, 1965, BR2, BR22; and John Mitzel and Steven Abbott, "The *Fag Rag* Interview [with Gore Vidal]," in Vidal, *Sexually Speaking: Collected Sex Writings* (San Francisco: Cleis Press, 1999), 194-218, 207, originally published in *Fag Rag* (Winter/Spring 1974).

13. Fredric Warburg, *All Authors Are Equal: The Publishing Life of Fredric Warburg, 1936-1971* (London: Hutchinson and Company, 1973), 129, 133. Burns and Warburg met in the late 1940s and eventually became close friends. When he and Burns first met, Warburg wrote Frank MacGregor of Harpers that he found Burns "personally a most charming man," though "still very young and rather in the stage of regarding the world as his oyster." Fredric Warburg to Frank S. MacGregor, June 14, 1949, in the John Horne Burns Collection, Selected Records of Harper and Brothers, 1909-60, box 6, folder 26, Manuscripts Division, Department of Rare Books and Special Collections, Princeton University. Cited hereafter as JHB Collection, Princeton.

14. "Uncle Dudley," in "All That Matters in the 20th Century," editorial, *Boston Globe*, November 8, 1953, n.p., clipping in JHB Collection, BU. "Uncle Dudley" was the name signed in countless *Globe* editorials, starting in the 1890s. Their usual style was indeed avuncular. According to Louis M. Lyons, the "Uncle Dudley" pieces were usually the work of *Globe* editorial writers Lucien Price and James Powers. Erwin Canham, review of *Newspaper Story: One Hundred Years of the Boston Globe* by Louis M. Lyons, *New England Quarterly* 45, no. 1 (March 1972): 125-27, 125.

15. Untitled "Uncle Dudley" article clipped from the *Boston Globe*, probably by Catherine or Cathleen Burns, n.d., John Horne Burns Collection, BU.

16. James Michener, *The World Is My Home: A Memoir* (New York: Ballantine Publishing Group, 1992), 345, 328.

17. "1999 Symposium Speakers Series—Joseph Heller," *James Jones Literary Society Newsletter* 9, no. 2 (Winter 1999-2000), http://www.jamesjonesliterarysociety.org/vol9-2.HTM.

18. Edward W. Hastings to Harper and Brothers, November 11, 1951, JHB Collection, Princeton, folder 28.

19. "Edward Hastings, Co-Founder of ACT, Dies at 80," *SF Gate*, July 7, 2011, www.sfgate.com; "Recent Alumni Deaths," September/October 2011, www.yalealumnimagazine.com.

20. See, e.g., Herbert Mitang, "Books of the Times," *New York Times*, July 9, 1954, 15; Frederic Morton, "Innocents Abroad," review of *The Facts of Love* by Stanley Baron, *New York Times Book Review*, September 30, 1956, BR 2; Mitang, "Publishing: Once an Australian," *New York Times*, November 26, 1977, 88; Charles J. Rolo, "Four Make a Scenario," review of *The Capri Letters* by Mario Soldati, *New York Times Book Review*, February 12, 1956, BR4; Mark Slonim, "The Roman Education of Jimmy," review of *Tempo di Roma* by Alexis Curvers, *New York Times Book Review*, June 7,1959, BR 5; Jon Saaric, "Arguing the Nobel Prize," Letters to the Editor, *New York Times*, October 28, 1984, online.

21. Bassett, "John Horne Burns: Toward a Critical Biography," 265.

22. Frank S. MacGregor to Robert Lichello, August 31, 1953, in the JHB Collection, Princeton, folder 31.

23. Warburg, *All Authors Are Equal*, 129.

24. Kenji Yoshino, *Covering: The Hidden Assault on Our Civil Rights* (New York: Random House, 2006).

25. Vidal, "John Horne Burns," 343.

26. Mitzel, *John Horne Burns: An Appreciative Biography*, 46, 47. Not averse to disclosure himself, Mitzel observed and wondered: "There are men alive today [in 1974, in Boston] who knew JHB sexually. Have I slept with any of them?" (16). Mitzel held that, Burns's evasions aside, "everyone who cared to know knew" Burns was gay (82). An early gay rights activist and owner for many years of Boston's Calamus Book Store, which stayed open long after small gay book stores in cities like New York and San Francisco had closed, Mitzel died of cancer at sixty-five in 2013. See "Writer and LGBT Bookstore Owner John Mitzel, 65, Has Died," http://www.lambdaliterary.org/features/rem/10/05/writer-and-lgbt-bookstore-owner-john-mitzel-65-has-died/.

27. Warburg, *All Authors Are Equal*, 128.

28. Margolick, *Dreadful: The Short Life and Gay Times of John Horne Burns*, 199.

29. Margolick, 207.

30. JHB to John S. Fischer, September 20, 1947, in the JHB Collection, Princeton, folder 21. Elizabeth Wilson Fischer's Scottish nationality is noted in "Guide to John Sylvester Fischer Papers," MS 850, Yale University Library, drs.library.yale.edu:8083.

31. Warburg, *All Authors Are Equal*, 128.

32. "*Holiday* By-Lines: John Horne Burns, Author of *The Gallery*, Writes First Series of Magazine Articles for *Holiday*," *Holiday* 5, no. 2 (February 1949): 32.

33. JHB to Ramona Herdman, November 22, 1948, JHB Collection, Princeton, folder 23.

34. Quoted in Margolick, *Dreadful: The Short Life and Gay Times of John Horne Burns*, 245.

35. JHB to Frank S. MacGregor, January 6, 1949, JHB Collection, Princeton, folder 24.

36. JHB to David MacMackin, May 29, 1942, in Bassett, "John Horne Burns: Toward a Critical Biography," 111–12; Margolick, *Dreadful: The Short Life and Gay Times of John Horne Burns*, 62–63. Of MacMackin's increasingly sad adult life before his 1993 death at sixty-eight, see Margolick, 371–72.

37. JHB to David MacMackin, June 28, 1945, in Bassett, "John Horne Burns: Toward a Critical Biography," 112.

38. Margolick, *Dreadful: The Short Life and Gay Times of John Horne Burns*, 157, 175.

39. JHB to Ramona Herdman, November 22, 1948, JHB Collection, Princeton, folder 23.

40. Eloise Perry Hazard, "John Horne Burns," *Saturday Review of Literature*, February 14, 1948, 7.

41. Quoted in Mitzel, *John Horne Burns: An Appreciative Biography*, 36.

42. An early passage in *The Gallery*, quoted by Paul Fussell in his introduction to a recent edition of *The Gallery* (New York: New York Review Books, 2004), vii–xi, vii.

43. See, e.g., JHB to Catherine Burns, March 9, 1944, JHB Collection, BU, "Wartime Correspondence" folders. One letter described Jack's wartime meeting with his brother Tom, the same meeting Tom described to me. Citing Tom's prodigious consumption of brandy while telling Jack's coworkers of "his adventures off the coast of France on his LCI," Jack noted that "all thought him quite nobly mad in the best Burns tradition." JHB to Catherine Burns, September 14, 1944, JHB Collection, BU, "War Correspondence." Unless otherwise noted, all of JHB's quoted wartime correspondence is from this location.

44. Quoted in Margolick, *Dreadful: The Short Life and Gay Times of John Horne Burns*, 98.

45. JHB to David MacMackin, May 9, 1942, quoted in Bassett, "John Horne Burns: Toward a Critical Biography," 109.

46. JHB to Joseph Burns Sr., July 29, 1945; JHB to Catherine Burns, December 14, 1943; JHB to Joseph Burns Sr., November 14, 1943. By no means did Burns's expressions of self-importance vanish during the war. He once wrote his mother that "I can't make up my mind whether I'm just a petty misanthrope or a reformer with a mind comparable to Jesus Christ." JHB to Catherine Burns, February 4, 1944.

47. JHB to Catherine Burns, January 3, 1944. Having lost their Andover home during the Depression, Burns's parents had had to move to a flat in downtown Boston, hence the reference to 89 Gainsboro.

48. Quoted in Margolick, *Dreadful: The Short Life and Gay Times of John Horne Burns*, 73.

49. Quoted in Margolick, 157.

50. JHB to Catherine Burns, July 14, 1945.

51. Margolick, *Dreadful: The Short Life and Gay Times of John Horne Burns*, 62.

52. JHB to David MacMackin, May 9, 1943, quoted in Bassett, "John Horne Burns: Toward a Critical Biography," 122; January 1, 1943, quoted in Bassett, 151; September 12, 1944, quoted in Bassett, 160.

53. JHB to Joseph Burns Sr., quoted in Margolick, *Dreadful: The Short Life and Gay Times of John Horne Burns*, 150. Mario is mentioned in Margolick, 173.

54. JHB to Cathleen Burns, October 19, 1942. Peter Paul O'Mara's novel was serialized in *Redbook*, beginning with the July 1942 issue. O'Mara's hometown paper, the *Saint Petersburg (Florida) Times*, reported that his work had begun to appear in *Redbook*, as the magazine's "rising young scribe"; the wedding ring Burns saw was from when O'Mara "was married here several months ago to Marjorie Kemp, a member of the *Times* staff." "City of Women," *Saint Petersburg Times*, May 31, 1942, 2.

55. JHB to Catherine Burns, November 1, 1944; February 21, 1944; September 7, 1943; December 30, 1943; January 17, 1944.

56. JHB to Cathleen Burns, April 25, 1945.

57. JHB to Catherine Burns, February 21, 1944; January 20, 1944; February 2, 1944; September 24, 1943; March 21, 1944.

58. JHB to Catherine Burns, November 30, 1943; December 4, 1943; September 14, 1943; January 13, 1944; September 1, 1945.

59. JHB to Catherine Burns, February 19, 1944; July 7, 1944, October 31, 1944; September 12, 1945.

60. Hazard, "John Horne Burns," 7.

61. JHB to Catherine Burns, August 16, 1945.

62. Galleria Umberto I, http://www.naplesldm.com/galumb.html.

63. JHB to David MacMackin, n.d., quoted in Bassett, "John Horne Burns: Toward a Critical Biography," 154.

64. Quoted in Bassett, 166.

65. JHB to Catherine Burns, March 24, 1944; March 25, 1944

66. JHB to Joseph Burns Sr., November 5, 1943; December 5, 1943.

67. JHB to Joseph Burns Sr., March 5, 1944; September 10, 1944; July 16, 1945.

68. JHB to Catherine Burns, July 10, 1944; May 11, 1945; June 1, 1945.

69. JHB to Holger Hagen, n.d., quoted in Margolick, *Dreadful: The Short Life and Gay Times of John Horne Burns*, 181.

70. Bassett, "John Horne Burns: Toward a Critical Biography," 251–52; Roslyn Rosenberg to Frank MacGregor, November 19, 1946, JHB Collection, Princeton, folder 19. Before he signed with Harpers, Burns wrote his father from Loomis, "I expect to sign a fabulous contract sometime this week or the next. At present the Vanguard Press, Harpers, and the Viking Press are all competing for my manuscript." JHB to Joseph Burns Sr., October 10, 1946, JHB Collection, BU, "Fan Letters and Other Epistolary Matters Re: *The Gallery*." Mitzel, *John Horne Burns: An Appreciative Biography*, 39. Harpers executive John S. Fischer was enthusiastic in reporting early sales figures to Burns. John S. Fischer to JHB, September 18, 1947; September 25, 1947, JHB Collection, Princeton, folder 21.

71. JHB to Frank MacGregor, March 1, 1947; February 3, 1947, JHB Collection, Princeton, folder 20, folder 19.

72. Norman Mailer, *The Naked and the Dead* (New York: Rinehart, 1948).

73. No less a figure than Edmund Wilson recommended *The Gallery* to Fredric Warburg, the book's eventual British publisher, who thought it "an extraordinary work" for which he had "immense admiration." Warburg, *All Authors Are Equal*, 129, 127; Fredric Warburg to (Harpers board chairman) Cass Canfield, November 27, 1947, JHB Collection, Princeton, folder 21.

74. Harrison Smith, "Thirteen Adventurers: A Study of a Year of First Novelists," *Saturday Review of Literature* 31, no. 7 (February 14, 1948): 6–8, 7.

75. Ramona Herdman to Frank MacGregor, December 13, 1948, JHB Collection, Princeton, folder 23.

76. John Dos Passos to Harpers Editorial Department, June 13, 1947, JHB Collection, Princeton, folder 21.

77. Lilo Juan Daves to JHB, June 2, 1947, JHB Collection, BU, "Fan Letters and Other Epistolary Matters Re: *The Gallery*"; Helen T. Arnold to JHB, May 14, 1947; Marie Whitbeck Clark to Harper and Company, January 10, 1948, JHB Collection, Princeton, folder 20, folder 22; Jim Tuck to JHB, September 2, 1947, JHB Collection, BU, "Fan Letters and Other Epistolary Matters Re: *The Gallery*"; Mary Squire Abbot to Evan Thomas (regarding the letter from Hobart Skidmore), June 24, 1948; Kenneth B. Marcom to Harpers, October 5, 1948, JHB Collection, Princeton, folders 22 and 23.

78. William Hogan, "A First Novel on Warped War Centers of Europe," review of *The Gallery*, *San Francisco Chronicle*, June 29, 1947, 10.

79. *New York Times* online obituary for William Hogan, February 24, 1996.

80. Unsigned review of *The Gallery*, *Times Literary Supplement*, July 24, 1948, 413.

81. Lawrence Grant White, "Portraits and Promenades," review of *The Gallery*, *Saturday Review of Literature*, July 19, 1947, 21. Other brief references to Momma's in reviews of *The Gallery* are Richard Sullivan, "Under the Shattered Roof of an Italian Galleria," *New York Times Book Review*, June 8, 1947, 7, 25; John Hallock, "Psychology of Total War," clipping with place of publication not shown, JHB Collection, BU, scrapbook, n.p.

82. For other reviews of *The Gallery*, see, e.g., unsigned review, *Kirkus Reviews*, March 1, 1947, 137; Charles Poore, untitled review, *New York Times*, June 7, 1947, 11; Richard Sullivan, "Under the Shattered Roof of an Italian Galleria," *New York Times Book Review*, June 8, 1947, 7, 25; John Hallock, "Psychology of Total War," clipping with place of publication not shown, JHB Collection, BU, scrapbook, n.p.; John F. Huth, "Ex-G.I. Describes

'War' among His Buddies in Naples," *Cleveland Plain Dealer*, June 8, 1947, 15B; John Far-relly, untitled review, *New Republic*, July 7, 1947, n.p.; William McFee, untitled review, *New York Sun*, July 9, 1947, 21.

83. Edmund Wilson, "The Americans in Italy: 'The Gallery,'" review of *The Gallery*, *New Yorker*, August 9, 1947, 60–62. Other affirmative reviews of *The Gallery* include Gerald D. Roscoe, "The Riddle of Life: Andover Young Author's Book Reveals One of the Finest Talents," *Boston Globe*, June 4, 1947, n.p.; Thomas E. J. Kenna, "Literature of Disillusion," *Hartford Courant Magazine*, June 8, 1947, 12; Jerome D. Ross, "From a War-Torn Naples," *New York Herald Tribune Weekly Book Review*, June 8, 1947, 3; "Homage to Naples," un-signed review, *Time*, June 9, 1947, 110; Anna C. Hunter, untitled review, *Savannah Morning News*, July 27, 1947, 26. See also Robert Halsband, "Victors and Vanquished: Nine Members of Motley Crowd in Postwar Naples," *Chicago Sun Book Week*, August 3, 1947, 8.

84. The indispensable work on this topic is still Allan Bérubé, *Coming Out under Fire: The History of Gay Men and Women in World War Two* (New York: Free Press, 1990).

85. *Gallery*, 133.

86. See esp. Bérubé, *Coming Out under Fire*, 142–43.

87. Margolick, *Dreadful: The Short Life and Gay Times of John Horne Burns*, 188–89.

88. *Gallery*, 130, 134–35, 149, 141, 151, 183, 144–45.

89. *Gallery*, 259, 338, 303, 304, 305.

90. *Gallery*, 99, 16, 4, 20, 306, 307.

Chapter Three

1.   A superb study of certain facets of the "troubled homecoming" of returning veterans is Thomas Childers, *Soldier from the War Returning: The Greatest Generation's Troubled Homecoming from World War II* (Boston: Houghton Mifflin Harcourt, 2009).

2.   JHB to Joseph Burns Sr., October 10, 1946, JHB Collection, BU.

3.   Letters to the Editor, *New York Times Book Review*, June 20, 1965, BR29. See also "John H. Burns," obituary, *Hartford Courant*, n.d., n.p., clipping in the JHB Collection, BU.

4.   Mark Travis Bassett, "John Horne Burns: Toward a Critical Biography" (PhD diss., University of Missouri, Columbia, 1985), 88–89, 122.

5.   David L. Goodrich, *My Well-Spent Youth: A Lucky Man's 1930-1960 New York-to-Paris Memoir* (Silver Spring, MD: Beckham Publications, 2009), 107, 108, 110, 106–7, 115.

6.   Bassett, "John Horne Burns: Toward a Critical Biography," 86.

7.   Back issues of the Loomis *Log*, Loomis Chaffee School Archives, Windsor, CT.

8.   Goodrich, *My Well-Spent Youth*, 115.

9.   David Margolick, *Dreadful: The Short Life and Gay Times of John Horne Burns* (New York: Other Press, 2013), 44.

10. Alfred Duhrrsen, *Memoir of an Aged Child* (New York: Holt, Rinehart, and Winston, 1967), 121–22, 125.

11. Loomis *Log*, October 10, 1947.

12. The story is told in Margolick, *Dreadful: The Short Life and Gay Times of John Horne Burns*, 42.

13. Paul F. Kneeland, "'Born Snob,' John Horne Burns Turned Down Hollywood Gold," *Boston Globe*, December 11, 1947, n.p., clipping JHB Collection, BU, scrapbook.

14. Stephen J. Whitfield, "Laughter in the Dark: Notes on American-Jewish Humor," *Midstream*, February 1978, 48–58, 58.

15. At Burns's behest, Harpers executive Cass Canfield wrote his friend Royden Dangerfield a "Dear Roy" recommendation for Burns for an English department position at the University of Oklahoma. Dangerfield was administrative assistant to the university's president. Cass Canfield to Royden Dangerfield, July 21, 1947, JHB Collection, Princeton, folder 21.

16. Kneeland, "'Born Snob.'"

17. Quoted in Margolick, *Dreadful: The Short Life and Gay Times of John Horne Burns*, 287.

18. Thomas D. Burns to the author, March 25, 2011.

19. "Lucifer with a Book," Loomis *Log*, April 22, 1949, 2.

20. L. W. Fowles, "The Harvest of Our Lives: The History of the First Half-Century of the Loomis Institute," a special issue of *Loomis Bulletin* 32, no. 3 (March 1964): 96. There was less at stake in *Lucifer*'s public memory at Phillips Academy; though Burns had attended prep school there, the novel seemed much more likely to have been based on Loomis. When the *Phillipian*, the Phillips Academy student newspaper, reported that Burns's parents had established an annual short-story prize in their son's memory in 1961, the paper merely noted that his "less successful" *Lucifer* was "a story of boarding school life," a subject that Burns was "well qualified to write . . . both from his days as a student here and from his six years as a teacher at Loomis." "New Prize for Short Story Instituted by Joseph Burns," *Phillipian*, October 3, 1961, 1, JHB Collection, Phillips Academy Archives, Andover, MA.

21. John G. Clark, "John Horne Burns: 'No Apples for Teacher,'" *Loomis Chaffee: The Magazine*, Winter 2003, Loomis Chaffee School Archives. The identical title, "No Apples for Teacher," had been used in a 1949 review of *Lucifer* in the *New York Times Book Review*. See note 51 below.

22. On his well-developed pedagogy, see JHB, "A Word with the Teacher of English," *English Leaflet* 47 (February, 1948): 17–24, 18, 19, 21.

23. JHB to Rose Orente, April 21, 1949, quoted in Bassett, "John Horne Burns: Toward a Critical Biography," 32.

24. Robert Phelps, with Jerry Rosco, eds., *Continual Lessons: The Journals of Glenway Wescott, 1937–1955* (New York: Farrar Straus Giroux, 1990), 214.

25. James Michener, *The World Is My Home: A Memoir* (New York: Ballantine Publishing Group, 1992), 344. A considerably less secure person than Michener, Burns unwisely had agreed to review *The Fires of Spring*, and the resulting review reveals less about the book than about Burns's resentment over losing the Pulitzer to Michener. JHB, "Adventurer in Life," review of *The Fires of Spring*, *Saturday Review of Literature*, February 12, 1949, 16.

26. On this passage from the *Inferno*, see Michael Camille, chapter 3, "The Pose of the Queer: Dante's Gaze, Brunetto Latini's Body," in *Queering the Middle Ages*, ed. Glenn Burger and Steven F. Kruger, 57–86 (Minneapolis: University of Minnesota Press, 2001).

27. MacMackin's adult life appears to have been a sad one, his memories of Burns bitter. See Margolick, *Dreadful: The Short Life and Gay Times of John Horne Burns*, 371–72.

28. JHB, *Lucifer with a Book* (New York: Harper and Brothers, 1949), 27, 128, 48–49, 46.

29. On the unconvincing relationship between Hudson and Blanchard, see, e.g., *Lucifer*, 274–75, 340.

30. Margolick, *Dreadful: The Short Life and Gay Times of John Horne Burns*, devotes 251–97 to *Lucifer*, yet Ralph appears in only two paragraphs, on 257–58.

31. *Lucifer*, 84, 85, 132–33.

32. On the trope in film, e.g., see Vita Russo, *The Celluloid Closet: Homosexuality in the Movies*, rev. ed. (New York: Harper and Row, 1987), 50, 84.

33. *Lucifer*, 287, 84.

34. *Lucifer*, 104, 118.

35. *Lucifer*, 47–48.

36. *Lucifer*, 185–86.

37. *Lucifer*, 42, 43, 50, 92.

38. *Lucifer*, 111–12, 131.

39. *Lucifer*, 279.

40. *Lucifer*, 192, 194, 195–96, 197, 281.

41. *Lucifer*, 280.

42. Philip Wylie, *Generation of Vipers* (New York: Rinehart, 1942).

43. *Lucifer*, 55–56.

44. Wylie, *Vipers*, 60–61.

45. M. H. Koenig to Harper and Brothers, August 25, 1949; Frank S. MacGregor to M. H. Koenig, September 2, 1949; Keonig to MacGregor, September 15, 1949, JHB Collection, Princeton, folder 26. Margolick quotes a little from Koenig, calling her simply "a doctor from Albany," erroneously identifying her as a man. Margolick, *Dreadful: The Short Life and Gay Times of John Horne Burns*, 291. Her full name and her identification with the Divine Metaphysical Science Church are in Albany city directories citied on ancestry.com.

46. Robert C. Barr to Orville Prescott (cc to Harper and Brothers), August 24, 1949, JHB Collection, Princeton, folder 36; Frank S. MacGregor to Robert C. Barr, September 2, 1949, JHB Collection, Princeton, folder 26. Barr's occupation as a publicist was noted in the 1930 US census and in the New Canaan city directory cited on ancestry.com.

47. E. D. Toland to Martha Nicholas (cc to Frank MacGregor), June 14, 1949, JHB Collection, Princeton, folder 26; E. D. Toland to Frank MacGregor, March 10, 1950, JHB Collection, Princeton, folder 27. In the margin of the letter, someone, presumably MacGregor, wrote, "Send same letter as sent to Mr. Barr attached." There then is a note in the folder accompanying the correspondence, directing that someone adapt the letter to Barr to Toland, "ignoring the questions." Toland was not one to give up easily. There is yet another long diatribe to MacGregor, dated March 18, 1950, in folder 27. There was a similar exchange between MacGregor and Katherine H. Swan of Vermont: Katherine H. Swan to Harper Brothers, April 16, 1949; Frank S. MacGregor to Katherine H. Swan, April 29, 1949, JHB Collection, Princeton, folder 26.

48. A. L. Johnsonius to Harper and Brothers, n.d., JHB Collection, Princeton, folder 26.

49. *1940 U.S. Federal Census*; *U.S. World War I Draft Registration Cards, 1917–1918*; *Find a Grave Index, 1777–2012*, all on ancestry.com. Another interesting reader's response to *Lucifer* is contained in a "Headmaster's File" on Burns that apparently was kept by Andover's new man in charge (since 1948), John M. Kemper. Eleanor Read Richards to

James R. Adriance (Andover's Admissions Officer), April 30, 1949; James R. Adriance to Eleanor Read Richards, May 11, 1949; JHB to Eleanor Read Richards, July 27, 1949, in "Headmaster's File," JHB Collection, Phillips Academy Archives. David Margolick fails to note Richards's praise of Andover, and characterizes her letter entirely as an expression of concern. Margolick, *Dreadful: The Short Life and Gay Times of John Horne Burns*, 293.

50. For Margolick's treatment of *Lucifer with a Book* and its critics, see Margolick, *Dreadful: The Short Life and Gay Times of John Horne Burns*, chapter 24, 275–88, and chapter 25, 289–97.

51. Unsigned review of *Lucifer with a Book*, *Atlantic Monthly*, April 1949, 89; R. D. Charques, review of *Lucifer with a Book*, *Spectator*, November 4, 1949, 616; for other reviews of *Lucifer*, also see unsigned review, *Kirkus Reviews* 17 (February 1, 1949), 66; William DuBois, "No Apples for Teacher," *New York Times Book Review*, April 3, 1949, BR4; unsigned review, *Altoona Mirror*, April 28, 1949, 17; unsigned review, *Catholic World* 169 (June 1949): 240; "Burns' Novel Is Portrait of Private School," unsigned review, *European Stars and Stripes*, July 10, 1949, 8; unsigned review, *Times Literary Supplement*, November 4, 1949, 709.

52. Hiram Haydn, "Satire Turns to Burlesque," review of *Lucifer with a Book*, *New York Herald Tribune Weekly Book Review*, April 3, 1949, 4; Orville Prescott, review of *Lucifer with a Book*, *New York Times*, April 1, 1949, n.p.

53. Theodore Kalem, "The Case of the Angry Novelist," review of *Lucifer with a Book*, *Christian Science Monitor*, April 28, 1949, 15.

54. Antonia White, review of *Lucifer with a Book*, *New Statesman and Nation*, November 5, 1949, 520; Steele Lindsay, "John H. Burns' Second Novel Bears Out His Earlier Promise," review of *Lucifer with a Book*, *Boston Post*, n.d., n.p.

55. Virginia Vaughn, review of *Lucifer with a Book*, *Commonweal*, April 29, 1949, 76–77; Ernest Dewey, "Not So Pretty Picture Painted of Conditions in Private School," review of *Lucifer with a Book*, *Hutchinson (Kansas) News Herald*, April 13, 1949, 6. See also John Broderick, review of *Lucifer with a Book*, *New Yorker*, April 16, 1949, 109.

56. See Colin R. Johnson, *Just Queer Folks: Gender and Sexuality in Rural America* (Philadelphia: Temple University Press, 2013).

57. Ben and Estelle Atkins, review of *Lucifer with a Book*, *Gaston (NC) Gazette*, April 23, 1949, 24; Marian Orgain, review of *Lucifer with a Book*, *Pacific Stars and Stripes*, June 18, 1949, 21. For other reviews of *Lucifer*, see also Gerald D. Roscoe, "Burns Tells Us," *Boston Globe*, n.d., n.p.; Donald Wasson, *Library Journal* 73 (March 15, 1949): 494; E. K. Brown, "Embattled Teachers: A Novel of Protest," *Winnipeg Free Press*, May 28, 1949, 12.

58. Maxwell Geismer, "Puritanism, Evil, and Malice," review of *Lucifer with a Book*, *Saturday Review of Literature*, April 2, 1949, 16; Victor P. Hass, "Prep School Sketched in an Acid Vein," review of *Lucifer with a Book*, *Chicago Tribune*, April 10, 1949, n.p.; see also Hass, *Leaves from a Bookman's Notebook* (Omaha, NE: Omaha World Herald, 1972), and "Looking Homeward: A Memoir of Small-Town Life in Wisconsin," *Wisconsin Magazine of History* 65, no. 3 (1981–82): 176–94; Frank Brookhouser, "Private Schools Satirized," review of *Lucifer with a Book*, *Philadelphia Inquirer*, April 3, 1949, 3; see also Brookhouser, *Our Philadelphia: A Candid and Colorful Portrait of a Great City* (Garden City, NY: Doubleday, 1957).

59. JHB to John S. Fischer, October 23, 1947, JHB Collection, Princeton, file 21.

60. John W. Aldridge, "The New Generation of Writers," *Harper's*, November 1947, 423–32, 432.

61. Aldridge, *After the Lost Generation: A Critical Study of the Writers of Two Wars* (New York: Arbor House, 1985; originally published, 1951), 142–43, 101, 105.

62. Aldridge, 142–43, 101–2, 100–101.

63. Margolick, *Dreadful: The Short Life and Gay Times of John Horne Burns*, 335.

64. JHB, untitled biographical sketch, JHB Collection, BU.

65. JHB, "Casablanca," *Holiday*, January 1949, 64–70, 130–31; "Algiers," *Holiday*, February 1949, 64–70, 131–34; "Tunis," *Holiday*, March 1949, 64–70, 122–24; "Naples," *Holiday*, May 1949, 64–70, 154–56; "Roman Family," *Holiday*, June 1949, 64–70, 132–34; "Tourist Washington," *Holiday*, February 1950, 102–13; "Andover," *Holiday*, March 1950, 56–61, 128–31; "Brighton," *Holiday*, September 1950, 52–55, 85–87; "Where the River Shannon Flows," *Holiday*, April 1951, 98–105, 139–46; "Belfast," *Holiday*, January 1952, 48–51; 85–87; "Florence," *Holiday*, October 1952, 44–47, 122–31. Margolick erroneously says that "there were eventually nine of the *Holiday* pieces"; there were eleven. Margolick, *Dreadful: The Short Life and Gay Times of John Horne Burns*, 267.

66. JHB, "Andover," 56, 128, 129; "Florence," 47, 129. The other use of *topolini*, in reference to young Italian men, is in JHB to Gore Vidal, March 18, 1948, in the Gore Vidal Papers, MS Am 2350, Series II, #1038, Correspondence, Houghton Library, Harvard College Library, Cambridge, MA.

67. Frank S. MacGregor to JHB, October 30, 1951, JHB Collection, Princeton, folder 28; Warburg, *All Authors Are Equal*, 130; JHB to Helen Strauss, October 1, 1951, JHB Collection, Princeton, folder 28; Frank S. MacGregor to JHB, American Cable and Radio System, March 10, 1952, JHB Collection, Princeton, folder 29; JHB to Frank S. MacGregor, March 18, 1952, May 21, 1952, JHB Collection, Princeton, folder 29; Warburg quoted in Mitzel, *John Horne Burns: An Appreciative Biography*, 117; Warburg, *All Authors Are Equal*, 130.

68. JHB Collection, Princeton, folder 29; Warburg, *All Authors Are Equal*, 129.

69. JHB, *A Cry of Children* (New York: Harper and Brothers, 1952).

70. *Children*, 17, 67, 192–93, 193.

71. *Children*, 192.

72. *Children*, 196.

73. *Children*, 213.

74. *Children*, 162.

75. *Children*, 143.

76. Margolick's unusually superficial treatment of *A Cry of Children* is chapter 29 of *Dreadful: The Short Life and Gay Times of John Horne Burns*, 318–34. As he had barely explored the relationship between Guy and Ralph in *Lucifer*, Margolick also shies away from examining in any detail the relationship between David and Fred.

77. William Weaver to Frank S. MacGregor, September 2, 1952, JHB Collection, Princeton, folder 30.

78. William Juengst, "'A Cry of Children' Mirrors Our Nylon-and-Zippered Era," review of *A Cry of Children*, *Brooklyn Eagle*, September 7, 1952, 19; Florence Haxton Bullock, "Love Affair as Battle," review of *A Cry of Children*, *New York Herald Tribune Book Review*,

September 7, 1952, 6; Charles White McGehee, "Man's Struggle for Art and Love," review of *A Cry of Children*, *Birmingham News*, September 7, 1952, E-6; information on McGehee from papers relating to an essay by McGehee on Minot Judson Savage, Andover-Harvard Theological Library, Harvard Divinity School, bMS 469, online; James Kelly, "No Way Out," review of *A Cry of Children*, *New York Times Book Review*, September 7, 1952, BR4.

79. Unsigned review of *A Cry of Children*, *Kirkus Reviews*, July 1, 1952, 381–82; for other reviews of *Children*, see also James Gray, "Omnibus of Depravity," *Saturday Review*, September 13, 1952, 23, 39; Whitney Balliett, "The Manic Moan," *New Republic*, September 15, 1952, 22; on Balliett, see Ben Ratliff, "Whitney Balliett, *New Yorker* Jazz Critic, Dies at 80," obituary, *New York Times*, February 3, 2007, online; Victor P. Hass, "Mr. Burns Should Raise His Sights above the Gutter," *Chicago Tribune*, September 21, 1952, n.p.; Charles S. Rolo, untitled review, *Atlantic Monthly*, October 1952, 104; R. D. Charques, untitled review, *Spectator*, October 31, 1952, 580; unsigned review, *Times Literary Supplement*, November 14, 1952, 737; Anthony Curtis, untitled review, *New Statesman and Nation*, November 29, 1952, 656.

80. Doris Grumbach, "Alas! Alack!," review of *A Cry of Children*, *Books on Trial*, November 11, 1952, 62; John A. Lynch, "Not without a Bang," review of *A Cry of Children*, *Commonweal*, October 3, 1952, 633–34.

81. Brendan Gill, review of *A Cry of Children*, *New Yorker* 28 (September 6, 1952): 104–5.

82. JHB to Frank S. MacGregor, January 11, 1953, JHB Collection, Princeton, folder 31.

83. See, e.g., "John Horne Burns, Novelist, 36, Dies," obituary, *New York Times*, August 14, 1953, online; "Body of Author to Arrive Today," *Boston Herald*, September 2, 1953, n.p.; "John H. Burns," obituary, *Boston Globe*, August 14, 1953, n.p.; "John Horne Burns Dies, Author of 'The Gallery,'" obituary, *New York Herald Tribune*, August 14, 1953, n.p. All are clippings, pagination removed, JHB Collection, BU.

84. Paul Fussell, introduction to *The Gallery* (New York: New York Review of Books, 2004), vii–xi, x; Bassett, "John Horne Burns: Toward a Critical Biography," 263.

85. Margolick, *Dreadful: The Short Life and Gay Times of John Horne Burns*, 321.

86. Scrapbook, JHB Collection, BU, n.p.

87. Daniel H. Edgerton, "The Ambiguous Heroes of John Horne Burns," *ONE* 1, no. 10 (October 1958): 6–12, 9, 10–11. See also John P. Diggins, "The American Writer, Fascism, and the Liberation of Italy," *American Quarterly* 18 (Winter 1966): 599–614; William Zinsser, "*The Gallery* Revisited," *Sewanee Review* 100, no. 1 (Winter 1992): 105–12, 109. Also see Zinsser, "No Second Act: John Horne Burns and *The Gallery*," Zinsser on Friday, *American Scholar* online, February 4, 2010.

88. Vidal, "John Horne Burns," BR 2.

89. JHB, "The Creative Writer in the Twentieth Century," typescript, n.d., JHB Collection, BU, 1.

Chapter Four

1. Auster was Howard's original name, later changed to Austen, reportedly at Vidal's urging, to sound less Jewish and thereby enhance Howard's chances for employment in the 1950s. Both of Vidal's major biographers, Fred Kaplan and Jay Parini, in their works cited

below, use "Austen." Vidal used "Austen" in his first memoir, cited below, and, perhaps in some spirit of restoration, used "Auster" in his later one, also cited below. I use the original name, "Auster."

2. Interview with Gore Vidal, Los Angeles, November 9, 2009. Following Buckley's calling Vidal a "queer" during their televised "debates" during ABC's coverage of the 1968 political conventions, Vidal went on to imply snidely in an article in *Esquire* that the same might be true of Buckley, leading Buckley to sue the magazine, whereupon Vidal countersued. See Gore Vidal (hereafter GV), "A Distasteful Encounter with William F. Buckley," *Esquire*, September 1969, 140–45, 150. On the lawsuit, see, e.g., Jay Parini, *Empire of Self: A Life of Gore Vidal* (New York: Doubleday, 2015), 190–91. Vidal apparently had considerable interest in Buckley's sex life: Michelangelo Signorile maintained that Vidal told him that Buckley "used to spend summers on Mykonos, which has always been a gay destination, especially in summer. Vidal told me there were rumors of Buckley's involvement with at least one particular man, and that there were people there who could help track it down. . . . But it wasn't anything I pursued." Quoted in Tim Teeman, *In Bed with Gore Vidal: Hustlers, Hollywood, and the Private World of an American Master* (Bronx, NY: Magnus Books, 2013), 208.

Bouthillette has begun a three-volume memoir of his own, chronicling his military career, his disillusionment with the country's foreign policy, and his time with Vidal. See Fabian Bouthillette, *Gore Vidal's Last Stand: Part One; My American Initiation* (Kindle, Amazon Digital Services, 2014). On Bouthillette's relationship with Vidal, see Michael Mewshaw, *Sympathy for the Devil: Four Decades of Friendship with Gore Vidal* (New York: Farrar, Straus, and Giroux, 2015), 181–82.

3. For a sample of Newman's affectionate, playful correspondence with Vidal, see GV, *Snapshots in History's Glare* (New York: Abrams, 2009), 154–55.

4. GV, *Point to Point Navigation: A Memoir, 1964–2006* (New York: Doubleday, 2006).

5. In his recent biography of Burns, David Margolick maintains that the two met at a party in New York in 1948 held by Burns's former student David MacMackin, and that Wescott invited them both to a party a few days after that initial meeting. David Margolick, *Dreadful: The Short Life and Gay Times of John Horne Burns* (New York: Other Press, 2013), 243–44. In his *New York Times Book Review* essay on Burns, Vidal recalled that they met in 1947 and that Burns was "then 26 [to Vidal's twenty-two] but looked older." In fact, Burns was thirty or thirty-one in 1947. GV, "Speaking of Books: John Horne Burns," *New York Times Book Review*, May 30, 1965, BR 2, BR 22, BR 2.

6. Teeman, "For Gore Vidal, a Final Plot Twist," *New York Times*, November 8, 2013, online.

7. In an interview with Charlie Rose that was broadcast in December 2009, Vidal appears sharper and more firmly in control than when I interviewed him early in November. Though broadcast in December, however, the interview with Rose had actually occurred in October, according to Bouthillette, during their visit to New York to promote *Snapshots in History's Glare*.

8. Gore Vidal, www.imdb.com.

9. Parini's *Empire of the Self* is the most recent biography; his friendliness with his subject shows. See also Fred Kaplan, *Gore Vidal: A Biography* (New York: Doubleday, 1999); Mewshaw, *Sympathy for the Devil*; Dennis Altman, *Gore Vidal's America* (Cambridge:

Polity Press, 2005); Parini, *Gore Vidal: Writer against the Grain* (New York: Columbia University Press, 1992); Donald Weise, ed., *Gore Vidal: Sexually Speaking: Collected Sex Writings* (San Francisco: Cleis Press, 1999); Richard Peabody and Lucinda Ebersole, eds., *Conversations with Gore Vidal* (Jackson: University Press of Mississippi, 2005); his two indispensable autobiographies: GV, *Palimpsest: A Memoir* (New York: Penguin Books, 1995) and *Point to Point Navigation*; and *Snapshots in History's Glare*. The definitive guide to writings by and about Vidal is Steven Abbott, *Gore Vidal: A Bibliography, 1940–2009* (New Castle, DE: Oak Knoll Press, 2009).

10. Teeman, *In Bed*, 35.

11. Quoted in Kaplan, *Vidal*, 714.

12. Mailer, of course, actually titled one of his books *The Prisoner of Sex* (Boston: Little, Brown, 1971).

13. GV, *Palimpsest*, 19. The Kennedy biography is Nigel Hamilton, *JFK: Reckless Youth* (New York: Random House, 1992).

14. *Palimpsest*, 20.

15. Jerry Rosco, ed., *A Heaven of Words: Last Journals, 1956–1984; Glenway Wescott* (Madison: University of Wisconsin Press, 2013), 29.

16. On the matter of graves and inheritance, see, e.g., Parini, *Empire*, 407–8; "Sheppard Mullin's Adam Streisand Defeats Trust Suit against Gore Vidal Estate," June 8, 2015, http://www.sheppardmullin.com/newsroom-pressreleases-414.html; Vidal, *Navigation*, 72–76.

17. GV, *Williwaw* (New York: E. P. Dutton, 1946); *In a Yellow Wood* (New York: E. P. Dutton, 1947).

18. On his mother, see, e.g., Kaplan, *Vidal*, 21, 28, 31, 38–39, 56, 289; Parini, *Empire*, 13, 15–16, 18, 21, 22, 27, 29, 33, 52, 77, 89, 98. On Vidal's hostility toward her, see, e.g., *Palimpsest*, 13–19, 23–26, 67–70, 266–69, 322–25, 384–85.

19. Unsigned review of *Williwaw, Bulletin Virginia Kirkus' Service* 14 (May 1, 1946): 203.

20. John W. Aldridge, *After the Lost Generation: A Critical Study of the Writers of Two Wars* (New York: Arbor House, 1985; originally published, 1951), 170, 171. For other reviews of *Williwaw*, see also Orville Prescott, *New York Times*, June 17, 1946, 19; Jonathan Daniels, "Dirty Weather," *Saturday Review of Literature*, July 6, 1946, 27–28, 27.

21. On the relationship with Nin, see Kaplan, *Vidal*, 202–8, 220–23; Parini, *Empire*, 51–55, 63–66. On Rosalind Rust, see Parini, *Empire*, 32, 36. On Cornelia Phelps Claiborne, see Parini, *Empire*, 51, 53, 57, 70.

22. *Yellow Wood*, 147, 75, 159, 66, 68, 79, 111, 5.

23. Nathan L. Rothman, "A Strange Sort of War Casualty," review of *In a Yellow Wood, Saturday Review of Literature*, May 31, 1947, 21; Aldridge, *Lost Generation*, 173, 174. For other reviews of *Yellow Wood*, see also unsigned review, *Bulletin Virginia Kirkus' Service*, January 15, 1947, 43; Robert E. Kingery, untitled review, *Library Journal*, March 15, 1947, 464; Donald Barr, "The Veteran's Choice," *New York Times Book Review*, March 16, 1947, 10; unsigned review, *New Yorker*, March 22, 1947, 115; Clinton Textor, "Returned Vet Wants Only Humdrum Life," *Chicago Sun Book Week*, April 27, 1947, 2; Mark Schorer, "The American Novel," *Kenyon Review* 9 (August 1947): 628–36, 630.

24. Victor R. Yanitelli, SJ, review of *In a Yellow Wood, Best Sellers* 7, no. 1 (April 1, 1947): 7.

25. GV, *The City and the Pillar* (New York: E. P. Dutton, 1948).

26. Kaplan, *Vidal*, 256.

27. Vidal insisted, however, that "although I am the least autobiographical of novelists, I had drawn the character of athlete Jim Willard so convincingly that to this day aging pederasts are firmly convinced that I was once a male prostitute, with an excellent backhand at tennis." GV, introduction to *The City and the Pillar*, rev. ed. (New York: Random House: 1995), xi–xix, xv.

28. *City and the Pillar*, 39, 47, 39, 48.

29. *City and the Pillar*, 125, 140–41.

30. *City and the Pillar*, 236–37, 238.

31. Craig M. Loftin, *Masked Voices: Gay Men and Lesbians in Cold War America* (Albany: SUNY Press, 2012).

32. Gore Vidal Papers, MS Am 2350, Series I Compositions, E. Essays, Houghton Library, Harvard College Library, Cambridge, MA, #2283–#2287 (hereafter GV Papers). While Vidal himself would claim that he received "something like a thousand letters" about the novel, the volume of the novel's mail in Harvard's Vidal Collection, while substantial, is more modest than that. GV, *Snapshots in History's Glare*, 62. Details about the letter-writers that are not contained in the letters themselves come from ancestry.com, which provides ready access to obituaries, city directories, military service records, and the US census of 1940.

33. George Gaillard to GV, n.d. (probably 1948), Greenwich, CT, GV Papers, #2283.

34. Joseph A. Bochert to GV, n.d. (probably 1948), Lancaster, OH, GV Papers, #2283.

35. Charles S. Marlor, n.d. (probably 1948), Oxford, OH, GV Papers, #2283; GV, *Snapshots in History's Glare*, 65.

36. Fred H. Howard, MD, to GV, January 13, 1948, Worcester, MA, GV Papers, #2283. Evelyn Hooker, "The Adjustment of the Male Overt Homosexual," *Journal of Projective Techniques* 21 (1957): 18–31.

37. Edmund R. Laine to GV, January 22, 1948, Stockbridge, MA, GV Papers, #2283.

38. Sheldon F. Eckfeld to GV, February 1, 1948, Columbus, OH, GV Papers, #2283.

39. Harry Miele to GV, March 22, 1951, Bethel, ME, in GV Papers, #2286.

40. Irvin S. Sterling to GV, December 10, 1950, Elgin Air Force Base, Florida, GV Papers, #2285.

41. Paul Edwards to GV, February 23, 1951, New Haven, CT, in GV Papers, #2286.

42. Charles Ruas, "Gore Vidal," in *Conversations with Gore Vidal*, ed. Richard Peabody and Lucinda Ebersole, 85–99 (Jackson: University Press of Mississippi, 2005), 91.

43. On the emergence and evolution of the "fairy," see esp. George Chauncey, *Gay New York: Gender, Urban Culture, and the Making of the Gay Male World, 1890–1940* (New York: Basic Books, 1995), esp. chapter 2, "The Fairy as an Intermediate Sex," 47–63. On forging the link between heterosexuality and manly strength, see, e.g., E. Anthony Rotundo, *American Manhood: Transformations in Masculinity from the Revolution to the Modern Era* (New York: Basic Books, 1994), esp. chapter 10, "Passionate Manhood," 222–46.

44. On more recent manifestations of the negative connotations of effeminacy, see Tim Bergling, *Sissyphobia: Gay Men and Effeminate Behavior* (Philadelphia: Haworth Press, 1997).

45. C. S. Maxon to GV, January 24, 1948, Sault Sainte Marie, MI, GV Papers, #2283.

46. Carl Selph to GV, April 9, 1952, New York, GV Papers, #2287. Selph went on to teach at Georgia Tech, Auburn, the University of Arkansas, and elsewhere. He currently lives in Mexico, still writing poetry and also designing houses. http://bookstore.xlibris.com/Author/Default.aspx?BookworksSId=SKU-0040298049. See Carl Selph, *A Boy Like Me: A Memoir* (Charleston, SC: CreateSpace, 2014), and *Spilt Milk: A Memoir* (Kindle, 2016).

47. Don Mackintosh to GV, Chicago, March 24, 1949, GV Papers, #2284.

48. Victor Andrzejewski to GV, Detroit, March 16, 1948, GV Papers, #2283.

49. Frank Peterson to GV, Santa Monica, CA, May 26, 1952, in GV Papers, #2287.

50. Laurence Poinsette to GV, New York, March 7, 1949, in GV Papers, #2284.

51. Charles Beckwith Jaqua to GV, Paterson, NJ, January 14, 1948, in GV Papers, #2283.

52. Richard Donald LaConte to GV, Worcester, MA, n.d. (ca. 1950, since he was seventeen and born in 1933), in GV Papers, #2285.

53. Bill Harclerode to GV, n.p., n.d. (ca. 1951), in GV Papers, #2286.

54. Jack Brenner to GV, Saint Petersburg, FL, n.d. (ca. 1951), in GV Papers, #2286. Shortly after the book's publication, well before Brenner wrote, Vidal wrote his friend Pat Crocker that the "fan mail has been amazing, but no enclosed pictures so far." GV to Pat Crocker, n.d., 1948, quoted in Kaplan, *Vidal*, 257.

55. Leonard H. Selzer to GV, Hancock, New York, August 27, 1951, in GV Papers, #2286.

56. Philip R. Macy to GV, Scarsdale, NY, January 1, 1949, in GV Papers, #2284.

57. C. W. Randolph Benson to GV, Charlottesville, VA, February 16, 1948, GV Papers, #2283.

58. Obituary, *Roanoke Times*, March 9, 2007, B5, and findagrave.com.

59. Charles K. Winter, Bridgeport, CT, March 6, 1948, GV Papers, #2283.

60. An anonymous person posted Winter's handsome high school graduation photograph on his findagrave.com page.

61. Mann's reaction is noted by Kaplan, *Vidal*, 256.

62. Kennard Lewis to GV, East Stroudsburg, PA, February 29, 1948, GV Papers, #2283.

63. Hathaway Turner to GV, Montour Falls, NY, February 23, 1950, GV Papers, #2285.

64. GV, introduction to *City and the Pillar*, rev. ed. (New York: Random House: 1995), xv. For other assertions that he was effectively blackballed as punishment for *The City and the Pillar*, see Kaplan, *Gore Vidal*, 259; Parini, "An Interview with Gore Vidal," *New England Review* 14, no. 1 (Fall 1991): 93–101, 95; Eugene Walter, "Conversations with Gore Vidal," in Peabody and Ebersole, *Conversations*, 3–15, 8.

65. Christopher Bram, *Eminent Outlaws: The Gay Writers Who Changed America* (New York: Twelve, 2012), 9, 10.

66. *Snapshots in History's Glare*, 70.

67. Bram, *Outlaws*, 9.

68. Unsigned review of *The City and the Pillar*, *Bulletin Virginia Kirkus' Service*, January 9, 1948, 608; Kingery, review of *The City and the Pillar*, *Library Journal*, December 1, 1947, 1686; L. A. G. Strong, review of *The City and the Pillar*, *Spectator*, April 29, 1949, 586, 588, 588; P. H. Newby, "New Novels," review of *The City and the Pillar*, *Listener*, May 5, 1949, 774.

69. Edward Dermot Doyle, "An Honest Approach," review of *The City and the Pillar*, *San Francisco Chronicle*, February 2, 1948, 14.

70. Unsigned review of *The City and the Pillar*, in "Briefly Noted," *New Yorker*, January 10, 1948, 81.

71. David Leavitt, "Territory," *New Yorker*, May 31, 1982, 34-42, 45-46; Elizabeth Kastor, "David Leavitt: A Young Lion in Literature," *Washington Post*, June 21, 1985, online.

72. Richard B. Gehman, "Abnormal Doom," review of *The City and the Pillar*, *New York Herald Tribune Weekly Book Review*, January 18, 1948, 6.

73. Leslie Fiedler, "The Fate of the Novel," *Kenyon Review* 10, no. 3 (Summer, 1948): 519-27, 523; Fiedler, "Come Back to the Raft Ag'in, Huck Honey!," *Partisan Review*, June 1948, 664-671.

74. Kaplan, *Vidal*, 259. Kaplan mistakenly places Fiedler's review in the *Hudson Review*, not the *Kenyan Review*. There was a cursory review in the *Hudson Review* as well, by J. S. Shrike, noting the novel's compatibility with Kinsey, and maintaining that "Mr. Vidal's hero is irrevocably corrupted by his initial adolescent experience." J. S. Shrike, "Recent Phenomena," *Hudson Review* 1, no. 1 (Spring 1948): 136-38, 140, 142, 144, 137. In the same review essay, Shrike superficially assessed Capote's *Other Voices, Other Rooms* and the Kinsey Report on *Sexual Behavior in the Human Male*.

75. Kaplan, *Vidal*, 259.

76. C. V. Terry, "The City and the Pillar," review of *The City and the Pillar*, *New York Times Book Review*, January 11, 1948, BR22.

77. Julia Strachey, review of *The City and the Pillar*, *New Statesman and Nation*, May 14, 1949, 510, 512; Charles J. Rolo, "Reader's Choice," review of *The City and the Pillar*, *Atlantic Monthly*, February 1948, 107-12, 110; Richard McLaughlin, "Precarious Status," review of *The City and the Pillar*, *Saturday Review of Literature*, January 10, 1948, 14-15.

78. GV, *The Season of Comfort* (New York: E. P. Dutton, 1949), 83, 103, 112-13, 116, 117, 120, 203, 209, 196, 248, 253.

79. Richard Cheatham, review of *The Season of Comfort*, *Carolina Quarterly* 1, no. 2 (March 16, 1949): 69-70; for other reviews of *Comfort*, see also unsigned review, *Bulletin of Virginia Kirkus' Bookshop Service*, November 1, 1948, 578; Robert E. Kingery, untitled review, *Library Journal*, January 1, 1949, 60; Emmett Dedman, "Gore Vidal's Novel Gives Hint of What Young Writers Think," *Chicago Sun-Times*, January 9, 1949, unsigned review, *Booklist*, February 1, 1949, 193; Charles Rolo, "Life with Mother," *Atlantic Monthly*, February 1949, 86-87; Edward Dermot Doyle, untitled review, *San Francisco Chronicle*, February 13, 1949, 14.

80. William Fense Weaver, "Mr. Vidal's Solver Cord," review of *The Season of Comfort*, *New York Times*, February 6, 1949, 12; Barbara Klaw, "A Dominating Mother," review of *The Season of Comfort*, *New York Herald Tribune Book Review*, January 9, 1949, 10.

81. John Broderick, "Strong Start, Weak Finish," review of *The Season of Comfort*, *New Yorker*, January 15, 1949, 77-78. Broderick, a bold and prolific Irish novelist almost exactly Vidal's age, was an interesting choice to review *The Season of Comfort*. At times describing himself as homosexual, and later in life as bisexual, Broderick appears to have had little actual sexual experience, living with his mother in Athlone until she died when he was fifty, an event that severely exacerbated the alcoholism that plagued him throughout his adult life. Patrick Maume, "John Broderick," *Dictionary of Irish Biography*, http://dib.cambridge.org/viewReadPage.do?articleId=a0974. He also reviewed Burns's *Lucifer with a Book* for the *New Yorker* just three months later, but that review was so brief and essentially sarcastic that I consigned it to note 55 in the previous chapter.

82. Aldridge, "A Boy and His Mom," review of *The Season of Comfort, Saturday Review of Literature*, January 15, 1949, 19-20; Aldridge, *Lost Generation*, 178-80.

83. *Comfort*, 252.

84. *Palimpsest*, 167.

85. Winnifred Rugg, review of *A Search for the King, Christian Science Monitor*, January 26, 1950, 11; Robert F. Kingery, review of *A Search for the King, Library Journal*, December 1, 1949, 1819; Edward Wegenknecht, "Brilliant 'Historical' by a 24-Year Old: Vidal's Fifth Is Legend of *Coeur de Lion*," review of *A Search for the King, Chicago Tribune Sunday Magazine of Books*, January 15, 1950, 3; George Miles, review of *A Search for the King, Commonweal*, January 27, 1950, 446; Robert Langbaum, "The Questing Hero," review of *A Search for the King, Nation*, April 15, 1950, 352; Aldridge, *Lost Generation*, 182. For other reviews of *King*, see also, Frederic Nelson Litten, "Delightful Romantic Tale from Pen of a 'High Brow,'" *Chicago Sun-Times*, January 26, 1950, 65; Leo Lerman, "The Legend of Richard," *New York Times Book Review*, January 15, 1950, 4, 16; unsigned review, *Bulletin of Virginia Kirkus' Bookshop Service*, November 15, 1949, 628. Vidal's often uncritical biographer, Fred Kaplan, expansively calls *A Search for the King* "a sophisticated anticipation of magical realism." Kaplan, *Vidal*, 227.

86. GV, *A Search for the King: A Twelfth Century Legend* (New York: E. P. Dutton, 1950), viii.

87. Samuel Putnam, "Animated Tapestry," review of *A Search for the King, Saturday Review of Literature*, January 14, 1950, 10; John J. Maloney, "Set in the Mold of Legend," review of *A Search for the King, New York Herald Tribune*, January 15, 1950, 8; see also unsigned review, *Booklist*, February 1950, 150. After having been so bothered by male involvements in *Pillar* and *Comfort*, the *New Yorker* could only celebrate male friendship in *A Search for the King*. Unsigned review, *New Yorker*, January 21, 1950, 97-98.

88. *Search for the King*, 140, 142. Vidal apparently could not resist teasing readers with the possibility of male sexual activity, when he had Blondel meet a giant with a "special fondness for the shepherd boys in these hills." As it turns out, the giant, however, does not practice anything as conventional as sexual activity: A cannibal, he finds the shepherds tasty eating. *King*, 83, 84.

89. *King*, 196.

90. *Palimpsest*, 305.

91. Those remaining novels were *Dark Green, Bright Red* (New York: E. P. Dutton, 1950), *The Judgment of Paris* (New York: E. P. Dutton, 1952), and *Messiah* (New York: E. P. Dutton, 1954). In *Dark Green, Bright Red*, there are no more than "veiled suggestions" (284) that the protagonist may once have had a sexual connection to the brother of his primary female sexual partner; the brother, conveniently, commits suicide. In the very widely reviewed *The Judgment of Paris*, the protagonist does no more than visit some queer gathering places.

92. GV, *A Thirsty Evil: Seven Short Stories* (New York: Zero Press, 1956); GV, *Julian: A Novel* (Boston: Little, Brown, 1964).

93. GV, *The City and the Pillar Revised* (New York: E. P. Dutton, 1965); New American Library published a paperback edition shortly thereafter. The revised edition also contained a short essay by Vidal that originally had appeared in the *Partisan Review* the previous year entitled "Sex and the Law." With wit and precision, he pointed to the "wild disarray" of state regulations, questioning whether the state should have any say in sex between

consenting adults. Curiously, in his *Gore Vidal*, a biography of notable detail and girth, Fred Kaplan does not mention the novel's 1965 revision, nor does Vidal himself mention the revision in either of his memoirs.

94. *Pillar*, 287, 140–41; *Pillar Revised*, 204, 108–9.

95. The conflicted quality of *The City and the Pillar*, even with its new ending, may be instructively contrasted with the much more affirmative contemporaneous portrayal of love between males young and older in Sanford Friedman's *Totempole* (San Francisco: North Point Press, 1984; originally published, 1965). Friedman was just three years younger than Vidal, a military policeman in Korea. Benjamin Ivry, "Sanford Freedman's 'Heroic or Meritorious Achievement,'" obituary, *Jewish Daily Forward*, May 24, 2010, online.

96. Document #659 in GV Papers.

97. *Palimpsest*, 102–3.

98. Martin Duberman, *Cures: A Gay Man's Odyssey* (New York: Dutton Books, 1991).

99. Larry Kramer, "The Sadness of Gore Vidal," in GV, *Sexually Speaking: Collected Sex Writings* (San Francisco: Cleis Press, 1999), 252–71, 259, 262. Originally published in *QW Magazine* 4 (October 1992).

100. On Vidal's sexual insecurities, see Parini, *Empire of Self*, 404; Parini merely notes, but characteristically does not examine, Vidal's use of "degeneracy" to describe same-sex sexuality (328). For a brief but convincing interpretation of Vidal's vulnerability and frequent unhappiness, especially during the last few decades of his life, see Mewshaw, *Sympathy for the Devil*. On Vidal's effort to characterize *The City and the Pillar* as a critique of the "romantic fallacy" unrelated to sexual orientation, see, e.g., Gerald Clarke, "The Art of Fiction: An Interview with Gore Vidal," *Paris Review* 15, no. 59 (Fall 1974): 130–65, 136–37; GV, introduction to 1995 publication of the revised edition of *The City and the Pillar*, xi–xix, xvi.

101. *Palimpsest*, 34–35; interview with Fabian Bouthillette, August 10, 2012. Vidal claimed, as usual on the defense, that he had no aspiration of growing old with Trimble, just growing up with him, before each might then have established more stable lives. *Palimpsest*, 35. But he was stirred to learn from Trimble's mother in the 1990s that during the war Jimmie had asked her to send him a copy of *Leaves of Grass*. *Palimpsest*, 25, 40. On friends' skepticism about Trimble's significance to Vidal, see Mewshaw, *Sympathy for the Devil*, 129–32; Parini, *Empire of Self*, 37, 48; and Teeman, *In Bed with Gore Vidal*, 36, 43, 44. For more of Vidal's own comments on Trimble, see *Palimpsest*, 23, 24, 26. Parini even claims that by the spring of 2010, the "Jimmie Trimble Obsession had, at last, faded." Parini, *Empire of Self*. Much of Vidal himself had faded by then.

An unusually tender and graceful evocation of Trimble distinguishes an otherwise lackluster work of Vidal's, the odd *Two Sisters*, a 1970 blending of autobiography and history that leaves it unclear whether Vidal sought to parody the genre or refine it. What is clear is how much Trimble dominated Vidal's postwar consciousness. GV, *Two Sisters: A Memoir in the Form of a Novel* (London: Heinemann, 1970).

102. *Palimpsest*, 26.

103. The partners' desk in Vidal's study, with the single chair that I purchased at the estate sale, appeared in Elizabeth Lambert, "With Panache: The Hollywood Home of Gore Vidal," *Architectural Digest*, September 1980, 86–91, 90.

104. *Snapshots in History's Glare*, 7.

105. *Point to Point Navigation*, 77, 82, 85, 87. Vidal kept Howard's room in the Hollywood Hills home intact after he died in 2003, referring to it as "the guest room." He offered the room to Fabian Bouthillette when Vidal's condition required that he spend much of his time at Vidal's home, but Bouthillette maintained his own separate residence in the Silver Lake district. Interview with Fabian Bouthillette, August 10, 2012.

Chapter Five

1. E. Anthony Rotundo, *American Manhood: Transformations in Masculinity from the Revolution to the Modern Era* (New York: Basic Books, 1994), chapter 1, "Community to Individual: The Transformation of Manhood at the Turn of the Nineteenth Century," 10–30; on "communal manhood," see esp. 10–25.

2. Howard Brotz and Everett Wilson, "Characteristics of Military Society," *American Journal of Sociology* 51 (March 1946): 371–75, 374, 375. See also Frederick Elkin, "The Soldier's Language," *American Journal of Sociology* 51 (March 1946): 414–22.

3. Jack Belden, *Still Time to Die* (New York: Harper and Brothers, 1944), 27.

4. Willard Waller, *The Veteran Comes Back* (New York: Dryden Press, 1944), 36, 37, 180, 30, 42, 43, 139.

5. Sebastian de Grazia, *The Political Community: A Study of Anomie* (Chicago: University of Chicago Press, 1948), 159.

6. For a useful survey, based on numerous memoirs and a survey by the Army War College, see Gerald F. Linderman, *The World within War: America's Combat Experience in World War II* (New York: Free Press, 1997), chapter 7, "The Appeals of Battle: Comradeship," 263–99. Relying on memoirs along with vernacular photographs, I have analyzed men's involvements with each other during World War II in Ibson, *Picturing Men*, chapter 7, "Men Set Free: World War II and the Shifting Boundaries of Male Association," 158–95. A broad treatment, not confined to a single war, is J. Glenn Gray's splendid *The Warriors: Reflections on Men in Battle* (Lincoln: University of Nebraska Press, 1970; originally published, 1959).

7. Leon Uris, *Battle Cry* (New York: G. P. Putnam's Sons: 1953), 295.

8. Allan Bérubé, *Coming Out under Fire: The History of Gay Men and Women in World War Two* (New York: Free Press, 1990), 186.

9. Bill Mauldin, *Up Front* (New York: Henry Holt, 1945), 4.

10. James Bradley, with Ron Powers, *Flags of Our Fathers* (New York: Bantam Books, 2000).

11. US Department of Veterans Affairs, "America's Wars" (2016), www.va.gov/opa/.../fs_americas_wars.pdf; Paul Waldman, "American War Dead, by the Numbers, *American Prospect*, May 26, 2014, http://prospect.org/article/american-war-dead-numbers.

12. Andrew J. Huebner, *The Warrior Image: Soldiers in American Culture from the Second World War to the Vietnam Era* (Chapel Hill: University of North Carolina Press, 2008), 17.

13. Gray, *The Warriors*, 93.

14. Pascale-Anne Brault and Michael Naas, eds., *The Work of Mourning: Jacques Derrida* (Chicago: University of Chicago Press, 2001), 107.

15. Willie Pep, obituary, *New York Times*, November 25, 2006, online.

16. Drew Gilpin Faust, *This Republic of Suffering: Death and the American Civil War* (New York: Vintage, 2008).

17. Moore's and DeMase's letters are quoted in a book by Redmann's younger brother Kerry, based largely on the abundant letters that Morris wrote home, where he had nine younger siblings. Kerry P. Redmann, *Unfinished Journey: A World War II Remembrance* (Guilford, CT: Lyons Press, 2006), 277, 279.

18. Therese Benedek, MD, *Insight and Personality Adjustment: A Study of the Psychological Effects of War* (New York: Ronald Press, 1946), chapter 13, "Mourning for the Soldier," 190–98.

19. Benedek, 68, 67.

20. Roy R. Grinker, MD, and John P. Spiegel, MD, *Men under Stress* (New York: McGraw Hill, 1945), 280, 281, ix, 114, 117.

21. Carol Schultz Vento, *The Hidden Legacy of World War II: A Daughter's Journey of Discovery* (Camp Hill, PA: Sunbury Press, 2011), 112–13.

22. Huebner, *Warrior Image*, 17; John Ellis, *World War II: A Statistical Survey* (New York: Facts on File, 1993), 257.

23. S. Kirson Weinberg, "The Combat Neurosis," *American Journal of Sociology* 51 (March 1946): 465–78.

24. *Combat Exhaustion*, official training film, US Army Service Forces, War Department, 1945.

25. James Agee, *Nation*, May 11, 1946, quoted in Agee, *Agee on Film: Criticism and Comment on the Movies* (New York: Modern Library, 2000; originally published, 1958), 191.

26. *Let There Be Light* (1946), National Archives and Records Administration, National Film Preservation Foundation (released to the general public, 1980). On the significance and suppression of the film, see Thomas Childers, *Soldier from the War Returning: The Greatest Generation's Troubled Homecoming from World War II* (Boston: Houghton Mifflin Harcourt, 2009), 323.

27. *Shades of Gray* (1948), US Army professional medical film #PMF 5047.

28. Kansas Historical Society, "The Menninger Clinic," https://www.kshs.org/kansapedia /menninger-clinic/12147.

29. William C. Menninger, MD, *Psychiatry in a Troubled World: Yesterday's War and Today's Challenge* (New York: Macmillan, 1948), vii; chapter 16, "Homosexuality," 222–31, 231, 222.

30. Menninger, 224, 225. For an earlier effort to trivialize "homosexual buffoonery," see Irving L. Janis, "Psychodynamic Aspects of Adjustment to Army Life," *Psychiatry* 8 (May 1945): 159–76.

31. E. B. Sledge, *China Marine: An Infantryman's Life after World War II* (New York: Oxford University Press, 2002), 149, xiv.

32. John F. Cuber, "Family Readjustment of Veterans," *Marriage and Family Living* 7 (May 1945): 28–30, 28. See also Reuben Hill, "The Returning Father and His Family," *Marriage and Family Living* 7 (May 1945): 31–34; Catherine MacKenzie, "Fathers Home from War," *New York Times*, February 4, 1945, 87; Virginia M. Moore, MD, "When Father Comes Marching Home," *Parents*, January 1945, 16–17, 112.

33. J. H. S. Brossard, "Family Problems and the Immediate Future," *Journal of Home Economics* 37 (September 1945): 383–84.

34. Edward C. McDonough, "The Discharged Serviceman and His Family," *American Journal of Sociology* 51 (March 1946): 451–44, 452.

35. In a box on the second page of Moore, "When Father Comes Marching Home."

36. Irvin L. Child and Marjorie Van Der Water, eds., *Psychology for the Returning Veteran* (Washington, DC: Infantry Journal/Penguin Books, 1945), 131, 72.

37. Howard Kitching, *Sex Problems of the Returned Veteran* (New York: Emerson Books, 1946).

38. William Chafe, "The Personal and the Political: Two Case Studies," in *U.S. History as Women's History: New Feminist Essays*, ed. Linda Kerber et al., chapter 9, 189–213 (Chapel Hill: University of North Carolina Press, 1995), 203–4; see also Chafe, *Never Stop Running: Allard Lowenstein and the Struggle to Save American Liberalism* (New York: Basic Books, 1993), 22–23.

39. Chafe, *Never Stop Running*, 71, 211, 216–27.

40. Chafe, 226. For David Harris's own unsympathetic and personally revealing treatment of Lowenstein, see Harris, *Dreams Die Hard: Three Men's Journey through the Sixties* (San Francisco: Mercury House, 1993).

41. In instructive contrast to Lowenstein is his lifelong friend, fellow alumnus of New York's Horace Mann prep school, novelist Sanford Friedman. Awarded the Bronze Star in Korea, contentedly partnered for several years with "the ebullient Cleveland-born Jewish poet Richard Howard," and author of *Totempole*, a remarkable mid-1960s novel about same-sex love, Friedman managed to escape Lowenstein's bedevilment, and is a reminder that such was not impossible, even then. Benjamin Ivry, "Sanford Friedman's 'Heroic or Meritorious Achievement,'" *Forward*, May 4, 2010, http://forward.com /the-assimilator/127712/sanford-friedmans-heroic-or-meritorious-achievemen/;Sanford Friedman, *Totempole* (New York: New American Library, 1966).

42. On Kerouac and Vidal, e.g., see Fred Kaplan, *Gore Vidal: A Biography* (New York: Doubleday, 1999), 368–69; Ann Charters, *Kerouac: A Biography* (New York: St. Martin's Press, 1994), 388; Joyce Johnson, *The Voice Is All: The Lonely Victory of Jack Kerouac* (New York: Viking, 2012), 185, 186.

43. Charters, *Kerouac*, 43.

44. Johnson (a former lover of Kerouac's), *The Voice Is All*, 164.

45. Johnson, 171.

46. Charters, *Kerouac*, 48–49.

47. Frank S. Adams, "Columbia Student Kills Friend and Sinks Body in Hudson River, *New York Times*, August 17, 1944, 1, 13.

48. Charters, *Kerouac*, 48, 50.

49. James Campbell, *This Is the Beat Generation* (Berkeley: University of California Press, 1999), 13.

50. Eric Homburger, "Lucien Carr: Fallen Angel of the Beat Poets, Later an Unflappable News Editor for United Press," *Guardian*, February 9, 2005, 29.

51. Campbell, *This Is the Beat Generation*, 30, 33.

52. Allen Ginsberg, *The Book of Martyrdom and Artifice: First Journals and Poems, 1937-1952*, reprint ed. (Cambridge, MA: DaCapo Press, 2008), 51; Allen Ginsberg, *Spontaneous Mind: Selected Interviews, 1958-1996*, ed. David Carter (New York: Harper Collins, 2001), 56.

53. Johnson, *Voice Is All*, 164, 166, 168; Ginsberg, *Spontaneous Mind*, 113–14.

54. Edie Kerouac-Parker, *You'll Be Okay: My Life with Jack Kerouac* (San Francisco: City Lights 2007), 150, 149.

55. Jack Kerouac, *Vanity of Duluoz* (New York: G. P. Putnam's Sons, 1968), 212, 195, 197, 229, 230.

56. Johnson, *Voice Is All*, 114.

57. Johnson, 133–38.

58. An indication of how conventional is Joyce Johnson's interpretation of Kerouac's sexuality is the fact that the entry in her book's index for "Kerouac, Jack, love life of" contains seventeen names, all women's. Johnson, 481. In a book that in other ways is insightful and rich in detail, her attention to his same-sex desires is highly superficial, if not evasive, betraying an unyieldingly binary sense of sexual orientation, as if it were something that might be conclusively and lastingly determined by, say, a blood test. Johnson, 66–67, 81, 98, 186. She recognizes but does not for a moment examine the implications of the fact that, to put it mildly, "He had his deepest relationships with his intimate circle of male friends" (186).

59. Miriam G. Reumann, *American Sexual Character: Sex, Gender, and National Identity in the Kinsey Reports* (Berkeley: University of California Press, 2005), 173.

60. Peter Silver, *Our Savage Neighbors: How Indian War Transformed Early America* (New York: W. W. Norton, 2009).

61. Kai Erikson, *Wayward Puritans: A Study in the Sociology of Deviance* (Boston: John Wiley and Sons, 1966), 22.

62. Longhand Note of President Harry S. Truman, September 19, 1946, Truman Papers—President's Secretary's Files, Harry S. Truman Library and Museum, online, https://www.trumanlibrary.org/whistlestop/study_collections/trumanpapers/psf/longhand/index.php?pagenumber=3&documentid=hst-psf_naid735241-01&documentVersion=both&documentYear=1946.

63. David K. Johnson, *The Lavender Scare: The Cold War Persecution of Gays and Lesbians in the Federal Government* (Chicago: University of Chicago Press, 2006).

64. For an insightful analysis of Liberace's being characterized as "the greatest lover since Valentino," see Colin Carman, "The Keeper and the Kept," a review of Steven Sonderbergh's HBO film *Behind the Candelabra*, *Gay and Lesbian Review*, September–October, 2013, 48–49. On Hunter and Hudson, see, e.g., Tab Hunter, with Eddie Muller, *Tab Hunter Confidential* (Chapel Hill, NC: Algonquin Books, 2005); *Tab Hunter Confidential*, Automat Pictures, produced and directed by Jeffrey Schwarz, 2015; Robert Hofter, *The Man Who Invented Rock Hudson* (New York: Carroll and Graf, 2005).

65. Ted Berkman, "The Third Sex—Guilt or Sickness?," *Coronet*, November 1955, 129–33, 131, 132, 133.

66. Victor Bockris, *Transformer: The Lou Reed Story* (New York: Simon and Schuster, 1994), 13, 15.

67. Legs McNeil, *Please Kill Me: The Uncensored Oral History of Punk* (New York: Grove Press, 1996), 3–4.

68. Bockris, *Transformer*, 248. On Reed's sexual ambiguity, see also 47–49.

69. "Kill Your Sons," lyrics, Sony/ATV Music Publishing LLC.

70. Betty Friedan, *The Feminine Mystique*, fiftieth anniversary ed. (New York: W. W. Norton, 2013; originally published, 1963), 385.

71. Bois Burk Papers, #1989-07, GLBT Historical Society, San Francisco.

72. John Gerassi, *The Boys of Boise: Fear, Vice, and Folly in an American City* (Seattle: University of Washington Press, 2001; originally published, New York: Macmillan, 1966). Neil Miller, *Sex Crime Panic: A Journey to the Paranoid Heart of the 1950s* (Los Angeles: Alyson Books, 2002), 109.

73. Miller, *Sex Crime Panic*, 110–11.

74. Donald Stewart Lucas Papers, #1997-25, GLBT Historical Society.

75. John Howard, *Men Like That: A Southern Queer History* (Chicago: University of Chicago Press, 1999), xi.

76. See esp. George Chauncey, "The Postwar Sex Crime Panic," chapter 10 in *True Stories for the American Past*, 3rd ed., ed. William Graebner, vol. 2, *Since 1865*, 160–78 (New York: McGraw-Hill, 2002).

77. Alfred C. Kinsey, Wardell B. Pomeroy, and Clyde E. Martin, *Sexual Behavior in the Human Male* (Philadelphia: W. B. Saunders, 1948), 610.

78. Walt Kelly, *The Pogo Papers* (New York: Simone Shuster, 1953.), foreword.

79. William M. Tuttle Jr., *"Daddy's Gone to War": The Second World War in the Lives of America's Children* (New York: Oxford University Press, 1993), 218. See chapter 12, "Daddy's Coming Home!," 212–30.

80. Francine Shapiro, "Baby Boomers and Distant Dads," *Huffington Post*, February 22, 2012, http://www.huffingtonpost.com/francine-shapiro-phd/ptsd-veterans_b_1228542.html.

81. "The Menace of the Maternal Father," *Hygeia* 20 (June 1942): 468–70, 469.

82. Tuttle, *"Daddy's Gone to War,"* 221.

83. Tuttle, 225.

84. Tim O'Brien, *If I Die in a Combat Zone: Box Me Up and Ship Me Home* (New York: Random House, 1975), 11.

85. Cf. David Stannard's insightful interpretation of the Puritans' keeping a "due distance" between themselves and their own children, as a means of emotional fortification in an era when the likelihood of a child's death was high. David E. Stannard, *The Puritan Way of Death: A Study in Religion, Culture, and Social Change* (New York: Oxford University Press, 1977), 58.

86. Ralph LaRossa has suggested that "the culture of fatherhood in the fifties" represented "something of a U-turn" from "the progressive path it had been on since the turn of the century." LaRossa, "The Culture of Fatherhood," *Journal of Family History* 29 (January 2004): 47–70, 57.

87. Benjamin Spock, MD, *Baby and Child Care* (New York: Pocket Books, 1957), 312–13, 316.

88. Spock, *The Pocket Book of Baby and Child Care* (New York: Pocket Books, 1946), 99.

89. Mary L. Dudziak, *War Time: An Idea, Its History, Its Consequences* (New York: Oxford University Press, 2012), 36.

90. As Michale A. Milburn and Sheree D. Conrad have reminded us, "denial is a common reaction to traumatic experiences such as natural disasters, wars, torture, or childhood abuse." Milburn and Conrad, *The Politics of Denial* (Cambridge, MA: MIT Press, 1996), 17. Apart from any issues regarding war, the emotional reserve that may accompany de-

nial can, of course, be a common way for American men to perform their masculinity. Add severe trauma to the mix, and a resulting reticence is hardly surprising.

91. Childers, *Soldier from the War Returning*.

92. Carol Schultz Vento, *The Hidden Legacy of World War II: A Daughter's Journey of Discovery* (Camp Hill, PA: Sunbury Press, 2011), 21, 8, 2, 37, 53, 56, 67, 74; foreword by Thomas Childers, 4-7, 6.

93. Karen Fisher-Alaniz, *Breaking the Code: A Father's Secret, a Daughter's Journey, and the Question That Changed Everything* (Naperville, IL: Sourcebooks, 2011), 176, 205, 309, 313, 314, v.

94. Julia Collins, *My Father's War: A Memoir* (New York: Four Walls, Eight Windows, 2002), 246, 9, 139-40, 132, 154, 215, 10, 248. For a powerful story of another quest by a veteran's daughter to understand the special trauma for American Jewish soldiers who witnessed Nazi concentration camps, see Leila Levinson, *Gated Grief: The Daughter of a Concentration Camp Liberator Discovers a Legacy of Trauma* (Brule, WI: Cable Publishing, 2011.)

95. Tom Matthews, *Our Fathers' War: Growing Up in the Shadow of the Greatest Generation* (New York: Broadway Books, 2005), 16, 159, 169, 171, 69, 65, 54-61, 43, 44, 17, 19, 25, 28, 29.

96. Recent uncertainty about whether Bradley's father John was actually in the famous flag-raising photograph or had in fact taken part in an earlier, similar photo is immaterial for my points and purposes. Thomas Gibbons-Neff, " 'Flags of Our Fathers' Author Now Says His Father Was Not in the Iconic Iwo Jima photo," *Washington Post*, May 3, 2016, online, https://www.washingtonpost.com/news/checkpoint/wp/2016/05/03/flags-of-our-fathers-author-now-says-his-father-was-not-in-iconic-iwo-jima-photo/.

97. James Bradley, with Ron Powers, *Flags of Our Fathers* (New York: Bantam Books, 2000), 4-5, 261, 343, 344, 345, 109, 110, 238, 259.

98. Tom Hayden, *Reunion: A Memoir* (New York: Random House: 1988), 80, 7-8. Hayden's second memoir sensitively explores the significance throughout his life of his cultural heritage as an Irish American. Hayden, *Irish on the Inside: In Search of the Soul of Irish America* (New York: Verso Books, 2001).

99. Ralph LaRossa, *Of War and Men: World War II in the Lives of Fathers and Their Families* (Chicago: University of Chicago Press, 2011), 110, 148.

100. Michael Messner, *King of the Wild Suburb: A Memoir of Fathers, Sons, and Guns* (Austin, TX: Plain View Press, 2011), 149, 148, 116.

101. Michael C. C. Adams, *The Best War Ever: America and World War II* (Baltimore: Johns Hopkins University Press, 1994). Cf. Studs Terkel, ed., *"The Good War": An Oral History of World War II* (New York: Ballantine Books, 1984); Tom Brokaw, *The Greatest Generation* (New York: Random House, 2004); Geoffrey C. Ward and Ken Burns, *The War: An Intimate History, 1941-1945* (New York: Knopf, 2007); *The War: A Film by Ken Burns and Lynn Novick* (PBS, 2007). Stephen Ambrose, *The Good Fight: How World War II Was Won* (New York: Atheneum Books for Young Readers, 2001).

102. Ambrose, *Comrades: Brothers, Fathers, Heroes, Sons, Pals* (New York: Simon and Schuster, 2000); Ambrose, *Band of Brothers: E Company, 506th Regiment, 101st Airborne from Normandy to Hitler's Eagle's Nest* (New York: Simon and Schuster, 2001).

103. Robert S. McNamara and Brian VanDeMark, *Retrospect: The Tragedy and Lessons of Vietnam* (New York: Vintage Books, 1996); James G. Blight and Janet M. Lang, *The Fog of*

War: Lessons from the Life of Robert S. McNamara (Lanham, MD: Rowman and Littlefield, 2005).

104. Karl Marlantes, *What It Is Like to Go to War* (New York: Grove Press, 2011), 60, 47.

105. J. Glenn Gray, *The Warriors: Reflections on Men in Battle* (Lincoln: University of Nebraska Press, 1970; originally published, 1959), xxiii, xv, xxii, 9, 15, xxiii, 6, 24, 27, 28, 29–58, 44, 45, 46–47, 51, 45–46, 61–79, 88–95, 93, 94, 95, 107.

106. Gore Vidal, *Palimpsest: A Memoir* (New York: Random House, 1995), 37.

107. Niobe Way, *Deep Secrets: Boys' Friendships and the Crisis of Connection* (Cambridge, MA: Harvard University Press, 2011), 184.

108. See, e.g., Elizabeth Fraterrigo, *Playboy and the Making of the Good Life in Modern America* (New York: Oxford University Press, 2009); Elaine Tyler May, *Homeward Bound: American Families in the Cold War Era*, rev. ed. (New York: Basic Books, 2008); Barbara Ehrenreich, *The Hearts of Men: American Dreams and the Flight from Commitment* (New York: Anchor, 1983); Susan Faludi, *Stiffed: The Betrayal of the American Man* (New York: William Morrow, 1999).

Coda

1. Gore Vidal, *Palimpsest: A Memoir* (New York: Penguin Books, 1995), 90.

2. Chauncey Mabe, "Knowles Now Thirty Years after He Wrote *A Separate Peace*," *Sun Sentinel* (Broward County, FL), March 15, 1987, online; William H. Honan, obituary for John Knowles, "John Knowles, 75, Novelist Who Wrote 'A Separate Peace,'" *New York Times*, December 1, 2001, online. Hallman Bell Bryant, *Understanding "A Separate Peace": A Student Case Book to Issues, Sources, and Historical Documents* (Westport, CT: Greenwood Press, 2002), introduction, xi.

3. John Knowles (hereafter JK), *A Separate Peace* (London: Seckler and Warburg, 1959; New York: Macmillan, 1960), 48, 19.

4. *Separate Peace*, 24, 62. Oddly, criticism of the novel has paid scant attention to the color of the shirt, the "fairy" remarks, or Gene's putting it on in private. One superficial interpretation is H. B. Bryant, "Phineas's Pink Shirt in *A Separate Peace*," *Notes on Contemporary Literature* 14, no. 5 (November 1984): 5–6.

5. John Ibson, *Picturing Men: A Century of Male Relationships in Everyday American Photography* (Chicago: University of Chicago Press, 2006), 156.

6. Mabe, "Now Thirty Years After."

7. Honan, obituary for Knowles.

8. JK, "A Special Time, a Special School," n.d., Phillips Exeter Academy website. See also JK, "My Separate Peace," *Esquire*, March 1985, 107–9.

9. His biographer, Penelope Nivens, is evasive on the subject. Penelope Nivens, *Thornton Wilder: A Life* (New York: Harpers, 2013), esp. 440. More informative and convincing was Robert Gottlieb, "Man of Letters: Thornton Wilder," *New Yorker*, January 7, 2013, online.

10. Dorothy Knowles Maxwell (via Robert Maxwell, her son) to the author, May 24, 2016.

11. See, e.g., James Holt McGavran, "Fears Echo and Unhinged Joy: Crossing Homosocial Boundaries in *A Separate Peace*," *Children's Literature* 30 (2002): 67–80; Eric Tribunella, "Refusing the Queer Potential: Crossing Homosocial Boundaries in *A Separate Peace*,"

Children's Literature 30 (2002): 81–95; Dedria Bryfonski, ed., *War in John Knowles' "A Separate Peace"* (Farmington Hills, MI: Greenhaven Press, 2011).

12. Dawn B. Sova, *Banned Books: Literature Suppressed on Social Grounds* (New York: Facts on File, 2011), 308.

13. Whitney Balliett, review of *A Separate Peace*, *New Yorker* 36 (April 2, 1950): 158–59; Donald Yates, "Dramatic First Novel of Life in a Prep School," review of *A Separate Peace*, *Chicago Tribune Sunday Magazine of Books*, March 27, 1960, 5; Granville Hicks, "The Good Have a Quiet Heroism," review of *A Separate Peace*, *Saturday Review* 43 (March 5, 1960): 15; unsigned review of *A Separate Peace*, *Booklist* 56 (February 1960): 353; unsigned review of *A Separate Peace*, *Bookmark* 19 (March 1960): 151; unsigned review of *A Separate Peace*, *Kirkus Reviews* 27 (December 1, 1959): 893.

14. Anne Duchene, "On the Dark Perimeters of Feeling and Fiction," review of *A Separate Peace*, *Manchester Guardian*, May 1, 1959, 6; Edmund Fuller, "Shadow of Mars," review of *A Separate Peace*, *New York Times Book Review*, February 7, 1960, 35; Simon Raven, "No Time for War," review of *A Separate Peace*, *Spectator*, May 1, 1959, 630; Douglas Aitken, "Tale of Two Schoolboys," review of *A Separate Peace*, *San Francisco Chronicle*, June 26, 1960, 29; unsigned review of *A Separate Peace*, *Christian Century*, June 8, 1960, 697; unsigned review *A Separate Peace*, *Horn Book Magazine*, October 1960, 421; Jean Hotzhauer, review of *A Separate Peace*, *Commonweal*, December 9, 1960, 284; "New Novels," unsigned review of *A Separate Peace*, *New Statesman*, May 2, 1959, 618.

15. Harding Lemay, "Two Boys and a War Within," review of *A Separate Peace*, *New York Herald Tribune Book Review*, March 6, 1960, 6; Thomas F. Houlihan, review of *A Separate Peace*, *Library Journal*, March 1, 1960, 987.

16. Philip Roth, *Goodbye, Columbus* (Boston: Houghton Mifflin, 1959).

Bibliography

SELECTED PRIMARY SOURCES

Manuscript Collections and Other Archival Material

Author's Private Collection of Vernacular Photographs of American Men Together, Mid-Nineteenth Century to Mid-Twentieth Century.

Bois Burk Papers #1989-07. GLBT Historical Society, San Francisco.

Cathleen Burns Elmer Collection. Howard Gottlieb Archival Research Center, Boston University, Boston.

Donald Stewart Lucas Papers #1997-25. GLBT Historical Society, San Francisco.

Gore Vidal Papers. Houghton Library, Harvard College Library, Cambridge, MA.

John Horne Burns Collection. Howard Gottlieb Archival Research Center, Boston University, Boston.

John Horne Burns Collection. Phillips Academy Archives, Andover, MA.

John Horne Burns Collection. Selected Records of Harper and Brothers, 1909-60. Box 6, C0103, Folder 19-32. Manuscript Division, Department of Rare Books and Special Collections, Princeton University, Princeton, NJ.

John Horne Burns Material. Loomis Chaffee School Archives, Windsor, CT.

Ralph Green Photo Albums, 91-11. Boxes A, C, D, 4. GLBT Historical Society, San Francisco.

Interviews Conducted by the Author

Fabian Bouthillette, Los Angeles, August 10, 2012.

Thomas D. Burns, Boston and Andover, MA, May 27, 2010; January 11, 2011; and April 23, 2012.

Gore Vidal, Los Angeles, November 9, 2009.

Interviews Conducted by Others

Carter, David, ed. Allen Ginsberg: *Spontaneous Mind: Selected Interviews, 1958-1996*. New York: Harper Collins, 2001.

Clarke, Gerald. "The Art of Fiction No. 50: Interview with Gore Vidal." *Paris Review* 15, no. 59 (Fall 1974): 130-65.

Grobel, Lawrence. *Talking with Michener*. Jackson: University Press of Mississippi, 1999.

Kloman, Harry. "An Interview with Gore Vidal." In Peabody and Ebersole, *Conversations with Gore Vidal*, 139-55.

Kramer, Larry. "The Sadness of Gore Vidal." In Vidal, *Sexually Speaking: Collected Sex Writings*, 252-71. Also in Peabody and Ebersole, *Conversations with Gore Vidal*, 156-72. First published in *QW Magazine* 4 (October 1992).

Mitzel, John, and Steven Abbott. "The Fag Rag Interview [with Gore Vidal]." In Vidal, *Sexually Speaking: Collected Sex Writings*, 194-218. Also in Peabody and Ebersole, *Conversations with Gore Vidal*, 16-35. First published in *Fag Rag*, Winter/Spring 1974.

Mitzel, John, and Thom Willenbecher. "The Gay Sunshine Interview [with Gore Vidal]." In Vidal, *Sexually Speaking: Collected Sex Writings*, 219-51. First published in *Gay Sunshine* (1974).

Parini, Jay. "An Interview with Gore Vidal." *New England Review* 14, no. 1 (Fall 1991): 93-101.

Peabody, Richard, and Lucinda Ebersole, eds. *Conversations with Gore Vidal*. Jackson: University Press of Mississippi, 2005.

Ruas, Charles. "Gore Vidal." In Peabody and Ebersole, *Conversations with Gore Vidal*, 85-99. First published in *Conversations with American Writers*, 57-74. New York: Random House, 1985.

Walter, Eugene. "Conversations with Gore Vidal." In Peabody and Ebersole, *Conversations with Gore Vidal*, 3-15. First published in *Transatlantic Review*, Summer 1960, 5-17.

Weiner, Jon. "The Scholar Squirrels and the National Security State." *Radical History Review* 44 (July 1988): 109-37. Also in Peabody and Ebersole, *Conversations with Gore Vidal*, 100-126.

Autobiographies and Memoirs

Bouthillette, Fabian. *Gore Vidal's Last Stand: Part One; My American Initiation*. Kindle, 2014.

Bradley, James, and Ron Powers. *Flags of Our Fathers*. New York: Bantam Books, 2000.

Bruce, Lenny. *How to Talk Dirty and Influence People: An Autobiography*. Chicago: Playboy Press, 1967.

Collins, Julia. *My Father's War: A Memoir*. New York: Four Walls, Eight Windows, 2002.

Dick, Gene. *Portholes to Life*. Bloomington, IN: Trafford Publishing, 2011.

Duberman, Martin. *Cures: A Gay Man's Odyssey*. New York: Penguin, 1991.

Duhrssen, Alfred. *Memoir of an Aged Child*. New York: Holt, Rinehart, and Winston, 1967.

Elmer, Cathleen Burns. "Roots" (Previously "What We Were"), n.d. Cathleen Burns Elmer Collection, Boston University.

Fahey, James J. *Pacific War Diary, 1942-1945*. Boston: Houghton Mifflin, 2003. First published 1963.

Fisher-Alaniz, Karen. *Breaking the Code: A Father's Secret, a Daughter's Journey, and the Question That Changed Everything*. Naperville, IL: Sourcebooks, 2011.

Fuess, Claude M. *Independent Schoolmaster*. Boston: Little, Brown, 1952.

Giles, Janice Holt, ed. *The G.I. Journal of Sergeant Giles*. Boston: Houghton Mifflin, 1965.

Goodrich, David L. *My Well-Spent Youth: A Lucky Man's 1930-1960 New York-to-Paris Memoir*. Silver Spring, MD: Beckham Publications, 2009.

Greene, Bob. *Duty: A Father, His Son, and the Man Who Won the War*. New York: Harper Collins, 2001.

Hass, Victor P. *Leaves from a Bookman's Notebook*. Omaha, NE: Omaha World Herald, 1972.

——."Looking Homeward: A Memoir of Small-Town Life in Wisconsin." *Wisconsin Magazine of History* 65, no. 3 (1981-82): 176-94.

Hayden, Tom. *Reunion: A Memoir*. New York: Random House, 1988.

Hunter, Tab, with Eddie Muller. *Tab Hunter Confidential*. Chapel Hill, NC: Algonquin Books, 2005.

Hynes, Samuel. *Flights of Passage: Recollections of a World War II Aviator*. New York: Penguin Books, 2003. First published 1988 by Naval Institute Press.

———. *The Soldiers' Tale: Bearing Witness to Modern War*. New York: Penguin Books, 1997.

Kerouac-Parker, Edie. *You'll Be Okay: My Life with Jack Kerouac*. San Francisco: City Lights, 2007.

Ladd, Dean, and Steven Weingartner. *Faithful Warriors: A Combat Marine Remembers the Pacific War*. Annapolis, MD: Naval Institute Press, 2009.

Leckie, Robert. *Helmet for My Pillow: From Parris Island to the Pacific*. New York: Bantam Books, 2010.

Levinson, Leila. *Gated Grief: The Daughter of a Concentration Camp Liberator Discovers a Legacy of Trauma*. Brule, WI: Cable Publishing, 2011.

Lord, James. *My Queer War*. New York: Farrar, Straus, and Giroux, 2010.

Kendal at Hanover Residents Association. *World War II Remembered*. Hanover, NH: Kendal at Hanover, 2012.

Knowles, John. "A Special Time, a Special School," n.d. http://separatepeacebook.com/as sets/essay-1.pdf.

Matthews, Tom. *Our Fathers' War: Growing Up in the Shadow of the Greatest Generation*. New York: Broadway Books, 2005.

Mauldin, Bill. *Back Home*. New York: William Sloane Associates, 1947.

———. *The Brass Ring: A Sort of a Memoir*. New York: W. W. Norton, 1971.

Mewshaw, Michael. *Sympathy for the Devil: Four Decades of Friendship with Gore Vidal*. New York: Farrar, Straus, and Giroux, 2015.

Messner, Michael A. *King of the Wild Suburb: A Memoir of Fathers, Sons and Guns*. Austin, TX: Plain View Press, 2011.

Michener, James. *The World Is My Home: A Memoir*. New York: Ballantine, 1982.

O'Brien, Tim. *If I Die in a Combat Zone: Box Me Up and Ship Me Home*. New York: Random House, 1975.

Phelps, Robert, with Jerry Rosco, eds. *Continual Lessons: The Journals of Glenway Wescott, 1937-1955*. New York: Farrar, Straus and Giroux, 1990.

Recollections of World War II: Andover, 1938. Chapel Hill, NC: Professional Press, 2000.

Redman, Kerry P. *Unfinished Journey: A World War II Remembrance*. Guilford, CT: Lyons Press, 2006.

Reich, Charles A. *The Sorcerer of Bolinas Reef*. New York: Random House, 1976.

Rosborough, James Douglas. *Confessions of a Boatbuilder*. Dibbs Ferry, NY: Sheridan House, 2000.

Rosco, Jerry, ed. *A Heaven of Words: Last Journals, 1956-1984; Glenway Wescott*. Madison: University of Wisconsin Press, 2013.

Sledge., E. B. *China Marine: An Infantryman's Life after World War II*. New York: Oxford University Press, 2002.

Terkel, Studs. *"The Good War": An Oral History of World War Two*. New York: Ballantine, 1984.

Vidal, Gore. *Palimpsest: A Memoir*. New York: Random House, 1995.

———. *Point to Point Navigation: A Memoir*. New York: Doubleday, 2006.

———. *Snapshots in History's Glare*. New York: Abrams, 2009.

Vento, Carol Schultz. *The Hidden Legacy of World War II: A Daughter's Journey of Discovery*. Camp Hill, PA: Sunbury Press, 2011.

Warburg, Fredric. *All Authors Are Equal: The Publishing Life of Fredric Warburg, 1936–1971*. London: Hutchinson, 1973.

White, Minor. *Mirrors, Messages, Manifestations*. New York: Aperture, 1969.

Fiction

Burns, John Horne. *A Cry of Children*. New York: Harper and Brothers, 1952.

———. *The Gallery*. New York: Harper and Brothers, 1947.

———. *Lucifer with a Book*. New York: Harper and Brothers, 1949.

Elmer, Cathleen Burns. *Bicentennial Bliss*. Floresville, TX: Burning Bridge, 2007.

Friedman, Sanford. *Totempole*. San Francisco: North Point Press, 1984. First published 1965.

Jones, James. *The Thin Red Line*. New York: Charles Scribner's Sons, 1962.

Knowles, John. *Indian Summer*. New York: Random House, 1966.

———. *The Paragon*. New York: Random House, 1971.

———. *A Separate Peace*. New York: Scribner, 1987. First published 1959.

Miller, Arthur. *All My Sons: A Drama in Three Acts*. New York: Penguin, 2000. First published 1947.

O'Mara, Peter Paul. "City of Women." *Redbook* 79, no. 3 (July 1942): 10–13, 68–73.

Riggs, Ransom. *Miss Peregrine's Home for Peculiar Children*. Philadelphia: Quirk Books, 2013.

Uris, Leon. *Battle Cry*. New York: Bantam Books, 1954.

Vidal, Gore. *The City and the Pillar*. New York: E. P. Dutton, 1948.

———. *The City and the Pillar Revised*. New York: E. P. Dutton, 1965.

———. *The City and the Pillar: A Novel*. New York: Random House, 1995.

———. *Dark Green, Bright Red*. New York: E. P. Dutton, 1950.

———. *In a Yellow Wood*. London: Abacus, 2009. First published 1947 by Dutton.

———. *The Judgment of Paris*. New York: E. P. Dutton, 1952.

———. *Julian: A Novel*. Boston: Little, Brown, 1964.

———. *Messiah*. New York: E. P. Dutton, 1954.

———. *A Search for the King: A Twelfth Century Legend*. New York: E. P. Dutton, 1950.

———. *The Season of Comfort*. New York: E. P. Dutton, 1949.

———. *A Thirsty Evil: Seven Short Stories*. New York: Zero, 1956.

———. *Two Sisters: A Novel in the Form of a Memoir*. Boston: Little, Brown, 1970.

———. *Williwaw*. Chicago: University of Chicago Press, 2003. First published 1946.

Windham, Donald. *Two People*. New York: Coward-McCann, 1965.

Reviews of Work by John Horne Burns

Reviews of *A Cry of Children*

Balliett, Whitney. "The Manic Moan." Review of *A Cry of Children*. *New Republic* 127 (September 15, 1952): 22.

Bullock, Florence Haxton. "Love Affair as Battle." Review of *A Cry of Children*. *New York Herald Tribune Book Review*, September 7, 1952, 6.

Charques, R. D. Review of *A Cry of Children*. *Spectator* 189 (October 31, 1952): 580.

Curtis, Anthony. Review of *A Cry of Children*. *New Statesman and Nation* 44 (November 29, 1952): 656.

Gill, Brendan. Review of *A Cry of Children*. *New Yorker* 28 (September 6, 1952): 104–5.

Gray, James. "Omnibus of Depravity." Review of *A Cry of Children*. *Saturday Review of Literature*, September 13, 1952, 23, 39.

Grumbach, Doris. "Alas! Alack!" Review of *A Cry of Children*. *Books on Trial*, November 11, 1952, 62.

Hass, Victor P. "Mr. Burns Should Raise His Sights above the Gutter." Review of *A Cry of Children*. *Chicago Tribune*, September 21, 1952.

Juengst, William. "'A Cry of Children' Mirrors Our Nylon-and-Zippered Era." Review of *A Cry of Children*. *Brooklyn Eagle*, September 7, 1952, 1.

Kelly, James. "No Way Out." Review of *A Cry of Children*. *New York Times Book Review*, September 7, 1952, BR4.

Kirkus Reviews. Unsigned review of *A Cry of Children*. 20 (July 1, 1952): 381–82.

Lynch, John A. "Not without a Bang." Review of *A Cry of Children*. *Commonwealth*, October 3, 1952, 633–34.

McGehee, Charles White. "Man's Struggle for Art and Love." Review of *A Cry of Children*. *Birmingham News*, September 7, 1952, E-6.

Rolo, Charles J. Review of *A Cry of Children*. *Atlantic Monthly* 190 (October 1952): 104.

Times Literary Supplement. Unsigned review of *A Cry of Children*. November 14, 1952, 737.

Reviews of *The Gallery*

Farrelly, John. Review of *The Gallery*. *New Republic*, July 7, 1947, 3.

Hallock, Joseph. "Psychology of Total War." Review of *The Gallery*, n.p., n.d. Clipping in John Horne Burns Collection, Boston University.

Halsband, Robert. "Victors and Vanquished: Nine Members of Motley Crowd in Postwar Naples." Review of *The Gallery*. *Chicago Sun Book Week*, August 3, 1947, 8.

Hart, H. W. Review of *The Gallery*. *Library Journal* 72 (June 6, 1947): 886.

Hogan, William. "A First Novel on Warped War Centers of Europe." Review of *The Gallery*. *San Francisco Chronicle*, June 29, 1947, 10.

"Homage to Naples." Unsigned review of *The Gallery*. *Time* 49 (June 9, 1947): 110.

Hunter, Anna C. Review of *The Gallery*. *Savannah Morning News*, July 27, 1947, 26.

Huth, John F. "Ex-G.I. Describes 'War' among His Buddies in Naples." Review of *The Gallery*. *Cleveland Plain Dealer*, June 8, 1947, 15B.

Keena, Thomas E. J. "Literature of Disillusion." Review of *The Gallery*. *Hartford Courant Magazine*, June 8, 1947, 12.

Kirkus Reviews. Unsigned review of *The Gallery*. March 1, 1947, 137.

McFee, William. Review of *The Gallery*. *New York Sun*, July 9, 1947, 21.

Poore, Charles. Review of *The Gallery*. *New York Times*, June 7, 1947, 11.

Roscoe, Gerald D. "The Riddle of Life: Andover Young Author's Book Reveals One of the Finest Talents." Review of *The Gallery*. *Boston Globe*, June 4, 1947.

Ross, Jerome D. "From a War-Torn Naples." Review of *The Gallery*. *New York Herald Tribune Weekly Book Review*, June 8, 1947, 3.

Sullivan, Richard. "Under the Shattered Roof of an Italian Galleria." Review of *The Gallery*. *New York Times Book Review*. June 8, 1947, 7, 25.

Time Literary Supplement. Unsigned review of *The Gallery*. July 24, 1948, 413.

White, Lawrence Grant. "Portraits and Promenades." Review of *The Gallery*. *Saturday Review of Literature*, July 19, 1947, 21.

Wilson, Edmund. "The Americans in Italy: 'The Gallery.'" Review of *The Gallery*. *New Yorker* 23 (August 9, 1947): 60–62.

Reviews of *Lucifer with a Book*

Atkins, Ben, and Estelle. Review of *Lucifer with a Book*. *Gaston Gazette*, April 23, 1949, 24.

Atlanta Mirror. Unsigned review of *Lucifer with a Book*. April 28, 1949, 17.

Atlantic Monthly. Unsigned review of *Lucifer with a Book*. 183 (April 1949): 89.

Broderick, John. Review of *Lucifer with a Book*. *New Yorker* 25 (April 16, 1949): 104.

Brookhouser, Frank. "Private Schools Satirized." Review of *Lucifer with a Book*. *Philadelphia Inquirer*, April 3, 1949, Books Section, 3.

Brown, E. K. "Embattled Teachers: A Novel of Protest." Review of *Lucifer with a Book*. *Winnipeg Free Press*, May 28, 1949, 12.

"Burns' Novel Is Portrait of Private School." Unsigned review of *Lucifer with a Book*. *European Stars and Stripes*, July 10, 1949, 8.

Catholic World. Unsigned review of *Lucifer with a Book*. 169 (June 1949): 240.

Charques, R. D. Review of *Lucifer with a Book*. *Spectator*, November 4, 1949, 646.

Dewey, Ernest. "Not So Pretty Picture Painted of *Conditions* in Private School." Review of *Lucifer with a Book*. *Hutchinson News Herald*, April 13, 1949, 6.

Du Bouis, William. "No Apples for Teacher." Review of *Lucifer with a Book*. *New York Times Book Review*, April 3, 1949, BR4.

"Further Education." Unsigned review of *Lucifer with a Book*. *Times Literary Supplement*, November 4, 1949, 709.

Geismer, Maxwell. "Puritanism, Evil, and Malice." Review of *Lucifer with a Book*. *Saturday Review of Literature*, April 2, 1949, 16.

Hass, Victor P. "Prep School Sketched in an Acid Vein." Review of *Lucifer with a Book*. *Chicago Tribune*, April 10, 1949.

Haydn, Hiram. "Satire Turns to Burlesque." Review of *Lucifer with a Book*. *New York Herald Tribune Weekly Book Review*, April 3, 1949, 4.

Kalem, Theodore. "The Case of the Angry Novelist." Review of *Lucifer with a Book*. *Christian Science Monitor*, April 28, 1949, 15.

Kirkus Reviews. Unsigned review of *Lucifer with a Book*. 17 (February 1, 1949): 66.

Langley, Dorothy. "School for Neurotics." Review of *Lucifer with a Book*. *Chicago Sun-Times*, July 7, 1949, 44.

Lindsay, Steele. "John H. Burns' Second Novel Bears Out His Earlier Promise." Review of *Lucifer with a Book*. *Boston Post*, n.d., n.p. Clipping in John Horne Burns Collection, Boston University.

Orgain, Marian. Review of *Lucifer with a Book*. *Pacific Stars and Stripes*, June 18, 1949, 21.

Prescott, Orville. Review of *Lucifer with a Book*. *New York Times*, April 1, 1949.

Roscoe, Gerald D. "Burns Tells Us." Review of *Lucifer with a Book*. *Boston Globe*, n.d., n.p. Clipping in John Horne Burns Collection, Boston University.

Vaughan, Virginia. Review of *Lucifer with a Book*. *Commonwealth* 50 (April 29, 1949): 76–77.

Wasson, Donald. Review of *Lucifer with a Book*. *Library Journal* 73 (March 15, 1949): 494.

White, Antonia. Review of *Lucifer with a Book*. *New Statesman and Nation* 38, no. 5 (November 5, 1949): 52.

Reviews of Work by Gore Vidal

Reviews of *The City and the Pillar*

"Briefly Noted." Unsigned review of *The City and the Pillar*. *New Yorker* 23 (January 10, 1948): 81.

Bulletin Virginia Kirkus' Service. Unsigned review of *The City and the Pillar*. 15 (January 9, 1948): 608.

Doyle, Edward Dermot. "An Honest Approach." Review of *The City and the Pillar*. *San Francisco Chronicle*, February 2, 1948, 14.

Gehman, Richard B. "Abnormal Doom." Review of *The City and the Pillar*. *New York Herald Tribune Weekly Book Review*, January 18, 1948, 6.

Kingery, Robert E. Review of *The City and the Pillar*. *Library Journal* 72 (December 1, 1947): 1686.

McLaughlin, Richard. "Precarious Status." Review of *The City and the Pillar*. *Saturday Review of Literature* 31 (January 10, 1948): 14–15.

Newby, P. H. "New Novels." Review of *The City and the Pillar*. *Listener* 41, no. 1058 (May 5, 1949): 774.

Rolo, Charles J. "Reader's Choice." Review of *The City and the Pillar*. *Atlantic Monthly* 181, no. 2 (February 1948): 107–12.

Shrike, J. S. "Recent Phenomena." Review of *The City and the Pillar*. *Hudson Review* 1, no. 1 (Spring 1948): 136–38, 140, 142, 144.

Stratchey, Julia. Review of *The City and the Pillar*. *New Statesman and Nation* 37, no. 949 (May 14, 1949): 510, 512.

Strong, L. A. G. Review of *The City and the Pillar*. *Spectator*, April 29, 1949, 586, 588.

Terry, C. V. "The City and the Pillar." *New York Times Book Review*, January 11, 1948: BR22 and 242.

Reviews of *The City and the Pillar Revised*

Donahugh, Robert H. Review of *The City and the Pillar Revised*. *Library Journal* 90 (May 15, 1965): 22, 89–90.

Kramer, Hilton. "Queer Affirmations." Review of *The City and the Pillar Revised*. *New Leader* 48 (August 30, 1965): 16–17.

Marcus, Steven. "A Second Look at Sodom." Review of *The City and the Pillar Revised*. *Book Week*, June 20, 1965, 5.

Mayne, Richard. "Make 'em Wait." Review essay including *The City and the Pillar Revised*. *New Statesman* 70 (October 1, 1965): 488–89.

Reviews of *Dark Green, Bright Red*

Barr, Donald. "From Patio to Jungle." Review of *Dark Green, Bright Red*. *New York Times*, October 8, 1950, online.

Booklist. Unsigned review of *Dark Green, Bright Red*. *Booklist* 47 (November 1950): 98.

Brooks, John. "Fighting Somebody Else's Revolution." Review of *Dark Green, Bright Red*. *Saturday Review of Literature* 33 (October 14, 1950): 15.

Bulletin Virginia Kirkus' Service. Unsigned review of *Dark Green, Bright Red*. 18 (October 9, 1950): 527.

Derleth, August. "Vidal Writes Vivid Tale of Revolution." Review of *Dark Green, Bright Red*. *Chicago Tribune*, October 8, 1950, 3.

Kingery, Robert E. Review of *Dark Green, Bright Red*. *Library Journal* 75 (October 11, 1950): 1662.

Math, Richard. "Loveless Life, Banana Land." Review of *Dark Green, Bright Red*. *New York Herald Tribune Book Review*, October 15, 1950, 10.

"Men, Women, and War." Unsigned review of *Dark Green, Bright Red*. *Times Literary Supplement*, August 25, 1950, 529.

New Yorker. Unsigned review of *Dark Green, Bright Red*. 26 (October 28, 1950): 130–31.

Shrapnel, Norman. Review of *Dark Green, Bright Red*. *Manchester Guardian*, August 11, 1950, 4.

Reviews of *In a Yellow Wood*

Barr, Donald. "The Veteran's Choice." Review of *In a Yellow Wood*. *New York Times Book Review*, March 16, 1947, 10.

Bulletin Virginia Kirkus' Service. Unsigned review of *In a Yellow Wood*. 15 (January 15, 1947): 43.

Kingery, Robert E. Review of *In a Yellow Wood*. *Library Journal* 72, no. 6 (March 15, 1947): 464.

New Yorker. Unsigned review of *In a Yellow Wood*. 23 (March 22, 1947).

Rothman, Nathan L. "A Strange Sort of War Casualty." Review of *In a Yellow Wood*. *Saturday Review of Literature* 30 (May 31, 1947): 21.

Schorer, Mark. "The American Novel." Review essay including *Williwaw* and *In a Yellow Wood*. *Kenyon Review* 9 (Autumn 1947): 628–36.

Stepanchev, Stephen. "Four Roads to Tomorrow." Review of *In a Yellow Wood*. *New York Herald Tribune Weekly Book Review*, March 16, 1947, 10.

Textor, Clinton. "Returned Vet Wants Only Humdrum Life." Review of *In a Yellow Wood*. *Chicago Sun Book Week*, April 27, 1947, 2.

Yanitelli, Victor R., SJ. Review of *In a Yellow Wood*. *Best Sellers* 7, no. 1 (April 1, 1947): 7.

Reviews of *The Judgment of Paris*

Aldridge, John W. "Three Tempted Him." Review of *The Judgment of Paris*. *New York Times*, March 9, 1952, online.

Atlantic. Unsigned review of *The Judgment of Paris*. 189 (April 1, 1952): 85.

Crane, Milton. "Plundered Myth." Review of *The Judgment of Paris*. *Saturday Review of Literature* 35 (March 22, 1952): 18.

Derleth, August. "Vidal's Latest Not His Best, nor Poorest." Review of *The Judgment of Paris*. *Chicago Tribune*, March 9, 1952, 4.

Kingery, Robert E. Review of *The Judgment of Paris*. *Library Journal* 77 (January 15, 1952): 144.

L.V. Review of *The Judgment of Paris*. *San Francisco Chronicle*, July 6, 1952, 10.

New Yorker. Unsigned review of *The Judgment of Paris*. 28 (March 15, 1952): 118.

Peterson, Virgilia. "Finding Love in Paris." Review of *The Judgment of Paris*. *New York Herald Tribune Book Review*, June 8, 1952, 11.

Theall, D. Bernard, OSB. Review of *The Judgment of Paris*. *Best Sellers* 11, no. 24 (March 15, 1952): 256.

Virginia Kirkus' Review. Unsigned review of *The Judgment of Paris*. 19 (December 15, 1951): 711.

Reviews of *Julian*

Allen, Walter. "The Last Pagan." Review of *Julian*. *New York Review of Books* 2 (July 30, 1964): 20–22.

"The Ascetic Pagan." Review of *Julian*. *Time* 83 (June 12, 1964): 122, 124–25.

Auchincloss, Louis. "The Best Man, Vintage 361 A.D." Review of *Julian*. *Life* 56, no. 24 (June 12, 1964): 19, 21.

Barrett, William. "Death of the Gods." Review of *Julian*. *Atlantic Monthly* 214, no. 1 (July 1964): 134–35.

Buckmaster, Henrietta. "Gore Vidal's Roman Emperor." Review of *Julian*. *Christian Science Monitor*, June 18, 1964, 7.

Burgess, Anthony. "A Touch of the Apostasies." Review of *Julian*. *Spectator* 213, no. 7112 (October 16, 1964): 518.

Davenport, Guy. "Caution: Falling Prose." Review of *Julian*. *National Review* 16 (July 14, 1964): 609–10.

David, Robert M. "Approach to the Apostate." Review of *Julian*. *Critic* 23 (August 3, 1964): 70–71.

Dolbier, Maurice. "Gore Vidal's Good, Solid Historical Novel." Review of *Julian*. *New York Herald Tribune*, June 8, 1964, 19.

Donahugh, Robert H. Review of *Julian*. *Library Journal* 89 (April 1, 1964): 1625–26.

Fitts, Dudley. "England in Life and in a Pagan Past." Review of *Julian*. *New York Times*, May 31, 1964, online.

Foller, Edmund. "An Idealistic Pagan." Review of *Julian*. *Wall Street Journal*, June 12, 1964, 6.

Green, Peter. "Resuscitated Emperor." Review of *Julian*. *New Republic* 3, no. 50 (June 13, 1964): 21.

Harvey, Mary Kersey. "The Author: Who Is the Real Gore Vidal?" *Saturday Review of Literature* 47 (June 6, 1964): 32.

Heineman, Larry Curtiss. "Lost in the Crowds." Review of *Julian*. *Times Literary Supplement*, November 12, 1964, 1013.

Hicks, Granville. "No Cross on Olympus." Review of *Julian*. *Saturday Review of Literature* 47 (June 6, 1964): 31–32.

Hill, William B., SJ. Review of *Julian*. *Best Sellers* 24, no. 6 (June 15, 1964): 113–14.

Hope, Francis. "I, Julian." Review of *Julian*. *New Statesman* 68 (November 13, 1964): 741–42.

Pickrel, Paul. "The Gods: Their Exits and Their Entrances." Review of *Julian. Harper's* 229 (July 1964): 99.

Pomer, Belle. "Echoes." Review of *Julian. Canadian Forum* 44 (September 1964): 144.

Prescott, Orville. "The Apostate Emperor." Review of *Julian. New York Times*, June 10, 1964, 43.

Steiner, George. "Vicisti, Galilaee." Review of *Julian. Reporter* 31 (July 16, 1964): 45.

Virginia Quarterly Review. Review of *Julian.* 40, no. 4 (Autumn 1964): cxlviii.

"Vitality." Review of *Julian. Newsweek* 63 (June 15, 1964): 106.

Warner, Rex. "Philosopher King—and Imperian Eagle Scout." Review of *Julian. Book Week*, June 7, 1964, 4.

Reviews of *Messiah*

Bulletin Virginia Kirkus' Bookshop Service. Review of *Messiah.* 22 (February 15, 1954): 130.

Geismar, Maxwell. "Deadly Altar." Review of *Messiah. New York Times*, April 25, 1954, 4.

Rugoff, Milton. "One Very Dark Look Ahead." Review of *Messiah. New York Herald Tribune Book Review*, April 25, 1954, 16.

Stone, Jerome. "Frightening Future." Review of *Messiah. Saturday Review* 37 (May 22, 1954): 34–35.

Sullivan, Richard. "Brilliant, Satiric Novel Marred by Its Mockery." Review of *Messiah. Chicago Tribune*, April 25, 1954, 4.

Vogler, Lewis. "A Mediocre Evangelist Fools His Fellow Men." Review of *Messiah. San Francisco Chronicle*, May 23, 1954, 17.

Reviews of *A Search for the King*

Booklist. Unsigned review of *A Search for the King. Booklist* 46, no. 16 (February 1950): 150.

Bulletin Virginia Kirkus' Bookshop Service. Review of *A Search for the King.* 17, no. 24 (November 15, 1949): 628.

Gravel, George. Review of *A Search for the King. Best Sellers* 9, no. 22 (February 15, 1950): 183–84.

Kingery, Robert E. Review of *A Search for the King. Library Journal* 74, no. 21 (December 1, 1949): 1819.

Langbaum, Robert. "The Questing Hero." Review of *A Search for the King. Nation* 170, no. 15 (April 15, 1950): 35.

Lerman, Leo. "The Legend of Richard." Review of *A Search for the King. New York Times Book Review*, January 15, 1950, 4, 16.

Litten, Frederic Nelson. "Delightful Romantic Tale from the Pen of a 'High-Brow.'" Review of *A Search for the King. Chicago Sun-Times*, January 26, 1950, 6S.

Maloney, John J. "Set in the Mold of Legend." Review of *A Search for the King. New York Herald Tribune*, January 15, 1950, 8.

Miles, George. Review of *A Search for the King. Commonwealth* 51, no. 16 (January 27, 1950): 446.

New Yorker. Unsigned review of *A Search for the King.* January 21, 1950, 97–98.

Putnam, Samuel. "Animated Tapestry." Review of *A Search for the King. Saturday Review* 33 (January 14, 1950): 10.

Rugg, Winnifred. Review of *A Search for the King. Christian Science Monitor*, January 26, 1950, 11.

Wagenknecht, Edward. "Brilliant 'Historical' by a 24-Year Old: Vidal's Fifth Is Legend of Coeur de Lion." Review of *A Search for the King. Chicago Tribune Sunday Magazine of Books*, January 15, 1950, 3.

Reviews of *The Season of Comfort*

Aldridge, John W. "A Boy and His Mom." Review of *The Season of Comfort. Saturday Review of Literature* 32 (January 15, 1949): 19–20.

Booklist. Unsigned review of *The Season of Comfort. Booklist* 45 (February 1, 1949): 193.

Broderick, John. "Strong Start, Weak Finish." Review of *The Season of Comfort. New Yorker* 24 (January 15, 1949): 77–78.

Bulletin of Virginia Kirkus' Bookshop Service. Unsigned review of *The Season of Comfort*. 16, no. 23 (November 1, 1948): 578.

Cheatham, Richard. Review of *The Season of Comfort. Carolina Quarterly* 1, no. 2 (March 16, 1949): 69–70.

Dedmon, Emmett. "Gore Vidal's Novel Gives Hint of What Young Writers Think." Review of *The Season of Comfort. Chicago Sun-Times*, January 9, 1949, 8X.

Doyle, Edward Dermot. Review of *The Season of Comfort. San Francisco Chronicle*, February 13, 1949, 14.

Kingery, Robert E. Review of *The Season of Comfort. Library Journal* 74 (January 1, 1949): 60.

Klaw, Barbara. "A Dominating Mother." Review of *The Season of Comfort. New York Herald Tribune Book Review*, January 9, 1949, 10.

Rolo, Charles. "Life with Mother." Review of *The Season of Comfort. Atlantic* 183, no. 2 (February 1949): 86–87.

Weaver, William Fense. "Mr. Vidal's Silver Cord." Review of *The Season of Comfort. New York Times*, February 6, 1949, 12.

Reviews of *A Thirsty Evil*

Hicks, Granville. "The Prize Short Stories of the Year and Three New Individual Collections." Review of *A Thirsty Evil. New Leader* 40, no. 6 (February 11, 1957): 21–22.

Malcolm, Donald. "At Home in a Gray Rubber Sack." Review of *A Thirsty Evil. New Republic* 136 (February 25, 1957): 20.

Peden, William. "On the Road to Self-Destruction." Review of *A Thirsty Evil. New York Times*, January 27, 1957, 33.

Quinton, Anthony. Review of *A Thirsty Evil. London Magazine* 6, no. 6 (June 8, 1959): 71.

Raven, Simon. "Brother Mountobank." Review of *A Thirsty Evil. Spectator* 201, no. 6800 (October 24, 1958): 560.

"Seven Stories by Gore Vidal." Review of *A Thirsty Evil. New York Herald Tribune*, February 17, 1957, 5.

Reviews of *Williwaw*

Bulletin Virginia Kirkus' Service. Unsigned review of *Williwaw*. 14 (May 1, 1946): 203.

Daniels, Jonathan. "Dirty Weather." Review of *Williwaw*. *Saturday Review of Literature* 29 (July 6, 1946): 7–8.

Fields, Arthur C. Review of *Williwaw*. *New York Herald Tribune Weekly Book Review*, June 23, 1946, 17.

Morgan, Rhea M. "'Williwaw': Gore Vidal's Novel of 'Big Wind' in Arctic." *Springfield Republican*, July 28, 1946, 46.

Prescott, Orville. Review of *Williwaw*. *New York Times*, June 17, 1946, 19.

Schorer, Mark. "The American Novel." Review essay including *Williwaw* and *In a Yellow Wood*. *Kenyon Review* 9 (Autumn 1947): 628–36.

Reviews of Work by John Knowles

Aitken, Douglas. "Tale of Two Schoolboys." Review of *A Separate Peace*. *San Francisco Chronicle*, June 26, 1960, 29.

Belliett, Whitney. Review of *A Separate Peace*. *New Yorker* 36 (April 2, 1960): 158–59.

Booklist. Unsigned review of *A Separate Peace*. 56 (February 15, 1960): 353.

Bookmark. Review of *A Separate Peace*. 19 (March 1960): 151.

Christian Century. Unsigned review of *A Separate Peace*. 77 (June 8, 1960): 697.

Duchene, Anne. "On the Dark Perimeters of Feeling and Fiction." Review of *A Separate Peace*. *Manchester Guardian*, May 1, 1959, 6.

Fuller, Edmund. "Shadow of Mars." Review of *A Separate Peace*. *New York Times Book Review*, February 7, 1960, 35.

Hicks, Granville. "The Good Have a Quiet Heroism." Review of *A Separate Peace*. *Saturday Review of Literature* 43 (March 5, 1960): 16.

Holzhauer, Jean. Review of *A Separate Peace*. *Commonwealth* 73 (December 9, 1960): 284.

Horn Book Magazine. Unsigned review of *A Separate Peace*. 36 (October 1960): 421.

Houlihan, Thomas F. Review of *A Separate Peace*. *Library Journal* 85 (March 1, 1960): 987.

Kirkus Reviews. Unsigned review of *A Separate Peace*. 27 (December 1, 1959): 893.

Lemay, Harding. "Two Boys and a War Within." Review of *A Separate Peace*. *New York Herald Tribune Book Review*, March 6, 1960, 6.

"New Novels." Unsigned review of *A Separate Peace*. *New Statesman* 57 (May 2, 1959): 618.

Raven, Simon. "No Time for War." Review of *A Separate Peace*. *Spectator*, May 1, 1959, 630.

Yates, Donald. "Dramatic First Novel of Life in a Prep School." Review of *A Separate Peace*. *Chicago Tribune Sunday Magazine of Books*, March 27, 1960, 5.

Nonfiction Works by Principal Characters

Burns, John Horne. "Adventurer in Life." *Saturday Review of Literature* 32 (February 12, 1949): 16.

——. "Algiers." *Holiday* 5, no. 2 (February 1949): 64–70, 131–34.

——. "Andover." *Holiday* 7, no. 3 (March 1950): 55–61, 128–31.

——. "Belfast." *Holiday* 11, no. 1 (January 1952): 48–51, 86–89.

———. "Brighton." *Holiday* 8, no. 3 (September 1950): 52–55, 85–87.

———. "Casablanca." *Holiday* 5, no. 1 (January 1949): 64–70, 130–31.

———. "The Creative Writer in the 20th Century." Typescript, n.d. John Horne Burns Collection at the Howard Gottlieb Archival Research Center. Boston University.

———. "Drunk with Ink." *Saturday Review of Literature* 32 (December 17, 1949): 9–10.

———. "Florence." *Holiday* 12, no. 4 (October 1952): 44–47, 122–31.

———. "Naples." *Holiday* 5, no. 5 (May 1949): 64–70, 154–56.

———. "Novel of Combat." *New York Times Book Review*, July 24, 1949, BR5.

———. "Promenade in Naples." *Harper's* 194, no. 1164 (May 1947): 402–7.

———. "Roman Family." *Holiday* 5, no. 6 (June 1949): 64–70, 132–34.

———. "The Sadness and Madness of Naples." *New York Times Book Review*, September 4, 1949, BR3.

———. To Ramona Herdman. November 1, 1946. From "The Creative Writer in the 20th Century." Typescript. John Horne Burns Collection at the Howard Gottlieb Archival Research Center. Boston University.

———. "Tourist Washington." *Holiday* 7, no. 2 (February 1950): 102–13.

———. "Tunis." *Holiday* 5, no. 3 (March 1949): 64–70, 122–24.

———. "Where the River Shannon Flows." *Holiday* 9, no. 4 (April 1951): 98–105, 139–46.

———. "A Word with the Teacher of English." *English Leaflet* 49 (February 1948): 17–24.

Vidal, Gore. "Making and Remaking." *New York Times*, November 14, 1965, online.

———. "Sex and the Law." In *The City and the Pillar Revised*, 229–41.

———. *Sexually Speaking: Collected Sex Writings*. San Francisco: Cleis Press, 1999.

———. "Speaking of Books: John Horne Burns." *New York Times Book Review*, May 30, 1965, BR22.

———. "Those Bleak Young Nihilists." *Wisconsin State Journal*, July 22, 1951, 8.

———. "Two Immoralists: Orville Prescott and Ayn Rand." *Esquire* 56, no. 1 (July 1961): 24, 26–27.

———. *United States: Essays, 1952–1992*. New York: Random House, 1993.

Film and Television

Combat Exhaustion. Official Training Film. US Army Service Forces, War Department, 1945.

Huston, John. *Let There Be Light* (1946). Narrated by Walter Huston. National Archives and Records Administration. National Film Preservation Foundation. Released 1980.

Shades of Gray. US Army Documentary. Professional Medical Film #5047. 1947.

Midcentury Newspapers, Magazines, and Journal Articles

Adams, Frank S. "Columbia Student Kills Friend and Sinks Body in Hudson River." *New York Times*, August 7, 1944, 1, 13.

"Andover Author Is Dead in Italy." Obituary. *Boston Post*, August 14, 1953. Clipping in John Horne Burns Collection. Boston University.

"Body of Author to Arrive Today." Obituary. *Boston Herald*, September 2, 1953. Clipping in John Horne Burns Collection. Boston University.

Bossard, J. H. S. "Family Problems of the Immediate Future." *Journal of Home Economics* 37 (September 1945): 383–84.

Brotz, Howard, and Everett Wilson. "Characteristics of Military Society." *American Journal of Sociology* 51 (March 1946): 371–75.

Burns Obituary. *Phillips Academy Bulletin*, November 1953. Clipping in John Horne Burns Collection. Boston University.

Cuber, John F. "Family Readjustment of Veterans." *Marriage and Family Living* 7 (May 1945): 28–30.

Eaton, Walter H. "Research on Veterans' Adjustment." *American Journal of Sociology* 51 (March 1946): 483–87.

Elkin, Frederick. "The Soldiers Language." *American Journal of Sociology* 51 (March 1946): 414–22.

Elkin, Henry. "Aggressive and Erotic Tendencies in Army Life." *American Journal of Sociology* 51 (March 1946): 408–13.

Farnum, Marynia F., MD. "The Tragic Failure of America's Women." *Coronet* 22 (September 1947): 5–9.

Fowles, L. W. "The Harvest of Our Lives: The History of The First Half-Century of the Loomis Institute." *Loomis Bulletin* 32, no. 3 (March 1964).

Harris, Eleanor. "Men without Women." *Look* 24, no. 24 (November 22, 1960): 124, 127–30.

Hill, Reuben. "The Returning Father and His Family." *Marriage and Family Living* 7 (May 1945): 31–34.

Hollingshead, August B. "Adjustment to Military Life." *American Journal of Sociology* 51 (March 1946): 439–47.

"John H. Burns." Obituary. *Boston Globe*, August 14, 1953. Clipping in John Horne Burns Collection. Boston University.

"John H. Burns." Obituary. *Hartford Courant*, n.d. Clipping in John Horne Burns Collection. Boston University.

"John Horne Burns Dies in Italy." Obituary. *Boston Herald*, August 14, 1953. Clipping in John Horne Burns Collection. Boston University.

"John Horne Burns Dies, Author of 'The Gallery.'" Obituary. *New York Herald Tribune*, August 14, 1953. Clipping in John Horne Burns Collection. Boston University.

"John Horne Burns, Novelist, 36, Dies," Obituary. *New York Times*, August 4, 1953. http://www.nytimes.com/1953/08/14/archives/john-horne-burns-novelist-36-dies-author-of-gallery-called-best-war.html.

Kneeland, Paul F. "'Born Snob,' John Horne Burns Turned Down Hollywood Gold." *Boston Globe*, December 11, 1947.

Mackenzie, Catherine. "Fathers Home from War." *New York Times*, February 4, 1945, 87.

"The Making of the Infantryman." *American Journal of Sociology* 51 (March 1946): 376–79.

"Mauldin Meets Son: The War's Best-Known GI Returns to See His Baby for the First Time." *Life*, July 9, 1945, 30–31.

McDonough, Edward C. "The Discharged Serviceman and His Family." *American Journal of Sociology* 51 (March 1946): 451–54.

"The Men from the Boys." *Boston Globe*, August 28, 1955. Clipping in John Horne Burns Collection. Boston University.

"The Menace of the Maternal Father." *Hygeia* 20 (June 1942): 468–70.

Moore, Virginia M., MD. "When Father Comes Marching Home." *Parents*, January 1945, 16–17, 112.

"Uncle Dudley." In "All That Matters in the 20th Century." *Boston Globe*, November 8, 1953. John Horne Burns Collection. Boston University.

Weinberg, S. Kirson. "The Combat Neurosis." *American Journal of Sociology* 51 (March 1946): 465–78.

Midcentury Literary Criticism

Aldridge, John W. *After the Last Generation: A Critical Study of the Writers of Two Wars*. New York: Arbor House, 1985. First published 1951 by McGraw-Hill.

———. *In the Country of the Young*. New York: Harper's Magazine Press, 1970.

———. "The New Generation of Writers." *Harper's* 195, no. 1170 (November 1947): 423–32.

Baumbach, Jonathan. "The Saint as a Young Man: A Reappraisal of *The Catcher in the Rye*." *Modern Language Quarterly* 25, no. 4 (December 1964): 461–72.

Brophy, Brigid. *Don't Never Forget: Collected Views and Reviews*. New York: Holtz Rinehart and Winston, 1966.

Edgerton, Daniel H. "The Ambiguous Heroes of John Horne Burns." *One* 1, no. 10 (October 1958): 6–12.

Fiedler, Leslie. "The Fate of the Novel." *Kenyon Review* 10, no. 3 (Summer 1948): 519–27.

Hazard, Eloise Perry. "John Horne Burns." *Saturday Review of Literature* 31, no. 7 (February 14, 1948): 7.

Mailer, Norman. Introduction to *After the Last Generation: A Critical Study of the Writers of Two Wars*, by John W. Aldridge, xvii–xxii. New York: Arbor House, 1985.

Mitgang, Herbert. "Books of the Times." *New York Times*, July 9, 1954, 15.

Morton, Frederic. "Innocents Abroad." Review of *The Facts of Love* by Stanley Baron. *New York Times Book Review*, September 3, 1956, BR2.

Poore, Charles. "Books of the Times." *New York Times*, May 31, 1956, 25.

Rolo, Charles J. "Four Make a Scenario." Review of *The Capri Letters* by Mario Soldati. *New York Times Book Review*, February 12, 1956, BR4.

Saal, Hubert. "John Horne Burns's Italy." *Yale Literary Magazine* 114, no. 9 (October 1947): 23–28.

Seng, Peter J. "The Fallen Idol: The Immature World of Holden Caulfield." *College English* 23, no. 3 (December 1961): 203–9.

Shrike, J. S. "Recent Phenomena." *Hudson Review* 1, no. 1 (Spring 1948): 136–38, 140, 142, 144.

Slonim, Mark. "The Roman Education of Jimmy." Review of *Tempo di Roma* by Alexis Curvers. *New York Times Book Review*, June 7, 1959, BR5.

Smith, Harrison. "Thirteen Adventurers: A Study of a Year of First Novelists." *Saturday Review of Literature* 31, no. 7 (February 14, 1948): 6–8.

Midcentury Social and Psychological Studies

Benedick, Therese, MD. *Insight and Personality Adjustment: A Study of the Psychological Effects of War*. New York: Ronald Press, 1946.

Child, Irvin L., and Marjorie Van De Water, eds. *Psychology for the Returning Serviceman.* Washington, DC: Infantry Journal/Penguin Books, 1945.

Cory, Donald Webster, and Albert Ellis. *The Homosexual in America: A Subjective Approach.* New York: Greenberg, 1951.

Cory, Donald Webster, and John P. LeRoy. *The Homosexual and His Society: A View from Within.* New York: Citadel Press, 1963.

de Grazia, Sebastian. *The Political Community: A Study of Anomie.* Chicago: University of Chicago Press, 1948.

Dumas, Alexander G., and Grace Keen. *A Psychiatric Primer for the Veteran's Family and Friends.* Minneapolis: University of Minnesota Press, 1945.

Dupuy, R. Ernest, and Herbert L. Bregstein. *Soldiers Album.* Boston: Houghton Mifflin, 1946.

Grinker, Roy R., MD, and John P. Spiegel, MD. *Men under Stress.* New York: McGraw-Hill, 1945.

Janks, Irving L. "Psychodynamic Aspects of Adjustment to Army Life." *Psychiatry* 8 (May 1945): 159–76.

Kitching, Howard. *Sex Problems of the Returned Veteran.* New York: Emerson Books, 1946.

Kinsey, Alfred C., Wardell B. Pomeroy, and Clyde E. Martin. *Sexual Behavior in the Human Male.* Philadelphia: W. B. Saunders, 1948.

Miller, Arthur. *Situation Normal . . .* New York: Reynal and Hitchcock, 1944.

Mills, C. Wright. *White Collar: The American Middle Classes.* New York: Oxford University Press, 1951.

Reich, Charles A. *The Greening of America.* New York: Random House, 1970.

Riesman, David, with Nathan Glazer and Reuel Denney. *The Lonely Crowd: A Study of the Changing American Character.* New Haven, CT: Yale University Press, 1950.

Slater, Philip. *The Pursuit of Loneliness: American Culture at the Breaking Point.* Boston: Beacon Press, 1970.

Waller, Willard. *The Veteran Comes Back.* New York: Dryden Press, 1944.

Whyte, William H. *The Organization Man.* Philadelphia: University of Pennsylvania Press, 2002. First published 1956.

Additional Midcentury Nonfiction

Baldwin, James. "Preservation of Innocence." In *Collected Essays*, 594–600. New York: Library of America, 1998. First published summer 1949 by Zero.

DePastino, Todd, ed. *Willie and Joe: Back Home.* New York: Fantagraphics Books, 2011.

———. *Willie and Joe: The WWII Years.* New York: Fantagraphics Books, 2011.

Lundberg, Ferdinand, and Marynia F. Farnum, MD. *Modern Woman: The Lost Sex.* New York: Harper and Brothers, 1947.

Mauldin, Bill. *Up Front.* New York: Henry Holt, 1945.

Spock, Benjamin, MD. *Baby and Child Care.* New York: Pocket Books, 1957.

———. *The Pocket Book of Baby and Child Care.* New York: Pocket Books, 1946.

Wylie, Philip. *Generation of Vipers.* New York: Rinehart, 1942.

SELECTED SECONDARY SOURCES

Books and Dissertations

Aarons, Mark, and John Loftus. *Unholy Trinity: The Vatican, the Nazis, and the Swiss Banks.* New York: St. Martin's Press, 1991.

Abbott, Steven. *Gore Vidal: A Bibliography, 1940–2009.* New Castle, DE: Oak Knoll Press, 2009.

Adams, Michael C. C. *The Best War Ever: America and World War II.* Baltimore: Johns Hopkins University Press, 1994.

Agee, James. *Agee on Film: Criticism and Comment on the Movies.* New York: Modern Library, 2000. First published 1958.

Aldridge, John W. *Talents and Technicians: Literary Chic and the New Assembly-Line Fiction.* New York: Charles Scribner's Sons, 1992.

Allis, Frederick S., Jr. *Youth from Every Quarter: A Bicentennial History of Phillips Academy, Andover.* Hanover, NH: University Press of New England, 1979.

Ambrose, Stephen E. *The Wild Blue: The Men and Boys Who Flew the B-24s over Germany, 1944–45.* New York: Simon and Schuster, 2002.

Austen, Roger. *Playing the Game: The Homosexual Novel in America.* Indianapolis: Bobbs-Merrill, 1977.

Bassett, Mark Travis. "John Horne Burns: Toward a Critical Biography." PhD diss., University of Missouri-Columbia, 1985.

Bedford, Victoria Hilkevitch, and Barbara Formaniak Turner, eds. *Men in Relationships: A New Look from a Life Course Perspective.* New York: Springer, 2006.

Bennett, Roger, and Jules Shell. *Camp: Where Fantasy Island Meets Lord of the Flies.* New York: Crown Archetype, 2008.

Bockris, Victor. *Transformer: The Lou Reed Story.* New York: Simon and Schuster, 1994.

Bodnar, John. *The "Good War" in American Memory.* Baltimore: Johns Hopkins University Press, 2010.

Bérubé, Allan. *Coming Out under Fire: The History of Gay Men and Women in World War Two.* New York: Free Press, 1990.

Bloom, Harold, ed. *John Knowles's "A Separate Peace."* Philadelphia: Chelsea House Publishers, 2000.

———. *John Knowles's "A Separate Peace."* New York: Bloom's Literary Criticism, 2009.

Bogdan, Robert, and Todd Weseloh. *Real Photo Postcard Guide: The People's Photography.* Syracuse, NY: Syracuse University Press, 2006.

Bolton, Richard. *The Contest of Meaning: Critical Histories of Photography.* Cambridge, MA: MIT Press, 1992.

Bram, Christopher. *Eminent Outlaws: The Gay Writers Who Changed America.* New York: Twelve, 2012.

Brault, Pascale-Ann, and Michael Naas, eds. *The Work of Mourning: Jacques Derrida.* Chicago: University of Chicago Press, 2001.

Brokaw, Tom. *The Greatest Generation.* New York: Random House, 2004.

Bronski, Michael. *A Queer History of the United States.* Boston: Beacon Press, 2011.

Bryant, Hallman Bell. *"A Separate Peace": The War Within.* Boston: Twayne Publishers, 1990.

———. *Understanding "A Separate Peace": A Student Casebook to Issues, Sources, and Historical Documents*. Westport, CT: Greenwood Press, 2002.

Bryfonsky, Dedria, ed. *War in John Knowles's "A Separate Peace."* Farmington Hills, MI: Greenhaven Press, 2011.

Bullough, Vern L., ed. *Before Stonewall: Activists for Gay and Lesbian Rights in Historical Context*. New York: Harrington Park Press, 2002.

Bunnell, Peter C. *Minor White: The Eye That Shapes*. Boston: Art Museum, Princeton University with Little, Brown, 1989.

Campbell, James. *This Is the Beat Generation*. Berkeley: University of California Press, 1999.

Chafe, William H. *Never Stop Running: Allard Lowenstein and the Struggle to Save American Liberalism*. New York: Basic Books, 1993.

Chalfen, Richard. *Snapshot Versions of Life*. Bowling Green, OH: Bowling Green State University Popular Press, 1987.

Charters, Ann. *Kerouac: A Biography*. New York: St. Martin's Press, 1994.

Childers, Thomas. *Soldier from the War Returning: The Greatest Generation's Troubled Homecoming from World War II*. Boston: Houghton Mifflin Harcourt, 2009.

Chovinard, Yvon, and Steve Pezman. *California Surfing and Climbing in the Fifties*. Santa Barbara, CA: T. Adler Books, 2013.

Collier, John, et al. *Visual Anthropology: Photography as a Research Method*. Albuquerque: University of New Mexico Press, 1986.

Cooney, John. *The American Pope: The Life and Times of Francis Cardinal Spellman*. New York: Dell Publishing, 1984.

Corber, Robert J. *Homosexuality in Cold War America: Resistance and the Crisis of Masculinity*. Durham, NC: Duke University Press, 1997.

Coviello, Peter. *Tomorrow's Parties: Sex and the Untimely in Nineteenth-Century America*. New York: New York University Press, 2013.

Cutshaw, Stacey McCarroll, and Ross Barrett. *In the Vernacular: Photography of the Everyday*. Boston: Boston University Art Gallery, 2008.

Dallek, Robert. *An Unfinished Life: John F. Kennedy, 1917–1963*. New York: Little, Brown, 2013. First published 2003.

de la Croix, St. Sukie. *Chicago Whispers: A History of LGBT Chicago before Stonewall*. Madison: University of Wisconsin Press, 2012.

D'Emilio, John D. *Sexual Politics, Sexual Communities: The Making of a Homosexual Minority in the United States, 1940–1970*. Chicago: University of Chicago Press, 1983.

DePastino, Todd. *Bill Mauldin: A Life Up Front*. New York: W. W. Norton, 2008.

Derrida, Jacques. *The Politics of Friendship*. London: Verso, 1997.

Devlin, Rachel. *Relative Intimacy: Fathers, Adolescent Daughters, and Postwar American Culture*. Chapel Hill: University of North Carolina Press, 2005.

Diggins, John Patrick. *The Proud Decades: America in War and Peace, 1941–1960*. New York: W. W. Norton, 1988.

Dorrien, Gary J. *The Making of American Liberal Theology: Crisis, Irony, and Postmodernity, 1950–2005*. Louisville, KY: Westminster John Knox Press, 2006.

Duberman, Martin. *Left Out: The Politics of Exclusion; Essays, 1964–2002*. Cambridge: South End Press, 2002.

Dudziak, Mary L. *War Time: An Idea, Its History, Its Consequences*. New York: Oxford University Press, 2012.

Dyer, Geoff. *The Missing of the Somme*. New York: Random House, 2011. First published 1994 by Hamish Hamilton Ltd.

Eberwein, Robert. *Armed Forces: Masculinity and Sexuality in the American War Film*. New Brunswick, NJ: Rutgers University Press, 2007.

Ellis, John. *The Sharp End: The Fighting Man in World War II*. New York: Charles Scribner's Sons, 1980.

——. *World War II: A Statistical Survey*. New York: Facts on File, 1993.

Engel, Steven, ed. *Readings in "The Catcher in the Rye."* San Diego: Greenhaven Press, 1998.

Faas, Ekbert. *Young Robert Duncan: Portrait of the Poet as Homosexual in Society*. Santa Barbara, CA: Black Sparrow Press, 1983.

Fraterrigo, Elizabeth. *Playboy and the Making of the Good Life in Modern America*. New York: Oxford University Press, 2009.

Freud, Sigmund. *Group Psychology and the Analysis of the Ego*. Lexington, KY: Empire Book, 2012.

Fulsom, Don. *Nixon's Darkest Secrets: The Inside Story of America's Most Troubled President*. New York: St. Martin's Press, 2012.

Gamwell, Lynn, and Richard Wells, eds. *Sigmund Freud and Art: His Personal Collection of Antiquities*. New York: Harry N. Abrams, 1989.

Gentry, Curt. *J. Edgar Hoover: The Man and the Secrets*. New York: W. W. Norton, 1991.

Gerassi, John. *The Boys of Boise: Furor, Vice, and Folly in an American City*. Seattle: University of Washington Press, 2001. First published 1966 by MacMillan.

Goldman, Albert, and Lawrence Schiller. *Ladies and Gentlemen, Lenny Bruce*. New York: Penguin Books, 1991. First published 1974.

Goranin, Nakki. *American Photobooth*. New York: W. W. Norton, 2008.

Gray, J. Glenn. *The Warriors: Reflections on Men in Battle*. Lincoln: University of Nebraska Press, 1970. First published 1959.

Hall, James Baker. *Minor White: Rites and Passages*. New York: Aperture, 1978.

Halperin, David M., and Valerie Traub, eds. *Gay Shame*. Chicago: University of Chicago Press, 2009.

Hamilton, Nigel. *JFK: Reckless Youth*. New York: Random House, 1992.

Harman, Robert, and John Louis Lucaites. *No Caption Needed: Iconic Photographs, Public Culture and Liberal Democracy*. Chicago: University of Chicago Press, 2007.

Heiferman, Marvin. *Now Is Then: Snapshots from the Maresca Collection*. New York: Princeton Architectural Press, 2008.

Herman, Arthur. *Joseph McCarthy: Reexamining the Life and Legacy of America's Most Hated Senator*. New York: Free Press, 2000.

Hayden, Tom. *Irish on the Inside: In Search of the Soul of Irish America*. New York: Verso, 2002.

Hofter, Robert. *The Man Who Invented Rock Hudson*. New York: Carroll and Graf, 2005.

Huebner, Andrew J. *The Warrior Image: Soldiers in American Culture from the Second World War to the Vietnam Era*. Chapel Hill: University of North Carolina Press, 2008.

Hunt, Nigel C. *Memory, War and Trauma*. Cambridge: Cambridge University Press, 2010.

Hurst, Michael, and Robert Swope, eds. *Casa Susanna*. New York: Powerhouse Books, 2014.

Ibson, John. *Picturing Men: A Century of Male Relationships in Everyday American Photography*. Chicago: University of Chicago Press, 2006.

Jarnot, Lisa. *Robert Duncan: The Ambassador from Venus*. Berkeley: University of California Press, 2012.

Jarvis, Christina S. *The Male Body at War: American Masculinity during World War II*. DeKalb: North Illinois University Press, 2004.

Johnson, Colin R. *Just Queer Folks: Gender and Sexuality in Rural America*. Philadelphia: Temple University Press, 2013.

Johnson, Joyce. *The Voice Is All: The Lonely Victory of Jack Kerouac*. New York: Viking, 2012.

Joshi, S. T. *Gore Vidal: A Comprehensive Bibliography*. Lanham, MD: Scarecrow Press, 2007.

Junger, Sebastian. *War*. New York: Twelve, 2010.

Kaplan, Fred. *Gore Vidal: A Biography*. New York: Doubleday, 1999.

Krich, A. M., ed. *Men: The Variety and Meaning of Their Sexual Experience*. New York: Dell Publishing, 1954.

LaRossa, Ralph. *Of War and Men: World War II in the Lives of Fathers and Their Families*. Chicago: University of Chicago Press, 2011.

Lawlor, William T., ed. *Beat Culture: Lifestyles, Icons, and Impact*. Santa Barbara, CA: ABC-CLIO, 2005.

Leggett, John. *Ross and Tom: Two American Tragedies*. New York: Simon and Schuster, 1974.

Lesy, Michael. *Dreamland: American at the Dawn of the Twentieth Century*. New York: New Press, 1997.

Lifshitz, Sebastian. *The Invisibles: Vintage Portraits of Love and Pride*. New York: Rizzoli, 2013.

Linderman, Gerald F. *The World within War: America's Combat Experience in World War II*. New York: Free Press, 1997.

Loach, Jennifer. *Edward VI*. New Haven, CT: Yale University Press, 2002.

Loftin, Craig M. *Masked Voices: Gay Men and Lesbians in Cold War America*. Albany: SUNY Press, 2012.

Loughery, John. *The Other Side of Silence: Men's Lives and Gay Identities; A Twentieth-Century History*. New York: Henry Holt, 1998.

Margolick, David. *Dreadful: The Short Life and Gay Times of John Horne Burns*. New York: Other Press, 2013.

Marlantes, Karl. *What It Is Like to Go to War*. New York: Grove Press, 2011.

Martineau, Paul. *Minor White: Manifestations of the Spirit*. Los Angeles: J. Paul Gerry Museum, 2014.

McGovern, James Holt, ed. *Literature and the Child: Romantic Continuations, Postmodern Contestations*. Iowa City: University of Iowa Press, 1999.

McNeil, Legs. *Please Kill Me: The Uncensored Oral History of Punk*. New York: Grove Press, 1996.

Meeker, Martin. *Contacts Desired: Gay and Lesbian Communications and Community, 1940s-1970s*. Chicago: University of Chicago Press, 2006.

Milburn, Michael A., and Sheree D. Conrad. *The Politics of Denial*. Cambridge, MA: MIT Press, 1996.

Miller, Neil. *Sex-Crime Panic: A Journey to the Paranoid Heart of the 1950s*. Los Angeles: Alyson Books, 2002.

Mitzel, John. *John Home Burns: An Appreciative Biography*. Dorchester, MA: Manifest Destiny Books 1974.

Morgan, Ted. *A Covert Life: Jay Lovestone; Communist, Anti-Communist, and Spymaster*. New York: Random House, 1999.

Muensterberger, Werner. *Collecting: An Unruly Passion; Psychological Perspectives*. New York: Harcourt Brace, 1995.

Nivens, Penelope. *Thornton Wilder: A Life*. New York: Harpers, 2013.

Parini, Jay. *Empire of Self: A Life of Gore Vidal*. New York: Doubleday, 2015.

———, ed. *Gore Vidal: Writer against the Grain*. New York: Columbia University Press, 1992.

Peden, William. *The American Short Story: Continuity and Change, 1940–1975*. Boston: Houghton Mifflin, 1975.

Perret, Geoffrey. *Jack: A Life Like No Other*. New York: Random House, 2002.

Pitts, David. *Jack and Lem: John F. Kennedy and Lem Billings; The Untold Story of an Extraordinary Friendship*. New York: Carroll and Graf, 2007.

Reay, Barry. *New York Hustlers: Masculinity and Sex in Modern America*. Manchester and New York: Manchester University Press, 2010.

Reumann, Miriam G. *American Sexual Character: Sex, Gender, and National Identity in the Kinsey Reports*. Berkeley: University of California Press, 2005.

Roberts, Mary Louise. *What Soldiers Do: Sex and the American GI in World War II France*. Chicago: University of Chicago Press, 2013.

Rosenheim, Jeff L. *Photography and the American Civil War*. New York: Metropolitan Museum of Art, 2014.

Sedgwick, Eve Kosofsky. *Between Men: English Literature and Male Homosexual Desire*. New York: Columbia University Press, 1985.

Seinfelt, Mark. *Final Drafts: Suicides of World Famous Authors*. Amherst, NY: Prometheus Books, 1999.

Serlin, David. *Replaceable You: Engineering the Body in Postwar America*. Chicago: University of Chicago Press, 2004.

Sherry, Michael S. *In the Shadow of War: The United States since the 1930s*. New Haven, CT: Yale University Press, 1995.

Sites, Kevin. *The Things They Cannot Say: Stories Soldiers Won't Tell You about What They've Seen, Done, or Failed to Do in War*. New York: Harpers, 2013.

Slide, Anthony. *Lost Gay Novels: A Reference Guide to the First Half of the Twentieth Century*. New York: Haworth Press, 2003.

Smith, Catherine, and Cynthia Greig. *Women in Pants: Manly Maidens, Cowgirls, and Other Renegades*. New York: Harry N. Abrams, 2003.

Smith, Shawn Michelle. *At the Edge of Sight: Photography and the Unseen*. Durham, NC: Duke University Press, 2013.

Sova, Dawn B. *Banned Books: Literature Suppressed on Social Grounds*. New York: Facts on File, 2011.

Stannard, David E. *The Puritan Way of Death: A Study in Religion, Culture, and Social Change*. New York: Oxford University Press, 1977.

Stecyk, C. R., and Don James. *Surfing San Onofre to Point Dume: Photographs by Don James: 1936–1942*. Santa Barbara, CA: T. Adler Books, 2008.

Sturken, Marita, and Lisa Cartwright. *Practices of Looking: An Introduction to Visual Culture.* New York: Oxford University Press, 2009.

Teeman, Tim. *In Bed with Gore Vidal: Hustlers, Hollywood, and the Private World of an American Master.* New York: Magnus Books, 2013.

Thomas, Evan. *The Very Best Men: The Daring Early Years of the CIA.* New York: Simon and Schuster, 2006. First published 1995.

Toker, Franklin. *Fallingwater Rising: Frank Lloyd, E. J. Kaufman, and America's Most Extraordinary House.* New York: Alfred A. Knopf, 2003.

Tripp, C. A. *The Homosexual Matrix.* New York: McGraw Hill, 1975.

———. *The Intimate World of Abraham Lincoln.* New York: Free Press, 2005.

Tuttle, William M., Jr. *"Daddy's Gone to War": The Second World War in the Lives of America's Children.* New York: Oxford University Press, 1993.

Van Ells, Mark D. *To Hear Only Thunder Again: America's World War II Veterans Come Home.* Lanham, MD: Lexington Books, 2001.

Vaule, Rosamond B. *As We Were: American Photographic Postcards, 1905-1930.* Boston: David R. Godine, 2004.

Von Hoffman, Nicholas. *Citizen Cohn: The Life and Times of Roy Cohn.* New York: Doubleday, 1988.

Waldie, D. J. *Close to Home: An American Album.* Los Angeles: Getty Museum, 2004.

Ward, Geoffrey C., and Ken Burns. *The War: An Intimate History.* New York: Alfred A. Knopf, 2007.

Way, Niobe. *Deep Secrets: Boys' Friendships and the Crisis of Connection.* Cambridge, MA: Harvard University Press, 2011.

Williams, Michael, Richard Cohan, and Nicholas Osborn. *Who We Were: A Snapshot History of America.* Chicago: CityFiles Press, 2008.

Willis, Deborah, and Barbara Krauthamer. *Envisioning Emancipation: Black Americans and the End of Slavery.* Philadelphia: Temple University Press, 2013.

Wood, Edward W., Jr. *Worshipping the Myths of World War II.* Washington, DC: Potomac Books, 2006.

Ziecher, Scott. *Band of Bikers.* New York: Powerhouse Books, 2010.

Zuromskis, Catherine. *Snapshot Photography: The Lives of Images.* Cambridge, MA: MIT Press, 2013.

Articles, Book Chapters, and Essays

Aldridge, John W. Introduction to *The Gallery*, by John Horne Burns, vii-xiii. New York: Arbor House, 1985.

Atwood, Thomas A., and Wade M. Lee. "The Price of Deviance: Schoolhouse Gothic in Prep School Literature." *Children's Literature* 35 (2007): 102-26.

"Beulah Wescott Hagen." Obituary. *Saint Louis Post-Dispatch*, February 11, 1994, 4B.

Bryant, H. B. "Phineas's Pink Shirt in *A Separate Peace*." *Notes on Contemporary Literature* 14, no. 5 (November 1984): 5-6.

Canham, Erwin. Review of *Newspaper Story: One Hundred Years of the Boston Globe* by Louis M. Lyons. *New England Quarterly* 45, no. 1 (March 1972): 125-27.

Coffey, Jerry. "MVP (Most Valuable Philanthropist): An Avid Collector of Baseball Autographs Goes to Bat for His Church." *Fort Worth Star Telegram*, July 8, 1991, E1, E5.

"The Correspondence of Ernest Hemingway and A. E. Hotchner." Kennedy Library Forums. November 28, 2005. http://jfklibrary.org/NR/rdonlyres/A9BA6BE2-F20A-4628-97C1 -4C65433B1C44/26253/thecorrespondenceofernesthemingwayandaehotchner999.pdf.

Digging, John P. "The American Writer, Fascism, and the Liberation of Italy." *American Quarterly* 18 (Winter 1966): 599–614.

Doherty, Thomas. "Pixies: Homosexuality, Anti-Communism, and the Army-McCarthy Hearings." In *Television Histories: Shaping Collective Memories in the Media Age*, edited by Gary R. Edgerton and Peter C. Rollins, 193–206. Lexington: University Press of Kentucky, 2001.

Duberman, Martin. "The 'Father' of the Homophile Movement." In Duberman, *Left Out: The Politics of Exclusion: Essays, 1964–2002*, 59–94.

Frangedis, Helen. "Dealing with the Controversial Elements in *The Catcher in the Rye*." *English Journal* 77, no. 7 (November 1988): 72–75.

Fussell, Paul. Introduction to *The Gallery*, by John Horne Burns, vii–xi. New York: New York Review Books, 2004.

Gottlieb, Robert. "Man of Letters: The Case of Thornton Wilder." *New Yorker*, January 7, 2013. http://www.newyorker.com/magazine/2013/01/07/man-of-letters-5.

Hamburger, Eric. "Lucien Carr: Fallen Angel of the Beat Poets, Later an Unflappable News Editor with United Press." *Guardian*, February 9, 2005.

Heiferman, Marvin. "Now Is Then: The Thrill and the Fate of Snapshots." In Heiferman, *Now Is Then: Snapshots from the Maresca Collection*, 40–52.

Honan, William H. "John Knowles, 75, Novelist Who Wrote 'A Separate Peace.'" *New York Times*, December 1, 2001. http://www.nytimes.com/2001/12/01/arts/john-knowles-75 -novelist-who-wrote-a-separate-peace.html.

Ibson, John. "Masculinity under Fire: Life's Presentation of Camaraderie and Homoeroticism before, during, and after World War II." In *Looking at "Life": Framing the American Century in the Pages of "Life" Magazine*, edited by Erika Doss, 178–99. Washington, DC: Smithsonian Institution Press, 2001.

LaRossa, Ralph. "The Culture of Fatherhood in the Fifties." *Journal of Family History* 29 (January 2004): 47–70.

Mabe, Chauncey. "Knowles Now Thirty Years after He Wrote *A Separate Peace*." *Sun Sentinel*, March 14, 1987. http://articles.sun-sentinel.com/1987-03-15/features/8701160400_1 _autobiography-readers-fiction/2.

Mamet, David. "Looking at War from Many Angles." *Wall Street Journal*, April 23, 2011. https://www.wsj.com/articles/SB10001424052748704529204576256922657278808.

Manning, Robert. "Hemingway in Cuba." *Atlantic Monthly*, August 1965, 101–8. https://www .theatlantic.com/magazine/archive/1965/08/hemingway-in-cuba/399059/.

McGovern, James Holt. "Fear's Echo and Unhinged Joy: Crossing Homosocial Boundaries in *A Separate Peace*." *Children's Literature* 30 (2002): 67–80.

McNichols, William Hart, SJ. "Cardinal Spellman and the Public." *New York Times*, November 25, 1984. http://www.nytimes.com/1984/11/25/books/l-cardinal-spellman-and-the -public-106570.html.

Metcalf, Stephen. "The Secret of *A Separate Peace*." *Slate*, December 31, 2009. http://www
.slate.com/articles/arts/the_dilettante/2009/12/the_secret_of_a_separate_peace.html.

Mitgang, Herbert. "Books of the Times; Fantasy amid the Reality of Naples." Review of *Thus
Spake Bellavista: Naples, Love, and Liberty* by Luciano De Crescenzo. *New York Times*,
February 28, 1989. http://www.nytimes.com/1989/02/28/books/books-of-the-times
-fantasy-amid-the-reality-of-naples.html.

———. "Books of the Times; Michener Memoir, 'World Is My Home.'" Review of *The World
Is My Home* by James A. Michener. *New York Times*, December 30, 1991. http://www
.nytimes.com/1991/12/30/books/books-of-the-times-michener-memoir-world-is-my
-home.html.

———. "Fifty Missions Brought Them Home." Review of *The Locust Fire* by Eugene Brown.
New York Times Book Review. Online.

———. "Publishing: Once an Australian." *New York Times*, November 26, 1977, 88.

Moore, Kevin. "Cruising and Transcendence in the Photographs of Minor White." In *More
Than One: Photographs in Sequence*, edited by Joel Smith, 66–79. Princeton, NJ, and New
Haven, CT: Princeton University Art Museum and Yale University Press, 2008.

Murray, Stephen O. "Donald Webster Cory." In Bullough, *Before Stonewall: Activists for Gay
and Lesbian Rights in Historical Context*, 333–42.

"New and Noteworthy." *New York Times*, June 12, 1977.

"1999 Symposium Speakers Series—Joseph Heller." *James Jones Literary Society Newsletter* 9,
no. 2 (Winter 1999–2000). http://www.jamesjonesliterarysociety.org/assets/vol9-2_page
source.html.

Parini, Jay. "Gore Vidal: The Writer and His Critics." In Parini, *Gore Vidal: Writer against the
Grain*, 1–30.

Saaric, Jon. "Arguing the Nobel Prize." Letter to the Editor. *New York Times*, October 26, 1984.

Sekula, Allan. "Reading an Archive: Photography between Labour and Capital." In *Visual
Culture: The Reader*, edited by Jessica Evans and Stuart Hall, 181–92. London: Sage,
1999.

Shannon, William V. "Guileless and Machiavellian." Review of *The American Pope: The Life
and Times of Francis Cardinal Spellman* by John Cooney. *New York Times*, October 28,
1984. http://www.nytimes.com/1984/10/28/books/guileless-and-machiavellian.html.

Shapiro, Francine. "Baby Boomers and Distant Dads." *Huffington Post*, February 22, 2012.
http://www.huffingtonpost.com/francine-shapiro-phd/ptsd-veterans_b_1228542.html.

Signorile, Michelangelo. "Cardinal Spellman's Dark Legacy." *New York Press*, May 7, 2002 (up-
dated November 11, 2014). http://www.nypress.com/cardinal-spellmans-dark-legacy.

Summers, Claude J. "*The City and the Pillar* as Gay Fiction." In Parini, *Gore Vidal: Writer
against the Grain*, 56–75.

Syrett, Nicolas L. "A Busman's Holiday in the Not-So-Lonely Crowd: Business Culture, Epistolary Networks, and Itinerant Homosexuality in Mid-Twentieth Century America."
Journal of the History of Sexuality 21 (January 2012): 121–40.

Tatum, James. "The *Romanitas* of Gore Vidal." In Parini, *Gore Vidal: Writer against the Grain*,
199–220.

Tribunella, Eric. "Refusing the Queer Potential: Crossing Homosocial Boundaries in *A Separate Peace*." *Children's Literature* 30 (2002): 81–95.

Vider, Stephen. "'Oh Hell, May, Why Don't You People Have a Cookbook?': Camp Humor and Gay Domesticity." *American Quarterly* 65, no. 4 (December 2013): 877–905.

West, Nancy Martha. "Telling Time: Found Photographs and the Stories They Inspire." In Heiferman, *Now Is Then: Snapshots from the Maresca Collection*, 78–89.

Woo, Elaine. "John Knowles, 75: Wrote 'A Separate Peace.'" Obituary. *Los Angeles Times*, December 31, 2001. http://articles.latimes.com/2001/dec/01/local/me-10289.

Zinsser, William. "*The Gallery* Revisited." *Sewanee Review* 100, no. 1 (Winter 1992): 105–12.

——. "No Second Act: John Horne Burns and *The Gallery*." Zinsser on Friday. *American Scholar*, February 4, 2011. https://theamericanscholar.org/no-second-act/#.WURLK uvyu70.

——. "Trapped by the Past: Finding a Different Take on John Horne Burns's Story." Zinsser on Friday. *American Scholar*, May 6, 2011. https://theamericanscholar.org/trapped-by-the -past/#.WURLmOvyu70.

Index

Page numbers in italics refer to figures.